SOUTH ASIA DEVELOPMENT FORUM

Hidden Potential

Rethinking Informality in South Asia

Editors
MAURIZIO BUSSOLO AND SIDDHARTH SHARMA

South Asia Development Forum

Home to a fifth of humankind, and to almost half of the people living in poverty, South Asia is also a region of marked contrasts: from conflict-affected areas to vibrant democracies, from demographic bulges to aging societies, from energy crises to global companies. This series explores the challenges faced by a region whose fate is critical to the success of global development in the early 21st century, and that can also make a difference for global peace. The volumes in it organize in an accessible way findings from recent research and lessons of experience, across a range of development topics. The series is intended to present new ideas and to stimulate debate among practitioners, researchers, and all those interested in public policies. In doing so, it exposes the options faced by decision-makers in the region and highlights the enormous potential of this fast-changing part of the world.

Contents

Boxes

Figures

Tables

Foreword

Countries in South Asia have enjoyed almost three decades of significant gross domestic product (GDP) growth. However, the lion's share of GDP in South Asia is generated by a small number of firms in the formal sector. Low-productivity informality remains widespread. Excluding agriculture, nearly 75 percent of workers and an even higher share of firms are still informal in South Asia. Informality is also prevalent in other regions, but it is not as extensive as in South Asia.

The recent COVID-19 (coronavirus) crisis and the increasingly more frequent climate-related disasters have been stark reminders of why informality is a major development issue. Informal workers and firms—who operate in restricted local markets, have limited access to capital and advanced technologies, and are not covered by formal labor contracts or social protection systems—have been more vulnerable to these shocks and have been more harshly affected by them.

The persistent gap between the formal and the informal sectors has resulted in stubborn inequality and limited upward mobility.

A large literature discusses the causes and consequences of informality, but there is no consensus on the most appropriate policy stance to deal with informality because the debate on informality tends to be polarized into two opposite views. One view sees informality as a manifestation of a dualistic economy, where entry barriers and other distortions enable formal, privileged insiders to exclude informal outsiders. The other view sees informal workers or firms as choosing to avoid regulations and taxation because of either their low productivity or their preferences (for part-time arrangements, for example).

The appeal of these two polarized views is that their policy recommendations are straightforward. In the first case, governments should remove barriers to competition, reduce distortions, and level the playing field. In the second case, governments should support workers or firms by providing training and access to input and output markets. Doing this would change the workers' intrinsic characteristics (such as their productivity), and they would then choose to participate in the formal economy.

As the studies in this book show, however, while policies based on either perspective can help to reduce informality, there are serious limitations on how far each of these approaches can go on its own. The presence of strong vested interests makes it difficult to lower barriers to entry in the formal sector within a short period of time. Increasing productivity in the informal sector is difficult because the informal sector is extremely diverse in terms of entrepreneurial ability, aspirations, geographic location, and other circumstances. In short, there is no single silver bullet.

The collection of studies in this edited volume proposes a framework that reconciles these two opposite views and highlights the heterogeneity of the informal sector. The framework—based on recent research (Kanbur 2017, 2021; Ulyssea 2018, 2020, among others)—considers informality as the outcome of firm dynamics in distorted economies. In other words, informality is the result of *both* intrinsic characteristics of the firms (or workers) *and* the barriers and distortions of the economic environment in which they operate.

Considering the impact of market liberalization on informality, one chapter in this volume shows that about one-half of the current size of India's informal sector can be explained by entry barriers and distortions. Addressing these would thus set in motion a significant transformation of the Indian economy, but it would not mean a complete eradication of its informality. In the same vein, a survey of the evidence on business registration reforms worldwide concludes that the impact of such reforms on informality is limited. At best, they lead to a modest and temporary increase in registration rates. The firms that register in response to such programs do not experience a significant increase in profits or other measures of performance after registration.

Efforts to support firms or workers also need to consider the heterogeneity of the informal sector. For example, new approaches to market access, such as those provided by e-commerce, show promise in increasing the sales and productivity of small firms selling through digital channels. This is because e-commerce platforms offer an infrastructure of marketing, warehousing, and commercial relations and thereby remove some of the intrinsic limitations that small and informal firms face in participating in larger markets and, ultimately, in becoming part of the formal sector. Nevertheless, many informal firms do not seem able to take advantage of e-commerce opportunities; in fact, a large share of them are still reliant on traditional brick-and-mortar retailing. Potential causes of this selective adoption of e-commerce include limited access to digital infrastructure among firms and their target customers, informational barriers to the adoption of new technologies by firms, and limited capability of firms to profit from e-commerce. Better data on informality should improve the understanding of which of these causes matter for which firms; these data will be needed for designing policies that can complement the generic expansion of the digital infrastructure.

Recognizing the heterogeneity of the informal sector and adapting policy interventions to different cases is also important when the objective is building resilience. In part because of the COVID-19 pandemic, all governments have become acutely aware of the challenges of extending protection to their whole population.

Expanding noncontributory schemes that currently cover only a small fraction of informal workers would be prohibitively expensive and may distort labor market choices. Semicontributory schemes would be more affordable but may not reach the poorest. Consequently, countries in the region have been experimenting with approaches that combine contributory and noncontributory schemes for both old-age risk as well as health and unemployment shocks. This experience is surveyed in one of the contributions in this book. It recommends a combined approach that would target the poorest through noncontributory schemes while reaching the rest of the informal sector through streamlined versions of existing schemes that better fit the informal sector, for example, by developing new savings instruments targeted to this segment.

In short, a multipronged strategy is needed to tackle the developmental challenges presented by informality. The essays in this collection provide much food for thought on how we at the World Bank can adapt our approaches—in private sector development as well as in the design of adaptive social assistance systems—to better take the heterogeneity of informal businesses and workers into account.

Martin Raiser
Regional Vice President for South Asia
The World Bank Group

References

Kanbur, S. M. Ravi. 2017. "Informality: Causes, Consequences, and Policy Responses." *Review of Development Economics* 21 (4): 939–61.

Kanbur, S. M. Ravi. 2021. "Introduction: The Long Discourse on Informality as Reflected in Selected Articles of the *International Labour Review*." *International Labour Review* 1 (July 27): 1–11.

Ulyssea, Gabriel. 2018. "Firms, Informality, and Development: Theory and Evidence from Brazil." *American Economic Review* 108 (8): 2015–47.

Ulyssea, Gabriel. 2020. "Informality: Causes and Consequences for Development." *Annual Review of Economics* 12 (August): 525–46.

Acknowledgments

This book's ideas originated from our discussions on informality as a key development challenge in South Asia with Hans Timmer, Chief Economist for this region at the World Bank. Accordingly, our first debt of gratitude is to him for his patience and guidance during the two-year life span of this project.

We are immensely grateful to all our contributors (please see the full list in the About the Editors and Authors pages); without them, this book would not exist. They not only provided valuable insights on a wide range of themes related to informality in South Asia, but also endured the long process of attending workshops, incorporating comments, and responding to all of our queries while always remaining accessible and committed to the final outcome.

Ravi Kanbur and Chris Woodruff played the key role of academic advisers for this project. We have had many meetings with them on the content and overall narrative of this volume. More than once, they have stirred us, as well as the contributors of the various chapters, to move in fruitful directions.

This project has benefited from the support and advice of many people, including those who contributed comments during the various seminars and conferences at which the authors presented their papers. For their remarks, suggestions, and peer reviews, we thank, in particular, these people. Hernan Winkler, Arti Grover, Ambar Narayan, and Mary C. Hallward-Driemeier were peer reviewers for the concept note of this project. At that initial stage or in subsequent authors' workshops, Zoubida K. Allaoua, Najy Benhassine, Guangzhe Chen, Cecile Fruman, Farris H. Hadad-Zervos, Henry G. R. Kerali, Maria Beatriz Orlando, Mercy M. Tembon, Margaret Ellen Grosh, Stefano Paternostro, and William F. Maloney provided helpful comments.

By commenting on one other's work, the authors of the individual chapters have also collectively improved the quality of this volume. In addition, the authors want to thank the following: Martha Chen, Ugo Panizza, Yi Huang, Sebastian Bedoya, Valerie Blackman, Luming Chen, Ding Ding, Paul Mathieu, Tianshi Mu, Nayantara Sarma,

Sam Asher, Anirudha Dutta, Kaushik Krishnan, Sutirtha Sinha Roy, Anurati Tandon, Qaiser Khan, Priyanka Kanth, and Melis U. Guven.

Special thanks go to the people who supported us during the crucial phase of the production of the book. William Shaw helped revise several parts of the initial drafts, contributing significantly to their final clarity. Robert Zimmerman painstakingly copy-edited all of the chapters. Jewel McFadden was our acquisitions editor. Mary Fisk was the production editor for the book; she managed the editing, typesetting, and proof-reading. Carlos Reyes and Gabriel Lora created the beautiful cover art and design. Yaneisy Martinez was the print and electronic conversion coordinator. The dedication and professionalism of the production team are what converted the manuscript into a finished book.

We gratefully acknowledge financial support from the Program for Asia Connectivity and Trade Window of the South Asia Regional Integration, Cooperation and Engagement Umbrella Trust Fund and the South Asia Regional Trade Facilitation Program Window of the AusAid-World Bank Partnership for South Asia Trust Fund. Cecile Fruman and Mandakini Kaul helped us in securing and managing this financial support.

Finally, our thanks go to the two vice presidents for South Asia, Hartwig Schafer and Martin Raiser, who supported us from the beginning to the end.

About the Editors and Authors

Editors

Maurizio Bussolo is a Lead Economist in the World Bank's Office of the Chief Economist for South Asia. His research interests include aging, trade, growth, poverty, and inequality. He led operational teams in the aftermath of the 2008–09 crisis. Earlier, he worked at the Organisation for Economic Co-operation and Development (OECD), the Overseas Development Institute in London, and Fedesarrollo and Los Andes University in Colombia. He has published extensively in academic journals; his recent monographs include "Toward a New Social Contract" and "The Impact of Macroeconomic Policies on Poverty and Income Distribution." He holds a PhD in economics from the University of Warwick.

Siddharth Sharma is a Lead Economist in the World Bank's Office of the Chief Economist for South Asia. His research interests include productivity, innovation, and labor markets; his recent work has examined how firms are affected by regulatory policies and new technology. He has coauthored several World Bank reports and was a core team member of the *World Development Report 2017*. He holds a PhD in economics from Yale University.

Authors

Miglena Abels has been a Research Analyst in the World Bank Social Protection and Labor Global unit since 2016. Her work has focused on providing analytical and policy support to client countries with respect to achieving pension system fiscal and social sustainability. Her experience in assessing the performance of pension programs spans all regions and income levels, including experience with building public sector pension programs in fragile, conflict, and violent countries. Prior to joining the Social Protection and Labor Global unit, she worked in the Europe and Central Asia Region of the World Bank from 2012 to 2016. She holds a Master of Arts in economics from the State University of New York at Buffalo.

Syud Amer Ahmed is a Senior Economist with the Social Protection and Jobs Global Practice for South Asia, leading the unit's engagement on jobs and migration in the region. He has been at the World Bank since 2008. He has published works in the areas of climate change, fiscal policy, labor, international trade, growth, and demographics. He has coauthored flagship publications, including the *Global Economic Prospects* report series and the *Global Monitoring Report 2015/2016* on the Millennium Development Goals and demographics. He holds a PhD in applied economics from Purdue University, where he specialized in international trade.

Pierre Bachas is an Economist in the Development Research Group (DECRG) of the World Bank. His research focuses on public finance, financial inclusion, and development economics. He is particularly interested in how to design efficient and equitable taxes and transfers in the context of informality and weaker administrative capacity. He holds a PhD in Economics from the University of California, Berkeley.

Emilio Basavilbaso is an international Senior Consultant on social protection and has worked on reforms in Saudi Arabia and Mexico with the World Bank. He is a professor of Public Policies at Universidad Austral, Buenos Aires. He is the former Executive Director of Argentina's National Social Security Agency (ANSES) and Head of the City of Buenos Aires' Housing Institute (IVC, Instituto de Vivienda de la Ciudad), with 12 and 10 years of experience in the public and private sector, respectively. In 2020, he launched the book *The Battle for Social Investment*.

Davi Bhering is a PhD candidate at the Paris School of Economics. His research focuses on tax policy in developing countries; he is particularly interested in how governments can make the value added tax more efficient.

Ernesto Brodersohn was a senior official at CONSAR, the Mexican pension's supervisor, from 2003 to 2016, where he was the General Director of Operational Regulation and Financial Inclusion, coordinating projects operationalizing multiple pension reforms. From 2017 to 2021, he worked as a consultant for the World Bank, the Inter-American Development Bank, and the Toronto Centre on projects in Africa, the Middle East, and Latin America, supporting policy makers, regulators, and agencies focused on efforts to extend pension coverage to the informal sector. He is currently a senior official at the social security development branch of the International Social Security Association.

Pinyi Chen has worked in several World Bank units, including the Development Economics Prospects Group; East Asia and Pacific Countries Economies; Finance, Competitiveness, and Innovation; and Social Protection and Jobs Global Practice, and has contributed to reports and working papers on topics ranging from demography to innovation to skill development since 2015. She coauthored research papers on the costs of the Israeli occupation of the West Bank, using satellite data at the Assistance to the Palestinian People Unit of the United Nations. She also conducted impact evaluations of capacity-building activities at the International Monetary Fund's Institute for Capacity Development. Her academic training was completed at Purdue, Cornell, and Yale universities. She is a PhD candidate in development economics at the Geneva Graduate Institute.

Gustavo Demarco is the Pensions and Social Insurance Global Lead at the World Bank. He also coordinates the Social Protection, Aging, Disability, and Inclusion at the World Bank. Over the past 20 years, he has led World Bank operations and policy dialogue on Social Protection and Labor in more than 30 countries. Before joining the World Bank, he served as Director of Operations, Planning, and Research at the Pension Supervision Authority of Argentina. He was a core member of the Argentine pension reform team in the 1990s. Earlier in his career, he was Professor of Economics at the Universities of Córdoba, La Rioja, and Buenos Aires (Argentina). He has authored or contributed to several books and articles on social protection and pension economics. He received his undergraduate degree in economics from the University of Córdoba (Argentina) and followed graduate studies at the Economic Commission for Latin America and the Caribbean, Chile, and the University of Córdoba.

Roberto N. Fattal Jaef is a Senior Economist in the Macroeconomics and Growth team of the World Bank's Development Research Department. His research interests cover various areas of macroeconomics, with a special emphasis on economic growth. Current and recent research topics include: (1) understanding the role of market distortions for firm-level behavior, entrepreneurship, and long-run macroeconomic outcomes; (2) investigating the micro and macro patterns of transition growth paths; and (3) studying the role of credit for business cycles. Before joining the World Bank, he worked at the International Monetary Fund's Research department from 2011 to 2013. He holds a PhD in economics from the University of California, Los Angeles.

Lucie Gadenne is an Associate Professor at Queen Mary University of London and a Research Fellow at the Institute for Fiscal Studies. Her research lies at the intersection of public finance and development economics, with a particular focus on the equity and efficiency implications of consumption taxes. She holds a PhD from the Paris School of Economics.

Clément Joubert is a Research Economist in the World Bank's Development Research Group (Human Development Team). An applied microeconomist, he is interested in how households work and save in high-informality settings, the economic risks they face, and how to optimally design social protection programs for them. His research also covers such topics as gender inequality, underemployment, and radicalization. Before joining the World Bank, he was an Assistant Professor at the University of North Carolina at Chapel Hill (2010–15). He holds a PhD in economics from the University of Pennsylvania and a Master of Science from HEC Paris.

Martin Kanz is a Senior Economist in the Development Research Group at the World Bank. His research focuses on banking, behavioral economics, and the political economy of the credit market. He served as the Deputy Director of the *World Development Report 2022* and has led numerous field studies and impact evaluations on financial sector topics, primarily in India and southeast Asia. His academic research has appeared in the *Quarterly Journal of Economics*, *Journal of Political Economy*, *Journal of Finance*, and other leading academic publications. He holds an AB in economics from Harvard University, an MSc in development economics from Oxford, and a PhD from Harvard University.

Radhika Kaul is a Consultant for the South Asia Region's Chief Economist Office and the Development Research Group at the World Bank. She is also a manager at Women in Econ/Policy, a nongovernmental organization based in India. She has worked on various projects related to public finance, informality, gender, and social protection. She holds a master's degree in public policy from Georgetown University and a BA in economics from Delhi University.

Ananya Kotia is a PhD candidate in the Department of Economics, London School of Economics. He is interested in combining microempirical methods and macroeconomic theory to study firm dynamics and economic growth in developing countries. He was a predoctoral research fellow at the Energy Policy Institute at the University of Chicago and an economist at the Ministry of Finance, Government of India. He holds a BA and an MPhil in economics from Cambridge and Oxford universities, respectively.

Zaineb Majoka is an Economist in the World Bank's Social Protection and Jobs Global Practice for South Asia, where she works on research and operations related to labor markets and human capital. She has made numerous contributions to regional and global analytical work on savings, labor markets, food subsidies, adaptive social protection, and poverty assessments. She has coauthored country flagships reports, including *Pakistan Jobs Diagnostic* and *Somali Poverty and Vulnerability Analysis.* Before joining the World Bank, she worked at Oxfam, studying the political economy of inequality. She holds a master's degree in public policy from Johns Hopkins University.

Romina Quagliotti is a predoctoral Research Assistant at Haas School of Business, University of California, Berkeley. Her fields of interest are public and development economics. She holds a BA and is pursuing an MA in economics from Universidad de la República, Uruguay.

Jyotirmoy Saha has been a Consultant at World Bank Social Protection and Jobs Global Practice for the past four years. He has more than 10 years of expertise as a statistician and econometrician. He formerly worked at the Population Council, where he oversaw quantitative research and the impact evaluation of various large-scale randomized control trial studies. His main research areas include machine learning, poverty analysis, labor market, social protection, financial economics, child marriage, and climate change. He has coauthored several scientific articles in peer-reviewed journals. He holds a master's degree in economics and applied statistics.

Yue Zhou is an Economist in the Fiscal Affairs Department at the International Monetary Fund. In this capacity, he provides technical assistance on wage bill management and energy subsidy reform to client countries and acts as Fiscal Economist for Sierra Leone. Before joining the International Monetary Fund, he was a consultant in the South Asia Chief Economist Office at the World Bank. His research interests include international finance, public finance, macroeconomics, and development. He holds a PhD in international economics from the Graduate Institute, Geneva, and a master's in economics and a bachelor's in international politics from Peking University.

Main Messages

Informality remains widespread in South Asia. Nearly three-quarters of South Asia's nonagricultural workers were informal between 2010 and 2017, the highest share among developing regions. The share of informal firms in the total number of firms in the nonfarm sector is even higher, reaching 99 percent in India. The recent two-and-a-half decades of strong gross domestic product (GDP) growth have not brought about a reduction of informality, casting doubts about the standard theories of development predicting a decline of informality with rising incomes.

Informality thus remains a major development issue because of its association with low earnings, high vulnerability, and a small tax base. Yet there is no consensus on its causes and consequences. The debate is polarized between a view that informality is a problem of regulatory evasion and should be eradicated, on the one hand, and another that equates informality with economic exclusion, blaming a small group of privileged insiders as the main cause for the backwardness of the informal outsiders, on the other hand.

These views are at odds with the heterogeneity observed among informal firms. These range from economic activities run by a single self-employed person with almost no other inputs, to small businesses that exclusively employ family members, and to slightly larger firms with a few employees and some assets. In addition, a large share of informal workers are employed by formal firms.

Recent advances in analyzing informality as the outcome of firm dynamics in distorted economic environments can help reconcile the two polarized views. Building on these advances, the approach adopted in this volume clarifies that there are different types of informality, with different drivers and consequences. The starting point of this approach is that firms inherently differ in their optimal size. Suppose all firms above a certain size are required to register and fulfill costly regulatory obligations. As explained by this volume's conceptual framework, some firms will underreport their size or hide their activities to evade this requirement, while others will avoid growing to their optimal size simply to remain under the regulatory threshold. The number of these informal firms (evaders and avoiders) can be linked directly to the distortion caused by (size-based) regulations. The informal sector, however, also includes many firms that are below the regulatory threshold because they are inherently small, not because they are evading or avoiding business regulations.

Using this approach, the chapters in this volume revisit old questions about the relationship of informality to regulation and taxation, and they pose new ones, such as how digital technologies and multifaceted policy designs can improve prospects in the informal sector. Rather than trying to identify a single major driver of informality and its associated silver bullet policy remedy, this volume presents new evidence on the heterogeneity of informality in South Asia and offers a guide to policy making by discussing how the effectiveness of interventions (taxation, education, investment) is affected by this heterogeneity.

Four main messages are derived from the studies collected in this volume.

- **First, informality in South Asia is dominated by firms that happen to be outside the purview of regulations because they are small, as opposed to those that remain small to escape regulations.** In this setting, the key is to understand the specific constraints that keep these firms from growing and performing well, such as limited access to skills, markets, capital, and technology.

- **Second, reforms of business regulations tend to have small direct effects on the informal sector, although they could have sizable indirect impacts on it if they succeed in removing major inefficiencies in the broader economy.** Regulatory reforms do not have large direct impacts on informality because relatively few informal firms in South Asia have chosen to remain suboptimally small only to avoid business regulations. If reforms succeed in leveling the playing field for firms, they could trigger broad resources reallocation and allow capable entrepreneurs from the informal sector to grow.

As estimated by one of the studies in this volume, relative to the United States, nearly one-half of the total informality in Indian manufacturing can be accounted for by the indirect general equilibrium effects of prevailing firm-level distortions, including large de facto business entry barriers. This finding implies that comprehensive business climate reforms could, in time, shrink the informal sector to one-half of its present size. However, governments cannot rely on this approach alone. Enacting such sweeping reforms will not be easy, and about one-half of the informal sector would persist even if the reforms were enacted.

- **Third, e-commerce platforms and similar technologies offer new opportunities to informal firms and workers, but many of these also need complementary skills or credit to benefit from such technologies.** This message presents the second major pathway to improving the livelihoods of workers and entrepreneurs in South Asia's informal sector. Small firms in the informal sector cannot afford the upfront costs of reaching out to a bigger market, which tends to limit their size and earnings potential. Digital platforms can boost market access at almost no cost to firms. In addition, firms on the platforms adopt improved business practices and technologies. Nevertheless, only a select group of informal firms appear to be using such platforms on a sustained basis. This could be because many of these firms lack the know-how or finance to benefit from market access. Such gaps may be met by complementary business training and financial support programs. A growing evidence base suggests that such interventions can be cost-effective if designed with the specific needs and aspirations of targeted firms in mind.

- **Fourth, a combination of contributory and noncontributory programs recognizing the heterogeneous saving capacities of informal workers may be necessary to achieve more universal coverage of social insurance and thereby allow informal workers to withstand the larger risks often associated with higher-return, higher-productivity jobs and activities.** Lacking access to formal social protection, those working in the informal sector are vulnerable to shocks and old age. The poorest among them can be helped by modifying existing non-contributory programs targeted to the poor. However, cost considerations limit the coverage of such programs. Individuals in the middle and upper segments of the income distribution in the informal sector can be reached through a lighter version of contributory schemes originally designed for the formal sector. Those who have the potential to save for retirement but lack the access to suitable financial instruments would benefit from innovative contributory schemes or savings instruments designed to unlock that potential.

In sum, a multipronged strategy is needed to tackle the developmental challenges presented by informality.

Abbreviations

ASI	Annual Survey of Industries
ASPIRE	Atlas of Social Protection Indicators of Resilience and Equity
CBS	Central Bureau of Statistics (Nepal)
CES	constant elasticity of substitution
CMIE	Center for Monitoring Indian Economy
CPHS	Consumer Pyramids Household Survey
EAP	East Asia and Pacific
EAP	Elderly Assistance Program
ECA	Eastern Europe and Central Asia
ETI	elasticity of taxable income
ETR	effective tax rate
GDP	gross domestic product
GST	goods and services tax
HSN	Harmonized System Nomenclature
IGNOAPS	Indira Gandhi National Old Age Pension Scheme
IHS	inverse hyperbolic sine
ILO	International Labour Organization
LAC	Latin America and the Caribbean
LMICs	low- and middle-income countries
LSS	Labor and Skills Survey (Pakistan)
Mbao	pension plan (Kenya)
MENA	Middle East and North Africa
MGNREGA	Mahatma Gandhi National Rural Employment Guarantee Program
OAA	Old Age Allowance
OABP	Old Age Basic Pension
OECD	Organisation for Economic Co-operation and Development
OLS	ordinary least squares

PAMA	Public Welfare Assistance Allowance
PSLM	Pakistan Social and Living Standards Measurement
SAR	South Asia
SMM	simulated method of moments
SSA	Sub-Saharan Africa
STEP	Skills toward Employment and Productivity Survey (Sri Lanka)
TFP	total factor productivity
UME	Unorganized Manufacturing Enterprises Survey
VAT	value added tax
WDI	World Development Indicators

CHAPTER 1

Rethinking Informality in South Asia: An Overview of the Findings

MAURIZIO BUSSOLO AND SIDDHARTH SHARMA

Introduction

Stubbornly prevalent informality among firms and workers is a key development issue in South Asia. Nearly three-quarters of South Asia's nonagricultural workers were informal between 2010 and 2017, the highest share among developing regions (figure 1.1). The share of informal firms in the total number of firms in the nonfarm sector is even higher, reaching 99 percent in India.[1] These shares have remained stable for a long time, including during the recent decades of strong economic growth in the region. In some cases, they even increased (Kanbur 2017; World Bank 2020a). This underscores that informality does not necessarily disappear with rising incomes as predicted by standard theories of development.[2]

Three main reasons make informality a major development issue: (1) informality is associated with low labor productivity and limited access to capital and advanced technologies; (2) it is related to poor working conditions and vulnerability; and (3) it implies a low tax base. Slow economic growth, persistent inequality and poverty, and limited government revenues are thus all linked with informality.

The link with informality does not mean that informality is the cause of these issues. In fact, the vast literature on informality has not reached a consensus on causes and consequences. The debate polarizes between a view that informality is a problem and should be eradicated and a view that informal firms and workers are discriminated

FIGURE 1.1 **Share of Informal Employment in Total Nonagricultural Employment**

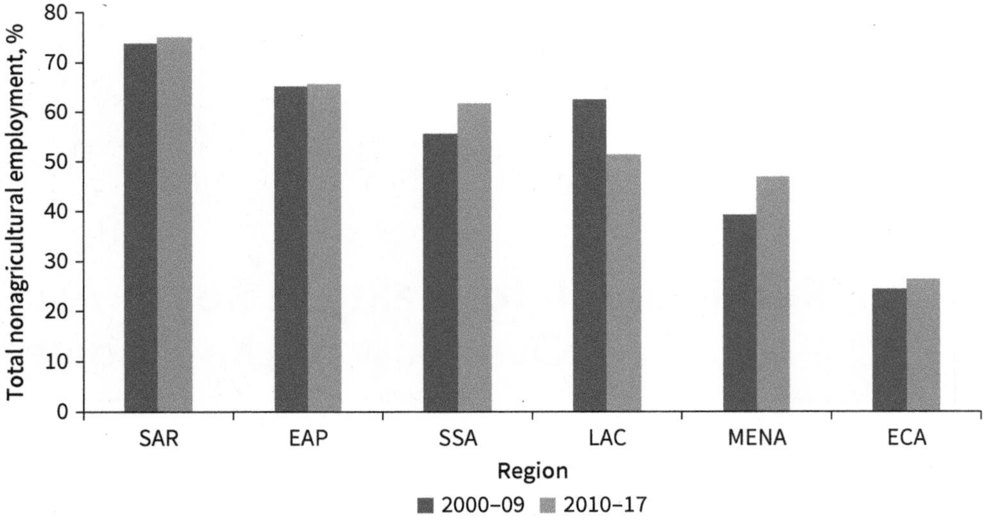

Source: WDI (World Development Indicators) (dashboard), World Bank, Washington, DC, https://datatopics
.worldbank.org/world-development-indicators/.
Note: Includes only low- and middle-income countries. EAP = East Asia and Pacific. ECA = Eastern Europe and
Central Asia. LAC = Latin America and the Caribbean. MENA = Middle East and North Africa. SAR = South Asia.
SSA = Sub-Saharan Africa.

against in a dualistic economy. In the first view, informal firms choose to remain small and avoid formal regulations and taxation. This may be because informality is better suited to their intrinsic characteristics, such as limited business skills, or because of their preference for flexibility. Clearly, the implication is that these intrinsic characteristics must be changed so that the hindrance to development caused by informality is removed or at least alleviated. In the second view, the characteristics or, rather, the privileges of the formal sector are the problem. High entry barriers in the form of regulatory burdens and above-market wages benefit a relatively small group of insiders, leaving a large group of outsiders with less access to resources. The policy advice deriving from this view is also clear: the removal of the entry barriers to promote deregulation and increased competition should be central in reform.[3]

These opposite views are influential because they provide unambiguous guidance for government interventions. However, they are also highly stylized and do not consider three features commonly observed in South Asian and other developing economies, as follows:

- The significant heterogeneity of informal firms, ranging from economic activities run by a single self-employed person with almost no other inputs, to small businesses that exclusively employ family members and to slightly larger firms with a few employees and some assets.

- The long-term coexistence of an informal sector and a formal sector, or the fact that there is a large overlap between formality and informality; for example, some formal firms may be registered because of certain aspects of the regulations but not others, or they may employ a large share of informal workers.

- The political economy of the existing institutional setting, which may constrain the possibility of meaningful reform.

This volume adopts an approach that encompasses these three features and, in a way, reconciles the two opposite views described. The approach highlights that there is not a single solution in tackling development issues in economies with a high degree of informality and that a multipronged strategy has a greater chance of success.

Before describing the approach, it is important to establish a clear definition of the informal sector. This volume defines a firm as informal if it is not registered with the relevant authorities. This legalistic definition of informality equates informality with operations on the margins of the relevant laws and regulations and is the dominant one in the literature.[4] It is also similar to the approach used by the International Labour Organization (ILO) and national statistical agencies in South Asia, which define informal enterprises as those that are not legally incorporated (ILO 2013).[5] In the South Asia context, because many regulations and tax obligations apply only to firms above a certain size threshold, there is a strong correspondence between firm size and formality status.[6] From the perspective of labor markets, this volume defines informal employment to include all individuals working in informal enterprises as owners, employees, or contributing family members, as well as individuals employed in formal firms as casual or temporary workers without formal contracts.[7]

The approach or conceptual framework of this volume follows recent research (Kanbur 2017, 2021; Ulyssea 2018, 2020) and may be summarized as follows. Consider a hypothetical economy in which, initially, there are no government interventions or regulations. Firms employ labor and capital to produce a homogeneous product and differ only in their total factor productivity (TFP). Market interactions, diminishing returns to scale in firms, and the initial distribution of TFP produce a natural size distribution of firms, ranging from very small to very large firms, whereby firms with higher TFP are larger in size.[8]

Then a government regulation is introduced that imposes on firms above a given size a fixed registration cost and an obligation to provide some benefits to their employees.[9] In effect, it segments the market into two parts. Firms with a natural size below the regulatory threshold are not affected directly by this policy and now constitute the informal sector. Firms with a natural size above the threshold, now in the formal sector, face a higher unit labor cost, net of regulatory obligations. In response, they reduce employment below their natural levels. The labor released from the formal sector is now employed in informal firms, an indirect consequence of the regulation. There is, in short, a distortion in labor allocation: informal firms employ too much labor relative to their natural levels; formal firms employ too little. As a result of this distortion, there is a gap in revenue per unit of labor between the formal and informal sectors.

Now, suppose the regulation is imperfectly enforced. The various possible responses thereby split firms into four groups:

- Type A firms with a natural size above the size threshold that comply with the regulation

- Type B firms with a natural size above the threshold that evade the regulation and risk a penalty (evaders)

- Type C firms that would naturally be slightly above the threshold but adjust their size downward to be below the threshold and avoid the regulation (avoiders)

- Type D firms outside the regulation because their natural size is well below the threshold (outsiders).

The firms in group A are formal, and groups B, C, and D are informal.[10] Group D, the outsiders, will also include the self-employed.

This approach clarifies that there are different types of informality, with different drivers and consequences. For example, the costs involved in complying with the regulation are clearly important for the evader and avoider firms and distort their choices, but they do not directly affect the outsider firms. Consequently, a reduction of the cost of complying with the regulation or a stricter enforcement of the regulation would reduce the shares of evaders and avoiders, but it would not change the share of outsiders directly. More precisely, the outsiders will not be affected directly by changes in the regulation, although they could be affected indirectly by general equilibrium effects (such as by absorbing the excess labor from the formal sector).

The TFP distribution plays a key role in determining the size and composition of the informal sector. TFP levels may vary across firms for a number of reasons. Potential causes include factors internal to firms, such as their management practices. They also include external factors in the operating environment of firms that prevent equal access to markets and to opportunities to make productivity-enhancing investments.[11] Policies that address the underlying causes of TFP variations could make a difference in the size and composition of the informal sector.

This discussion highlights the importance of considering the composition of informality, that is, the relative size of the various components. The impact of policies will depend on tackling the appropriate driver(s) of each specific type of informality. This shift of focus, from a reduction of informality toward the removal of the underlying constraints, should also contribute to the design of more effective development policies. In settings in which informality is mainly composed of outsider-type firms, the key is to understand the specific constraints to the performance of such firms and the wider economic conditions that allow so many outsider-type firms to coexist with type A firms in the same industry.

Collectively, the studies in this volume contribute to this shift of focus and demonstrate that, by using appropriate interventions, it is possible to improve the lives of informal workers and the growth opportunities of informal firms.

It is possible to extract four key messages from the eight chapters of this volume, as follows:

- A large share of informality in South Asia comprises firms and self-employed individuals who are outsiders; avoiders and evaders exist, but are much smaller components of the informal sector.

- Reforms in business licensing and regulation tend to have small direct effects on the informal sector, although they could have sizable indirect effects on the informal sector if they succeed in addressing major sources of distortions in the economy.

- E-commerce and related digital platform technologies can improve the growth opportunities of informal firms by easing their market access. However, many informal firms lack the requisite skills or credit to benefit from e-commerce and may be better served by interventions that provide skills and credit.

- Workers in the informal sector are disproportionately vulnerable to shocks, and a combination of contributory and noncontributory social protection systems recognizing the heterogeneous saving capacities of informal workers would be preferable to expanding the existing formal worker programs.

MESSAGE 1: OUTSIDERS

The first message is self-explanatory, given the preceding discussion of the framework; the section entitled "South Asia's informal firms: outsiders, evaders, or avoiders?" provides more detail. The first part of the second message—that regulatory changes tend to have small direct effects on informality—is a consequence of the small share of evaders and avoiders in the informal sector.

The message about indirect effects needs some elaboration. Essentially, it says that market conditions in the informal sector, such as the demand for informally produced goods, may change significantly because of reforms in regulatory and tax policies that have sizable economy-wide productivity impacts, even if the reforms do not target informality. Thus, hypothetically, a reform that removes distortive subsidies in the ready-made garment industry may make it possible for capable garment manufacturers in the informal sector to compete on a more equal footing and grow.

MESSAGE 2: DIRECT AND INDIRECT EFFECTS OF REFORM

This complex interplay of informality with regulatory and tax policies is examined in chapters 2–4, in which the findings emphasize the importance of considering the heterogeneity of the informal sector and both direct and indirect channels of interaction.

The analysis in chapter 2 estimates the de facto distortions in resource allocation in Indian manufacturing, including the de facto entry barriers to firms, and predicts what would happen to economy-wide productivity and the informal sector if these distortions were reduced. It finds that, relative to the United States, nearly one-half of the total informality in Indian manufacturing may be accounted for by the indirect effects of prevailing firm-level distortions, including large de facto entry barriers. Although the chapter findings imply that there is sizable scope for indirectly reducing the inefficiencies associated with a large informal sector by reducing de facto distortions, it does not identify the specific policies or institutions that may cause these distortions. Discovering these causes would prove challenging, as would implementing reforms to tackle the causes in the face of potential political economy constraints.

Chapter 3 examines a specific policy lever: the replacement of the sales tax by the value added tax (VAT). This switch can reduce the tax burden on firms and eliminate the distortions caused by the double taxation in value chains. The chapter finds that in the case of India, the VAT had a sizable impact on total output and productivity. Because most informal firms are in the outsider group (type D), however, the VAT's impact on the informal sector—a reduction by 2 percent in the output of the sector—was limited and predominantly indirect.

Chapter 4 examines the relationship of informality and the elasticity of formal firm sales to the VAT rate. It finds that the VAT rate elasticity, an important parameter in the optimal design of tax rates, does not seem to depend on informality.

MESSAGE 3: EFFECTIVE INTERVENTIONS

The third message of this volume underscores that new technologies, such as e-commerce platforms, by lowering the transaction costs related to market search, transportation, and tracking and verification (Goldfarb and Tucker 2019), may allow small informal firms to grow and expand by easing demand-side constraints. Chapter 5 shows that these platforms offer a digital infrastructure that boosts market access at no cost to firms that are joining. In addition, firms on the platforms adopt improved business practices and technologies. The evidence in chapter 5 is part of a small but growing empirical literature on the impacts of digital technologies on informality.[12]

A common thread in this nascent literature is the fact that a subset of informal firms self-select into adopting digital technology or joining e-commerce platforms, underlining, once more, the heterogeneity of the informal sector. Chapter 5—as well as a recent case study of e-commerce platform sellers in Bangladesh, Nepal, Pakistan, and Sri Lanka (Bussolo et al. 2022)—shows that informal firms selling on e-commerce platforms are a select group that includes owners who are better educated and younger than average. It may be that e-commerce platforms yield benefits only to those informal entrepreneurs who have sufficient skills and capital and are constrained mainly on the demand side.[13] Hence, while policies to expand the internet infrastructure are useful, there is also a need for complementary policies that reach out to informal workers and firms that are not yet ready to join e-commerce.

Chapter 6 contributes to the evidence base on interventions that address supply-side constraints, that is, skills and credit constraints.[14] In the case of the extreme poor, chapter 6 describes the promising results of programs that simultaneously address multiple constraints to self-employment. A big push along multiple fronts is needed in such cases.

MESSAGE 4: SOCIAL PROTECTION SYSTEMS

The fourth message emerges from chapters 7 and 8. Chapter 7 illustrates the excess vulnerability of informal workers during the early phase of the COVID-19 (Coronavirus) crisis. Informal wage workers were significantly more likely than their formal counterparts to lose a job during the early period of the pandemic (April–May 2020). This gap cannot be explained by differences in location, occupation, or industry and hence appears to be caused by factors inherent to informality.

Against this backdrop, chapter 8 tackles the problem of universalizing social protection, focusing on the case of old-age pensions. Informal workers lack access to social insurance for risks such as job loss, illness, and old age. Noncontributory social assistance programs help bridge the gap, but only among the extreme poor, leaving a large missing middle in the informal sector uncovered by social programs. While some of the workers in this segment need social assistance, others have the capacity to build precautionary savings but lack access to suitable savings instruments. Given this heterogeneity, the chapter calls for a multipronged strategy to help cover the informal sector by expanding the coverage of existing noncontributory pension schemes for the adequate coverage of the extreme poor, while creating innovative contributory schemes or savings products for the missing middle.

The rest of this overview is organized as follows. The next section presents in more detail the conceptual framework of the volume. The following section describes the composition of the informal sector in South Asia, providing evidence on the relative size of outsiders, avoiders, evaders, and formal groups. Subsequent sections summarize the main findings and policy implications of the various chapters of this volume by organizing them around the main messages. The final section offers concluding remarks.

Conceptual Framework

The framework described in this section follows recent research (Kanbur 2017, 2021; Ulyssea 2018) on informality and, building on the insight that firms may have heterogeneous returns from formalization, reconciles the opposing views of informality.[15]

THE UNDISTORTED ECONOMY AND THE NATURAL DISTRIBUTION OF FIRM SIZE

Suppose that the output of firm i depends on the firm's total factor productivity (z) and inputs of capital (k) and labor (h): $y_i = z_i F(k_i, h_i)$. The production function is characterized by diminishing returns to scale.

Efficient and undistorted markets will allocate resources so as to equalize marginal returns across firms. Consider, for example, the allocation of labor. In equilibrium, each firm optimally employs labor to the point where the marginal product (*MP*) equals the marginal cost, which is the equilibrium wage rate $w*$, as follows:

$$MP_i^h = w*. \tag{1.1}$$

Because firms face the same wage rate, the marginal product of labor is equalized across firms.[16]

If firms differed in MP^h, there would be scope to increase aggregate output by shifting resources from low to high MP^h firms. Hence, in this undistorted economy, the equilibrium allocation of labor across firms is optimal from the perspective of aggregate productivity, with no scope left to increase aggregate output by shifting labor from one firm to another.

Firm size is proportional to TFP, for, otherwise, firms with higher TFP would not have the same marginal returns as those with lower TFPs. Given diminishing returns, the optimum allocation thus entails giving more inputs to higher TFP firms. This generates the optimal (or natural) firm size distribution, given the distribution of TFP among firms and the production technology.

In equilibrium, firms also have the same output per unit of input (labor or capital), regardless of the TFP differences. This, too, is a consequence of the firm's optimal input choices in undistorted markets. The intuition for this is that firms with higher TFP are larger in size in equilibrium and their TFP advantage is exactly counteracted by diminishing returns to scale. Box 1.1 illustrates this equilibrium with a specific production function.

BOX 1.1 Natural Firm Size in the Undistorted Economy: An Example

Suppose firms have a constant elasticity of substitution production function. Omitting the firm subscript for concision, firm level output is given by the following:

$$y = z[\alpha k^p + (1 - \alpha)h^p]^{\mu/p}. \tag{B1.1.1}$$

The parameters are the same for all firms. The parameter μ indicates the returns to scale and is smaller than 1 (decreasing returns).

This production function can be rewritten as follows:

$$y = zx^\mu, \tag{B1.1.2}$$

with x a composite input. This is possible for almost all production functions where the returns-to-scale parameter can be separated. In this constant elasticity of substitution case, the formula for x is as follows:

$$x = [\alpha k^p + (1 - \alpha)h^p]^{1/p}. \tag{B1.1.3}$$

(Box continues next page)

BOX 1.1 Natural Firm Size in the Undistorted Economy: An Example *(continued)*

If r is the factor price for k, and w is the factor price for h, then cost minimization by the firm implies a certain optimal ratio of inputs, leading to the following unit cost for x, denoted by c:

$$c = \left[\alpha r^{1-\sigma} + (1-\alpha) w^{1-\sigma} \right]^{1/(1-\sigma)}; \quad \sigma = \frac{1}{1-\rho}. \tag{B1.1.4}$$

These unit costs of x are the same for all firms.

Taking y as numeraire (that is, the output price is 1), the optimal size of a firm is as follows:

$$y_i^* = z_i \left(\mu \frac{z_i}{c} \right)^{\mu/(1-\mu)}. \tag{B1.1.5}$$

So, the optimal size of a firm is larger if the firm's productivity level is higher, but smaller if the market-determined unit cost of x is larger. If one of the firms increases its productivity, all firms will face a higher unit cost of x and thus the optimal size of all other firms will decline. In this optimum, the following condition also holds:

$$\frac{y_i}{x_i} = \frac{c}{\mu}. \tag{B1.1.6}$$

So, the observed productivity (level, not only marginal) is the same for all firms. Because the relation between k and x and between h and x is the same for all firms, the observed labor and capital productivity, too, are equal across firms.

INFORMALITY AND DISTORTIONS

Now, imagine that the government introduces a law that requires firms with employment levels above a threshold Q to formalize by registering with the government. Firms in the formal sector have to incur ongoing expenses to comply with labor regulations, such as mandated employer contributions to the social security benefits of workers and workplace safety requirements. These ongoing regulatory costs associated with the formal sector may be framed as an ad valorem tax on labor, τ^h_{formal}.[17]

Firms with a natural size below Q are not directly affected by the law because they have no reason to increase employment above this threshold and incur additional costs. These firms now constitute the informal sector. In contrast, firms with a natural size above Q now face a higher effective wage rate, net of the regulatory labor tax, and they reduce employment to the point where the marginal product of labor equals the new equilibrium wage rate, plus the labor tax as follows:[18]

$$MP^h_{formal} = \left(1 + \tau^h_{formal}\right) w^o \tag{1.2}$$

Because the labor released from the formal sector must be employed in the informal sector, the new equilibrium wage w^o has to be lower than the undistorted equilibrium wage w^* to induce informal firms to exceed their natural employment level. This general equilibrium impact of the regulation indirectly affects informal firms.

The regulatory wedge in labor costs between the two sectors implies that the marginal product of labor is higher in the formal sector:

$$MP^h_{formal} = \left(1 + \tau^h_{formal}\right) w^o > w^o = MP^h_{informal} \tag{1.3}$$

There is a misallocation of labor because there is scope to increase aggregate output by simply reallocating labor to the formal sector.

Firms in the formal sector now have a higher output per unit of labor than firms in the informal sector. Even with differences in TFP across firms, there were no differences in their labor productivities in equilibrium before the distortion—the regulatory wedge—was introduced.

OUTSIDERS, EVADERS, AND AVOIDERS: DIFFERENT TYPES OF INFORMALITY

Now, suppose that, while firms with employment greater than Q face a large fine if they do not register, the enforcement of this fine is not perfect.[19] Firms larger than Q weigh the costs and benefits of formalizing; they may decide not to register and risk the fine if the costs sufficiently outweigh the benefits.

Suppose also that, in addition to the labor tax, there is a one-time cost of entry into the formal sector that includes registration fees, as well as the effort expended in dealing with the paperwork and other procedures involved in the process of firm registration. Although formalizing entails higher regulatory costs, there are also potential benefits. Registration is often a precondition for bidding on government contracts and making loan applications. Accordingly, formalization may raise profits by enabling better access to markets and capital.

As in the case examined by Ulyssea (2018), suppose that the net gain from formalizing is larger among firms that have a larger natural size. This can be motivated by two mechanisms. First, firms with a larger natural size have more to gain from accessing a larger market. Second, larger firms are more visible to authorities and may therefore face a larger expected fine if they do not comply with the registration law.

The relationship between the net benefits of formalization and firm size is depicted in figure 1.2, in which the x-axis represents the natural size of the firm (in terms of employment) and the y-axis shows the net benefits of formalization (the benefits, minus the costs in present discounted value). As explained by Kanbur (2017), the effect of imperfectly enforced, size-dependent registration requirements is to create three types of informal firms depending on how firms alter their behavior in response to the requirements.

FIGURE 1.2 Formal and Informal Sectors with Entry Costs and Size-Based Registration Rules

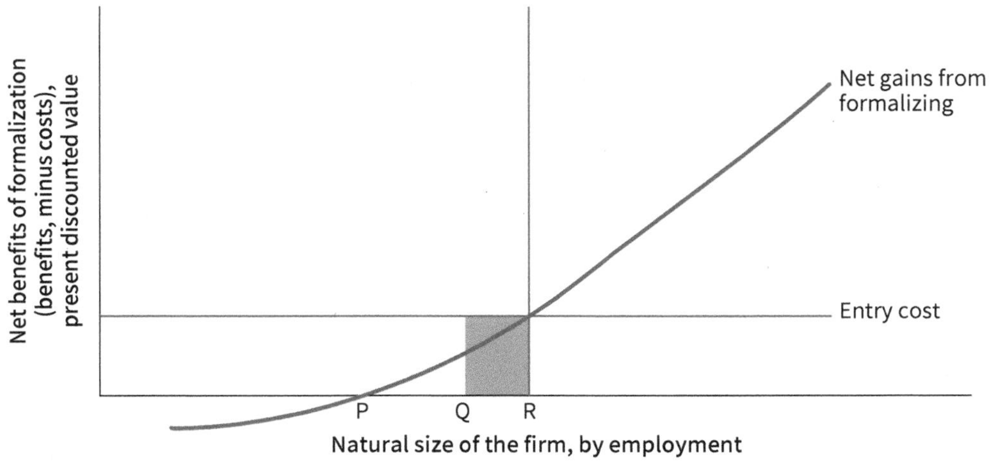

Source: Original figure produced for this publication.
Note: Q is the official threshold for registration. P is the level at which the net gains from formalizing become positive, and R the level at which they are sufficient to cover the entry cost.

Firms with a natural size greater than R (type A) will register. Firms with a natural size between Q and R will not want to register because the net benefits they accrue from formalization will not cover the entry costs. They will either avoid or evade the regulation. Specifically, firms that have a natural size significantly above Q but below R (type B) will find that remaining at their natural size, while evading the labor regulation by not registering, is optimal. Firms with a natural size slightly above Q (type C) will find that avoiding the regulation by remaining slightly below the size threshold Q is optimal. These firms will choose not to reach their full natural size and thereby remain legally outside the regulatory net.

As before, firms with a natural size below Q do not need to alter their behavior because of the size-dependent registration requirement. These type D firms—the outsiders—are arguably informal because of their small natural size and not because the owners wish to avoid or evade regulations. Given their current productivity levels, changing the cost of labor regulations or the intensity with which those regulations are enforced is unlikely to alter their decision to remain informal. This is especially true of firms with natural size below P, which have negative gains from formalization even after excluding entry costs.

Evasion and avoidance behaviors add to the distortions in the economy. Avoiders remain inefficiently small. This distortion in firm size because of size-dependent regulation and its toll on aggregate productivity is a major concern of economists. It is likely that evaders resort to suboptimal practices to hide their noncompliance, such as hiring workers informally to keep them off their rolls, impeding the performance of the firms and the workers.

POLICY LEVERS INFLUENCING INFORMALITY

The conventional policy levers for reducing informality involve reforms to business licensing requirements and product and factor market regulations that begin to apply at the threshold of the formal sector. Their impact depends on the extent to which the informal sector consists of evader and avoider firms. They have little direct impact on outsider firms.

For example, suppose there is a fall in the cost of compliance with labor regulations that start binding at size Q. This will shift the curve representing the net gains from formalizing upward at points Q and above, thereby inducing some type B and type C firms to formalize. Type D firms, however, will be largely untouched because the change in the regulatory cost will not affect their natural size or their gains from formalization.

Another option is to increase the intensity of regulatory enforcement among likely evaders. In terms of the framework, this would increase the expected penalty for evaders. Some evaders will start complying with the regulations, while others may choose to avoid the regulations altogether by shrinking to the point where they are legally outside the enforcement net, that is, by turning into avoiders. The total level of informality and the distortions caused by regulatory evasion will decrease, but the distortion caused by firms choosing to stay below their natural size to avoid the regulatory threshold may increase.

The price for achieving meaningful reductions in regulatory compliance costs and strengthening enforcement has to be weighed, too, in considering such policies. In lowering the costs of complying with regulations, not compromising the achievement of the intended impact of the regulations is important. Doing this may involve sizable investment in regulatory redesign and capacity-building measures, such as staff training and information technology system upgrades. Increasing enforcement intensity may likewise require expensive investments in enforcement capacity.

In addition to regulations, other levers are available to policy makers that do not target informality directly, but may still improve conditions in the informal sector and raise the productivity of the economy. Their impact is not restricted to those informal firms that are evading or avoiding regulations.

Reforms that reduce distortions in the formal sector may affect the informal sector indirectly. The impacts depend on the nature of product market links between the two sectors. If informal firms produce goods that are substitutes for those produced by formal firms, this will decrease the demand for informally produced goods, causing the least profitable informal firms to either shed workers or shut down. Thus, if the two sectors compete, productivity growth in the formal sector will tend to shrink informality. In contrast, if the two sectors produce complementary goods, growth in the formal sector will tend to increase informality.

Access to capital, managerial skills, and technology is another lever for enabling substantive change. For example, a government program that effectively addresses informational barriers to the adoption of better business practices could boost the earnings of informal entrepreneurs. Such an intervention might also induce formalization by removing managerial constraints on firm size and increasing the natural size of informal firms. It could make formalization more attractive because better-managed firms may have more to gain from access to government contracts. The main challenge for policy makers is to diagnose underlying market or institutional failures correctly and devise programs that can address them in a cost-effective manner.

South Asia's Informal Firms: Outsiders, Evaders, or Avoiders?

This chapter's framework has emphasized the heterogeneity among firms in the informal sector and how that matters in policy design. For effective policy design, it would be useful to know how many informal firms are informal because they are trying to avoid or evade regulations and how many only happen to be in the informal sector because of other constraints to productivity growth and market access.

The share of outsider-, avoider-, and evader-type firms in the informal sector of South Asian countries is ultimately an empirical question. It hinges on the distribution of the hypothetical natural firm size, that is, the size distribution that would naturally emerge if business regulations and taxes applied uniformly to all firms regardless of size. This natural size distribution is not observed directly. Nevertheless, examining the actual size distribution of formal and informal firms can throw some light on this issue. Although better and more frequent data collection on informal activities would be useful in settling this empirical issue, a main conclusion from the available incomplete data is that the share of the outsiders (type D) is large in South Asia; thus, policies that deal with distortions and enforcement capacity, while still relevant, should not be the only policies pursued in the region.

South Asian firms are predominantly small. In Nepal, according to the official census of firms, 91 percent of all firms engaged in nonfarm activities employ only five or fewer persons (figure 1.3). This share is even higher in Bangladesh and India. In general, firms with more than 10 persons account for fewer than 5 percent of all nonfarm firms in these countries.

FIGURE 1.3 **South Asian Firms Are Predominantly Small**

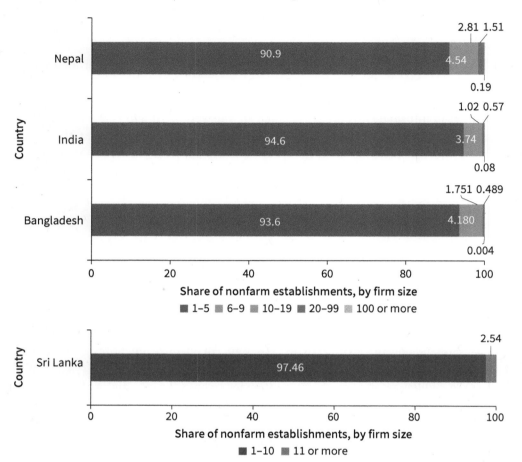

Sources: Based on tables published in government reports on Bangladesh Economic Growth Institute census (2009) microdata and the India Economic Census (2013–14), the Nepal Economic Census (2018), and the Sri Lanka Economic Census (2013–14).
Note: The Economic Growth Institute census covers only urban locations in 19 districts.

The size distribution of informal firms is dominated to an even greater extent by tiny firms. In Nepal, among firms in nonfarm activities that are not registered with any government agency, nearly 99 percent employ only five or fewer persons (figure 1.4). In Bangladesh, among firms in nonfarm activities that do not possess the most basic type of business license, a municipal trade license, 98.1 percent employ only five or fewer persons.

Chatterjee and Kanbur (2014) infer the shares of factories evading and avoiding the Factories Act, a law in India under which all manufacturing factories with more than

FIGURE 1.4 **Informal South Asian Firms Are Predominantly Microenterprises**

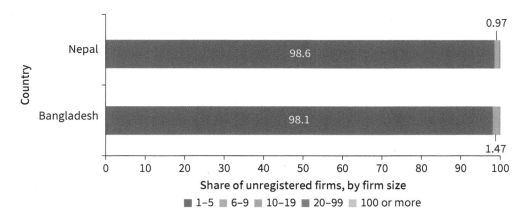

Sources: Based on tables published in government reports on Bangladesh Economic Growth Institute census (2009) microdata and the Nepal Economic Census (2018).
Note: The Bangladesh Economic Growth Institute census covers only urban locations in 19 districts. Registration in the Economic Growth Institute census refers to firms registered for a trade license with a municipality. Registration in the Nepal Economic Census refers to any type of registration with a government agency.

10 workers are required to register. They do so by pooling data from the Annual Survey of Industries, which captures factories registered under this Act, with that from the National Sample Survey Office survey of unregistered factories.[20] Factories that appear in the latter survey (and are therefore unregistered), but that have more than 10 workers, must be evading the act, while some of those that are slightly below the regulatory size threshold are likely avoiders. By this estimate, only 1.5 percent of all manufacturing firms are evaders and fewer than 1.0 percent are avoiders.[21] About 97 percent of factories appear to be outsiders.

Firms in the informal sector also appear to differ in the extent to which they perceive the benefits of formalization. For example, in Bangladesh, informal firms employing more than five individuals are more likely than firms with fewer than five individuals to perceive benefits from tax formalization (figure 1.5). The differences in the perceived benefits from tax registration are most evident in regard to access to credit and the attainment of a greater scale in operations. While neither of these groups perceive a significant benefit in terms of access to export markets or government programs or of better contract enforcement, the gaps between smaller and larger informal firms are sizable. These patterns are consistent with the idea expressed in the framework of the analysis here that naturally smaller firms may have less to gain from formalizing.

There is substantial heterogeneity in revenue per worker within the informal sector and between the formal and informal sectors. In India's manufacturing sector,

FIGURE 1.5 Larger Firms Are More Likely to Perceive Benefits from Obtaining a Tax ID

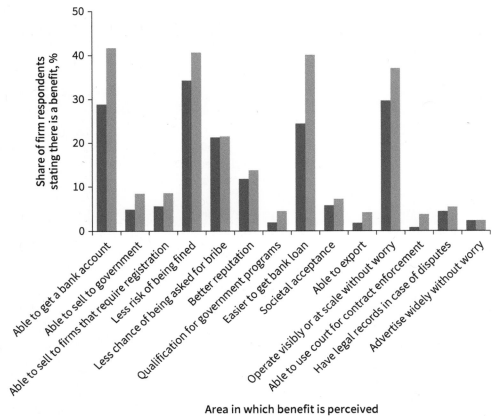

Area in which benefit is perceived

Firm size: ■ 1–5 ■ 5+

Source: Data of Informal Firms Survey 2010: Bangladesh, 2010 (dashboard), Microdata Library, World Bank, Washington, DC, https://doi.org/10.48529/sne5-np62.

the distribution of value added per worker in informal factories employing 5–10 persons looks different from the corresponding distribution in formal factories, although there is substantial overlap in the ranges. The difference is starker in considering informal factories with fewer than 5 workers (figure 1.6).[22] The mean value added per worker in informal factories employing 5–10 persons is about one-third the corresponding mean in formal factories, while the mean in informal factories employing 1–5 persons is about one-eighth the mean in formal factories. These differences in mean value added per worker may reflect distortions caused by how

FIGURE 1.6 **Informal Firms Have Lower Output per Worker**

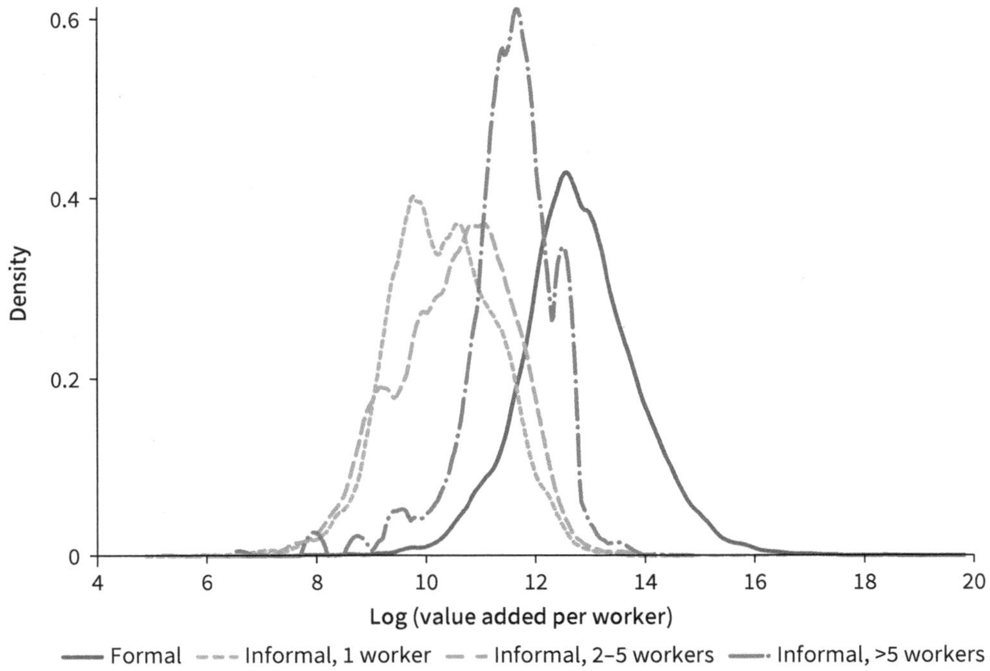

Source: Estimates based on pooled microdata from ASI (Annual Survey of Industries) (dashboard), Industrial Statistics Wing, National Statistical Office, Ministry of Statistics and Program Implementation, Kolkata, http://www .csoisw.gov.in/CMS/En/1023-annual-survey-of-industries.aspx; "India: Unincorporated Non-Agricultural Enterprises (Excluding Construction), July 2015–June 2016, 73 round" (data portal), National Data Archive, National Sample Survey Office, Ministry of Statistics and Program Implementation, New Delhi, http://www.icssrdataservice.in /datarepository/index.php/catalog/148.

firms respond to regulations, as well as differences in access to capital, product markets, and skills.

The variation in the earnings of informal workers echoes the patterns observed in informal firms. The informal sector is mostly poor, but there is much heterogeneity within it and also some overlap with the formal sector. Figure 1.7 shows the share of informal and formal workers at different income percentiles of the wage-earning population in Bangladesh and Pakistan as estimated from labor force survey data. As expected, informal workers predominate in the lower half of the earnings distribution. More than 80 percent of wage workers at the median income level in these countries are in the informal sector. However, there is also a sizable presence of informal workers at the upper end of the earnings distribution. In Bangladesh, at least 50 percent of workers at the 90th earnings percentile are informal; in Pakistan, the share is more than 20 percent.

FIGURE 1.7 Informal and Formal Workers, by Earnings Percentile, Bangladesh and Pakistan

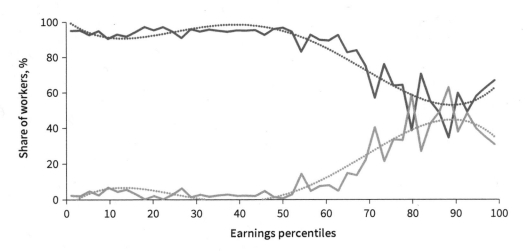

a. Bangladesh: distribution of informality

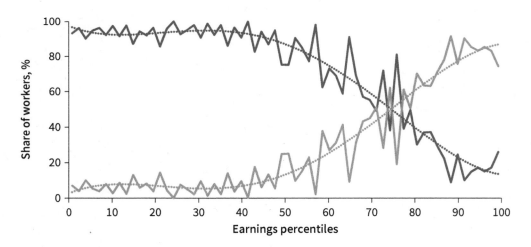

b. Pakistan: distribution of informality

Sources: Bangladesh: Labour Force Survey 2016–2017: Bangladesh, 2016–2017, Bangladesh Bureau of Statistics, Dhaka, Bangladesh; Pakistan: Labor Force Survey 2017, Labour Force Statistics (dashboard), Pakistan Bureau of Statistics, Islamabad, Pakistan, https://www.pbs.gov.pk/content/labour-force-statistics.

Likely Effect of Reforms on the Informal Sector: Productivity Impacts

Regulatory and tax policy reforms are important because of their potential economy-wide productivity impact; however, as shown in chapters 2–4, they have limited potential to transform the informal sector directly. One reason is that a large group of firms will not benefit directly from these reforms because they are far from the size thresholds that trigger compliance. This may explain why business licensing reforms have had limited effect on the informal sector. Nevertheless, the wider productivity impacts of such reforms may have sizable spillovers on informality in the long run. As is explained in chapter 2, the total potential for such long-run indirect impacts may be large given the sheer extent of the distortions in resource allocation that still characterize South Asian economies.

Identifying specific reforms with the potential for a large impact on aggregate productivity, however, remains a challenging policy research agenda. One such reform is the implementation of the VAT system. As is estimated in chapter 3, this reform had sizable economy-wide productivity effects, including indirect effects on the informal sector, but limited direct impacts on informal firms. It thus remains important to find ways to address directly the demand- and supply-side constraints to the growth of informal firms, particularly outsider firms.

BUSINESS ENTRY REFORMS HAVE LIMITED EFFECT

The exclusion view of informality emphasizes the potential of reforms that lower entry barriers to the formal sector to help informal firms formalize and grow. As described in the framework, this impact depends on the number of informal firms poised at the threshold of formality.

Perhaps motivated by the exclusion view, the simplification of business entry procedures has recently been among the most common types of regulatory reforms enacted by low- and middle-income countries, including South Asian ones. For example, in 2004–11, governments and stakeholders in 54 countries introduced new technology to simplify company registration processes (Wille et al. 2011). In 2004, 124 countries required entrepreneurs to deposit a fixed minimum paid-in capital amount legally with banks or notaries before incorporating a business. By 2019, more than half of these countries had eliminated this requirement (World Bank 2020b).

The evidence on the impact of such reforms on informality is sobering (Bruhn and McKenzie 2014; Jayachandran 2020). Several studies find that efforts to ease the registration process among firms can lead to a modest increase in registration rates, but not all do. For example, in a randomized controlled trial in Bangladesh, the delivery of information to informal firms on registration procedures had no significant impact on formalization (De Georgi and Rahman 2013). Similarly, when randomly selected groups of informal firms in Sri Lanka were provided information about the registration process and reimbursement of the direct costs of registration, their registration rate did not increase (de Mel, McKenzie, and Woodruff 2013).

Such modest impacts have been observed not only in interventions targeting small firms but even in reforms that could potentially affect a much larger range of firm types. For example, a large-scale reform in Mexico that reduced the number of days taken to start a business from 30 to 1 increased firm registration by only 5 percent (Bruhn 2011; Kaplan, Piedra, and Seira 2011).

Even if firms can be induced to formalize if compensated sufficiently for the registration expenses, few appear to benefit much from registration. This finding suggests that most informal firms do not have much to gain from registering formally. In the Sri Lankan randomized study, when given payments equivalent to one-half a month to one month of the median firm's profits, one-fifth of the firms registered. Raising the payment amount increased the registration rate. Within 15–31 months, the firms that had been induced to register had higher mean profits, but this was driven by a few select firms that grew rapidly after registration (de Mel, McKenzie, and Woodruff 2013).

This heterogeneity in the potential to benefit from formalizing may partly derive from differences in the personal characteristics of informal business owners. In Sri Lanka, 70 percent of informal business owners have personal characteristics similar to wage earners, and 30 percent are similar to formal business owners (de Mel, McKenzie, and Woodruff 2010). In Mexico, relative to informal business owners who shared personal characteristics with formal business owners, informal business owners who shared characteristics with wage workers were much less likely to formalize in response to a licensing reform and more likely to become wage workers (Bruhn 2013).

Though business entry reforms have not delivered on the promise of making informal firms formalize and grow, it would be premature to disregard such reforms. First, it is possible that there are significant hidden costs of business entry that are not being addressed in licensing reforms. Second, making entry more accessible to ordinary firms may have other positive impacts on aggregate productivity by increasing competition and efficiency in the formal sector (Charlot, Malherbet, and Terra 2015; Ulyssea 2018). This may create better employment opportunities for workers who are stuck in precarious jobs in the informal sector. Such indirect impacts of entry reforms on the informal sector are not well researched in South Asia.

REFORMS TO ECONOMIC DISTORTIONS: SIZABLE IMPACTS ON THE INFORMAL SECTOR

Although the direct impacts of regulatory reforms on the informal sector may be limited to the relatively small segment of evader- and avoider-type firms, the gains in aggregate productivity that are achieved by major economic reforms may, in time, have sizable indirect effects on the informal sector. This channel is highlighted in chapter 2, which measures the magnitude and impacts of de facto entry barriers and firm-level misallocation in Indian manufacturing.[23]

Chapter 2 finds that more than half the current size of India's informal sector can be explained in equal measure by entry barriers and distortions. Specifically, distorting the benchmark US economy by introducing India's higher level of entry costs and distortions would raise the share of the informal sector to 54 percent, more than halfway to the actual share of 85 percent in India.

How can this large outcome be reconciled with the small impacts of simplifying business entry observed in randomized trials? One reason is that chapter 2 considers the broader, long-run economic impacts of addressing distortions and entry barriers and their indirect impacts on informality. These indirect impacts are caused by an increase in the aggregate productivity of the economy and the resulting price effects. Lowering entry barriers and reducing size-dependent distortions induce the most able entrepreneurs to invest in productivity-enhancing improvements and innovations, which drives out the less able entrepreneurs in both the formal and informal sectors. The indirect impact on informal manufacturing depends on the demand links with formal manufacturing.

Another reason the analysis in chapter 2 predicts a large impact from the elimination of entry barriers is that it finds the de facto firm entry cost to be considerably higher than the explicit procedural costs of business licensing. It may be that the business entry reforms investigated in randomized studies have had a limited impact on de facto entry barriers. This suggests that policy makers should advance beyond business licensing reforms and address other access costs, such as the cost of procedures to obtain an electricity connection, that may be prohibitive for small firms, or less explicit sources of entry barriers and distortions, such as corruption in regulatory enforcement.[24]

However, this will not be an easy agenda. First, identifying specific sources of entry barriers and size-dependent distortions is a challenge. In their survey of recent research on distortions and productivity, Restuccia and Rogerson (2017) note that the specific policies and regulations identified in this body of research as causes of distortion do not explain a large share of the observed magnitudes of distortion. Second, even if the sources of distortions were identified, efforts to tackle them could run into opposition from powerful groups with vested interests.

Specific sources of direct and indirect distortions may reside, for example, in tax systems. Because taxes on corporate profits, sales, or value added increase the ongoing costs of formality, a reduction in tax rates might reduce informality by making formalization more attractive.[25] Changes in the tax structure, too, can have an impact on the informal sector. An important development in this respect is the replacement of the sales tax by the VAT in much of South Asia. Indian states gradually replaced sales taxes with the VAT during 2002–14. Building on these reforms, in 2017, India adopted a nationwide unified goods and services tax (GST), which is structured as a VAT. The stated objectives of this tax reform included the expansion of the tax net among informal firms and growth in the manufacturing sector (KPMG 2017; Rao and Mukherjee 2019).

The VAT eliminates cascading or double taxation along the value chain, potentially reducing the deadweight losses from taxation and making formalization more attractive.[26] Chapter 3 examines this channel in the case of the introduction of the

VAT in the Indian state of West Bengal. It finds that the direct impact of the VAT reform on informality was quite limited. The estimates imply that, if the cascading sales tax had been replaced by a VAT while keeping the tax rate the same, only 0.3 percent of informal firms would have registered.[27] This muted impact arose because of the prevalence of outsider-type firms in the informal sector. For such firms, a lower tax burden did not generate a major incentive to formalize.

Chapter 3 also finds that, even though the switch from the sales tax to the VAT did not have a major impact on formalization, it did have a significant positive impact on total output, profits, and wage income by reducing distortions caused by double taxation. A switch to a VAT system while keeping the tax rate the same would have increased formal sector output by 12 percent and reduced informal sector output by 2 percent, the latter predominantly through indirect channels.

Although the direct response of informal firms to tax policy changes may be restrained, the existence of a large informal sector may influence how formal firms respond to changes in tax policy. For instance, widespread informality may enable formal firms to evade the tax increase. Greater competition from informal firms may make the demand for the goods of formal firms more price elastic, thereby rendering the revenue more sensitive to tax rates. Widespread informality may thus dilute the impact of changes in tax rates. Should this be a major consideration in the design of tax policy?

Chapter 4 makes a new contribution to the limited evidence base on this question in the context of the multiple tax rates prevailing in India's GST system. These multiple rates exist mainly because, in addition to raising tax revenue, the GST is used to improve the equity of the tax system by imposing lower tax rates on necessity goods (such as fresh produce) and higher rates on luxuries.

Using detailed data on product-level GST returns from the state of Karnataka and exploiting the natural policy experiment generated by the multiplicity of GST rate changes, chapter 4 estimates the sensitivity of reported sales to the tax rate and considers whether the presence of informal firms affects this sensitivity.[28] The estimated elasticity is high. Firms report 2.6 percent fewer sales when the tax rate they face increases by 1 percent. This finding suggests that the inefficiency caused by multiple rates may be sizable. However, the elasticity of the reported sales to the GST rate is not significantly higher in sectors with a large share of informality, suggesting that there is no efficiency rationale for applying lower tax rates in sectors with more informality.

Can Digital Platforms Address Demand Constraints on Informality?

Digital platforms can help informal firms transcend constraints posed by limited access to markets. More generally, digital technologies shift the cost-benefit balance of investing, growing, and becoming more visible among informal firms. E-commerce platforms provide an infrastructure of marketing, warehousing, and commercial relations at no cost to firms that participate. The requirements of registration with tax authorities to operate on these platforms do not offset these benefits; in some cases, as shown by the emerging evidence presented in chapter 5 and other recent studies, informal firms actively formalize soon after joining the platforms.

Yet, digital platform technologies are not a silver bullet. Not all informal firms have smooth access to online platforms. Moreover, such platforms mainly address the demand-side constraints on small firms. The heterogeneity of the informal sector means that not all informal firms or workers would necessarily benefit from easing only market access. Small businesses also face other constraints, such as those related to credit, skills, access to technology, and managerial expertise.[29] Among firms in which the relevant constraint relates to such factors, supply-side interventions addressing these constraints might be more useful.

E-COMMERCE CAN IMPROVE GOODS MARKET ACCESS TO THE INFORMAL SECTOR

The market share of e-commerce in South Asia is small, but it is growing rapidly. For example, the share of online channels in total retail sales expanded from 1.6 percent in 2015 to about 5.0 percent in 2020 (IBEF 2021). This trend accelerated during the COVID-19 crisis. Total e-commerce revenues in Bangladesh thus reportedly rose by 70 percent to 80 percent during 2020 (Hasan 2020). In addition to retail, digital platforms are also increasingly active in other service industries, such as in transportation and domestic services and in agriculture. The Collabrex digital platform in Pakistan, for instance, connects farmers to markets. Such industries have large informal sectors. However, there is a dearth of rigorous evidence on the impacts of these developments on the informal sector.

Digital platforms reduce transaction costs related to search, replication, transportation, tracking, and verification (Goldfarb and Tucker 2019), which may be especially important for small and informal firms. By joining an e-commerce platform, small firms can gain access to a large customer base without incurring prohibitively expensive investments in marketing and distribution channels. As their online transactions grow, they may become better able to prove their creditworthiness to banks through verifiable digital records of sales and payments. This may improve their access to credit (Klapper, Miller, and Hess 2019). Joining a platform may also enable productivity growth in small firms by improving the access of the firms to information on new technologies and business practices and helping them generate data to track their revenues, costs, and other performance indicators.

Chapter 5 uncovers new evidence on this issue by analyzing previously unexplored data from a large e-commerce platform in India.[30] The chapter describes the impacts on small and informal firms of joining such a platform by analyzing information from transactions on the platform (quantity, prices, and the locations of individual sales over a period of four years), in combination with data from a survey on the businesses and entrepreneurs selling on the platform.

The analysis in chapter 5 suggests that e-commerce platforms can help firms grow by enabling access to a wider market. Most of the firms selling on the platform analyzed are located in the major metropolitan areas of Delhi and Mumbai, but they are selling to a much more spatially dispersed customer base. The states of Karnataka, Maharashtra, Tamil Nadu, and Uttar Pradesh (mostly postal codes outside greater Delhi) account for the largest shares of sales, and none of them have shares of more than 15 percent of total purchases. Businesses selling on the platform experience a steady increase in sales and in the number of postal codes to which they sell. They also experience an expansion in the number of product types sold.

Informal firms on the e-commerce platform are generally doing as well as their formal counterparts on the platform in terms of growth. There is no difference between formal and informal firms in the growth rates of the monthly number of sales transactions, total revenue, number of products offered, and geographic reach (as measured by the number of postal codes to which they sell).

Informal businesses even outperform formal businesses in some dimensions of productivity on the platform. On average, a formal business has 34 fewer sales per employee than an informal business with similar characteristics, and the revenue per worker of the formal business is nearly one-half the corresponding revenue of the informal firm. This suggests that informal businesses have relatively more to gain than formal businesses by joining a platform. It may be that joining the platform allows smaller businesses to gain access to a larger market without any of the overhead costs—such as those involved in advertising and building networks of sales agents—that larger businesses may have already incurred.

The platform also provides a relatively stable source of demand, a feature that may be especially desirable to informal firms because of their limited cash buffers. More than 65 percent of the firms on the platform experience almost no months with zero sales. Large month-on-month fluctuations in sales are also relatively rare; 32 percent of the firms experience no month in which their sales dropped 50 percent relative to the previous month.

These positive findings have potential implications beyond e-commerce. Digital platforms are also increasingly active in South Asia in markets for low-skilled services, such as transportation, food delivery, personal care, and domestic help. For example, there are numerous ride-hailing and food delivery apps operating in the region. The personal care and domestic help services industry, too, is seeing the entry of apps, such as the Hellotask platform in Bangladesh that connects domestic help workers and potential employers.[31]

Such platforms could enhance earnings among low-skilled workers in South Asia's informal sector. The market for personal or domestic services is predominantly local and informal, and there are almost no modern firms supplying such services. Digital platforms could ease frictions in these markets by making it easier to match demand and supply and by enabling workers to build a reputation for good work. For instance, in a randomized experiment involving data entry operators on an international online task platform, providing a rating and feedback to inexperienced workers on the platform almost tripled their income and reduced their level of unemployment (Pallais 2014). Although encouraging, such evidence is mostly from high-income country contexts and may not translate to informal labor markets in South Asia.

Flexibility is another potential benefit of digital platforms that deserves more careful examination in South Asia. In the United States, Uber drivers are found to benefit significantly from the flexibility in work hours that the service enables and are even willing to earn less as long as they get to choose when they work. It is estimated that this flexibility is worth more than twice the surplus they would earn in less-flexible arrangements (Chen et al. 2019). Flexibility in choosing when and where to work could be particularly valuable to women in the informal sector who may be struggling to balance work with childcare responsibilities and undertaking long, unsafe commutes to and from work.

Whether online lending platforms can change how informal businesses obtain loans in South Asia is also worth examining. Such platforms use automated processes to screen loan applicants and match them with lenders. This potentially enables the lenders to lend more quickly and more optimally than traditional banks; the fact that they do not take deposits reduces their regulatory requirements and allows them to lend without collateral (Beaumont, Tang, and Vansteenberghe 2021). These attributes make the platforms particularly well suited for extending credit to small and young firms, which often lack collateral and credit history with traditional banks.[32] Some evidence on South Asia suggests that small firms that already use digital payments are more likely to benefit from online lending platforms.[33]

Not all the findings in chapter 5 are good news for the informal sector. Two observations suggest that many informal firms are currently not in a position to benefit from selling on e-commerce platforms. First, there is significant attrition among both formal and informal firms; 8.6 percent of firms exited the platform within one month of registering. Only about 50 percent of firms remained active on the platform for more than two years.

Second, firms that sell on the platform are also notably different from the average firm. They are, for instance, disproportionately located in two major metropolitan areas, Delhi and Mumbai. Some other key differences with typical firms become apparent if they are compared with the sample of entrepreneurs in a large survey that is representative of the population of family business owners in age, sex, and educational attainment.[34] Entrepreneurs selling on the e-commerce platform are substantially younger, better educated, and more likely to be women than the general population of family business owners. While the average age of sellers in the sample is about 32, it is around 44 in the general population. The majority of entrepreneurs on the platform has a university degree, while the range is 15 percent to 40 percent in the general population depending on the size of the firm. The share of women entrepreneurs in the sample—only 20 percent—is much higher than the 2 percent to 4 percent share in the general population of entrepreneurs. This degree of self-selection into the use of online sales channels suggests that the observed experience of online sellers in the study sample may not be representative of the experience of the typical small and informal business in South Asia if it were to join the platform. It may be that younger, better educated, and women entrepreneurs are in a better position to harness the benefits of online sales channels.

Among the firms that are not able to adopt and use digital platforms effectively, this new technology may represent a threat rather than an opportunity. As such platforms make deeper inroads into markets traditionally served by informal firms, such firms may find that survival is increasingly difficult. Another concern is that digital platforms tend to accumulate market power because of inherent economies of scale in this technology and because they can acquire a hold on consumers because of behavioral biases in the way people shop online.[35] The growing market power of digital platforms may squeeze profit margins among informal producers and constrain their growth possibilities. Understanding the factors that prevent informal firms from using digital platforms effectively is important.

Barriers to Skills and Capital Accumulation in the Informal Sector

Informal enterprises are constrained not only by product markets but also by limited access to skills and capital. The evidence is promising on interventions that provide capital or business skills to microenterprises and small businesses in the informal sector. Some programs seem to work.[36] For example, a randomized study found that the Start-and-Improve Your Business Program, one of the most widely implemented business training programs in developing countries, had a positive impact on woman-owned microenterprises in Sri Lanka (de Mel, McKenzie, and Woodruff 2014). Providing grants in cash or in kind, too, has been found to have a positive impact on informal microenterprises, consistent with the hypotheses that a large segment of informal firms is credit constrained. Grants worth US$100 or US$200 significantly increased profits among microenterprises in Sri Lanka, and the positive impacts lasted for at least five years (de Mel, McKenzie, and Woodruff 2012).[37]

In the design of such interventions, the aspirations of the target group should matter. As with e-commerce platforms, it may be the case that only some informal business owners want to grow their businesses substantially; others may only wish to earn a good living, while staying small. Consider, for example, the fact that fewer than one-third of the informally self-employed in Sri Lanka resemble small and medium enterprises owners in terms of attributes such as cognitive ability, motivation, and a competitive attitude (de Mel, McKenzie, and Woodruff 2010). Most resemble wage workers rather than small and medium business owners.[38]

In this sense, interventions among informal microenterprises can be broadly divided into two types. The first type of program selectively targets informal entrepreneurs who want to grow their firms substantially and aims to help them grow into small or medium formal businesses. Targeting such a program well is critical. For example, it could be structured as a business plan competition for aspiring entrepreneurs (McKenzie 2017). Information from peers or psychometric data analysis could also be used for better targeting. For instance, Hussam, Rigol, and Roth (2022) use a cash grant experiment in India to demonstrate that peer knowledge can help target microentrepreneurs with high growth potential.

The second type of intervention helps informal business owners improve their earnings potential without necessarily expecting them to grow into big firms. Such programs should not have to be selective; rather, they should be seen as part of a multifaceted strategy to reduce the precariousness of livelihoods in the informal sector.[39]

Here, graduation or economic inclusion programs that simultaneously target multiple constraints to earnings growth among extreme poor households also show promise. Based on the idea that the extreme poor need a big push along multiple dimensions to be able to change their economic prospects sustainably, the programs provide productive asset transfers, intensive training and coaching, consumption support, and other support, such as health services. The pioneering Targeted Ultra-Poor Program run by BRAC, a Bangladesh nongovernmental organization, has been found to help rural women who were dependent on casual wage labor activities in agriculture to diversify into self-employment in the nonfarm sector and increase their incomes (Bandeira et al. 2013).[40]

In this context, chapter 6 examines whether multifaceted programs to raise earnings potential in the informal sector should also emphasize socioemotional skills. This question is motivated by growing evidence, mostly from high-income countries, that personal traits, such as perseverance, self-control, trust, self-esteem, empathy, hostility, and the ability to engage productively in society are changeable and matter to labor market outcomes (Acosta and Muller 2018; Heckman, Stixrud, and Urzua 2006). Using new survey data from Pakistan and Sri Lanka, chapter 6 finds that, unlike cognitive ability and formal education, socioemotional traits do not have a consistent positive association with labor market returns. These findings suggest that the labor market returns to socioeconomic skills depend on economic structure and institutions and might be greater in the formal sector. More context-specific evidence on which of these skills really matter will be important in program design.

Programs intended for women microentrepreneurs may also need to address norms. In Pakistan, women were found to learn as much as men from business training, but only the latter saw an improvement in business outcomes (Giné and Mansuri 2021). This finding may be because the women lacked the agency to implement what they had learned in the business training. Leveraging peer support among women to complement training and strengthen confidence and business aspirations made a difference in a business training program in India (Field et al. 2016).

Building Resilience: Offering Social Insurance in the Informal Sector

INFORMAL WORKERS ARE VULNERABLE TO SHOCKS

Informal sector workers are disproportionally vulnerable to shocks. Because they are not covered by formal employment protection laws and social insurance programs and are concentrated within microenterprises and small firms that have limited cash reserves, they are more highly exposed to job loss during negative shock events. Possessing fewer savings and poorer access to credit than formal workers, informal sector workers are also less able to cope with labor market shocks.

The COVID-19 crisis has made the vulnerability of South Asia's informal sector all too evident. Chapter 7 uses a large panel data set on India to assess how informal workers have weathered the crisis compared with formal workers. Difference in differences event study regressions show that informal wage workers were significantly more likely than their formal counterparts to lose a job during the early period of the pandemic (April–May 2020). The likelihood that informal workers would lose a job was 6 percent higher relative to formal workers in the same location (district) and industry (figure 1.8, panel a). Because the analysis controls for location and industry-specific variation in the shock, this excess vulnerability among informal workers is not driven by the concentration of these workers in specific industries, such as tourism and hospitality, which were disproportionately affected by the lockdown, but likely reflects the inherently greater risk faced by informal workers. To a lesser extent, self-employed individuals were also more vulnerable than formal workers (figure 1.8, panel b).

OFFERING SOCIAL INSURANCE IN THE INFORMAL SECTOR: A MULTIFACETED APPROACH

Individuals working in South Asia's informal sector typically lack access to social insurance programs that help cover risks such as job loss, illness or injury, and old age. The heterogeneity of income and savings capacity among informal sector workers calls for a multifaceted approach to extending social insurance to these workers.

Chapter 8 examines ways to extend pension arrangements to informal sector workers in South Asia, an issue that will become increasingly urgent as the population starts to age. There are two traditional approaches to this problem. The first is to start from the bottom and move up, that is, by expanding and deepening the coverage of targeted social assistance programs. The second is to start from the top and move down, that is, by trying to include more of the informal sector into the net of tax-funded insurance programs. New evidence on the heterogeneity of savings capacity among informal

FIGURE 1.8 **The COVID-19 Lockdown Affected Informal Workers More**

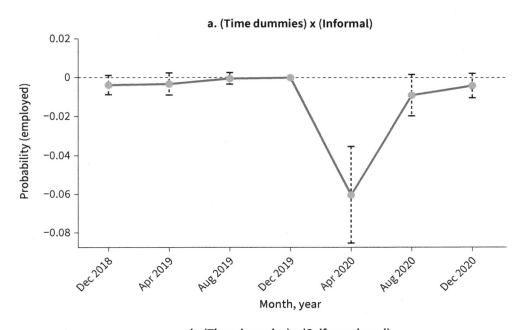

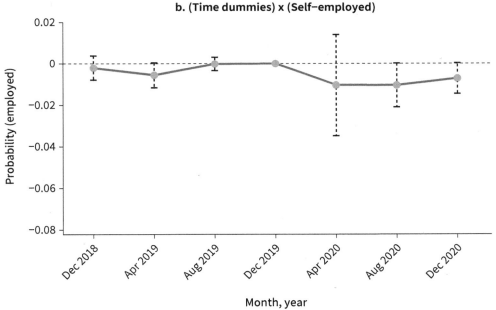

Source: Calculations based on CMIE CPHS data.
Note: The charts depict difference in differences event study estimates of the likelihood of employment among informal workers (panel a) and the self-employed (panel b) relative to formal workers. December 2019 is the baseline period. Informal, self-employed and formal denote employment status as of December 2019. The dashed vertical lines depict the 95 percent confidence intervals of the estimates.

workers suggests that these approaches should be complemented with new interventions, such as introducing flexible, low-cost savings instruments for those informal workers who have some capacity to save. The lessons of this analysis are also relevant for other types of social insurance programs, such as those addressing unemployment or health shocks.

Five countries in the region run noncontributory pension schemes that target the elderly and are mostly means tested. For example, in Bangladesh the old-age social pension scheme targets old persons who do not receive any other governmental or nongovernmental allowance and whose annual income does not exceed Tk 10,000 (equivalent to US$120). The income ceilings and benefit levels vary across the region.

Simulations show that expanding the coverage and benefit levels of noncontributory schemes to cover the informal sector fully could become prohibitively expensive as the population ages. Keeping coverage rates and benefits constant, population aging alone implies a 200 percent to 300 percent increase in the total cost of these programs (as a share of gross domestic product) by 2050. A large expansion of noncontributory schemes may also cause incentive-related problems. As benefit levels rise and targeting thresholds become looser, such schemes could distort labor market choices.

Countries that have tried the alternate approach—simply extending contributory schemes designed for the formal sector to the informal sector—have experienced mixed results. Social security agencies and their programs were designed to reach a relatively small formal workforce and may lack the implementation capacity to scale up programs to the self-employed and the informal wage workers in a cost-effective and user-friendly manner.

Efforts to modify existing programs to make them more suitable for the informal sector have been relatively more successful. These cases, many of which are in Latin America, are characterized by simple enrollment processes, low costs, and the bundling of social insurance and other benefits to make the schemes sufficiently attractive to encourage informal workers and employers to join.

Some of the individuals in the missing middle of the informal sector in South Asia may have the capacity to save for retirement. A growing share of Pakistan households are accumulating sizable assets over the life cycle. In 2018, the median net worth of households headed by a 60- to 65-year-old was equivalent to 36.8 months of household consumption, almost twice the net worth in 2001. This accumulation (relative to a household's monthly consumption) occurs at a comparable pace across urban and rural households from all but the poorest quintile of the population, perhaps in response to the forces of population aging and weakening family and village risk-sharing networks.

Chapter 8 concludes that households possessing the ability to save for retirement seem to lack access to suitable financial instruments. Nearly 80 percent of the wealth accumulated by age 60–65 consists of residential buildings, a comparatively illiquid and undiversified asset portfolio. Accordingly, there is room to introduce innovative contributory schemes or retirement savings instruments for this segment of the informal sector.

Conclusion

This volume makes the case that the developmental challenges associated with widespread informality are unlikely to be solved by an approach focused solely on bringing the informal sector into the ambit of formal sector regulations. These challenges—low productivity, vulnerable jobs, and a limited tax base—have multiple, complex causes that are more suitably addressed through policy reforms and programs that recognize the heterogeneity of informal firms and workers.

Perhaps realizing that decades of growth and business formalization programs have had little impact on the problems associated with informality, policy makers in South Asia have begun to try new approaches to improving the prospects of informal workers. A major development in this direction is the growing recognition of the need for a multifaceted approach to provide social protection in the informal sector. For example, Nepal's most recent (15th) economic development plan seeks to universalize social protection, expanding noncontributory social assistance programs as well as contributory programs to the informal sector (NPC 2020).

The growing use of digital technology to expand the reach of public services to the informal sector is another notable development. Recognizing that data are necessary in designing an effective social protection system in the informal sector, the Indian government introduced, in 2020, an online portal on which informal workers can register for access to programs.[41]

However, it is unclear if the overall approach to the issues associated with informality has changed substantively. Policy documents continue to mention informality in broad terms and as a problem to be eradicated. However, as argued in this volume, there is a need for a shift of focus from the desire merely to reduce the extent of informality to an effort to remove the various causes and negative consequences. Barring exceptions, such as the clarity with which the goal of universalizing social insurance is being formulated, the underlying objectives of many regulatory and tax-related policies associated with informality are not specified adequately. A case in point is VAT programs, which are apparently being used to achieve formalization, efficiency, and equity objectives simultaneously.

Technology-driven programs are promising, but more evidence on specific technologies and the associated channels of impact is required. Inducing informal firms to register for business licenses has not automatically caused them to grow and prosper. Likewise, enrolling firms and workers through digital portals and other, similar applications of technology may not lead to real change unless it fills specific institutional gaps or reduces binding frictions. For instance, e-commerce may be useful for informal firms that are constrained by market access but not for those facing other types of constraints.

This overview chapter stresses the need for more policy research and discussion on issues that are explored in this volume.

- First, how can various types of digital platforms address market frictions that lower productivity and reduce the resilience of informal firms and workers, and what complementary interventions may be needed to unlock positive impacts?

- Second, how can new ways of gathering and analyzing data on the traits and behavior of entrepreneurs and workers be used to tailor and target programs to the heterogeneous segments of the informal sector?

- Third, how can the extreme poor who are self-employed be better served by multidimensional economic inclusion programs?

- Fourth, how can the various segments of the informal sector be provided with some form of social insurance, whether publicly or by public-private partnerships?

The studies included in this volume present some early answers on these issues, but they also raise additional questions.

Notes

1. Estimates using pooled data from the Annual Survey of Industries and the National Sample Survey of Unincorporated Enterprises of 2015–16. In this estimate, own-account enterprises (those without any hired workers) in the National Sample Survey are considered informal firms. See ASI (Annual Survey of Industries) (dashboard), Industrial Statistics Wing, National Statistical Office, Ministry of Statistics and Program Implementation, Kolkata, http://www.csoisw.gov.in/CMS/En/1023-annual-survey-of-industries.aspx; "India: Unincorporated Non-Agricultural Enterprises (Excluding Construction), July 2015–June 2016, 73 round" (data portal), National Data Archive, National Sample Survey Office, Ministry of Statistics and Program Implementation, New Delhi, http://www.icssrdataservice.in/datarepository/index.php/catalog/148.

2. For example, see Lewis's (1954) dual economy framework in which the modern (formal and urban) sector grows and absorbs workers from the shrinking traditional (informal) sector. Also see Harris and Todaro's (1970) two-sector model whereby the minimum wage regulation in the formal sector generates excess labor supply that ends up in the informal sector. Deregulation in this model reduces informality.

3. See de Soto (1989) and Djankov et al. (2002) for examples of those who argue for an insider-outsider dualistic view of informality and Levy (2008) and Maloney (2004) among the proponents of the incentives-choice approach. For a recent excellent survey, see Ulyssea (2020).

4. A similar definition is adopted by Ulyssea (2020) in a recent literature review on informality. La Porta and Shleifer (2008, 2014) use registration with authorities in their definition of firm informality. Gelb et al. (2009) and Steel and Snodgrass (2008) use registration with tax authorities as the criterion in their definition of informal firms. They argue that the informal sector is an entity unknown to the fiscal authorities. Medvedev and Oviedo (2016) use

compliance with four regulations to identify formal firms. A firm is formal if (1) it has a tax ID, (2) it has a municipal license, (3) it requests receipts on its purchases, and (4) the majority of its employees are registered with the social security authority.

5. A key characteristic of such enterprises is that they are unincorporated and that there is no clear separation between the assets linked to the production activity of the firm and the assets of the firm owner.

6. Given their specific institutional arrangements, other regions may emphasize different aspects of the relationship with governments to define informality. For example, in the case of Latin America, Levy (2008) explains that the relationship between employer and employee is the core criterion in distinguishing formality and informality. Workers registered for social security, no matter the size of the firm that employs them, are considered formal workers.

7. This definition is consistent with the one established by the International Labour Organization (ILO 2013), and it has also been adopted by the national statistical offices of the countries in the region.

8. See Lucas (1978). Most papers concerned with the size distribution of firms have their origins in this seminal work.

9. This is an example of a size-dependent regulation. For example, the Factory Act (1947) in India requires all manufacturing units with at least 10 workers (20, if they do not use electricity) to register with the Registrar General of Industries. These factories have to comply with certain special regulations.

10. Firms may choose to register formally, but evade labor regulations by hiring workers on an informal basis. This intensive margin of informality (Ulyssea 2020) most closely corresponds to firms in group B in the framework.

11. See, for example, Syverson (2011) for a review of the knowledge base on the determinants of productivity in firms.

12. Online lending (financial technologies or fintech) platforms that use automated processes and nontraditional creditor data to screen loan applicants and match them to lenders could help expand access to credit among informal firms that are outside the formal banking sector. Digital task apps, such as HelloTask—the Bangladeshi app that matches women domestic workers and potential employers—may enable low-skilled workers in the informal sector to find employment that is better paying, safer, and more flexible.

13. More evidence is also needed to understand if unlocking the potential of digital platforms in the informal sector requires complementary public interventions. For example, because fintech relies on the digital footprint of firms in assessing loans, informal firms that have adopted other digital technologies, such as cashless payments or e-commerce, may find accessing fintech easier (see Ghosh, Vallee, and Zeng 2021). Government initiatives to open access to digital payments by informal firms might thereby have positive spillovers on access to credit among these firms.

14. Business training programs and grant programs in kind and in cash have been found to be cost-effective in improving the performance of informal microenterprises and small firms, though not always. Some successful program designs are also influenced by a context-specific understanding of peer effects, gender norms, or psychological factors, such as entrepreneurial mindset. See Jayachandran (2020), McKenzie and Woodruff (2014), and Woodruff (2018) for reviews of this evidence.

15. This recent strand of research on informality follows the literature on firm-level heterogeneity and the misallocation of resources, which is reviewed, for instance, in Restuccia and Rogerson (2017).

16. The marginal product in revenue terms is equalized. The analysis abstracts away from this by assuming that the firms are price takers in the output market and by setting the output as the numeraire.

17. In reality, governments have multiple registration requirements, ranging from local or municipal business registration to federal tax registration. These requirements have different compliance thresholds and are associated with different types of regulatory costs and taxes. To simplify, the framework in this chapter focuses on one major regulatory threshold.

18. Strictly speaking, firms with natural size at or slightly above Q will optimally choose to keep employment slightly below Q and avoid the regulatory costs, without any illegality on their part. This is discussed in more detail in the next subsection.

19. Business registration laws are often not enforced on microenterprises and small firms in South Asia. Sometimes, key business registration requirements and the associated regulatory costs explicitly apply only to firms above a specific size threshold. For example, in India, the Factory Act (1947) requires all manufacturing establishments employing 10 or more workers to register as factories. In other cases, even though all firms are supposed to register, the degree of enforcement intensity among small firms is practically nil. For instance, among firms with 1–10 workers in Sri Lanka, only 5 percent reported that they had any interaction with a public official in the previous year. Among unregistered firms with 1–10 unregistered workers, fewer than 0.5 percent reported that they had to pay a fine, penalty, or bribe because of their unregistered status (de Mel, McKenzie, and Woodruff 2013).

20. See ASI (Annual Survey of Industries) (dashboard), Industrial Statistics Wing, National Statistical Office, Ministry of Statistics and Program Implementation, Kolkata, http://www .csoisw.gov.in/CMS/En/1023-annual-survey-of-industries.aspx; "India: Unincorporated Non-Agricultural Enterprises (Excluding Construction), July 2015–June 2016, 73 round" (data portal), National Data Archive, National Sample Survey Office, Ministry of Statistics and Program Implementation, New Delhi, http://www.icssrdataservice.in/datarepository /index.php/catalog/148.

21. The low prevalence of avoiders does not imply that the costs associated with crossing the regulatory size threshold are trivial. Based on the observed distortion in the firm size distribution at the 10-worker threshold in India, Amirapu and Gechter (2020) estimate this cost to be 35 percent of unit labor costs. Although the threshold cost is high, the share of firms avoiding it may be low if the natural size distribution of firms is such that most firms are too small to be close to the threshold.

22. Some of the observed dispersion in value added per worker may derive from temporary idiosyncratic shocks faced by firms.

23. A fresh contribution of chapter 2 to the evidence base on informality in South Asia is that, instead of relying on measures of explicit regulatory entry costs, de facto entry barriers and distortions are quantified according to the model, combined with observed distortions in the firm size distribution and input usage patterns. Chapter 2 thereby builds on a large literature on the causes and consequences of firm-level resource misallocation. Hsieh and Klenow (2009), for example, estimate that, if capital and labor were reallocated

as efficiently in India's manufacturing sector as they are in the United States, the gains in manufacturing TFP would be in the range of 40 percent–60 percent. Size-dependent distortions—distortions that effectively tax a firm more and more as it grows in size—are particularly costly to productivity growth (Hseih and Klenow 2014; Restuccia and Rogerson 2017). This is because they disincentivize firms from making investments in physical and human capital.

24. In a similar vein, Amirapu and Gechter (2020) estimate that crossing the 10-worker size threshold is associated with a 35 percent increase in de facto unit labor costs in Indian manufacturing. This high cost cannot be explained by de jure regulatory costs.

25. However, total tax revenue could decline if this increase in the tax base is not sufficiently large to offset the reduced tax incidence on already formal firms. In Brazil, for instance, a large-scale formalization program that reduced taxes after business registration costs had already been reduced led to greater formalization by informal firms, although at the cost of a loss in total tax revenue (Rocha, Ulyssea, and Rachter 2018).

26. Another channel through which replacing sales tax with a VAT can affect informality relates to the self-enforcing feature embedded in this tax system. The VAT is often implemented through a tax credit system along the value chain whereby each firm receives a tax credit for inputs purchased from upstream firms to ensure that it only pays taxes on value added. This generates a paper trail and an incentive for firms to report purchases accurately from other firms (Pomeranz 2015). This process can lead to a transmission of formality (respectively, informality) along value chains that are already more formal (respectively, informal), as firms that are transacting predominantly with formal firms can only take advantage of the VAT credit by becoming formal (de Paula and Scheinkman 2010). In India, the introduction of the GST had a larger impact on firm registration in industries with more backward and forward links (Hoseini and Briand 2020).

27. The new VAT rates were generally higher than previous sales tax rates. Because the VAT does not involve double taxation along the value chain, VAT rates typically need to be higher than sales tax rates to generate the same total revenue. Chapter 3 finds that, if the VAT tax rate had dropped to zero, only about 3.5 percent of informal firms would have formalized.

28. The estimation of the elasticity of sales to the tax rates is carried out by employing a difference in differences approach that compares trends in sales among firms selling products affected by a rate change versus firms not affected, before and after the rate change.

29. For instance, see Woodruff (2018) for a review of evidence on the various constraints faced by small businesses.

30. The median firm in the dataset has three employees and an estimated annual revenue of about Rs 3 million (US$40,000).

31. See Hellotask (dashboard), HelloTask Platform Ltd., Dhaka, Bangladesh, https://hellotask.app/.

32. In the United States, for example, fintech companies are a major source of loans to small firms and may have played an important role in the recovery from the 2008 financial crisis (Gopal and Schnabl 2022). In France, the use of fintech is disproportionately high in locations with fewer bank branches, lower incomes, and a larger minority share of the population, as well as in industries with limited bank lending to small businesses (Erel and Liebersohn, 2020).

33. Using data from an Indian fintech lender that serves small businesses, Ghosh, Vallee, and Zeng (2021) find that small firms that make greater use of digital payments are more likely to be approved for fintech loans and obtain a lower interest rate.

34. See CPHS (Consumer Pyramids Household Survey) (dashboard), Consumer Pyramids$_{dx}$, Centre for Monitoring Indian Economy, Mumbai, https://consumerpyramidsdx.cmie.com/. The chapter uses data from surveys conducted in 2020.

35. See Stigler Center (2019) for a review of such evidence on market power and competition in digital platforms.

36. See Jayachandran (2020), McKenzie and Woodruff (2014), and Woodruff (2018) for reviews of the evidence base on microenterprise and small business development programs. Although not targeted on the informal sector, the beneficiaries of the programs are generally small and informal.

37. In comparison with grants, microcredit has been found to have limited impact on enterprise performance, with relatively few recipients benefiting from the loans (Jayachandran 2020).

38. Differences in measured ability can predict the future growth of small businesses, although the predictive power is low (Fafchamps and Woodruff 2017; McKenzie and Sansone 2017). Some evidence suggests that the potential to benefit from credit or similar interventions varies. In Hyderabad, for instance, entrepreneurs who were in business before microfinance was widely available experienced large and lasting gains in business performance from randomized access to microfinance, while those without a prior business did not experience any significant gains, an outcome that may derive from inherent variations in the potential to benefit from microcredit (Banerjee, Karlan, and Zinman 2015).

39. Interventions that address entrepreneurial orientation, motivation, and aspiration are also being tested. They sit somewhere in the middle of these types. For instance, personal initiative training increased profits by 30 percent among microentrepreneurs in Togo (Campos et al. 2017).

40. Banerjee et al. (2015) report similar results from randomized evaluations of six graduation programs implemented in different countries.

41. See e-Shram (dashboard), Ministry of Labour and Employment, New Delhi, https://eshram.gov.in.

References

Acosta, Pablo A., and Noël Muller. 2018. "The Role of Cognitive and Socio-emotional Skills in Labor Markets." IZA World of Labor 453 (October), Institute of Labor Economics, Bonn, Germany.

Amirapu, Amrit, and Michael Gechter. 2020. "Labor Regulations and the Cost of Corruption: Evidence from the Indian Firm Size Distribution." *Review of Economics and Statistics* 102 (1): 34–48.

Bandiera, Oriana, Robin Burgess, Narayan Das, Selim Gulesci, Imran Rasul, and Munshi Sulaiman. 2013. "Can Basic Entrepreneurship Transform the Economic Lives of the Poor?" IZA Discussion Paper 7386 (May), Institute of Labor Economics, Bonn, Germany.

Banerjee, Abhijit Vinayak, Esther Duflo, Nathanael Goldberg, Dean S. Karlan, Robert Osei, William Parienté, Jeremy Shapiro, Bram Thuysbaert, and Christopher R. Udry. 2015. "A Multifaceted Program Causes Lasting Progress for the Very Poor: Evidence from Six Countries." *Science* 348 (6236): 772–89.

Banerjee, Abhijit Vinayak, Dean Karlan, and Jonathan Zinman. 2015. "Six Randomized Evaluations of Microcredit: Introduction and Further Steps." *American Economic Journal: Applied Economics* 7 (1): 1–21.

Beaumont, Paul, Huan Tang, and Eric Vansteenberghe. 2021. "The Role of FinTech in Small Business Lending." Paper presented at the 4th IMF Macro-Financial Research Conference (virtual), September 29–30, 2021.

Bruhn, Miriam. 2011. "License to Sell: The Effect of Business Registration Reform on Entrepreneurial Activity in Mexico." *Review of Economics and Statistics* 93 (1): 382–86.

Bruhn, Miriam. 2013. "A Tale of Two Species: Revisiting the Effect of Registration Reform on Informal Business Owners in Mexico." *Journal of Development Economics* 103 (July): 275–83.

Bruhn, Miriam, and David J. McKenzie. 2014. "Entry Regulation and the Formalization of Microenterprises in Developing Countries." *World Bank Research Observer* 29 (2): 186–201.

Bussolo, Maurizio, Akshay Dixit, Anne Golla, Ananya Kotia, Jean N. Lee, Prema Narasimhan, and Siddharth Sharma. 2022. "How Selling Online Is Affecting Informal Firms in South Asia." World Bank, Washington, DC.

Campos, Francisco, Michael Frese, Markus P. Goldstein, Leonardo Iacovone, Hillary C. Johnson, David J. McKenzie, and Mona Mensmann. 2017. "Teaching Personal Initiative Beats Traditional Training in Boosting Small Business in West Africa." *Science* 357 (6357): 1287–90.

Charlot, Olivier, Franck Malherbet, and Cristina Terra. 2015. "Informality in Developing Economies: Regulation and Fiscal Policies." *Journal of Economic Dynamics and Control* 51 (February): 1–27.

Chatterjee, Urmila, and S. M. Ravi Kanbur. 2014. "Regulation and Noncompliance: Magnitudes and Patterns for India's Factories Act." Policy Research Working Paper 6755, World Bank, Washington, DC.

Chen, M. Keith, Peter E. Rossi, Judith Ann Chevalier, and Emily Oehlsen. 2019. "The Value of Flexible Work: Evidence from Uber Drivers." *Journal of Political Economy* 127 (6): 2735–94.

De Giorgi, Giacomo, and Aminur Rahman. 2013. "SME's Registration: Evidence from an RCT in Bangladesh." *Economics Letters* 120 (3): 573–78.

de Mel, Suresh, David J. McKenzie, and Christopher M. Woodruff. 2010. "Who Are the Microenterprise Owners? Evidence from Sri Lanka on Tokman versus De Soto." In *International Differences in Entrepreneurship*, edited by Josh Lerner and Antoinette Schoar, 63–87. Chicago: University of Chicago Press.

de Mel, Suresh, David J. McKenzie, and Christopher M. Woodruff. 2012. "One-Time Transfers of Cash or Capital Have Long-Lasting Effects on Microenterprises in Sri Lanka." *Science* 335 (6071): 962–66.

de Mel, Suresh, David J. McKenzie, and Christopher M. Woodruff. 2013. "The Demand for, and Consequences of, Formalization among Informal Firms in Sri Lanka." *American Economic Journal: Applied Economics* 5 (2): 122–50.

de Mel, Suresh, David J. McKenzie, and Christopher M. Woodruff. 2014. "Business Training and Female Enterprise Start-Up, Growth, and Dynamics: Experimental Evidence from Sri Lanka." *Journal of Development Economics* 106 (January): 199–210.

de Paula, Áureo, and José A. Scheinkman. 2010. "Value-Added Taxes, Chain Effects, and Informality." *American Economic Journal: Macroeconomics* 2 (4): 195–221.

De Soto, Hernando. 1989. *The Other Path: The Invisible Revolution in the Third World*. New York: Harper and Row.

Djankov, Simeon, Rafael La Porta, Florencio López-de-Silanes, and Andrei Shleifer. 2002. "The Regulation of Entry." *Quarterly Journal of Economics* 117 (1): 1–37.

Erel, Isil, and Jack Liebersohn. 2020. "Does FinTech Substitute for Banks? Evidence from the Paycheck Protection Program." NBER Working Paper 27659 (August), National Bureau of Economic Research, Cambridge, MA.

Fafchamps, Marcel, and Christopher M. Woodruff. 2017. "Identifying Gazelles: Expert Panels vs. Surveys as a Means to Identify Firms with Rapid Growth Potential." *World Bank Economic Review* 31 (3): 670–86.

Field, Erica M., Seema Jayachandran, Rohini Pande, and Natalia Rigol. 2016. "Friendship at Work: Can Peer Effects Catalyze Female Entrepreneurship?" *American Economic Journal: Economic Policy* 8 (2): 125–53.

Gelb, Alan, Taye Mengistae, Vijaya Ramachandran, and Manju Kedia Shah. 2009. "To Formalize or Not to Formalize? Comparisons of Microenterprise Data from Southern and East Africa." Working Paper 175 (July 20), Center for Global Development, Washington, DC.

Ghosh, Pulak, Boris Vallee, and Yao Zeng. 2021. "FinTech Lending and Cashless Payments." Working Paper, Harvard Business School, Boston.

Giné, Xavier, and Ghazala Mansuri. 2021. "Money or Management? A Field Experiment on Constraints to Entrepreneurship in Rural Pakistan." *Economic Development and Cultural Change* 70 (1): 41–86.

Goldfarb, Avi, and Catherine E. Tucker. 2019. "Digital Economics." *Journal of Economic Literature* 57 (1): 3–43.

Gopal, Manasa, and Philipp Schnabl 2022. "The Rise of Finance Companies and FinTech Lenders in Small Business Lending." *Review of Financial Studies*. Published ahead of print, June 13, 2022. https://doi.org/10.1093/rfs/hhac034.

Harris, John R., and Michael P. Todaro. 1970. "Migration, Unemployment, and Development: A Two-Sector Analysis." *American Economic Review* 60 (1): 126–42.

Hasan, Abir. 2020. "The Growth of e-Commerce during the Pandemic in Bangladesh." *Mindspeak* (blog), August 23, 2020. https://www.newagebd.net/article/114200/the-growth-of-e-commerce-during-the-pandemic-in-bangladesh.

Heckman James J., Jora Stixrud, and Sergio S. Urzua. 2006. "The Effects of Cognitive and Noncognitive Abilities on Labor Market Outcomes and Social Behavior." *Journal of Labor Economics* 24 (3): 411–82.

Hoseini, Mohammad, and Océane Briand. 2020. "Production Efficiency and Self-Enforcement in Value-Added Tax: Evidence from State-Level Reform in India." *Journal of Development Economics* 144 (May), 102462.

Hsieh, Chang-Tai, and Peter J. Klenow. 2009. "Misallocation and Manufacturing TFP in China and India." *Quarterly Journal of Economics* 124 (4): 1403–48.

Hsieh, Chang-Tai, and Peter J. Klenow. 2014. "The Life Cycle of Plants in India and Mexico." *Quarterly Journal of Economics* 129 (3): 1035–84.

Hussam, Reshmaan, Natalia Rigol, and Benjamin N. Roth. 2022. "Targeting High Ability Entrepreneurs Using Community Information: Mechanism Design in the Field." *American Economic Review* 112 (3): 861–98.

IBEF (India Brand Equity Foundation). 2021. "Indian E-Commerce Industry Analysis." *Indian E-Commerce Industry Report*, July 2021. IBEF, New Delhi. https://www.ibef.org/industry /ecommerce-presentation.

ILO (International Labour Organization). 2013. *Informal Economy and Decent Work: A Policy Resource Guide, Supporting Transitions to Formality*. Geneva: Employment Policy Department, International Labour Office.

Jayachandran, Seema. 2020. "Microentrepreneurship in Developing Countries." NBER Working Paper 26661 (January), National Bureau of Economic Research, Cambridge, MA.

Kanbur, S. M. Ravi. 2017. "Informality: Causes, Consequences, and Policy Responses." *Review of Development Economics* 21 (4): 939–61.

Kanbur, S. M. Ravi. 2021. "Introduction: The Long Discourse on Informality as Reflected in Selected Articles of the *International Labour Review*." *International Labour Review* 1 (July 27): 1–11.

Kaplan, David S., Eduardo Piedra, and Enrique Seira. 2011. "Entry Regulation and Business Start-Ups: Evidence from Mexico." *Journal of Public Economics* 95 (11–12): 1501–15.

Klapper, Leora F., Margaret Miller, and Jake Hess. 2019. "Leveraging Digital Financial Solutions to Promote Formal Business Participation." Working Paper, World Bank, Washington, DC.

KPMG. 2017. "Catalysing MSME Entrepreneurship in India: Capital, Technology, and Public Policy." Whitepaper (June), KPMG, Mumbai. https://assets.kpmg/content/dam/kpmg/in /pdf/2017/07/Catalysing-MSME-Entrepreneurship-India.pdf.

La Porta, Rafael, and Andrei Shleifer. 2008. "The Unofficial Economy and Economic Development." NBER Working Paper 14520 (December), National Bureau of Economic Research, Cambridge, MA.

La Porta, Rafael, and Andrei Shleifer. 2014. "Informality and Development." *Journal of Economic Perspectives* 28 (3): 109–26.

Levy, Santiago. 2008. *Good Intentions, Bad Outcomes: Social Policy, Informality, and Economic Growth in Mexico*. Washington, DC: Brookings Institution Press.

Lewis, W. Arthur. 1954. "Economic Development with Unlimited Supplies of Labour." *Manchester School* 22 (2): 139–91.

Lucas, Robert E., Jr. 1978. "On the Size Distribution of Business Firms." *Bell Journal of Economics* 9 (2): 508–23.

Maloney, William F. 2004. "Informality Revisited." *World Development* 32 (7): 1159–78.

McKenzie, David J. 2017. "How Effective Are Active Labor Market Policies in Developing Countries? A Critical Review of Recent Evidence." *World Bank Research Observer* 32 (2): 127–54.

McKenzie, David J., and Dario Sansone. 2017. "Man vs. Machine in Predicting Successful Entrepreneurs: Evidence from a Business Plan Competition in Nigeria." Policy Research Working Paper 8271, World Bank, Washington, DC.

McKenzie, David J., and Christopher M. Woodruff. 2014. "What Are We Learning from Business Training and Entrepreneurship Evaluations around the Developing World?" *World Bank Research Observer* 29 (1): 48–82.

Medvedev, Denis, and Ana María Oviedo. 2016. "Informality and Profitability: Evidence from a New Firm Survey in Ecuador." *Journal of Development Studies* 52 (3): 412–27.

NPC (National Planning Commission, Nepal). 2020. *The Fifteenth Plan (Fiscal Year 2019/20–2023/24)*. March. Kathmandu, Nepal: NPC, Government of Nepal.

Pallais, Amanda. 2014. "Inefficient Hiring in Entry-Level Labor Markets." *American Economic Review* 104 (11): 3565–99.

Pomeranz, Dina. 2015. "No Taxation without Information: Deterrence and Self-Enforcement in the Value Added Tax." *American Economic Review* 105 (8): 2539–69.

Rao, R. Kavita, and Sacchidananda Mukherjee. 2019. *Goods and Services Tax in India*. With the contribution of Amaresh Bagchi. Cambridge, UK: Cambridge University Press.

Restuccia, Diego, and Richard Rogerson. 2017. "The Causes and Costs of Misallocation." *Journal of Economic Perspectives* 31 (3): 151–74.

Rocha, Rudi, Gabriel Ulyssea, and Laísa Rachter. 2018. "Do Lower Taxes Reduce Informality? Evidence from Brazil." *Journal of Development Economics* 134 (September): 28–49.

Steel, William F., and Donald Snodgrass. 2008. "Raising Productivity and Reducing Risks of Household Enterprises: Diagnostic Methodology Framework." Africa Region Analysis on the Informal Economy (November 4), World Bank, Washington, DC.

Stigler Center. 2019. *Stigler Committee on Digital Platforms: Final Report*. Chicago: Stigler Center for the Study of the Economy and the State, Booth School of Business, University of Chicago.

Syverson, Chad. 2011. "What Determines Productivity?" *Journal of Economic Literature* 49 (2): 326–65.

Ulyssea, Gabriel. 2018. "Firms, Informality, and Development: Theory and Evidence from Brazil." *American Economic Review* 108 (8): 2015–47.

Ulyssea, Gabriel. 2020. "Informality: Causes and Consequences for Development." *Annual Review of Economics* 12 (August): 525–46.

Wille, John R., Karim O. Belayachi, Numa de Magalhaes, and Frederic Meunier. 2011. "Leveraging Technology to Support Business Registration Reform: Insights from Recent Country Experience." Investment Climate in Practice Note 7 (July), World Bank, Washington, DC.

Woodruff, Christopher M. 2018. "Addressing Constraints to Small and Growing Businesses." IGC Working Paper (October 24), International Growth Centre, London.

World Bank. 2020a. *Beaten or Broken? Informality and COVID-19*. South Asia Economic Focus, Fall 2020 (October). Washington, DC: World Bank.

World Bank. 2020b. *Doing Business 2020: Comparing Business Regulation in 190 Economies*. Washington, DC: World Bank.

CHAPTER 2

Formal Sector Distortions, Entry Barriers, and the Informal Economy: A Quantitative Exploration

ROBERTO N. FATTAL JAEF

Introduction

The goal of this chapter is to revisit the role of formal-sector distortions in accounting for the size of informal production.

The predominant view in the literature is that reforms that reduce regulatory hurdles to formalization have little success. These conclusions have been found both at the empirical microlevel, in studies that evaluate the impact of government reforms (Bruhn and McKenzie 2014), as well as at the quantitative macrolevel, in studies that feed regulation based proxies of entry barriers in models of firm dynamics to assess their explanatory power in predicting informal production.

This chapter revisits this view, leveraging a new methodology (Fattal Jaef 2019) to identify allocative distortions and entry barriers. The main question that we ask is: Does this novel measure of distortions portray a different picture with respect to the role of entry and allocative frictions in explaining the rise of the informal sector? To answer this question, we build a two-sector model where the size of the informal sector is endogenous and responds to distortions in the formal sector. Feeding our novel measure of entry barriers and idiosyncratic distortions in the model, we find that these are able to account for more than one-half of the observed informal employment share in India and to generate total factor productivity (TFP) losses of 15 percent.

The idiosyncratic distortions and entry barriers that are fed into the model are comprehensive model-based measures of the myriad of policies and market frictions constraining firm behavior in a given economy. It is instructive, prior to delving into further details, to outline concrete examples of what those policies and frictions could be. Further examples are discussed in annex 2B. A prominent example of a policy that misallocates resources across firms is the size-dependent enforcement of taxation. Limited by weak tax capacity, governments in developing countries concentrate taxation on the largest firms, where the enforcement is facilitated by the visibility. Doing this creates a distortion. Firms are encouraged to remain small, to not engage in innovation and capital accumulation, or even to remain outside the formal sector. Another salient example of a size-dependent policy, which used to be prominent in India, is licensing. Licensing requirements explicitly limited firm size, creating an incentive to curb investment and innovation and discouraging formalization. On the entry barrier front, a natural example is given by registration costs imposed by the government for the establishment of new firms. According to the World Bank and the Organisation for Economic Co-operation and Development (OECD), these registration costs are notoriously higher in less developed economies, constituting a plausible explanation for the lack of competition and the proliferation of large informal sectors.[1]

The model is a two-sector extension of the endogenous firm dynamics model of Fattal Jaef (2019). Consumers exhibit constant elasticity of substitution (CES) preferences over baskets of formal and informal goods. Within each sector, there is free entry and exit of a continuum of heterogeneously productive firms. In the formal sector, firm growth is endogenous, as firms invest resources in innovation. Informal firm dynamics are exogenous, but they are calibrated to match properties of the size distribution of informal firms in India.

The mechanisms generating a large share of informal production in response to distortions are intricately related to general equilibrium responses of wages and the relative price of formal and informal goods. Consider first the case of entry barriers to the formal sector. Here, the mechanism is easier to appreciate. With barriers to entry, fewer firms enter the formal sector. A decline in the number of producers reduces competition and translates into a decrease in wages and an increase in the relative price of formal goods. Consumers, then, switch expenditure to informal goods, mediated by their elasticity of substitution. Combined with the reduction in wages, entry is redirected to the informal sector, thereby increasing the informal employment share.

Idiosyncratic distortions—namely, distortions in the business environment that misallocate resources from the more to the less productive firms in the economy[2]—also increase the informal employment share through similar general equilibrium channels, albeit with different implications for firm dynamics in the formal sector. These distortions, by disproportionately affecting high productivity entrepreneurs, discourage firms from investing in innovation and misallocate resources to less efficient producers. As a result, aggregate productivity in the formal sector falls, and hence the relative price of formal goods increases relative to informal ones. This general equilibrium effect triggers a similar reallocation of entry and employment toward the informal sector, as in the case of entry barriers. At the microlevel, however, firm dynamics and the firm-size distribution in the formal sector respond very different, leading to a number of testable implications. According to the model, average firm size should go down in the informal sector, and firms exhibit a slower profile of growth over the life cycle, as a result of their subdued investment in innovation. These responses are consistent with the data.

The chapter then focuses on the aggregate implications of distortions and informal production.

Under a plausible calibration of the productivity distribution of informal firms, and given the endogenous reduction in the productivity distribution of formal establishments, we find that aggregate TFP falls by 15 percent. Naturally, the formal sector's value added and TFP fall significantly more. The aggregate effect is mitigated by the rise of informal varieties. However, the 15 percent reduction can only be compared with empirically observed TFP gaps in so far as we assume that all the value added in the economy, both formal and informal, is captured in the national statistics. The more the undermeasurement of informal value added, the higher the fall in measured aggregate productivity explained by the model.

At the end of the chapter, we discuss the policy implications of our results. Entry barriers are commonly associated with regulatory hurdles to registering formal firms. A similar effect can arise due to difficulties in the access to electricity, assuming this is a necessary input of any formal firm to operate. We assess the extent to which entry registration costs and barriers to accessing electricity, as measured by the World Bank's Doing Business Indicator, can account for the overall measure of entry barrier we identify from our model. We find that these can account for about 40 percent of the overall barrier to entry.

Model

Consumers derive utility from baskets of formal and informal goods, which they combine with a CES demand system

$$Q = \left[Q_1^{\frac{\lambda-1}{\lambda}} + Q_2^{\frac{\lambda-1}{\lambda}} \right]^{\frac{\lambda-1}{\lambda}}, \tag{2.1}$$

where Q is the final good consumer demand, and Q_1 and Q_2 are formal and informal good baskets that go in the production of the final good.[3] In a country with no distortions, which throughout this chapter we shall take to be the US, parameters will be set so that the equilibrium expenditure and employment share in the informal sector is low, targeting values of the informal sector share in the US economy. When distortions are identified and fed into the model, the elasticity of substitution λ will be a key determinant of the strength of the response of the informal sector to the distortions.

Within each sector, there is a continuum of monopolistically competitive producers of differentiated varieties. These producers operate a constant return to scale technology

$$y_i(\omega) = (A_i)^{\frac{1}{\theta-1}} (e^{\omega})^{\frac{1}{\theta-1}} l(\omega), \qquad (2.2)$$

where A_i constitutes a sector wide productivity component, e^{ω} is the idiosyncratic productivity of the producer of variety ω, and $l(\omega)$ is the labor input. The number of producers in each sector is endogenous. Both sectors face free entry from an infinite pool of potential entrants. In the formal sector, exit is endogenous, as firms confront fixed operation costs, which make a subset of all producers able to profitably run their businesses. Those whose productivity level falls below a threshold opt out of production. In the informal sector, where production is concentrated in two or three worker firms and exit is more random, we assume an exogenous death rate.

Prior to characterizing the trade-offs involved in entering each sector and describing the process of innovation for formal firms, consider an incumbent firm's static problem of setting prices and deciding how many workers to hire:

$$max_{p_i(\omega), l_i(\omega)} \{(1 - \tau_{\omega}) p_i(\omega) y_i(\omega) - w l_i(\omega)\}, \qquad (2.3)$$

subject to the demand function for a given variety ω in sector i:

$$y_i(\omega) = \left(\frac{p_i(\omega)}{P_i} \right)^{-\theta} \left(\frac{P_i}{P} \right)^{-\lambda} Q, \qquad (2.4)$$

and subject to the production technology defined earlier.

An important element of the profit function is given by the term $(1 - \tau_{\omega})$, which is the way we model the idiosyncratic distortions in the economy. These are introduced as revenue taxes, and their indexing by the productivity of the firm denotes their idiosyncratic nature. Their participation as revenue taxes is not motivated in that we think of these literally as taxes but, rather by how they distort efficient allocation of labor across firms. To see this, notice that the first order condition of the firm with respect to the labor input is given by:

$$(1 - \tau_{\omega}) MRPL_i(\omega) = w. \qquad (2.5)$$

The equation establishes that the marginal revenue product of labor (MRPL) multiplied by the distortion is equal to the prevailing wage rate in the market. It follows from this condition that in an undistorted economy, where τ_{ω} is equal to zero for all firms, the marginal revenue products are equalized across all firms, a result that can be seen easily by noting that all firms are assumed to confront the same wage rate in the market. Therefore, the revenue-tax form of the idiosyncratic distortion is just a reduced form specification to capture the idea that these distortions bring about the implication of breaking the principle of equalization of marginal revenue products across firms.[4]

An important property of equation 2.5 is that one could back out the value of $(1 - \tau_\omega)$ if equipped with firm-level data and after imposing a certain functional form for the revenue function of the firm. In our case, we adopted a revenue function that combines a CES demand system with a linear production function in labor. Equipped with firm-level data from India's Annual Survey of Industries (ASI), we can compare the marginal revenue product of each firm in a four-digit industry relative to the industry average,[5] and back-out $(1 - \tau_\omega)$ as the difference between each firm's and the average marginal revenue product

$$\frac{1}{(1-\tau_\omega)} = \frac{MRPL_i(\omega)}{\overline{MRPL}}.$$
(2.6)

While, according to the theory, any dispersion in $(1 - \tau_\omega)$ is indicative of resource misallocation, we acknowledge that there could be dispersion for many reasons, such as model specification or measurement error. Therefore, in the rest of the chapter, we focus on a particular statistic of the distribution of $(1 - \tau_\omega)$ across firms, which is less likely to be affected by these concerns. This statistic refers to the degree of correlation, or rather the elasticity, between $\log\left(\frac{1}{1-\tau_\omega}\right)$ and $log(e^\omega)$, namely, the elasticity between the idiosyncratic distortion and the idiosyncratic productivity of the firm.

This is a useful statistic because it measures the extent to which the distortions are reallocating resources from the high to the low productivity firms. As can be seen from equation 2.6, when $\left(\frac{1}{1-\tau_\omega}\right)$ is high, it means its marginal revenue produce is above the industry average. Given diminishing marginal returns of revenue, this has to imply that the firm is hiring fewer workers than it would otherwise do had there been no distortions. If, in turn, $\left(\frac{1}{1-\tau_\omega}\right)$ is increasing in e^ω, it would be implying that the firms hiring fewer workers are the most productive ones.

FIRM DYNAMICS

We endow the formal sector with a number of endogenous margins of adjustments to the distortions, so as to equip the theory with endogenous channels through which resources could be reallocated toward informal production. Importantly, these endogenous channels will deliver testable implications, which can be validated with the microdata and therefore provide empirical support for our implications regarding informality. These endogenous margins of adjustment relate to endogenous innovation and exit decisions of firms, as well as free entry into the sector. The testable implications that we will seek to validate in the microdata refer to the size distribution and lifecycle growth of firms in the formal sectors.

Informal firm dynamics are exogenous. We assume that informal firms enter with a given productivity level, grow deterministically over time, and exit exogenously due to death shocks. Both these parameters—the growth and exit rates—will be calibrated so as to replicate the size distribution of informal firms in India, which concentrates most of its production and employment in producers with less than five workers. The story we are trying to understand, then, is how distortions in the formal sector, through a rich set of channels, expel resources toward an informal sector where not many things can happen besides concentrating production in a large number of small producers.

Formal sector firm dynamics are given by the following innovation process. Upon entry, firms draw a productivity level from an exogenous distribution $\Gamma(\omega)$. Thereafter, a firm with current productivity e^{ω} jumps up to productivity $e^{\omega+\Delta}$ with probability $q(\omega)$, and jumps down to $e^{\omega-\Delta}$ with probability $(1 - q(\omega))$. The key is that firms choose $q(\omega)$. Firms can allocate workers to innovation purposes so as to achieve a particular level of $q(\omega)$, confronting the following innovation cost function:

$$\chi(q_t, \omega)\, e^{\omega} \times \eta(e^{\phi q_t} - 1). \tag{2.7}$$

This cost function is convex, and is scaled by the current productivity level of the firm, a feature that is introduced to make firm growth independent of firm size in the undistorted model, consistent with the US data.

Informal firms, in turn, enter the market with productivity level $e^{\omega(0)}$ normalized to 1, and then grow deterministically as they age

$$e\omega(a) = e^{\gamma a}. \tag{2.8}$$

We assume informal firms exit exogenously at rate δ, so that the fraction of entrants that remain active at age a is given by

$$f(a) = e^{-\delta a}. \tag{2.9}$$

In our calibration, μ and δ will be chosen so that few firms reach an older age and, those that do, have grown at a sufficiently low pace so as to replicate properties of the firm-size distribution of informal firms in India.

ENTRY

As discussed, there is free entry to each sector from an infinite pool of potential entrants. Entering a sector involves a labor-denominated sunk cost f_{e1} and f_{e2}. In the distorted economy, entry further entails surpassing an entry barrier, which takes the form of an entry tax. Because of free entry, then, in equilibrium it must hold that the entry cost in each sector is exactly equal to the expected net present value of profits of an entrant

$$wf_{e1}\,(1 + \tau_e) = NPV_1 \tag{2.10}$$

$$wf_{e2} = NPV_2,$$

where NPV_i stands for the expected net present value (NPV) of profits in each sector. (See the right-hand side of equation 2C.4 in annex 2C for a formal definition of NPV and for more details on the functional form of these net present value to profits.) Although we defer a formal definition of these objects to the annex, one can anticipate that idiosyncratic distortions and their associated effect on innovation decisions of firms have a first-order effect on the expected profitability of formal entrants, whereas the productivity growth and the death rates are key determinants of expected profitability in the informal sector. Entry barriers and idiosyncratic distortions in the formal sector interact in shaping the entry decision of prospective firms.

EQUILIBRIUM

The stationary equilibrium of the model, which we characterize formally in annex 2C, involves solving for individual outcomes, the distribution of firms across productivity levels in both sectors, the wage rate, and the relative price of formal and informal goods, so that decisions are optimal and markets are clear. Two key equilibrium objects, then, which will subsume the information of how distortions affect outcomes and which will signal the reallocation of production to the informal sector, are the wage rate and the relative price.

MECHANISMS

Consider the mechanisms underlying the economy's response to each type of distortion. Suppose there is an entry barrier τ_e, but there are no idiosyncratic distortions. The entry barrier increases the cost of entering the formal sector, and the number of formal firms falls, and so does the aggregate productivity in the sector. The relative price of formal goods increases, inducing a reallocation of expenditure, entry, and employment to the informal sector.

Consider the effect of idiosyncratic distortions that misallocate resources from the high to the low productivity firms. There are two sources through which aggregate productivity in the formal sector declines. First, there is the misallocation effect, which reduces allocative efficiency. Second, firms are discouraged from innovating, anticipating that the productivity-dependent distortion reduces the rate of return of growing their productivity. Similar to the entry barrier case, then, the relative price of formal goods increases, and firms and employment reallocate from the formal to the informal sector.

Stylized Facts

Prior to delving into the main quantitative exercise of the chapter, it is instructive to review a few empirical regularities characterizing the formal and informal sectors in India.

Informal production accounts for about 80 percent of total employment in the manufacturing sector, far higher than the 8 percent share exhibited in a developed economy like the US. Furthermore, an exploration of the size distribution of establishments in the informal sector reveals that informality is mostly a microentrepreneurship production activity.

Figure 2.1, panel a shows that 80 percent of informal employment is concentrated in firms with fewer than five employees. This pattern of the firm-size distribution is in sharp contrast with the formal sector's firm-size distribution (figure 2.1, panel b) where almost one-half of employment is accounted for by firms with 500 workers or more.

Despite the large share of employment at the top of the size distribution of formal firms, the average firm size in the sector is below the average firm size of more developed economies. Figure 2.2 shows the average firm size conditional on firms with 10 or more workers around the world, hence covering formal sector enterprises, and it shows a

FIGURE 2.1 Formal and Informal Sector Firm-Size Distribution

a. Informal firms

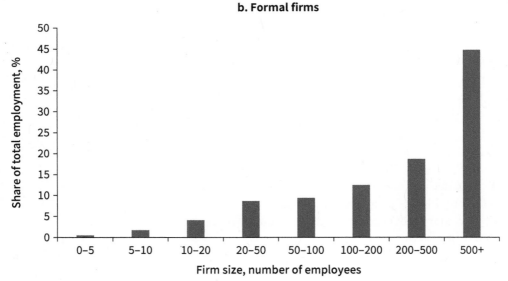

b. Formal firms

Source: Annual Survey of Industries (ASI) and National Sample Survey (NSS) data from 2015–16.

positive relationship between firm size and economic development. In India, the average formal firm size amounts to 70 workers, about 60 percent of the size of the average firm in the US. Figure 2.2 shows a more general stylized fact in the development literature, namely, that of a positive relationship between average firm size and income per capita.

The methodology in Fattal Jaef (2022) leverages the cross-country differences in average firm size to back-out estimates of entry barriers from the model. The idea is that idiosyncratic distortions, which can be measured directly from the firm-level data through the inference strategy outlined earlier, and entry distortions, interact in shaping the average firm size in the economy. Equipped, then, with an estimate of the productivity elasticity of distortions, the methodology then solves for the entry barrier so that in the model's stationary equilibrium, the average firm size in India (and in every country with firm-level data), the average firm size matches exactly the one observed in the data.

Figure 2.3 illustrates the estimate of the productivity-elasticity of idiosyncratic distortions and the model-based entry barrier against the income per capita for the 21 countries in our database, highlighting the relative position of India.

The figure shows a strong negative relationship between both types of distortions and the level of economic development. This finding is reassuring with respect to the methodology of identification of distortions, which is capable of finding little to no

FIGURE 2.2 **Average Firm Size and Economic Development**

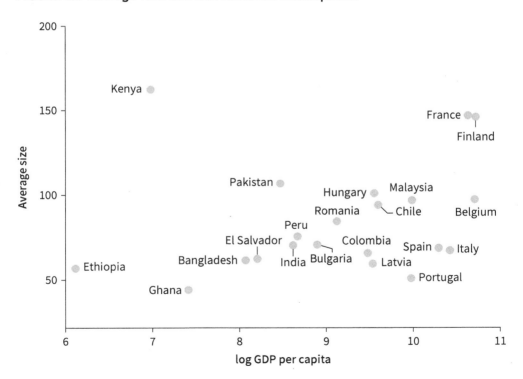

Source: Fattal-Jaef 2022.

FIGURE 2.3 Idiosyncratic Distortions and Entry Barriers

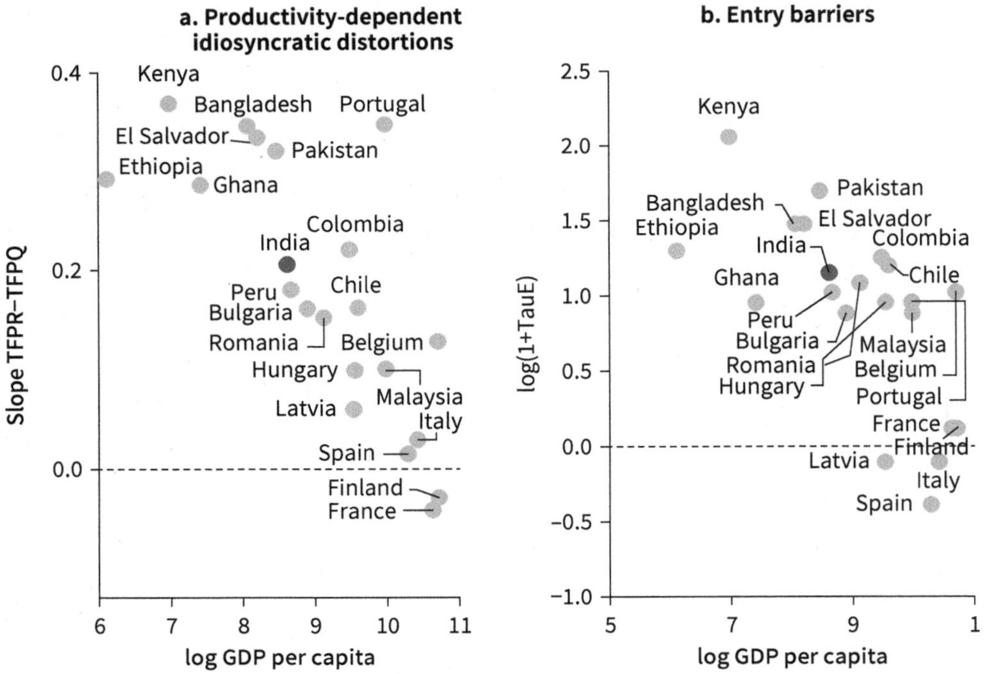

Source: Fattal-Jaef 2022.
Note: TauE = entry tax or barrier in the undistorted economy in the model. TFPQ = quantity total factor productivity. TFPR = revenue total factor productivity.

evidence of allocative or entry distortions in the most developed countries. India, however, exhibits a very high level of both productivity-dependent idiosyncratic distortions and barriers to firm entry. The question we ask in this chapter is: to what extent can this combination of distortions account for the observed levels of informality in India?

PRODUCTIVITY DIFFERENCES BETWEEN FORMAL AND INFORMAL FIRMS: THE ROLE OF CAPITAL

Prior to delving into the quantitative analysis, it is useful to address a particular concern with respect to our approach for modeling the informal sector. Our inference from the differences between the firm-size distribution of formal and informal producers in India are indicative of large productivity differences between formal and informal firms. However, it may be argued that the smaller size of informal firms may not conform to underlying productivity differences but rather to barriers in the access to physical capital. It is plausible in theory that an informal firm is as productive as a formal one but remains small because the informal status precludes the access to capital. The ultimate answer to this conjecture is empirical and would be provided by a measurement of the TFP distribution among informal firms. To my knowledge, this cannot be done.

However, one can construct a series of equally reasonable arguments that would help rule out, or at least tone down, the access to capital story. The first argument is that, if informal firms were indeed more productive, they would manage to grow out of the borrowing constraints through internal savings and eventually access the needed capital. Empirically, then, we would observe somewhat of a steep growth of informal firms' size over the life cycle. The evidence on this subject from Mexico (Busso, Levy, and Torres-Coronado 2019) and Brazil (Ulyssea), however, is quite the opposite: life-cycle growth is flat among informal producers. The second argument is that if informality were indeed precluding productive firms from accessing capital, reforms that alleviate registration and formalization costs would trigger a burst of formalization and firm-growth thereafter. Once again, the quasi-experimental evidence in various contexts (see Bruhn and McKenzie 2014; Ulyssea 2020) is not supportive of this prediction: formalization is virtually zero in response to changes in the regulatory environment.

In short, the hypothesis that the biggest constraint to the size of informal firms is not lower productivity but rather poorer access to capital is a very reasonable one that cannot be entirely ruled out or validated until estimates of informal firms' TFP are available. However, indirect arguments based on implied behavior that would have to be observed if that were to be the case do not support the argument; therefore, this chapter loads all the differences in size on differences in productivity.

QUANTIFYING INFORMALITY

Our goal now is to address the main quantitative question of the chapter: how much of the observed informal production in India can be accounted for by formal sector distortions? These are not simply proxies of a particular distorting policy or the outcome of a specific policy reform, which were the object of study in the earlier literature. The distortions we are considering are comprehensive measures that are inferred based on the observed behavior of firms in India; accordingly, they have the potential to exert a more notable effect than those policy interventions or regulations that are based on indicators studied earlier in the literature.

Our quantitative exploration is conducted in the following steps. First, we calibrate structural parameters in the model—such as those governing the elasticities of substitution, the entry costs, and the innovation cost function—to match salient firm-level properties of the US. In particular, we require the relative entry costs, f_{e1} and f_{e2}, and the relative sector-wide productivity levels A_1 and A_2 to be consistent with an informal employment share of 8 percent in the US. The innovation cost function in the formal sector is parameterized to replicate the life-cycle growth and the employment share in the top 10 largest firms in the US manufacturing sector. The growth and exit rate in the informal sector, in turn, are set so as to replicate the pattern of the informal sector's firm-size distribution in India. Parameter values associated with this calibration strategy are reported in annex 2A.

The second step is to introduce the estimate of the productivity elasticity of distortions and the entry barrier in India into the model, and solve for the associated stationary equilibrium. Figure 2.4 presents the results from this exercise. Panel a reproduces the informal

FIGURE 2.4 Model's Implications for Informal Employment Shares

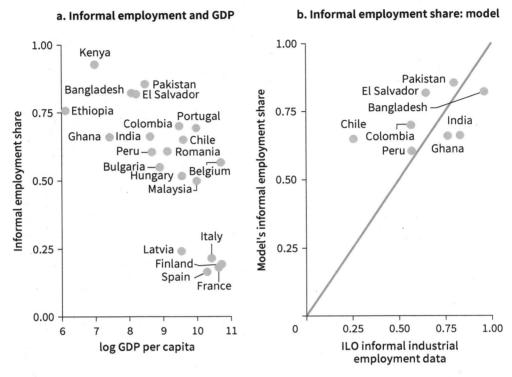

Source: World Bank calculations; ILOSTAT Database, International Labour Organization, Geneva, http://www.ilo
.org/ilostat/.
Note: ILO = International Labour Organization.

employment share in a stationary equilibrium with each country's pair of distortions along-side the level of economic development of the country. Panel b assesses the model's predictive power plotting the model's implied informal employment share against the informal employment share in industrial sectors from the International Labour Organization (ILO). In this case, data availability narrows the intersection of countries to eight.

As we expected, figure 2.4 shows a strong negative relationship between informal employment and economic development. This finding is expected in light of the lower prevalence of both type of distortions in advanced economies. Quantitatively, the model is capable of generating large informal sectors. In the case of India, the informal employment share amounts to 55 percent, about three-quarters of the overall informal employment share documented by the ILO (77 percent).

Figure 2.4, panel a shows that the model offers a good fit with the data. Although the model is simple and applies a common calibration strategy around the world, particularly with respect to the calibration of firm dynamics in the informal sector, the predicted informal employment shares line up quite closely to the data. In India, the model falls short of generating the observed degree of informality; in Chile, the model's prediction is about twice as high.

Turning to the aggregate implications of the distortions, figure 2.5 illustrates the TFP gains associated with the removal of all distortions. To do so, we start from each country's distorted stationary equilibrium and then compute a new equilibrium if all distortions were lifted. Then, we measure the TFP in this undistorted equilibrium relative to the initial one. It is important to remember that in this undistorted equilibrium, the informal employment share would have declined to the calibrated value for the US, equal to 8 percent.

Figure 2.5 uncovers sizable gains from dismantling distortions and reducing informality.

Naturally, TFP gains decrease with economic development, as do the underlying distortions. In India, the aggregate gains amount to 16 percent; between the poorest and richest countries, the aggregate gains range from 0 percent to 25 percent.

An interpretation of the TFP gains from reducing informality is that, while sizable, these surely do not capture the overall welfare gains from formalizing the labor force, and that these gains need not manifest as improvements in aggregate productivity. Most likely, the biggest sources of welfare arise from the many benefits associated with formal jobs, such as having access to social safety nets, credit markets, and insurance; these mechanisms are not accounted for in the model. So, while there are many efficiency gains to be reaped from reversing policies that promote informality, it is very likely that these are simply lower bounds to the overall welfare improvement of the workforce.

FIGURE 2.5 **TFP Gains from Reversing Informality**

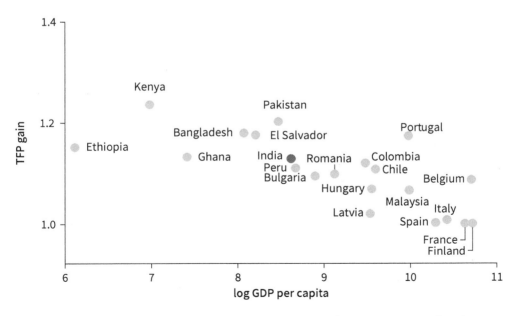

Sources: TFP gains calculated from the model's equilibrium; the logarithm of GDP per capita stems from the Penn World Table Database, version 10.0.
Note: TFP = total factor productivity.

REGULATION-BASED INDICATORS OF ENTRY BARRIERS AND INFORMALITY

Prior to concluding the analysis, we provide a quantification of the extent to which regulation-based indicators of the costs of entry, presumably an important component of the model-based measure of entry barrier that we have worked with so far, can account for the observed distribution of informal employment shares. To this end, we appeal to the costs of registering a new firm and accessing electricity as measured by the World Bank's Doing Business Indicators.[6]

Panel a of figure 2.6 illustrates the regulation-based estimates of entry barriers against the model-based ones. It follows from the figure that while the regulatory hurdles and the

FIGURE 2.6 **Informality under Regulation-Based Indicators of Entry Barriers**

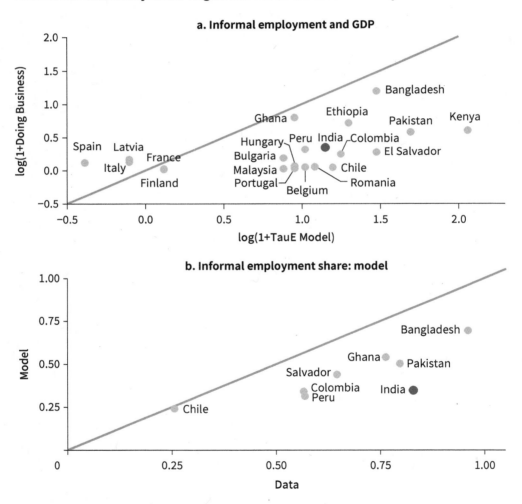

Sources: The informal employment share is based on ILO; the entry barrier in the vertical axis of panel A is based on the World Bank's Doing Business Database.
Note: The entry barrier comprises the sum of the costs of registering a new business and the cost of accessing electricity. TauE = entry tax or barrier in the undistorted economy in the model.

barriers in accessing electricity explain a reasonable share of the total value of the entry barrier identified by the model, a substantial unexplained component remains. Some of the complementary components are explored in annex 2B. In panel b of figure 2.6, we compute the informal employment shares that would be generated by the model if we fed it with the regulation-based estimates of entry barriers. As can be readily seen, while the model's mechanisms still respond strongly to the regulation-based component of barriers to entry, the majority of the dots fall well below the 45-degree line, dictating that the model can capture a substantially lower share of the observed degrees of informality. In the concrete example of India, the informal share generated by the regulation-based indicators is one-half as high as the one in the data. Still, the implication from the figure is that efforts aimed at simplifying entry and ensuring easier access to electricity can go a long way in reducing informality and fostering formal entry.

Conclusion

This chapter proposed a theory of informality combined with novel measures of formal sector distortions to account for the observed levels of informality in India and around the developing world. The model is disciplined by firm-level data on the informal sector's firm-size distribution in India, and it is fed with distortions that are identified from the formal sector's firm-level data alongside a theory-based inference strategy.

The model shows that distortions in the formal sector can account for three-quarters of the observed informality in India and that they follow quite closely the distribution of informal shares in the rest of the countries in the sample. The mechanism underlying the rise of informality is that formal sector distortions, in the form of barriers to entry and size-dependent policies, increases the relative price of formal goods and triggers a substitution of production, employment, and expenditure toward informal ones. Quantitatively, the mechanisms in the model dictate that these distortions are capable of explaining why informality is so prevalent in the developing world.

In future research, we seek to provide further insights on the properties of informal firms that rationalize their microscale. The model now interprets the informal firms' size distribution as indicative of a productivity distribution with low levels of productivity. Competing alternatives can be developed in which the real constraint on size does not stem from the lower productivity of informal firms but rather from their lack of access to capital. Exploring this hypothesis further, both empirically and quantitatively, is left for future work.

Annex 2: Calibration Strategy, Concrete Examples of Idiosyncratic Distortions and Entry Barriers, and Formal Characterization of the Equilibrium

Annex 2A: Calibration of Parameter Values in the Model

TABLE 2A.1 **Parameter Value**

Parameter	Values	Target
δ_1, δ_2	0.025; 0.0125	Exit rate large formal firms; exit rate informal firms
$\dfrac{\mu}{\delta_1}$	0.3	Employment share of top 10 largest firms in informal sector = 20%
λ	3	Bachas et al. 2021
ϑ	4	Hsieh and Klenow 2009
ζ	4.5	Average size of entrant relative to incumbent US manufacturing
η, φ	15 and 0.00056	Life-cycle growth and employment share in the top 10% of largest firms in the US
$\dfrac{f_{e1}}{f_{e2}}, \dfrac{A_1}{A_2}$	2.56; 7.15	Average firm size formal relative to informal and informal employment share –8%

Annex 2B: Further Examples of Idiosyncratic Distortions and Entry Barriers

Idiosyncratic distortions disrupt the allocation of physical and human capital across firms. In the model presented, these are modeled as firm-specific revenue taxes which depend on the firm's idiosyncratic productivity, τ_ω. This diagnostic tool is measured directly from the firm-level data based on the structural equation 2.6, which allows us to back-out the idiosyncratic distortion as the wedge that rationalizes the differences between marginal revenue products of labor and capital across firms.

Although it is useful to assess the extent of misallocation, it is instructive to consider a few examples of concrete policies or frictions that would manifest empirically as an idiosyncratic revenue tax. Following are a few such examples that were investigated in the literature.

- Financial frictions: banks lend up to proportion λ of assets: *Loan* $\leq \lambda a$

    - For example, a young but very productive firm (high z) has low assets

    - Then this firm will not be able to attract optimal K, L $\Rightarrow$ will exhibit high marginal product

- Size-dependent labor regulation: for example, France has a policy whereby firms with 50+ workers confront a series of higher labor taxes.

- Size-dependent tax enforcement: low compliance of taxes among small firms (low z), enforcement concentrated on large (high z) firms ⇒ misallocation from high to low productivity firms

- Firing and hiring taxes: when firms confront a fixed cost of firing a worker, there will be ranges of productivity and demand shocks for which the firm would have liked to fire the worker, but it does not, creating an excess demand of labor relative to what would occur had there not been such taxes. Similarly, anticipating difficulties in firing, firms will constrain their hiring even when profitable in an undistorted scenario. The effect of this type of policy on allocative efficiency and welfare has been studied in Hopenhayn and Rogerson (1993).

Examples of entry barriers are as follows:

- Regulation and bureaucratic hurdles for starting a firm (for example, those measured in Doing Business Indicators)

- Other sunk costs of starting a formal firm. For example, costs of accessing electricity are usually considered an entry barrier to formal operation

- Barriers in access to distribution networks

- Incumbents blocking entry of competitors:

  - For example, colluding with providers of key intermediate inputs

- In general, entry barrier is a label to capture all policies that inflate the cost of entry to an industry, beyond the "technological cost" of implementing a business idea.

- Not to be confused with industries where initial setup costs are high, these are technologically high setup costs, not driven by distortions.

Annex 2C: Formal Definition of Firm-Level Outcomes and Equilibrium Conditions

Given the formal firm's static optimization problem, the solution of which is characterized by equation 2.6, the dynamic decisions of how much to invest in innovation and whether to stay or exit operations is given by the following:

$$v_{1,t}^0(\omega) = \max_{q_t(\omega)} \left\{ \begin{array}{c} \pi_{1,t}^0(\omega) - w_t \chi(q_t, \omega) - w_t f_c \\ + R_t(1-\delta)[q_t(\omega)v_{1,t+1}(e^{\omega+\Delta}) + (1-q_t(\omega))v_{1,t+1}(e^{\omega-\Delta})] \end{array} \right\}, \qquad (2C.1)$$

where $v_{1,t}^{0}(\omega)$ is the value of an operating formal firm with current productivity e^{ω}, and $\pi_{1,t}^{v}(\omega)$ is the indirect profit function under optimal factor demands given prices and distortions, given by

$$\pi_{1,t}^{v}(\omega) = \frac{(\theta-1)^{\theta-1}}{\theta^{\theta}} P_{1}^{(\theta-\lambda)} \frac{Q}{w^{\theta-1}} e^{\omega} A_{1}(1-\tau_{\omega})^{\theta}.$$

The term f_{e} denotes the labor-denominated fixed cost of production, which the firm must confront if it decides to remain in operations. The continuation value of the firm, in turn, reflects the probability of jumping up or down in the innovation ladder, an outcome that is endogenous and governed by the endogenous probability $q_{t}(\omega)$.

The value of the formal firm prior to deciding whether to continue with production or exit is:

$$v_{1,t}(\omega) = max_{l_{1,t}(\omega)}\{v_{1,t}^{0}(\omega),0\}, \qquad (2C.2)$$

where $\iota_{1,t}(\omega)$ encodes the firm's exit decision, equal to one if it operates and equal to zero if it exits.

The value of an informal firm is more easily characterized, given the deterministic nature of its growth process and the exogenous exit. Given the exogenous growth process specified in the text, the value of an informal firm of age $\bar{a}$ is:

$$v_{2,t}(a) = \int_{a>=\bar{a}} \pi_{2,t}^{v}(a)e^{-(\rho+\delta)a}\,da, \qquad (2C.3)$$

where, again, $\pi_{2}^{v}(a)$ denotes the indirect profit of the informal firm, δ stands for the exit shock, and ρ is the discount factor of future profit streams.

Having defined the values of formal and informal firms, the free entry conditions to formal and informal sectors require that

$$w_{t}f_{e}(1+\tau^{e}) = R_{t}(1-\delta)\int v_{1t+1}(\omega)d\Gamma(\omega)$$

$$wf_{e2} = R_{t}(1-\delta)\int_{a>=0} \pi_{2,t+1}^{v}(a)e^{-(\rho+\delta)a}\,da. \qquad (2C.4)$$

Notice that the formal-sector entrant is ignorant, ex-ante, about her productivity upon entry, which is drawn from the known distribution $\Gamma(\omega)$. Lastly, notice that there is a one period time to build lag between the confrontation of the entry cost and the beginning of production.

EQUILIBRIUM AND AGGREGATE VARIABLES

A *stationary competitive equilibrium* in the model consists of (1) consumption, firm entry in each sector, and saving decisions of the household $[c, a, M_{e1}, M_{e2}, M_1, M_2]$; (2) labor demands and prices for each variety, and innovation and exit decisions of formal firms $[l_1(\omega), p_1(\omega), l_2(\omega), p_2(\omega), q_t(\omega), \iota_t(\omega)]$; (3) demand functions for intermediate inputs and final output $[y_1(\omega), Y_1, y_2(\omega), Y_2]$; (4) the age distributions of informal firms, the productivity distribution of formal firms, schedules of idiosyncratic distortions, and the entry barrier: $[M_t(\omega), f_2(a), [1 - \tau_\omega], \tau^E]$; and (5) interest rate and wages such that: (1) solves households' optimization problem, subject to the budget constraint, the law of motion for the number of firms, and taking as given the interest rate, the wage rate, aggregate demand, and the profile of idiosyncratic distortions; (2) solves each producer's intermediate goods static profit maximization problem; taking as given wages, the demand functions for individual varieties, and the laws of motion for idiosyncratic productivity; (3) solves the final good's static profit maximization problem, taking as given the price of intermediate varieties; and the labor market clears, net asset demand is equal to zero, and the free-entry conditions are satisfied.

Notes

This chapter was commissioned by the World Bank's Chief Economist Office for South Asia, in support of a flagship report on informality in South Asia. The views presented here are solely the author's and do not represent the World Bank Group's or any of its member countries.

1. OECD-World Bank Group Product Market Regulation database, 2013–18.

2. Examples of idiosyncratic distortions are: financial frictions, size dependent labor regulations, and size-dependent tax enforcement, among others.

3. One could have directly defined Q to be the aggregate consumption, where the aggregation is done at the level of the household. This is isomorphic to our specification of Q as a good produced by a final good aggregator.

4. To fix ideas, consider the effect of a particular type of financial friction, a collateral constraint whereby firms can only borrow up to a proportion λ of their assets in order to pay for the wage bill. In this case, there would not be a $(1 - \tau_\omega)$ in the profit function, but would rather be a constraint $l(\omega) < \lambda a$ affecting the demand for labor. If the constraint binds, then, the first order condition with respect to labor would take the form $(1 - multiplier) * MRPL = w$, where multiplier is the multiplier of the financial friction. This shows that the modeling of the distortion, in this case a collateral constraint, as a revenue tax is in many cases equivalent in terms of their implication for optimality conditions.

5. Since the assumption of the theory is that firms confront the same wage rate, we think that this is most likely to be the case in reality across firms within a narrow industry, but it is less likely across firms in very different industrial categories. Accordingly, it is to maximize the plausibility of the assumption that we assess the degree of dispersion in marginal revenue products across firms within a narrow industry classification.

6. The World Bank Doing Business Indicators underwent a serious investigation for potential manipulation of some of its values in certain countries starting in 2018, and for this reason its development has been suspended. To minimize the risk that the value of the indicators that we use in our assessment were subject to manipulation, we constrain the analysis to the indicators in 2014, sufficiently before the period under scrutiny.

References

Bachas, P., L. Gadenne, and A. Jensen. 2020. "Informality, Consumption Taxes, and Redistribution." Policy Research Working Paper 9267, World Bank, Washington, DC.

Bruhn, M., and D. McKenzie. 2014. "Entry Regulation and the Formalization of Microenterprises in Developing Countries." *World Bank Research Observer* 29 (2): 186–201.

Busso, M., S. Levy, and J. Torres-Coronado. 2019. "Labor Regulations and Resource Misallocation in Mexico." Manuscript, Inter-American Development Bank, Washington, DC.

Fattal Jaef, R. N. 2019. "Entry Barriers, Idiosyncratic Distortions, and the Firm-Size Distribution." Policy Research Working Paper Series 9027, World Bank, Washington, DC.

Fattal-Jaef, Roberto N. 2022. "Entry Barriers, Idiosyncratic Distortions, and the Firm Size Distribution." *American Economic Journal: Macroeconomics* 14 (2): 416–68.

Hopenhayn, H., and R. Rogerson. 1993. "Job Turnover and Policy Evaluation: A General Equilibrium Analysis." *Journal of Political Economy* 101 (5): 915–38.

Klenow, P., and C. T. Hsieh. 2009. "Misallocation and Manufacturing TFP in China and India." *Quarterly Journal of Economics*, Vol. CXXIV: 4.

Ulyssea, G. 2020. "Informality: Causes and Consequences for Development." *Annual Review of Economics* 12: 525–46.

CHAPTER 3

The Value Added Tax, Cascading Sales Tax, and Informality

YUE ZHOU

Introduction

Because informal firms do not pay taxes, a large informal sector constrains domestic revenue mobilization and tends to favor small, low-productivity firms. Accordingly, tackling informality can contribute to promoting state capacity and growth-enhancing structural change.

This chapter uses a structural model and Indian data to study how the adoption of a value added tax (VAT) affects informality. This appears to be the first chapter that quantifies the effect on informality of a VAT tax reform. A key finding of the analysis is that most informal firms are too unproductive to react to tax policy changes. Even if taxes were brought to zero, more than 90 percent of informal firms would remain unregistered. However, the analysis also finds that VAT adoption has an important positive impact on the most productive firms and hence contributes to the expansion of formal sector output.

It has been shown that, because of its self-enforcing nature, a VAT can reduce tax avoidance (Pomeranz 2015). However, studying the link between VAT adoption and informality is daunting because VAT reforms are often implemented together with other policy measures aimed at simplifying registration procedures and lowering registration costs (Kanbur and Keen 2014). It is therefore difficult to separate these effects on informality from those of complementary policies. Moreover, studying the effect of the

VAT on informality requires micro-level data on informal sector firms. Such data are hard to collect because informal firms tend to be small and, by definition, unregistered.

The chapter develops a structural model that builds on de Paula and Scheinkman (2010) and then applies the model to the data to study how VAT adoption has affected informality in India. The model assumes two stages of production characterized by upstream and downstream firms. Firms with different observed levels of productivity choose between operating in the formal or informal sector by comparing the benefits of avoiding taxes with the risk of being detected and punished for operating in the informal sector. Because the analysis assumes that the probability of detection increases with firm size and that the punishment is large, only firms that do not expect to become large choose to remain informal. It also assumes that there are no restrictions on trading across sectors: formal and informal firms can trade with both types of firms.

In the model, exit is determined by random idiosyncratic productivity shocks, and, in steady state, the number of entrants in each sector equals the number of firms that exit. Unlike de Paula and Scheinkman (2010), the model here includes entry and exit costs. This feature endogenizes the size of the formal and informal sectors (and the size of the economy) because firm choices are driven by entry costs, tax rates, and the tax regime. These elements allow for structural estimation of the impact of VAT adoption on informality.

A key prediction of the model is that VAT adoption does not have a large effect on the total number of formal firms, but VAT adoption does have an important effect on the incentive of productive firms to register and expand. As a consequence, VAT adoption leads to an expansion of formal sector output.

India is an ideal laboratory for studying the effect of VAT adoption on informality because, over 2002–14, Indian states gradually replaced the sales tax with a VAT. (In 2017, India adopted a broadbased goods and services tax.) The stated objectives of this tax reform included encouraging tax compliance by informal firms and boosting the manufacturing sector (KPMG 2017; Rao and Mukherjee 2019).

India is one of the few countries that collects detailed data on informal firms. The data here are sourced from the Unorganized Manufacturing Enterprises Survey (UME), which provides a representative sample of informal firms in the manufacturing sector.[1] The UME is based on the economic census, which is a complete count of all economic units, including establishments and firms that are not registered with the tax authorities.

After estimating the model, the research undertakes a counterfactual analysis aimed at comparing the VAT with the cascading sales tax, while keeping the tax rate constant. The finding is that only 0.3 percent of informal firms would register after the cascading tax is replaced with the VAT. This represents an increase of 2.0 percent in the number of formal firms. However, the effect of this tax reform is larger among more productive firms, leading to a nearly 12 percent expansion in formal sector output. The study also examines the effect of the tax reform on firms that were already in the formal sector. It finds that a VAT is particularly beneficial for large firms. This result is driven by the fact that large firms tend to buy a larger share of inputs from formal suppliers. Hence, they benefit more from the possibility of deducting the VAT paid on their purchases.

If tax rates and formal economic activity are kept constant, moving from a cascading sales tax to a VAT leads to lower tax revenues. However, other factors are not constant. For example, VAT adoption has a positive effect on labor income and formal sector profits. The analysis shows that higher corporate and income tax revenues more than offset the loss in tax revenue associated with the transition from the cascading sales tax to the VAT. According to the estimates, a switch to the VAT will lead to a drop of 27 percent in sales tax revenue; it will also lead to a 1 percent decrease in total tax revenue.

The analysis is closely related to several strands in the literature on VAT adoption and informality.[2] Relevant papers include Pomeranz (2015), who shows that the VAT facilitates tax enforcement by generating paper trails; Rocha, Ulyssea, and Rachter (2018), who show that lower tax rates and registration costs promote the formalization of Brazilian firms; and Emran and Stiglitz (2005), who study the welfare gains associated with replacing duties with VAT. The work of Hoseini and Briand (2020) is closest to the analysis here. The authors also study the link between VAT adoption and informality in India. The key difference is that this analysis develops a structural model and counterfactual analysis on both margins of informality, while the estimates of Hoseini and Briand are based on reduced form regressions that focus only on the share of informal firms.

This study is also related to the literature that portrays informal firms as capitalists-in-waiting who cannot join the formal sector because of high entry costs (for example, De Soto 1989; Tokman 2007). This literature suggests that formalizing informal firms by reducing tax burdens and entry costs will unleash the energy of the informal sector.[3] The results of the analysis here are closer to those of Kanbur (2017), La Porta and Schleifer (2014), Levy (2008), Maloney (2004), and Ulyssea (2018), who show that low-return firms have limited incentives to register even if taxes are reduced or enforcement tightened.

The remainder of the chapter is organized as follows: the second section describes the main characteristics of the informal sector in India. The third section builds a structural model with two stages of production and VAT. The fourth section structurally estimates the model. The fifth section presents the counterfactual analysis, and the sixth section provides the conclusion.

Stylized Facts on Informality

DATA

The analysis illustrated in this chapter relies on the Annual Survey of Industries (ASI) and the Unorganized Manufacturing Enterprises Survey (UME), which provide representative samples of formal and informal firms, respectively, in India's manufacturing sector.[4] The ASI consists of manufacturing establishments registered under the 1948 Factories Act, which covers all manufacturing firms that employ more than 10 workers if industrial power is used and at least 20 workers otherwise.[5] These ASI firms account for one-half of the formal firms that are defined in the analysis as firms registered with tax authorities.

The UME surveys are conducted every five years. The UME sample design is based on the most recent economic census, a complete count of all economic units in India that is synchronized with the household listing operations of the population census. The survey identifies the tax registration status of firms. Firms in the UME survey that are registered with the tax authorities are classified as formal; others are classified as informal firms.

Combining the ASI and UME datasets, a representative sample of all manufacturing firms in India was constructed for the analysis. Table 3.1 compares financial variables between registered and unregistered firms in fiscal year 2015.

Complementing the firm-level datasets, the analysis used transaction-level data in the state of West Bengal to calculate the intersectoral trade structure. VAT-paying firms in West Bengal must report their purchases from and sales to other VAT-paying firms. The transaction data contain information on 4.8 million transactions among formal firms during 2010 and 2016. Each supplier-client pair observation contains the tax code of both parties conducting the transactions.

STYLIZED FACTS

This subsection presents key stylized facts on the informal sector that are indispensable in implementing the simulated method of moments estimator in annex 3F. The analysis uses the combined ASI-UME dataset for 2015 and restricts the sample to manufacturing firms in West Bengal with more than two employees. For a description of the complete sample, see annex 3C.

TABLE 3.1 Annual Survey of Industries and Unorganized Manufacturing Enterprises Survey, 2015

Indicator	Number	Total labor, millions	Total revenue, Rs billions	Average labor	Average revenue, Rs millions
Tax registration					
Formal	817,944	19	68,718	25	84
Informal	5,325,092	26	6,224	5	1
Survey					
ASI	203,459	13	64,566	86	317
UME	5,939,577	31	10,376	5	2
Size					
>10 workers	591,592	21	67,094	39	113
<10 workers	5,551,444	24	7,848	4	1

Source: Based on data from the Annual Survey of Industries (ASI) and the Unorganized Manufacturing Enterprises (UME) Survey.

Several stylized facts on informality show that (1) informal firms are pervasive, but they only produce a small portion of total output; (2) most informal firms are small relative to an average formal firm; and (3) formal firms mainly trade with other formal firms, and informal firms mainly trade with other informal firms.

Size of the informal sector

Informal firms are prevalent in the Indian manufacturing sector, particularly in downstream industries. Following Antràs and Chor (2013), the downstream index is calculated for each four-digit Indian National Industrial Classification industry using the Indian input-output table for 2015. Industries with a downstream index above the median value are categorized as downstream industries, and the rest as upstream industries. Annex 3A documents the construction of the downstream index at the four-digit industry level. Figure 3.1 shows that 95 percent of firms in the manufacturing sector are informal. The share of informal firms is 98 percent among downstream industries compared with 92 percent among upstream industries. Despite their large share, however, informal firms only produce 21 percent of the total output (measured by revenue) in the manufacturing sector. The share of informal output is 31 percent among downstream industries compared with 16 percent among upstream industries. The result is consistent with the finding of Medina and Schneider (2018) that the informal sector produces 18 percent of gross domestic product (GDP) in India. In addition, 77 percent of workers are employed in the sector.

FIGURE 3.1 Informal Firms, by Share in Total Firms and in Total Output, West Bengal, 2015

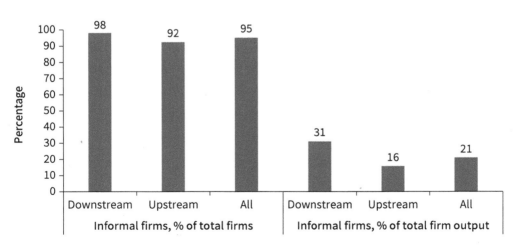

Source: Based on data of the Annual Survey of Industries and the Unorganized Manufacturing Enterprises Survey.
Note: The downstream category includes firms with downstream indexes above the median value. The upstream category includes firms with downstream indexes below the median value. The downstream indexes are calculated according to the method of Antràs and Chor (2013).

The distribution of informal firms. The analysis ranks all informal firms by their output and selects the firms at the 5th, 25th, 50th, 75th, and 95th percentiles to calculate their size measured by output relative to an average formal firm.

On average, an informal firm produces 1.5 percent and 2.4 percent as much revenue as an average formal firm in downstream and upstream industries, respectively. The median informal firms only produce 0.5 percent to 0.6 percent as much revenue as an average formal firm, while the 75th percentile informal firm produces around 1.5 percent of the revenue of an average formal firm (figure 3.2).

Figure 3.3 illustrates the output distribution of formal firms relative to informal firms. Most informal firms produce less than the small formal firm in the 10th percentile. The overlap in output distribution between formal and informal firms is limited, implying that informal firms are smaller and substantially different from formal firms. Farrell (2004) documents a bunching problem whereby a productive informal firm restricts its revenue below a certain threshold to avoid being detected. Annex 3E plots the histogram of the size of informal firms and does not find evidence of bunching near that threshold.

Trade structure

A less well-documented feature of the informal sector is the trade pattern. A key constraint in the analysis of domestic trade is the lack of interfirm transaction data.

FIGURE 3.2 Informal Firms Relative to the Average Formal Firm, by Revenue, West Bengal, 2015

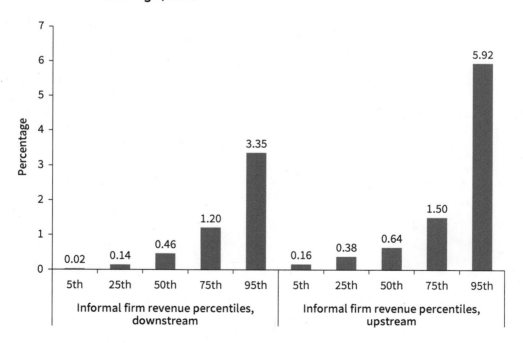

Source: Based on data of the Annual Survey of Industries and the Unorganized Manufacturing Enterprises Survey.

FIGURE 3.3 **Distribution of Output, Formal and Informal Firms, West Bengal, 2015**

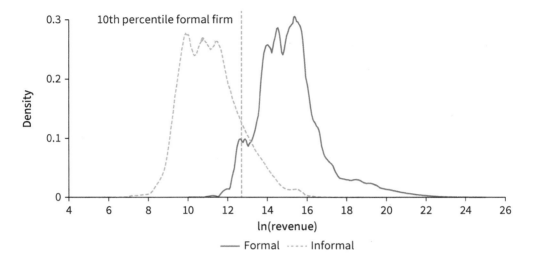

Source: Based on data of the Annual Survey of Industries and the Unorganized Manufacturing Enterprises Survey.

Combining transaction-level data with firm-level data, the study calculates the share of input from formal sector suppliers and the share of output to formal sector clients. (For details on the calculation procedure, see annex 3B).

Figure 3.4 illustrates the segmented trade structure. Formal firms purchase 80 percent of their inputs from formal sector suppliers, while informal firms purchase 29 percent of their inputs from formal sector suppliers. In addition, formal firms sell 48 percent of their total output to formal sector buyers, while informal firms sell 16 percent of their total output to formal sector buyers.

DESCRIPTIVE EVIDENCE

This subsection provides a descriptive analysis of the effect of the adoption of VAT on informality. Since 2003, Indian states have gradually adopted the VAT to replace the existing sales tax; 10 states or union territories did so before 2005, 19 did so in 2005, and 4 more did so between 2006 and 2008.[6] Annex 3C supplies a detailed description of the VAT reform. The variations in the timing of VAT adoption provide a natural experiment to study the effect of VAT reforms across Indian states and union territories.

First, the firm-level sample is aggregated into a state-level sample and a state-industry-level sample. The data on the state-level sample includes the number of formal (informal) firms; the formal (informal) sector output measured by total revenue; and the number of workers employed in the formal (informal) sector in 2000, 2005, 2010, and 2015.

FIGURE 3.4 Trade Pattern, Formal and Informal Firms, West Bengal, 2015

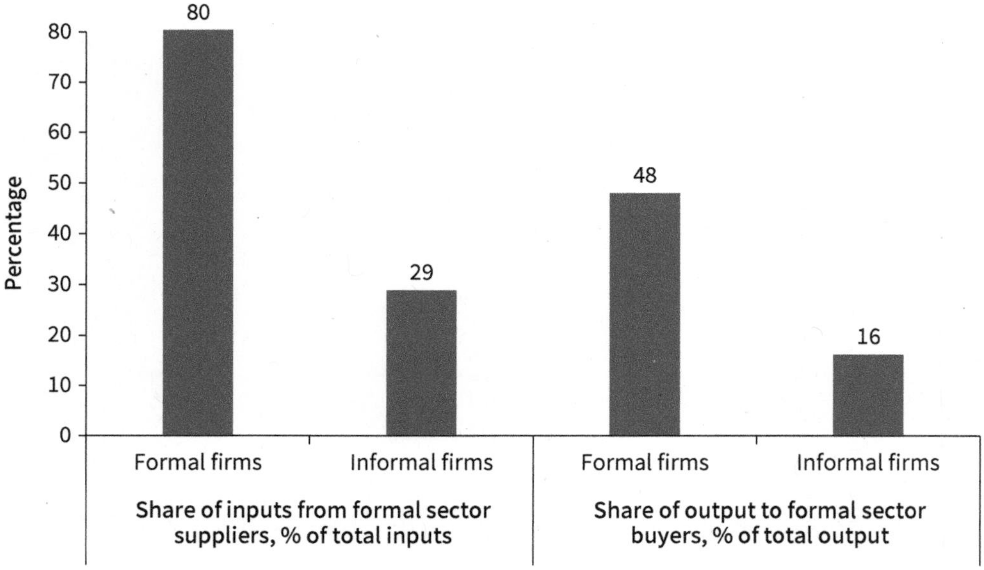

Source: Based on transaction-level data of the Annual Survey of Industries and the Unorganized Manufacturing Enterprises Survey.

Table 3.2 offers summary statistics of informality indicators in the state-level sample. On average, fewer than 7 percent of the observations on informal firms are registered with tax authorities, varying from 0.1 percent in Arunachal Pradesh to 60.0 percent in Daman and Diu, the former union territory. Meanwhile, the formal sector accounts for more than 70 percent of total output and employs 28 percent of all firm workers. The share of formal firms ranges from 7.4 percent to 5.8 percent after VAT adoption, but the t-statistics are insignificant. The share of formal sector output rises significantly, from 56 percent to 84 percent, and the share of formal sector employment increases from 26 percent to 31 percent. The state-industry-level sample shows similar results except that the share of formal firms increases by 5 percent after VAT adoption. The share of formal sector output and employment expanded by 18.4 percent and 7.8 percent, respectively.

EMPIRICAL RESULTS

The analysis takes advantage of the various dates of VAT adoption by Indian states to test the effect of the adoption on the share of informality at the extensive and intensive margins. Unlike previous work, the approach involves the calculation, that is, not only the share of formal firms but also the share of formal sector output and the share of formal sector employment relative to informal firms. This helps in determining both margins of informality.

TABLE 3.2 Summary Statistics: Informality Indicators, 2015

Indicator	Observations	Mean	Standard deviation	Before	After	Difference
State-year sample						
Share of formal firms	138	0.065	0.117	0.074	0.058	−0.016
Share of formal output	138	0.710	0.309	0.559	0.838	0.279***
Share of formal labor	138	0.286	0.235	0.259	0.309	0.050*
State-industry-year sample						
Share of formal firms	1614	0.261	0.376	0.232	0.281	0.049***
Share of formal output	1589	0.677	0.336	0.570	0.754	0.184***
Share of formal labor	1598	0.460	0.380	0.415	0.493	0.078***

Source: 2000–15 data of the Annual Survey of Industries and the Unorganized Manufacturing Enterprises Survey.
Note: Before = before VAT adoption. After = after VAT adoption. VAT = value added tax.
*p < .1 **p < .05 ***p < .001.

Following Hoseini and Briand (2020), the firm-level data are first aggregated to two-digit state-industry-year data to increase the identification power. The difference in differences specification is then used to reveal the effect of VAT reform on informality. The model is given by equation 3.1:

$$y_{sit} = \beta_0 + \beta_1 \cdot VAT_{st} + \alpha_{si} + \tau_t + \varepsilon_{st}, \tag{3.1}$$

where y_{sit} is a measurement of formality—share of formal firms, share of formal sector output, share of workers employed in the formal sector—in state s and year t; VAT_{st} is a VAT adoption dummy that equals 1 if state s adopts VAT in year t; and α_{si} and τ_t are a state-industry dummy and a year dummy, respectively.

Table 3.3 reports the results. After VAT adoption, the share of formal firms increases by 2.9 percentage points (the extensive margin), and the share of formal sector employment expands by 4.3 percentage points (the intensive margin). The share of formal sector employment also rises by 4 percentage points. This suggests that the VAT benefits incumbent formal firms and expands the production and employment among these firms. Annex 3C provides more robustness checks and empirical results from global experience.

More than 50 countries have adopted a VAT in the past 30 years; some did so with the explicit goal of encouraging formalization. Taking advantage of this natural experience, the analysis next examines the links between VAT adoption and informality in this international experience.

Medina and Schneider (2018) calculate the share of the informal economy across 165 countries in 1991–2017. The analysis here combined this dataset with a dataset on the timing of VAT adoption in 109 countries. The resulting sample includes 109 developing countries, of which 55 countries adopted a VAT from 1991 to 2017.

TABLE 3.3 **Difference in Differences Specification, India**

Indicator	Dependent variables		
	(1) ShareN	(2) ShareY	(3) ShareL
VAT	0.029** (0.012)	0.043*** (0.014)	0.040** (0.017)
Constant	0.161*** (0.004)	0.651*** (0.008)	0.434*** (0.007)
State-industry fixed effects	Y	Y	Y
Year fixed effects	Y	Y	Y
Observations	2,100	2,027	2,046
R-squared	0.886	0.914	0.883

Sources: Based on data of the Annual Survey of Industries and the Unorganized Manufacturing Enterprises Survey, 2000, 2005, 2010, 2015.
Note: ShareN = the share of formal firms. ShareY = the share of formal output. ShareL = the share of workers employed in the formal sector. VAT is a dummy variable that equals 1 if a state adopted VAT and 0 otherwise. VAT = value added tax. Robust standard errors are in parentheses.
**p < .05 ***p < .01.

Replicating the estimation in equation 3.1, table 3.4 reports the impact of VAT adoption on informal output based on this international experience. The adoption of VAT reduces the share of informal output by 0.33 percentage points (column 1). To capture the time lag, the analysis augments an interaction term between the number of years before and after VAT adoption into the baseline regression.[7] The share of informality does not change significantly in the first four years after VAT adoption, but decreases by 0.5 percentage points after five years (column 2).

Columns 3 and 4 replace the share of informality with the log value of informal outputs as the dependent variable. This captures the change in the total volume of informal output. The adoption of VAT has a negative impact of 4.6 percent on informal output in developing countries. The effect is significant only in the longer term.

Theory and Model

This section develops a structural model that builds on de Paula and Scheinkman (2010) to determine the respective size of the formal and informal sectors. The model assumes two stages of production. First, upstream firms, which have a unique observed level of productivity, use labor to produce intermediate goods for downstream firms. The labor market is assumed to be competitive, and the intermediate goods market involves monopolistic competition. Firms choose between operating in the formal or informal sector by comparing the benefits of avoiding the VAT and extra labor costs with the risks of detection and punishment for operating in the unregistered informal sector.

TABLE 3.4 Difference in Differences Specification Based on International Experience, 1991–2017

Indicator	Dependent variables			
	(1)	(2)	(3)	(4)
	Share of informal output		Ln(Informal output)	
	Baseline	Postreform	Baseline	Postreform
VAT adoption effect	−0.003*		−0.046**	
	(0.002)		(0.019)	
Treatment*1 year before VAT adoption		0.001		0.006
		(0.004)		(0.034)
Treatment*0 year after VAT adoption		0.000		0.020
		(0.004)		(0.034)
Treatment*1 year after VAT adoption		−0.001		−0.006
		(0.004)		(0.035)
Treatment*2 years after VAT adoption		0.001		−0.024
		(0.004)		(0.035)
Treatment*3 years after VAT adoption		−0.002		−0.046
		(0.004)		(0.036)
Treatment*4 years after VAT adoption		0.003		−0.042
		(0.004)		(0.037)
Treatment*5 years after VAT adoption		−0.005**		−0.048**
		(0.241)		(0.024)
Country fixed effect	Y	Y	Y	Y
Year fixed effect	Y	Y	Y	y
Observations	2,916	2,916	2,825	2,825
R-squared	0.966	0.966	0.987	0.987

Sources: Calculations based on data pooled from a dataset on 109 countries and data of Medina and Schneider 2018.
Note: Robust standard errors are in parentheses. Log form of total revenue by informal firms. VAT = value added tax.
*p < .1 **p < .05.

Second, downstream firms, which also have a unique observed level of productivity, use intermediate goods to produce homogeneous final products. The final goods market is assumed to be competitive. Downstream firms are therefore price takers, and they face the same trade-off between operating in the formal or informal sector.

To enter the formal and informal sectors, firms must pay a one-time fixed sum, the entry cost, which is higher in the case of the formal sector. In each period, there is a set number of potential entrants with heterogeneous productivity available to join either sector. Successful entrants replace dead firms that have exited the market after being affected by random productivity shocks. In equilibrium, the number of productive entrants equals the number of productive firms that exit. In equilibrium, upstream and downstream firms can have positive profits because the number of firms is limited.

The VAT induced in the model is an ad valorem tax that applies to each sale by formal firms. The difference between a VAT and a cascading sales tax is that the latter still applies to intermediate goods, while the VAT removes taxes on inputs. Tax incidence is shared by upstream and downstream firms according to the elasticity of supply and demand.

DOWNSTREAM FIRMS

Formal and informal downstream firms use the same technology to produce final goods. The analysis assumes a constant elasticity of substitution production function, which is increasing, concave, and twice continuously differentiable.

A formal firm's cost minimization problem is given by the following:

$$min \int_0^N x(i)p^f(i)[1-\tau(i)]di, \tag{3.2}$$

$$s.t. y_0 = (1-\tau^{corp})\theta^d \left[\int_0^N x(i)^\rho \beta(i)d \right]^{\frac{\alpha}{\rho}}, \tag{3.3}$$

where θ^d is the observed productivity of downstream firms; $x(i)$ is the quantity of inputs from upstream supplier i; $p^f(i)$ is the price paid to the upstream supplier i; y_0 is the total output that maximizes the profit. $\beta(i)$ captures the quality difference between formal and informal inputs.[8] A smaller $\beta(i)$ indicates the lower quality of the product from supplier i. $\beta(i)$ is normalized to 1 for all formal suppliers and β for all informal suppliers. $\frac{1}{1-\rho}$ is the elasticity of substitution parameter, and α is a production coefficient between 0 and 1. In addition to the VAT, formal firms pay the VAT at the rate of τ and the corporate tax on their profits at the rate of τ^{corp}.

Informal firms avoid paying taxes, but they will lose all the profits if they are detected. The analysis adds an extra cost, b_i, on the total inputs of informal firms. This is associated with the size of the firms. A more general form of b_i may be adopted as a function of firm size. However, for simplicity and following de Paula and Scheinkman (2010), the analysis assumes b_i is infinite if the observed productivity of an informal firm exceeds that of the smallest formal firm and 1 if the informal firm is below the threshold.

The cost minimization problem for an informal firm is given by the following:

$$min \int_0^N b_i x^i(i)p^i(i)di, \tag{3.4}$$

$$s.t. y_0^i = \theta^d \left[\int_0^N x^i(i)^\rho \beta(i)di \right]^{\frac{\alpha}{\rho}}. \tag{3.5}$$

UPSTREAM FIRMS

The upstream market is characterized by firms that produce intermediate goods using labor. The analysis assumes a simple linear production function of labor so that a firm's sales to various buyers are separable. It also assumes that formal firms pay additional labor costs, such as benefits, pensions, and social security. The upstream market is a monopolistic competition whereby firms have sufficient market power to set the prices of their products.

If a formal upstream firm sells to a formal downstream firm, its profit maximization problem is given by the following:

$$max(1-\tau^{corp})\left[(1-\tau)p_f^f x_f^f - w(1+\tau_l)\iota(x_f^f)\right],$$ (3.6)

$$s.t. x_f^f = \theta^u \iota.$$ (3.7)

If a formal upstream firm sells to an informal downstream firm, its profit maximization problem is as follows:

$$max(1-\tau^{corp})\left[(1-\tau)p_f^i x_f^i - w(1+\tau_l)\iota(x_f^i)\right],$$ (3.8)

$$s.t. x_f^i = \theta^u \iota,$$ (3.9)

where p_f^f and p_f^i are the demand function of the formal and informal downstream firms, respectively; τ_l is the additional labor cost; θ^u is the observed productivity; and ι is the number of workers hired by the upstream firm.

If an informal upstream firm sells to a formal downstream firm, the profit maximization problem is given by the following:

$$max\ p_i^f x_i^f = wb_l \iota(x_i^f),$$ (3.10)

$$s.t. x_i^f = \theta^u \iota.$$ (3.11)

If an informal upstream firm sells to an informal downstream firm, the profit maximization problem is as follows:

$$max\ p_i^i x_i^i - wb_l \iota(x_i^i),$$ (3.12)

$$s.t. x_i^f = \theta^u \iota,$$ (3.13)

where b_l is the extra cost accruing to informal firms based on the same assumption made in the analysis of downstream industries.

ENTRY AND EXIT

The analysis assumes that the market involves endogenous entries but exogenous exits. There are M potential entrants in upstream and downstream industries in each period. Potential entrants observe their preentry productivity, θ^d, which follows the distribution $\theta^d \sim G^d$. In each period, there is an ad hoc productivity shock after which a fixed proportion of firms will randomly exit the market. The exit rate is different in the formal and informal sectors, reflecting the different levels of resilience of the sectors to productivity shocks. Hence, the value function based on the observed productivity, θ, may be written as follows:

$$\tilde{V}_s = max\left\{\frac{\pi_s(\theta)}{1-\kappa_s}, 0\right\}, \qquad (3.14)$$

where $\pi_s(\theta)$ is the profit of the firm with productivity θ in sector s; κ_s is the probability of exit from sector s; and the discount rate is normalized to 1.

The realized productivity v follows a random process, $v = \varepsilon\theta$, and remains constant in subsequent periods; ε is a random variable. The expected present value function is given by the following:

$$V_s = \int \tilde{V}_s \, df(v \mid \theta), \qquad (3.15)$$

where $F(v|\theta)$ is the cumulative distribution function of realized productivity conditional on the observed productivity.

Firms will enter the formal sector if the expected value of formality is larger than the expected value of informality, plus the difference in entry costs between the formal downstream sector and the informal downstream sector. Hence, a necessary condition of becoming formal is the following:

$$V_f > V_i + E_f = E_i, \text{ with } \overline{V}_f \text{ as the cutoff present value.} \qquad (3.16)$$

If a firm's expected present value is less than the entry cost of formal sector E_f, but higher than the entry cost of informal sector E_i, then it may choose to enter the informal sector. The necessary condition of informality is as follows:

$$E_i < V_i < E_f. \qquad (3.17)$$

However, if the firm is surprised with a low-productivity draw such that the present value based on the realized productivity is less than the corresponding entry costs, it will exit the market immediately. This condition can be written as follows:

$$V_s^r < E_s, \qquad (3.18)$$

where V_s^r is the realized present value of the firm in sector s, and E_s is the entry cost.

EQUILIBRIUM

To close the model, it is necessary to specify consumer demand. The analysis assumes a representative household with a utility function, $U = u(x)$. It is also assumed that total consumption, x, is the sum of labor income $(1 + \tau_t)wL^f + wL^i$, firm profit Π, and total tax T. Fines on informal firms are treated as sink costs or a compensation for law enforcement. It is likewise assumed that the total labor supply is fixed at $L = L^f + L^i$. All the consumption components are endogenously determined by the model except the fixed total labor supply, L. Total consumption is calculated as follows:

$$Consumption = (1 + \tau_t)wL^f + wL^i + \Pi + T. \tag{3.19}$$

The equilibrium is determined by the following conditions: (1) the intermediate goods market clears, (2) the final goods market clears, (3) the labor market clears, and (4) a stationary equilibrium.

The intermediate goods market clears. The demand for intermediate goods by buyer i from supplier j must equal the supply from supplier j to buyer i. This determines the optimal prices charged by upstream suppliers to downstream buyers.

The final goods market clears. The total supply of final goods by downstream firms equals the total demand of final consumers. Because the model does not allow for investment, household income is equal to the consumption of final goods.

The labor market clears. The total labor employed by upstream firms must equal the total labor supplied by households, $l(x_1^f) + l(x_2^f) + l(x_1^i) + l(x_2^i) = L$. This condition determines the equilibrium wage.

Stationary equilibrium. Stationary equilibrium requires that all aggregate variables remain constant. The number of entrants in each sector therefore equals the number of exits in the corresponding sector.

$$M_f^d = \frac{1 - F^d\left(\overline{v_f^d} \mid \overline{\theta_f^d}\right)}{\kappa_f} M\left[G^d\left(\overline{\theta_f^d}\right) - G^d\left(\overline{\theta_i^d}\right)\right], \tag{3.20}$$

$$M_i^d = \frac{1 - F^d\left(\overline{v_f^d} \mid \overline{\theta_f^d}\right)}{\kappa_i} M \cdot \left[G^d\left(\overline{\theta_i^d}\right) - G^d\left(\underline{\theta_i^d}\right)\right], \tag{3.21}$$

$$M_f^u = \frac{1 - F^u\left(\overline{v_f^u} \mid \overline{\theta_f^u}\right)}{\kappa_f} M \cdot \left[G^u\left(\overline{\theta_f^u}\right) - G^u\left(\overline{\theta_i^u}\right)\right], \tag{3.22}$$

$$M_i^u = \frac{F^u\left(\overline{v_f^u} \mid \overline{\theta_f^u}\right)}{\kappa_i} M \cdot \left[G^u\left(\overline{\theta_t^u}\right) - G^d\left(\underline{\theta_i^u}\right)\right].$$ (3.23)

In equations 3.20–3.21, M is the total number of potential entrants; $\overline{\theta_f^d}$ is the upper bound of the observed productivity of formal downstream firms; $\overline{\theta_t^d}$ is the upper bound of the observed productivity of informal downstream firms; $\underline{\theta_i^d}$ is the lower bound of the observed productivity of informal downstream firms; $\overline{v_f^d}$ is the upper bound of the realized productivity of formal downstream firms; and M_f^d is the total number of incumbent formal firms downstream. A corresponding notation applies to formal and informal upstream and downstream firms in equations 3.21–3.23.

In addition, $M[G^d(\overline{\theta_f^d}) - G^d(\overline{\theta_i^d})]$ is the ex ante number of downstream firms that decide to enter the formal sector before drawing their realized productivity, and $1 - F^d(\overline{v_f^d} \mid \overline{\theta_f^d})$ is the share of successful entrants into the formal sector among the total number of firms that decide to enter. Thus, equation 3.20 requires that the number of successful entrants into the downstream formal sector in each period equals the total number of firms that exit.

There is a positive relationship between productivity and present value, but the shape of the relationship differs between the formal and informal sectors. Firms at the lowest productivity levels have a negative present value if they are formal because their net profits are not sufficient to cover the fixed costs of formality. However, they have a positive present value if they are informal because they can avoid paying taxes and the high entry costs of the formal sector. These low-productivity firms will therefore choose to enter the informal sector.

As productivity rises, present value rises more quickly among formal firms than among informal firms because informal firms must face the risk of detection and coercive intervention because of the lack of compliance with the law. There is a threshold of productivity below which firms choose to enter the informal sector and above which firms choose to enter the formal sector. The number of formal and informal firms thus depends on the distribution of productivity in the economy.

Figure 3.5 illustrates this framework by plotting the relationship between firm productivity and the counterfactual present values of firms entering the formal and informal sectors (net of entry costs). The solid blue line shows the value of firms entering the informal sector for each level of productivity, and the dotted blue line similarly shows the value of firms entering the formal sector. If all other factors are held constant, an economy that has many low-productivity firms, that is, those with productivity below θ in figure 3.5, will exhibit a relatively high level of informality.

Because the model does not generate an analytical solution, the estimation is based on the numerical solution of the model. Annex 3D shows the detailed model solution.

FIGURE 3.5 Illustrative Analysis of the Formalization Choice

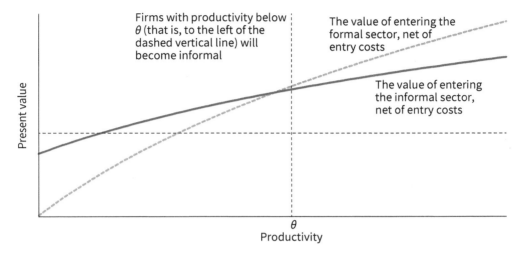

Source: Original figure for this publication.

Calibration and Estimation

This section specifies the functional form and discusses the estimation of the full model in an equilibrium setting. The equilibrium outcome should capture the key stylized facts presented above. The analysis relies on the simulated method of moments (SMM) to estimate the parameters of the model.

PARAMETERIZATION

First, the distribution function of the observed productivity, $G(\cdot)$, and the realized productivity, $F(\cdot)$, are specified. The distribution of observed productivity, $G(\cdot)$, is assumed to follow the Pareto distribution. The distribution of the observed productivity is allowed to vary between downstream and upstream industries, which is given by the following:

$$G^d(\theta \geq x) = \begin{cases} \left(\dfrac{v_0}{x}\right)^{\xi^d} & \text{for } x \geq v_0 \\ 1 & \text{for } \text{for } x \leq v_0 \end{cases}, \tag{3.24}$$

$$G^u(\theta \geq x) = \begin{cases} \left(\dfrac{v_0}{x}\right)^{\xi^u} & \text{for } x \geq v_0 \\ 1 & \text{for } \text{for } x \leq v_0 \end{cases}, \tag{3.25}$$

where v_0 is the minimum possible value of the Pareto distribution, and ξ is the shape parameter. The only difference in the preentry productivity distribution between the upstream and the downstream is the parameter ξ, which governs the right tail of the distribution. This setting requires the same minimum firm size among both upstream and downstream firms, while the maximum firm size (large firms) may differ. This is consistent with the data of the analysis whereby the minimum firm size is three employees, but there is no maximum firm size.

The realized productivity distribution follows a simple process, $v = \theta\varepsilon$. The misperception of productivity ε is assumed to have a log-normal distribution with a mean at zero and a variance of σ^2. Realized productivity, v, is therefore the product of a log-normal and a Pareto random variable, which follows the Pareto–log-normal distribution. The three-parameter distribution has a log-normal body and a Pareto right tail. Luttmer (2007) and Ulyssea (2018) prove that the Pareto–log-normal distribution fits many salient features of the size distribution of firms in developing countries.

THE CALIBRATION AND ESTIMATION OF PARAMETERS

The model parameters are divided into two sets. The first set includes three parameters that are calibrated from the real data. These parameters are as follows:

$$\psi = \left\{ \tau, \tau^{corp}, \kappa_f \right\}$$

The VAT rate in West Bengal was 12.5 percent in 2015, and the effective corporate tax rate was around 30 percent. The exit rate among formal firms has been calibrated from 2014–15 ASI data. After controlling for the industry fixed effect, one may calculate the exit rate of formal firms at 8 percent. The Pareto distribution scale parameter, v_0, is set at 0.7 so that the minimum number of employees is three. This parameter only affects the scale of the key variables.

The second set of model parameters includes 12 parameters, which are estimated using the SMM. These parameters are as follows:

$$\varphi = \left\{ \beta, \xi^d, \xi^u, E_i^d, E_f^d, E_i^u, E_f^u, \alpha, \rho, \tau_l, \kappa_i, \sigma \right\}$$

From a set of parameters, the SMM generates moments that may then be fit to the real data. The SMM estimator is the set of parameters that best approximate the moments calculated from the real data. For any given set of parameters, the model will generate a full set of observations that simulate the behavior of firms, including tax status, outputs, and trade structure. This set of observations is then used to produce a set of moments that may be compared with the set of moments from the real data.

First, the real data are bootstrapped 500 times to generate 500 bootstrapped datasets. The analysis calculates a vector of moments for each of these datasets and then determines the mean and the standard deviation of all vectors of moments, as follows:

$$\widehat{m_N} = \frac{1}{N} \sum_{i=1}^{N} m_i,$$

where m_i is the vector of moments in the ith dataset, and $\widehat{m_N}$ is the mean of all vectors of moments.

Next, an initial set of parameters, φ_0, is chosen that is used to generate a vector of moments from the model. The process is then replicated 50 times, and the mean of all vectors of moments is calculated, as follows:

$$\widetilde{m_N} = \frac{1}{N} \sum_{i=1}^{N} \widetilde{m_t}(\psi, \varphi_0), \tag{3.26}$$

where $\widetilde{m_t}(\psi, \varphi_0)$ is the vector of moments from the ith replication, and $\widetilde{m_N}$ is the mean of all vectors of moments.

Finally, the distance between the moments, $\widehat{m_N}$, of the real data and the moments, $\widetilde{m_N}$, of the model is represented as $g(\psi, \varphi_0) = \widehat{m_N} - \widetilde{m_t}(\psi, \varphi_0)$. The SMM estimator is therefore as follows:

$$\tilde{\varphi} = argmin\{g(\psi, \varphi_0)'\widehat{W_N}g(\psi, \varphi_0)\}, \tag{3.27}$$

where $\widehat{W_N}$ is a positive, semidefinite $r \times r$ matrix, and r is the length of the vector of moments $\widehat{m_N}$. Under suitable regularity conditions, the estimator is consistent and asymptotically normal, and the weighting matrix $\widehat{W_N}$ is chosen optimally to minimize the asymptotic covariance. The variance of real moments is used as $\widehat{W_N}$. Annex 3F provides a detailed discussion of the SMM estimator.

To estimate the parameters, 26 moments are selected, including the following: (1) the share of informal firms in downstream industries, the share of informal firms in upstream industries, the share of informal sector output in downstream industries, and the share of informal sector output in upstream industries (4 moments); (2) the ratios of the output of informal firms in each of the 5th, 25th, 50th, 75th, and 90th percentiles to the output of the average formal firm in downstream industries, and the corresponding ratios in the case of upstream industries (10 moments); the ratios of the output of informal firms in the 5th and in the 10th percentiles to the output of the average formal firm in downstream industries, and the corresponding ratios in upstream industries (4 moments); (3) the share of the inputs of formal suppliers in the formal sector, the share of the inputs of formal suppliers in the informal sector, the share of the output going to formal buyers in the formal sector, and the share of output going to formal buyers in the informal sector (4 moments); (4) the standard deviation in outputs, divided by the mean output (coefficient of variance) downstream and upstream (2 moments); (5) the share of intermediate goods in total expenditures (1 moment); and (6) the share of labor employed in the informal sector (1 moment).

According to an intuitive analysis, the distribution of informal and formal firms in upstream and downstream industries determines the Pareto shape parameter. A more clustered distribution of informal firms indicates a larger Pareto shape parameter.

The share of informal firms in upstream and downstream industries determines the entry costs in the formal sector, in which higher entry costs lead to a larger informal sector. The relative size of large informal firms helps in estimating separately the entry costs and the exit probabilities (Ulyssea 2018). Higher entry costs in the formal sector raise the size of informal firms that are barely able to enter, while the exit probability of informal firms increases the size of all informal firms.

The structure of trade determines the quality of formal input, β. The higher quality of formal input induces formal and informal buyers to purchase more from formal suppliers. The trade structure and the share of labor employed by the informal sector jointly determine the extra cost of formal worker τ_l. Fewer purchases from formal suppliers and a larger share of workers in the informal sector are signs of the higher extra cost of labor in the formal sector. The share of labor in the informal sector separates τ_l from β. The relative size of informal and small formal firms helps separate the exit parameter κ_i and the entry costs. While a higher exit rate among informal firms reduces the size of all informal firms, a higher entry cost in the formal sector only reduces the size of small formal firms.

ESTIMATES AND THE MODEL FIT

Table 3.5 exhibits the results of the calibration and estimation. The entry cost in the formal sector is 1.1 and 1.8 times the average annual profit of a formal firm in downstream industries and a formal firm in upstream industries, respectively. This suggests that it is more difficult to enter the formal sector downstream than upstream, which is consistent with the larger share of informal firms in downstream industries. Moreover, the entry costs in the formal sector are 90 and 37 times greater than the average annual profit of an informal firm in downstream and upstream industries, respectively. This suggests that informal firms are too unproductive to overcome the entry cost in the formal sector. The Pareto shape parameter is 2.35 downstream and 1.40 upstream, respectively.

The quality parameter of formal input β is 1.15, which indicates that formal sector input quality is 15 percent higher than informal sector input quality. The difference in labor cost between the formal and informal sectors is 10.7, meaning that firms pay workers 11 times more in the formal sector than in the informal sector.

Table 3.6 compares the moments generated from the real data and from the model using the above parameters. The model captures the share of informal firms and the share of informal output, as well as the trade structure. But the model does not fit well with the relative size of small formal firms, partly because of the constraints or advantages associated with small formal firms.

According to the model prediction, the share of informal firms in downstream and upstream industries is 98 percent and 93 percent, respectively, and the deviation from the real data is less than 1 percent. Around 30 percent of the downstream output and 14 percent of the upstream output are produced by informal firms, which is similar to

TABLE 3.5 **Estimated Parameters Based on the Simulated Method of Moments**

Parameter	Description	Value	Standard error
Calibrated			
τ	VAT rate	0.125	—
τ^{corp}	Corporate tax rate	0.3	—
τ_f	Formal exit probability	0.08	—
Simulated method of moments estimate			
β	Formal input quality	1.15	0.09
ξ^d	Pareto shape parameter (downstream)	2.35	0.03
ξ^u	Pareto shape parameter (upstream)	1.40	0.03
E_i^d	Downstream informal entry cost scaled by average informal downstream profit	0.51	0.01
E_f^d	Downstream formal entry cost scaled by average formal downstream profit	1.08	0.04
E_i^u	Formal upstream entry cost scaled by average informal upstream profit	1.22	0.06
E_f^u	Informal upstream entry cost scaled by average formal upstream profit	1.80	0.16
α	Production function coefficient	0.62	0.01
ρ	Substitution parameter	0.64	0.00
τ_l	Wage gap	10.7	1.10
κ_i	Informal exit probability	0.15	0.01
σ	Postentry shock variance	0.10	0.01

Source: Original compilation for this publication.
Note: — = not available. VAT = value added tax.

TABLE 3.6 **Model Fit: Moments from the Real Data and from the Estimated Model**
percent

Moments	Data	Model
Share of informality, total		
Downstream	98	98
Upstream	92	93
Share of informality, outputs		
Downstream	31	30
Upstream	16	14
Share of input from formal suppliers		
Formal firms	80	80
Informal firms	29	43
Share of output to formal buyers		
Formal firms	48	48
Informal firms	16	28

(continued)

TABLE 3.6 **Model Fit: Moments from the Real Data and from the Estimated Model** (*continued*)

percent

Moments	Data	Model
Distribution of downstream informal firms, by size relative to the average formal firm		
5th percentile	0.02	0.06
25th percentile	0.14	0.22
50th percentile	0.46	0.31
75th percentile	1.20	0.66
95th percentile	3.35	3.33
Distribution of upstream informal firms, by size relative to the average formal firm		
5th percentile	0.16	0.05
25th percentile	0.38	0.09
50th percentile	0.64	0.19
75th percentile	1.50	0.72
95th percentile	5.92	7.92
Distribution of downstream formal firms, by size relative to the average formal firm		
5th percentile	7.91	15.15
10th percentile	9.70	16.12
Distribution of upstream formal firms, by size relative to the average formal firm		
5th percentile	1.42	0.65
10th percentile	2.07	0.72
Standard deviation divided by mean		
Downstream	24.5	27.8
Upstream	24.4	37.8
Inputs/revenue		
Downstream	71	53
Share of informal labor		
Upstream	77	81

Source: Original compilation for this publication.

the results based on the real data. The model generally captures the pervasive number of informal firms that, together, contribute a small fraction of the total output.

In the model, the relative size of an informal firm in each quantile downstream is 0.22 percent, 0.31 percent, and 0.66 percent of the average formal firm in downstream industries. This is similar to the moments from the real data. Among upstream informal firms, the model predicts the relative size in each quantile at 0.09 percent, 0.19 percent, and 0.72 percent of the average formal firm, which deviates from the moments in the real data by one or two standard deviations. Annex 3G reports the standard deviation of these moments. The model captures the relative size of a large informal firm at the 95th percentile. Among small formal firms, the model prediction deviates one or two standard deviations from the real data.

The model predicts a segmented trade structure whereby formal firms purchase 80 percent of their inputs from formal suppliers, while informal firms purchase 43 percent of their inputs from formal suppliers. The share of sales to formal buyers is 48 percent and 28 percent in the model for formal and informal firms, respectively, compared with 48 percent and 16 percent in the real data. The model generally captures the trade structure of formal firms, but it overestimates informal sector trade with formal partners.

IDENTIFYING THE TYPES OF INFORMAL FIRMS

The existence of various perspectives on the informal sector implies that different sorts of behavior are embraced across informal firms in response to tax reforms. This subsection discusses a perspective that explains most accurately the response of informal firms to VAT adoption.

Informal firms may be divided into three types: reservoir, parasite, and unproductive informal firms. Reservoir firms become formal after all tax burdens (VAT and corporate taxes) are removed. Parasite firms can survive as formal firms if all tax burdens are removed, but they nonetheless remain informal. Unproductive-type firms can survive only as informal firms. If the tax rate falls to zero, the present value of formal status is negative, but the present value of informal status is positive.

If tax rates drop to zero, around 3.50 percent (downstream) and 0.03 percent (upstream) of informal firms will formalize (figure 3.6). Only 5.10 percent and 0.25 percent of informal firms can survive as formal firms (but choose not to) in downstream and upstream industries, respectively. Unproductive firms make up the majority of informal firms and are too unproductive to formalize even after the tax burden is removed, that is, if tax rates drop to zero.

Counterfactual Analysis

The availability of the estimated parameters allows the model to be used to compare the VAT and the cascading sales tax at any tax rate. For the analysis, the tax rate is set at 7.5 percent, which is consistent with the statutory sales tax rate in the state of West Bengal. Two other scenarios—VAT rates of 9.5 percent and 10.1 percent—are also considered, the first because it generates the same number of formal firms, and the latter because it generates the same level of tax revenue after VAT adoption. Respectively, these are the informality-neutral scenario and the revenue-neutral scenario.

FIGURE 3.6 **The Three Types of Informal Firms**

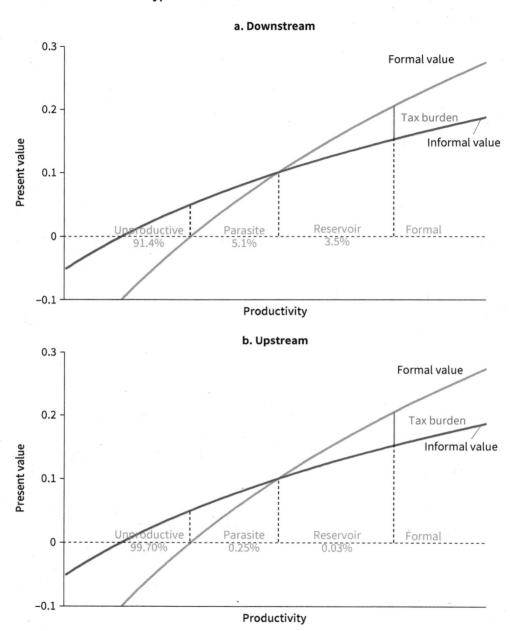

INFORMALITY: NUMBER AND OUTPUT

Table 3.7 shows the share of informality after VAT adoption. The replacement of the cascading sales tax with the VAT causes the share of formal firms to increase slightly, from 5.5 percent to 5.7 percent, while the share of formal output rises from 87 percent to 89 percent. In addition, the share of workers in the formal sector also rises, from 11.3 percent to 13.3 percent, suggesting that a substantial reallocation of labor has occurred from the informal sector to the formal sector; the share of workers employed in the formal sector increases by 17 percent, while the share of workers in the informal sector decreases by 2 percent.[9] If the VAT rate rises to the level in the informality-neutral scenario, the share of formal firms in the economy remains similar, at 5.6 percent, which accounts for 89 percent of total output. If the VAT rate climbs farther, to the level in the revenue-neutral scenario, the share of formal firms is 5.5 percent, and the share of formal output is 89 percent.

However, the share of informality neglects the absolute change number and output. Table 3.8 shows that about 0.6 percent of informal firms become formal after VAT adoption, which corresponds to a 2 percent increase in the number of formal firms if the tax rate remains the same. Yet, VAT adoption has a significant impact on formal sector output. Formal sector output rises by 12 percent, while informal sector output shrinks slightly, by 2.8 percent. In the informality-neutral scenario, the number of formal firms remains unchanged, but the number of informal firms increases by 0.2 percent. The output of the formal and informal sectors rises by 10 percent and –2 percent, respectively. In the revenue-neutral scenario, the output of formal and informal firms increases 10 percent and 1 percent, respectively. The results suggest that VAT adoption does not have a large effect on the total number of formal firms, but it does have an important effect on the incentive of productive firms to expand production.

TABLE 3.7 **The Share of Informality**
percent

Tax	Number share		Revenue share		Labor share	
	Formal	Informal	Formal	Informal	Formal	Informal
ST, 7.5	5.54	94.46	87.34	12.66	11.34	88.66
VAT, 7.5	5.68	94.32	89.21	10.79	13.30	86.70
VAT, 17.5	5.10	94.90	86.98	13.02	11.61	88.39
VAT, informality neutral	5.55	94.45	88.91	11.09	12.97	87.03
VAT, revenue neutral	5.52	94.48	88.72	11.28	12.88	87.12

Source: Original compilation for this publication.
Note: ST = cascading sales tax. VAT = value added tax. The informality-neutral rate is 9.5 percent; the number of formal firms is thus the same as in the benchmark scenario of a cascading sales tax at 7.5 percent. The revenue-neutral rate is 10.1 percent; the total value added tax revenue is thus the same as with the total cascading sales tax revenue.

TABLE 3.8 **Changes in the Formal and Informal Sectors after VAT Adoption**
percent

Tax	Number		Revenue	
	Formal	Informal	Formal	Informal
ST, 7.5	0	0	0	0
VAT, 7.5	2.0	−0.6	11.9	−2.8
VAT, 17.5	−7.3	1.3	1.3	6.4
VAT, informality neutral	−0.1	−0.2	9.9	−1.8
VAT, revenue neutral	0.0	0.4	10.4	0.6

Source: Original compilation for this publication.
Note: ST = cascading sales tax. VAT = value added tax. The informality-neutral rate is 9.5 percent; the number of formal firms is thus the same as in the benchmark scenario of a cascading sales tax at 7.5 percent. The revenue-neutral rate is 10.1 percent; the total value added tax revenue is thus the same as the total cascading sales tax revenue. The change in number or revenue is the percent change from the benchmark scenario of a cascading sales tax at 7.5 percent.

The fully cascading sales tax is the baseline scenario. This assumes that all intermediate inputs are subject to the sales tax. In reality, a sales tax often lies somewhere between a noncascading tax and a cascading tax; the extent of cascading depends on the enforcement of the sales tax. If more sellers are able to distinguish final goods from intermediate goods in selling to customers, then the sales tax leans toward a noncascading tax, and vice versa. This chapter therefore estimates the upper limit on the impact of VAT adoption on informality.

The expansion of formal sector output is mainly driven by large, high-productivity firms.[10] In downstream industries, small firms below the median size grow at less than 2.5 percent, while firms at the 90th percentile grow by 4.3 percent. In upstream industries, firms at the 10th and 90th percentiles grow by 9 percent and 15 percent, respectively (figure 3.7).

Figure 3.7 shows that small formal firms at the 10th percentile purchase 53 percent of their inputs from formal suppliers, while large firms at the 90th percentile purchase 62 percent of inputs from formal suppliers. Large firms tend to purchase a larger share of inputs from formal suppliers. Similarly, small formal upstream firms at the 10th percentile sell 39 percent of their output to the formal sector, while large firms at the 90th percentile sell 44 percent of their output to the formal sector. If the VAT removes tax costs on formal intermediate goods, large downstream firms will lower more of the taxes they have paid on purchases, while large upstream firms sell more to downstream firms.

Now that a segmented trade structure between the formal and informal sectors has been found, the extent to which segmented trade can be attributed to the VAT can be evaluated. Table 3.9 compares the share of inputs from and outputs to formal sector partners. In the baseline scenario, the formal sector purchases 74 percent of inputs from formal suppliers and sells 46 percent of output to formal buyers. After VAT adoption

FIGURE 3.7 **Revenue Growth after VAT Adoption, by Size**

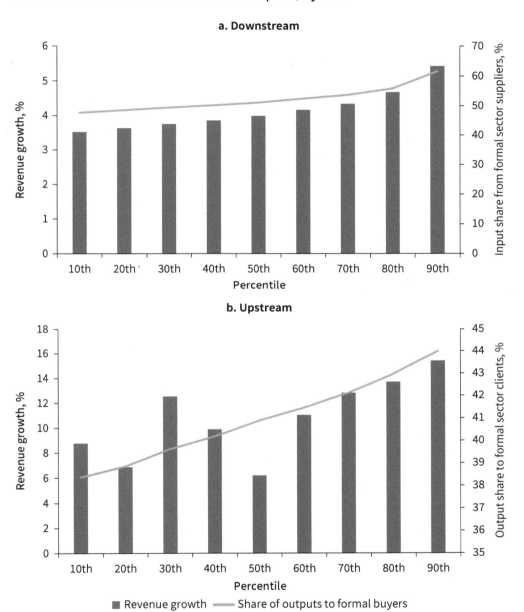

Source: Original figure produced for this publication.
Note: The figure plots the counterfactual size growth after VAT adoption using the estimated model. VAT = value added tax.

at the same tax rate, the share of inputs from formal suppliers rises to 78 percent, and the share of output going to formal buyers rises to 48 percent. Varying the VAT tax rate (the informality-neutral rate or the revenue-neutral rate) does not substantially affect the magnitude of the change.

TABLE 3.9 **Trade Pattern: VAT versus Sales Tax**

percent

Tax	Inputs		Output	
	Formal from formal	Informal from formal	Formal from formal	Informal from formal
ST, 7.5	74.1	44.9	46.2	29.9
VAT, 7.5	78.0	44.9	47.7	29.9
VAT, 17.5	77.9	38.3	43.0	24.7
VAT, informality neutral	78.4	43.9	46.8	28.8
VAT, revenue neutral	76.3	41.9	46.5	28.5

Source: Original compilation for this publication.
Note: ST = cascading sales tax. VAT = value added tax. The informality-neutral rate is 9.5 percent; the number of formal firms is thus the same as in the benchmark scenario of a cascading sales tax at 7.5 percent. The revenue-neutral rate is 10.1 percent; the total value added tax revenue is thus the same as the total cascading sales tax revenue.

TAXATION, CORPORATE PROFITS, AND HOUSEHOLD INCOME

One concern about the existence of a large informal sector is the potential loss of tax revenue that could be used to finance public goods. Besley and Persson (2013) argue that a main development issue associated with taxation relates to ways a government might increase the ratio of tax revenue to GDP from around 10 percent to around 40 percent.

If the tax rate remains the same, less sales tax revenue is generated by VAT adoption than by the cascading sales tax. However, the adoption of VAT has a positive effect on labor income and formal corporate profits. Table 3.10 shows that labor income among formal workers rises by 20 percent after VAT adoption, while the income of informal workers is unchanged.

Formal sector corporate profits increase by 8 percent after VAT adoption, while informal sector profits shrink by 2 percent. For informal firms, the border is blurred between corporate profits and individual wages. A loss in corporate profits negatively affects informal workers despite unchanged wage income. That the profit loss in the informal sector is less than 2 percent after VAT adoption suggests limited welfare loss among informal households.

Higher corporate and income tax revenues offset the loss from other tax revenues (see table 3.10). If the composition of tax revenues remains unchanged, a switch to the VAT will lead to a 27 percent drop in sales tax revenues but a 1 percent decline in total tax revenue. As the tax rate increases, the net gain in total tax revenue becomes more significant (figure 3.8).

TABLE 3.10 **Changes in Tax Revenue, Labor Income, and Corporate Profits**
percent

Tax	VAT/ST	Total tax	Household income		Corporate profit	
	Formal	Formal	Formal	Informal	Formal	Informal
ST, 7.5	0	0	0	0	0	0
VAT, 7.5	−27	−1	20	0	8	−2
VAT, 17.5	73	25	−1	−4	−1	7
VAT, informality neutral	−7	4	15	−1	6	−2
VAT, revenue neutral	0	7	15	−1	7	0

Source: Original compilation for this publication.
Note: ST = cascading sales tax. VAT = value added tax. The informality-neutral rate is 9.5 percent; the number of formal firms is thus the same as in the benchmark scenario of a cascading sales tax at 7.5 percent. The revenue-neutral rate is 10.1 percent; the total value added tax revenue is thus the same as with the total cascading sales tax revenue. Change is the percent change from the benchmark scenario of a cascading sales tax at a 7.5 percent rate.

FIGURE 3.8 **Tax Revenue and the Tax Rate: The VAT versus the Sales Tax**

a. Total tax revenue

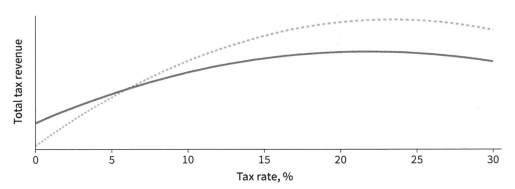

b. Sales tax/VAT revenue

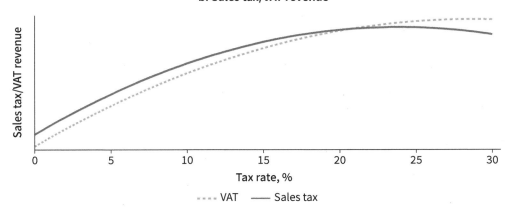

- - - - VAT ——— Sales tax

Source: Original figure produced for this publication.
Note: The figure plots the counterfactual relationship between the tax rate and tax revenue with the cascading sales tax and the VAT using the estimated model. VAT = value added tax.

Conclusion

In the past 30 years, more than 50 countries have adopted a VAT. In some of these countries, the VAT has been adopted with the explicit objective of improving compliance and reducing informality. Yet, we do not know much about the impact of the VAT on informality.

This chapter presents a structural framework for studying the relationship between VAT adoption and informality. Using data on Indian manufacturing firms, the chapter shows that, although VAT does not have a large impact on low-productivity informal firms, it is associated with a significant increase in formal sector output. The chapter finds that replacing a cascading sales tax with a VAT would have a relatively small effect on the number of formal firms (a 2 percent rise, according to the estimates here), but it would have a much larger effect on formal sector output (a 12 percent increase, according to the estimates). It also finds that the VAT is particularly beneficial for larger firms that tend to buy a larger share of their inputs from formal suppliers.

Although the results are in line with the literature that finds that unproductive firms have limited incentives to register even if taxes are reduced or enforcement tightened (La Porta and Schleifer 2014; Levy 2008; Maloney 2004; Ulyssea 2018), the findings here suggest that VAT adoption can be beneficial for productive firms. By streamlining the tax system to avoid double taxation at every stage of production, the VAT promotes the expansion of productive formal firms, leading them to absorb labor and capital from the informal sector. It is through this reallocation process that VAT adoption can have a positive effect on economic growth and structural transformation.

Annex 3A: The Downstream Index

Using the input-output table, Antràs and Chor (2013) propose a measure to capture the "downstreamness" of an industry in the value chain. Following is a sketch of their measurement and details of an application to the Indian input-output table. The basic input-output identity is as follows:

$$Y_i = F_i + Z_i, \tag{3A.1}$$

where Y_i is the total output in industry i; F_i is the output of i that goes toward final use; and Z_i is the use of i's output as inputs in other industries. In a world with N industries, this identity can be expanded as:

$$Y_i = F_i + \sum_{j=1}^{N} d_{ij} F_j + \sum_{j=1}^{N} \sum_{k=1}^{N} d_{ik} d_{kj} F_j + \sum_{j=1}^{N} \sum_{k=1}^{N} \sum_{l=1}^{N} d_{il} d_{lk} d_{kj} F_j + \dots \tag{3A.2}$$

where d_{ij} for a pair of industries is the amount of i used as an input in producing a dollar's worth of industry j's output. $\sum_{j=1}^{N} d_{ij} F_j$ captures the value of i's direct use as an input at industry j to produce output that immediately goes to final use. The remaining terms $\sum_{j=1}^{N} \sum_{K=1}^{N} d_{ik} d_{kj} F_j + \sum_{j=1}^{N} \sum_{K=1}^{N} \sum_{l=1}^{N} d_{il} d_{lk} d_{kj} F_j + \dots$ that involve higher-order summations reflect the indirect use of i as an input. These indirect inputs enter the value chain for future production at least two production stages away from final use.

The downstream index measures the distance of an industry to the final products consumed by final consumers. In practice, the index is calculated by dividing the direct use of industry i's product as an input for final use production by the total use of i's product as inputs in other industries. The higher the ratio in a given industry i, the more intensive is its use as a direct input for final use production, so that the industry is closer to the downstream stage of the value chain. Conversely, a lower ratio indicates that most of the contribution of input i to production processes occurs indirectly and that the industry is located closer to the upstream stage of the value chain.

Based on their methodology, the analysis relies on the Indian input-output table to calculate the relative position of each industry. The input-output table has been constructed for the year 2013–14, which is consistent with the national accounts estimates provided in the 2015 national accounts statistics. The input-output table contains 140 rows (products) and 67 columns (sectors), which have been collapsed and expanded to make the 130*130 input-output table of Singh and Saluja (2018).

First, the analysis calculates the N*N direct requirement matrix D and the N*1 final use vector F by summing over the value of each industry i's output purchased for consumption and investment by private or government entities and the N*1 output vector Y as the summation of all entries in row i in the input-output table. Then, the analysis calculates the direct use of each industry as DF, and the total input use for each industry as $Y-F$. The ith element of the direct use vector DF is divided by the corresponding ith element of the input vector $Y-F$, which generates the downstream index of industry i.

Table 3A.1 shows the downstream index and the share of informality in the 10 largest industries (Table 3A.2 presents the downstream index for all industries). Informal firms are prevalent among the miscellaneous food producers, textile producers, and leather producers, whose shares of informal firms are 89 percent, 94 percent, and 93 percent, respectively, and whose shares of total output are 17 percent, 8 percent, and 31 percent, respectively. These industries are also closer to final consumers; their downstream indexes are higher than average. Meanwhile, less informal firms occur among petroleum producers and metallic mineral producers (iron, steel, and ferroalloys). The shares of informal firms are 48 percent and 27 percent (less than 1 percent of total output) in these two industries, respectively. The two industries operate mainly in the upstream production stages.

There is a weakly positive correlation between the downstream index and the share of informality (figure 3A.1). The correlation may not be a coincidence. Hoseini and Briand (2020) find that informality is more salient in downstream industries. They calculate the backward link as a proxy for the position of an industry in the production chain. The larger the backward link, the longer the chain of inputs, which is similar to the downstream index used in this chapter. They argue that a cascading sales tax distorts product prices, an effect that tends to accumulate as the value chain moves toward downstream industries. Because downstream industries typically have strong backward links associated with their more numerous production stages, their product prices deviate more from the optimal prices as a result of cumulative taxes. The higher prices of formal sector products allow more space for cheaper informal sector products, the prices of which are not distorted by tax wedges. Hence, informal firms are more prevalent in downstream industries than in upstream industries.

However, the link between the downstream index and informality is beyond the scope of this chapter, which treats the differences in informality upstream and downstream as stylized facts without causal analysis. For an illustrative description of tax cascading, see annex 3C.

TABLE 3A.1 Share of Informal Firms in the 10 Largest Manufacturing Industries, 2015

Industry	Downstream index	Share of informal firms, %	Share of informal sector output, %
Petroleum products	0.85	48	0
Miscellaneous food products	1.20	89	17
Iron, steel, and ferroalloys	0.65	27	0
Motor vehicles	0.37	63	1
Miscellaneous manufacturing	0.76	89	11
Miscellaneous metal products	0.44	80	21
Drugs and medicines	1.69	55	0
Cotton textiles	1.12	94	8
Plastic products	1.00	64	4
Leather and leather products	1.20	93	31

Source: Based on data of the Annual Survey of Industries and the Unorganized Manufacturing Enterprises Survey.

FIGURE 3A.1 **The Share of Informal Firms and the Downstream Index, 2015**

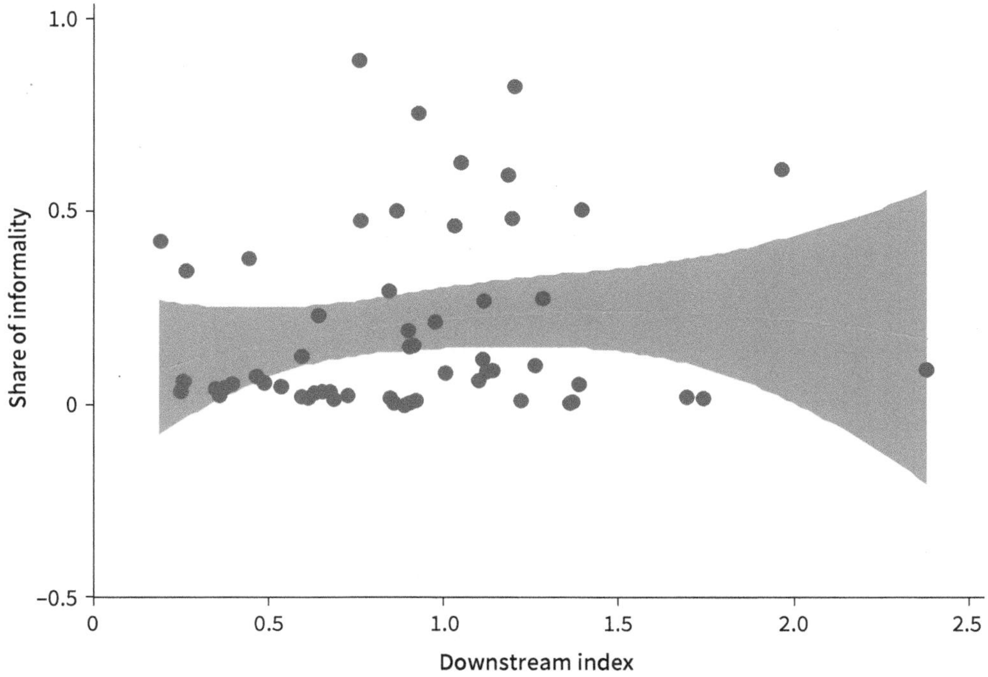

Source: Based on data of the Annual Survey of Industries and the Unorganized Manufacturing Enterprises Survey.

TABLE 3A.2 **The Downstream Index and the Share of Informal Firms, 2015**

Industry	Downstream index	Share of informal firms, %	Share of informal sector output, %
Petroleum products	0.85	48	0
Miscellaneous food products	1.20	89	17
Iron, steel, and ferroalloys	0.65	27	0
Motor vehicles	0.37	63	1
Miscellaneous manufacturing	0.76	89	11
Miscellaneous metal products	0.44	80	21
Drugs and medicines	1.69	55	0
Cotton textiles	1.12	94	8
Plastic products	1.00	64	4
Leather and leather products	1.20	93	31
Nonferrous basic metals	0.25	38	1
Other nonmetallic mineral products	0.90	87	23

(Continued)

TABLE 3A.2 **The Downstream Index and the Share of Informal Firms, 2015** *(continued)*

Industry	Downstream index	Share of informal firms, %	Share of informal sector output, %
Cement	1.22	24	0
Other nonelectrical machinery	0.84	65	4
Organic heavy chemicals	0.36	82	0
Motorcycles and scooters	0.86	3	0
Edible oils other than hydrogenated oil (vanaspati)	1.26	54	1
Beverages	1.28	82	2
Industrial machinery (others)	0.68	94	51
Electrical industrial machinery	0.64	62	2
Paper, paper products, and newsprint	0.59	71	4
Sugar	1.11	98	13
Soaps, cosmetics, and glycerin	0.91	75	3
Fertilizers	1.37	55	0
Synthetic fibers, resin	0.92	43	1
Iron and steel casting and forging	0.25	69	1
Rubber products	1.12	58	2
Miscellaneous textile products	1.39	94	48
Art silk, synthetic fiber textiles	1.10	86	1
Electrical wires and cables	0.63	77	2
Tractors and agricultural implements	2.38	62	4
Printing and publishing	0.26	74	21
Tobacco products	1.97	98	14
Wood and wood products	1.19	93	46
Structural clay products	0.90	79	43
Other chemicals	0.68	35	1
Electrical appliances	0.39	58	2
Paints, varnishes, and lacquers	0.90	9	0
Silk textiles	0.93	99	21
Pesticides	1.36	31	0
Leather footwear	0.97	96	17
Furniture and fixtures (wooden)	0.76	92	77
Readymade garments	0.19	91	13
Communication equipment	0.61	18	1
Batteries	0.59	57	13
Electronic equipment (including televisions)	0.46	53	0

(Continued)

TABLE 3A.2 **The Downstream Index and the Share of Informal Firms, 2015** *(continued)*

Industry	Downstream index	Share of informal firms, %	Share of informal sector output, %
Hand tools, hardware	0.86	77	16
Hydrogenated oil (vanaspati)	1.74	56	0
Other electrical machinery	0.72	76	7
Industrial machinery	0.53	60	9
Machine tools	0.35	68	1
Carpet weaving	1.03	91	13
Jute, hemp, mesta textiles	1.39	48	2
Bicycles, cycle-rickshaws	0.49	58	8
Woolen textiles	1.05	41	4
Other transport equipment	2.55	86	4
Ships and boats	4.52	75	3
Khandsari, boora	1.14	93	4
Rail equipment	0.89	0	0

Source: Based on data of the Annual Survey of Industries and the Unorganized Manufacturing Enterprises Survey.

Annex 3B: Calculating the Share of Formal Inputs and Output

The first step is to restrict the firm-level data to the manufacturing sector in West Bengal State where transaction data are available from local tax authorities. The second step is to divide firms into four categories: formal downstream firms, informal downstream firms, formal upstream firms, and informal upstream firms. Total revenue and total expenditure are then aggregated for each category using the sample weights of each firm. Revenue F denotes the total revenue of formal firms. Revenue I denotes the total revenue of informal firms. Expense F denotes the total expenditure of formal firms. Expense I denotes the total expenditure of informal firms.

The share of sales from formal sellers to formal buyers. Within the total revenue of formal firms (Revenue F), the share of revenue from sales by formal firms to formal buyers needs to be calculated. Revenue FF denotes the revenue from such sales. Transaction-level data from tax authorities are used in the analysis that cover all the transactions of formal firms in the state. Formal firms report all their sales to other formal firms as required by regulations. The total sales by formal sellers to formal buyers (Revenue FF) are aggregated and divided by the total revenue of formal firms (Revenue F). This yields the share of sales from formal sellers to formal buyers (figure 3B.1).

The share of inputs provided to formal firms by formal sellers. Among the total inputs of formal firms (Expense F), the share of inputs supplied to formal firms by

FIGURE 3B.1 **Measuring Transactions between the Formal and Informal Sectors**

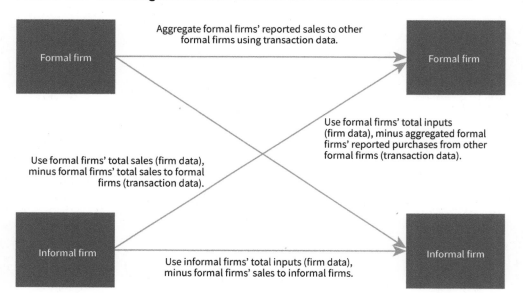

Source: Original figure produced for this publication.

formal sellers needs to be calculated. Expense FF denotes the total inputs going to formal firms from formal sellers. Formal firms have to report all their purchases from other formal firms to the tax authority. The total inputs provided to formal buyers by other formal sellers (Expense FF) are aggregated and divided by the total inputs of formal firms (Expense F). This yields the share of inputs supplied to formal firms by formal sellers.

The share of sales by informal firms to formal buyers. Within the total revenue of informal firms (Revenue I), the share of revenue received by informal firms from formal buyers needs to be calculated. Revenue IF denotes the total revenue received by informal sellers from formal buyers. Because transaction-level data on informal firms are not available, it is not possible to use the same aggregation to obtain the total revenue received by informal firms from formal buyers. However, the total revenue received by formal firms from formal buyers (Revenue FF) and the total inputs of formal firms (Expense F) can be calculated. Formal firms purchase inputs from either formal sellers or informal sellers. This means Expense F = Revenue FF + Revenue IF. The analysis uses this identity and subtracts the inputs of formal buyers (Expense F) from the total sales of formal sellers to formal buyers (Revenue FF). This yields the total sales by informal sellers to formal buyers (Revenue IF). Dividing the sales by informal sellers to formal buyers (Revenue IF) by the total sales of informal firms (Revenue I) yields the share of sales from informal sellers to formal buyers.

The share of inputs supplied to informal firms by formal sellers. Within the total inputs of informal firms (Expense I), the share of inputs going to informal firms from formal sellers needs to be calculated. Because there are no transaction-level data on informal firms, aggregation is not possible for informal firms. However, the total inputs of informal firms (Expense I), the total sales of formal sellers (Revenue F), and the total sales by formal sellers to formal buyers (Revenue FF) can be calculated. The total sales of formal sellers to informal buyers (Revenue FI) are calculated (Revenue FI + Revenue FF = Revenue F). Dividing the revenue received by formal sellers from informal buyers (Revenue FI) by the total inputs of informal buyers (Expense I), the share of inputs going to informal buyers from formal sellers can be calculated.

Households also purchase products from upstream suppliers. It is assumed that a fixed share of upstream sales goes to households. This equals the share of final consumption in the input-output table.

Annex 3C: Background on Indian Tax Reform

The various states of India adopted value added taxation between 2003 and 2014. Both direct taxes and indirect taxes are levied in India. Except for taxes associated with professions and property taxes, direct taxes are collected by the central government. Indirect taxes are levied by the central government and state governments. The service tax, customs duties, and union excise duties, including taxes on manufacturing products, are the prerogative of the federal government. The only indirect tax at the state level is the VAT, which accounts for more than half of all state tax revenue.

Prior to the adoption of VAT, the main source of tax revenue among states was the sales tax. This explains the reluctance of states to undertake tax reform despite the frequent commentary on the flaws of the tax system. The sales tax in Indian states was typically a cascading tax even under the two general rules that were aimed at distinguishing between intermediate and final consumption. According to the physical ingredient rule, an input is a material or component that is physically incorporated in goods intended to be sold. According to the direct use rule, items used directly in the production of goods are exempt from the sales taxes. However, these rules were not easy to apply, and they did not guarantee that business inputs would not be taxed.

The tax treatment of inputs is heterogeneous across the states and union territories of India. Raw materials are tax exempt in only a few states and union territories (such as Delhi and Gujarat); however, because of the widespread adoption of the physical ingredient rule in these states, fuel, tools, machinery, and equipment are also not considered inputs. NIPFP (1994) and Ring (1999) estimate that 30 percent to 40 percent of sales tax revenue is collected through intermediate inputs.

The VAT reform has been accompanied by other policies, such as a change in the tax rate, lower registration costs, and a change in the registration threshold (figures 3C.1 and 3C.2). In most Indian states and union territories, the VAT rates after the reform were higher than the sales tax rates before the reform. The threshold of VAT registration was also higher than the sales tax registrations, which suggests that there is greater tolerance of informality under the VAT regime.

West Bengal is a large state with 90 million inhabitants in East India. The total GDP in West Bengal was US$210 billion in 2019–20, which represents 7 percent of the national GDP. West Bengal implemented a VAT with a tax regime border on June 1, 2003 (rediff. com 2003). All firms with a turnover of more than 500,000 INR (threshold) are required to remit tax to the state. Firms with a turnover of less than Rs 5 million (border) can opt to remit the tax under a simplified tax scheme whereby they only pay a 0.025 percent tax on their total sales. However, firms in the simplified scheme cannot deduct from their tax liabilities the taxes paid by their suppliers.

Firms face different VAT rates depending on the goods they sell: 75 percent sell goods on the reduced tax schedule that are taxed at 4.0 percent; 21 percent sell goods on the main tax schedule that are taxed at 12.5 percent; and the remainder are taxed at super-reduced rates of 0 percent–1 percent. In 2014, the VAT rates for the main and reduced schedules increased by 1 percentage point. For simplicity, the chapter does not distinguish among the tax schedules and assumes that all firms pay a flat VAT rate of 12.5 percent.

FIGURE 3C.1 **Tax Rates before and after the VAT Reform, by State and Union Territory**

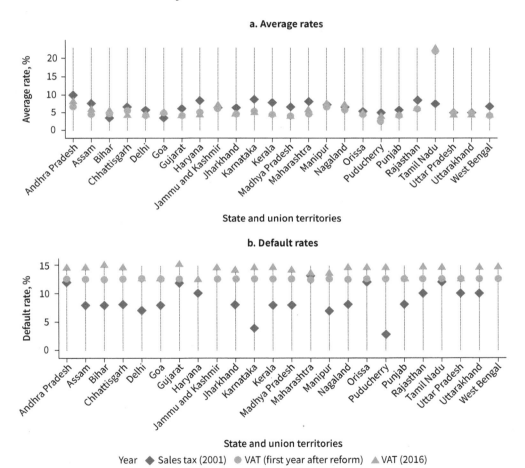

Source: Agrawal and Zimmermann 2019.
Note: VAT = value added tax.

FIGURE 3C.2 Tax Registration Threshold before and after the VAT Reform, by State and Union Territory

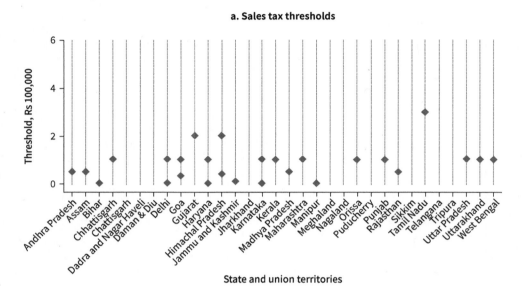

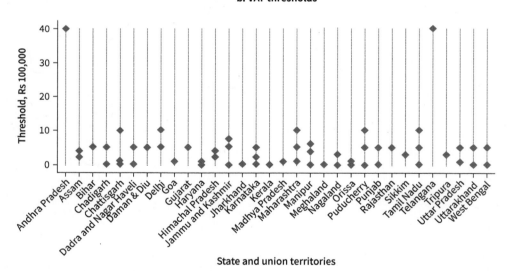

Source: Agrawal and Zimmermann 2019.
Note: VAT = value added tax.

Annex 3D: Model Solution

FORMAL DOWNSTREAM FIRMS

Formal sector buyers receive tax credits for formal sector inputs at the rate of t but do not receive credits for informal sector inputs. The VAT and the corporate tax are here imposed into the model (Investment Yogi 2015). The corporate tax is imposed on the net profit of formal firms both downstream and upstream. The VAT is levied on the gross margin downstream, along with a tax deduction if a formal buyer purchases from a formal supplier. Informal buyers and final consumers cannot deduct the taxes on intermediate inputs. The VAT is levied on the sales of formal firms, but the tax can be deducted by purchasing from other formal sellers. This creates an incentive for formal buyers to purchase from formal sellers rather than informal sellers if the price difference between the formal inputs and the informal inputs is less than the tax deduction. This might lead to market segmentation between the formal and informal sectors as depicted in the stylized facts.

Solving equations 3.2 and 3.3, the demand function of $x(i)$ for upstream firm i is as follows:

$$x^f(i) = [1-\tau(i)]^{\frac{1}{\rho-1}} \beta(i)^{-\frac{1}{\rho-1}} \left[\frac{y_0^f}{\theta^d}\right]^{\frac{1}{\alpha}} \left[\frac{p^f(i)}{P^f}\right]^{\frac{1}{\rho-1}}. \tag{3D.1}$$

The price index for formal downstream firms, p^f, becomes as follows:

$$P^f = \left[\int_0^N \left[(1-\tau(i))\,p^f(i)\right]^{\frac{\rho}{\rho-1}} \beta(i)^{-\frac{1}{\rho-1}}\,di\right]^{\frac{\rho-1}{\rho}}, \tag{3D.2}$$

$$P^f = \left[\int_{\underline{\theta^u}}^{\overline{\theta^u}} N\left[p_i^f\right]^{\frac{\rho}{\rho-1}}\,dF(\delta) + \int_{\overline{\theta^u}}^{\infty} N\left[(1-\tau)\,p_f^f\right]^{\frac{\rho}{\rho-1}} \beta^{-\frac{1}{\rho-1}}\,dF(\theta^u)\right]^{\frac{\rho-1}{\rho}}, \tag{3D.3}$$

where θ^u denotes the productivity of an upstream firm that sells to the buyer. It is assumed that downstream firms can observe the preentry productivity of upstream firms and form an initial expectation of the tax status of upstream suppliers, which coincides with the preentry productivity in the equilibrium. Specifically, downstream firms expect an upstream firm to be formal if the preentry productivity of the latter exceeds the upper bar of $\overline{\theta^u}$, and an upstream firm is expected to be informal if its productivity exceeds the lower bar of $\underline{\theta^u}$, but is below the higher bar of $\overline{\theta^u}$. In the equilibrium, $\underline{\theta^u}$ is the realized lower bar of the preentry productivity of informal firms, and $\overline{\theta^u}$ is the realized lower bar of the preentry productivity of formal firms.

Then firms choose the optimal output to maximize their profits:

$$max\left(1-\tau^{corp}\right)\left\{y_0-\int_0^N x(i)\,p^f(i)\left[1-\tau(i)\right]di\right\}, \tag{3D.4}$$

which yields the optimal output:

$$y_0^f=\theta^d\left[\frac{(1-\tau)\theta^d\alpha}{P^f}\right]^{\frac{\alpha}{1-\alpha}}. \tag{3D.5}$$

The net profit of formal downstream firms is thus:

$$\pi_f^d-\left(1-\tau^{corp}\right)\left\{y_0^f-\int_0^N x(i)\,p^f(i)[1-\tau(i)]\,di\right\}. \tag{3D.6}$$

INFORMAL DOWNSTREAM FIRMS

Solving the cost minimization problem in equations 3.4 and 3.5 yields the demand function of $x(i)$ for an informal upstream firm i:

$$x^i(i)=\beta(i)^{-\frac{1}{\rho-1}}\frac{y_0^{i\frac{1}{\alpha}}}{\theta^d}\left[\frac{p^i(i)}{P^i}\right]^{\frac{1}{\rho-1}}, \tag{3D.7}$$

with the price index P^i as follows:

$$P^i=\left[\int_0^N [p^i(i)]^{\frac{\rho}{\rho-1}}\beta(i)^{\frac{1}{\rho-1}}di\right]^{\frac{\rho-1}{\rho}}, \tag{3D.8}$$

$$P^i=\left\{\int_{\underline{\theta^u}}^{\overline{\theta^u}} N\left[p_i^i\right]^{\frac{\rho}{\rho-1}}dF\left(\theta^u\right)+\int_{\theta^u}^{\infty} N\left[p_f^i\right]^{\frac{\rho}{\rho-1}}\beta^{-\frac{1}{\rho-1}}dF\left(\theta^u\right)\right\}^{\frac{\rho-1}{\rho}}. \tag{3D.9}$$

Then, downstream firms choose the optimal output to maximize their profit:

$$max\left\{y_0-b_i\int_0^N x(i)\,p^f(i)\left[1-\tau(i)\right]di\right\}. \tag{3D.10}$$

And the optimal output is as follows:

$$y_0^i=\frac{\theta^d}{b_i}\left[\frac{\theta^d\alpha}{P^i}\right]^{\frac{\alpha}{1-\alpha}}. \tag{3D.11}$$

Hence, the maximized profit of an informal downstream firm is the following:

$$\pi_i^d=y_0^i-\int_0^N b_i x^i(i)\,p^i(i)\,di. \tag{3D.12}$$

FORMAL UPSTREAM FIRMS

The solution to the maximization problem in equations 3D.6 and 3D.7 yields the optimal output of a formal firm i going to a formal buyer as follows:

$$x_f^f = \left[\frac{w(1+\tau_l)}{\theta^u \rho \beta p^f} \right]^{\frac{1}{\rho-1}} \left[\frac{y_0^f}{\theta^d} \right]^{\frac{1}{\alpha}}. \tag{3D.13}$$

Solving equations 3D.8 and 3D.9 yields the optimal output for a formal seller to an informal buyer as follows:

$$x_f^i = \left[\frac{w(1+\tau_l)}{(1-\tau)\theta^u \rho \beta P^i} \right]^{\frac{1}{\rho-1}} \left[\frac{y_0^i}{\theta^d} \right]^{\frac{1}{\alpha}}. \tag{3D.14}$$

Equations 3D.13 and 3D.14 show the optimal sale by a formal supplier to a single formal firm and a single informal firm. It is assumed that upstream firms can observe the preentry productivity of downstream firms and then draw an initial expectation of the tax status of downstream buyers. The realized tax status in the equilibrium coincides with the initial guess. Specifically, upstream firms expect a downstream firm to be formal if the productivity of the latter exceeds the upper bar of $\overline{\theta^d}$; and a downstream firm is expected to be informal if its productivity exceeds the lower bar of $\underline{\theta^d}$, but is below the higher bar of $\overline{\theta^d}$. In the equilibrium, $\underline{\theta^d}$ is the realized lower bar of the preentry productivity of informal firms, and $\overline{\theta^d}$ is the realized lower bar of the preentry productivity of formal firms. With the initial guess of the tax status of downstream firms, the profit of an upstream formal firm is as follows:

$$\pi_f^u = \int_{\underline{\theta^d}}^{\overline{\theta^d}} x_f^i p_f^i - w(1+\tau_l) \left(\frac{x_f^i}{\theta^u} \right) dF(\theta^d) + \int_{\overline{\theta^d}}^{\infty} (1-\tau) x_f^f p_f^f - w(1+\tau_l) \left(\frac{x_f^f}{\theta^u} \right) dF(\theta^d). \tag{3D.15}$$

INFORMAL UPSTREAM FIRMS

Solving equations 3D.10 and 3D.11 yields the optimal sales to a formal buyer as follows:

$$x_i^f = \left[\frac{w(1+b_i)}{\theta^u \rho \beta P^f} \right]^{\frac{1}{\rho-1}} \left[\frac{y_0^f}{\theta^d} \right]^{\frac{1}{\alpha}}. \tag{3D.16}$$

The optimal sale to an informal buyer is the following:

$$x_i^i = \left[\frac{w(1+b_i)}{\theta^u \rho P^i} \right]^{\frac{1}{\rho-1}} \left[\frac{y_0^i}{\theta^d} \right]^{\frac{1}{\alpha}}. \tag{3D.17}$$

Equations 3D.16 and 3D.17 show the optimal sale by an informal supplier to a single formal buyer and a single informal buyer. Informal upstream firms may also observe the preentry productivity of downstream firms and then form an initial expectation of the tax status of downstream buyers. The realized tax status in the equilibrium coincides with the initial guess. With the initial guess of the tax status of downstream firms, the profit of an upstream informal firm is the following:

$$\pi_i^u = \int_{\underline{\theta^d}}^{\overline{\theta^d}} x_f^i p_f^i - w\left(\frac{x_i^i}{\theta^u}\right) dF(\theta^d) + \int_{\theta^d}^{\infty} x_i^f p_i^f - w\left(\frac{x_i^f}{\theta^u}\right) dF(\theta^d). \qquad (3D.18)$$

Annex 3E: A Granular Look at the Informal Sector

The analysis plotted the share of informal employment and the share of informal firms by state and union territory, sorted by GDP per capita from high to low. As Ulyssea (2018) suggests, informal employment and informal firms do not necessarily advance and slide back together in different places. Similar results are found using Indian data. The share of informal employment surpassed 95 percent in Andaman, Lakshadweep, and Mizoram, but barely reached 40 percent in Arunachal and in Daman and Diu. The share of informal firms, meanwhile, was highest in Andaman, Manipur, and Meghalaya, but lowest in Dadra, Daman and Diu, and Goa. The distribution of informal workers and informal firms varies largely, but firm informality and employment informality do not necessarily trend in the same direction. Delhi, for example, ranks 4th lowest in the share of informal firms, but only 18th lowest in the share of informal employment.

The correlation between income level and the share of informality is also not obvious (figure 3E.1) Rich states and union territories, such as Lakshadweep, also have a large share of informal firms and informal employment, implying that there are multiple causes of informality across India.

The analysis uses the subsample of firms with fewer than 10 employees in the UME survey to plot the distribution of informal firms by number of employees (figure 3E.2). The share of informal firms decreases as the number of employees in the firms grows. Among one-person establishments, 99 percent are informal. The share of informal firms drops to 96 percent, 88 percent, and 84 percent, respectively, among firms with two, three, or four employees. Among firms with more than five employees, informal firms only account for less than 80 percent of the firms.

The combined ASI and UME dataset shows that there are many more informal firms than formal firms (figure 3E.3). However, the typical informal firm is much smaller than the typical formal firm. Informal firms with only one or two workers account for more than 85 percent of all firms, but only generate 6 percent of the total output of firms.

The revenue produced by the average informal firm with more than three employees is Rs 14 million, which is 11 percent of the revenue of the average formal firm (figure 3E.4). The revenue of the average informal firms with fewer than or equal to three employees is only 1.3 percent of the revenue of the average formal firm. The average number of employees in formal firms, informal firms with more than three employees, and informal firms with fewer than three employees is 19.9, 4.8, and 1.3 employees, respectively.

Figure 3E.5 plots the size distribution of informal for example, firms with annual revenues of Rs 0–Rs 8 million. In the state of West Bengal, for example, firms with annual revenues above Rs 5 million are required to register with the tax authorities. If the owners of informal firms wish to keep their annual revenues below this level to avoid penalties, there should be bunching near the threshold. However, the number of informal firms with annual revenues near the threshold is not significant.

FIGURE 3E.1 **Informal Firms and Informal Employment, by State and Union Territory**

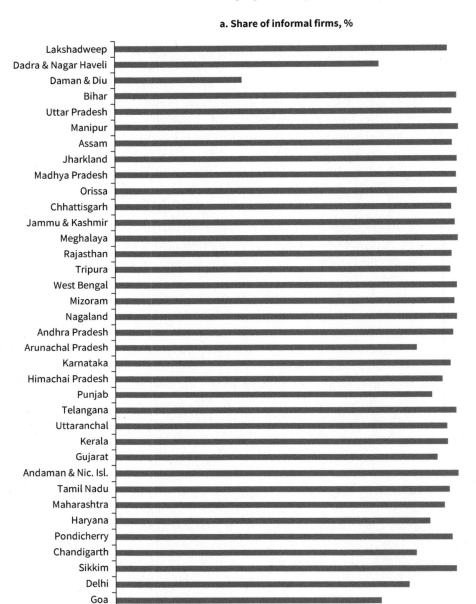

a. Share of informal firms, %

(continued)

FIGURE 3E.1 Informal Firms and Informal Employment, by State and Union Territory *(continued)*

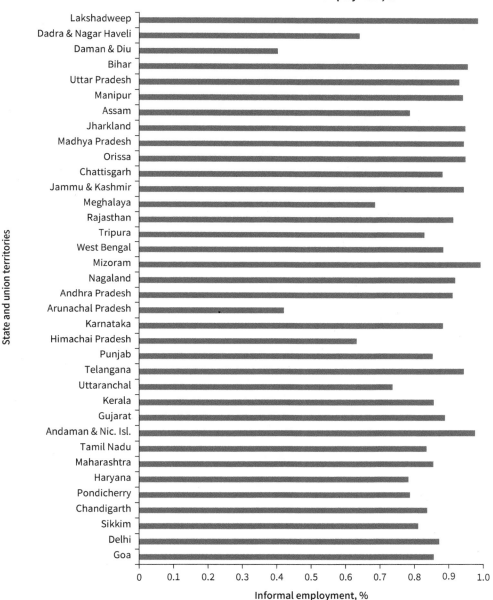

b. Share of informal employment, %

Sources: Based on data of the Annual Survey of Industries and the Unorganized Manufacturing Enterprises Survey, 2015; Labor Force Survey, 2017–18.

FIGURE 3E.2 **Share of Informal Firms, by Number of Employees in All Firms, 2015**

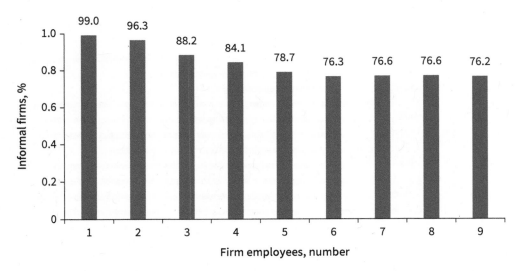

Source: Based on data of the Annual Survey of Industries and the Unorganized Manufacturing Enterprises Survey.

FIGURE 3E.3 **The Formal and Informal Firm Profile in Manufacturing, 2015**

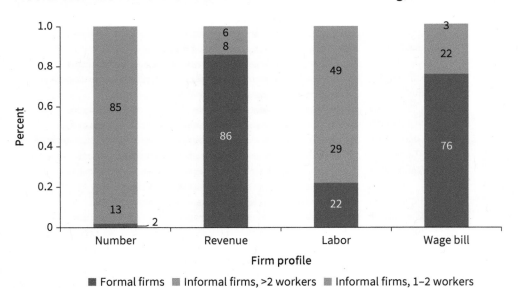

Source: Based on data of the Annual Survey of Industries and the Unorganized Manufacturing Enterprises Survey.

FIGURE 3E.4 Informal and Formal Firms, by Revenue and Number of Employees, 2015

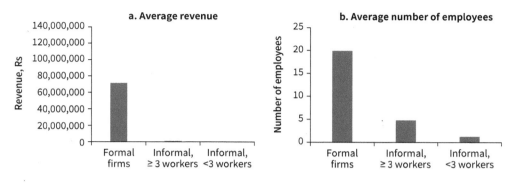

Source: Based on data of the Annual Survey of Industries and the Unorganized Manufacturing Enterprises Survey.

FIGURE 3E.5 Distribution of Informal Firms, by Revenue, 2015

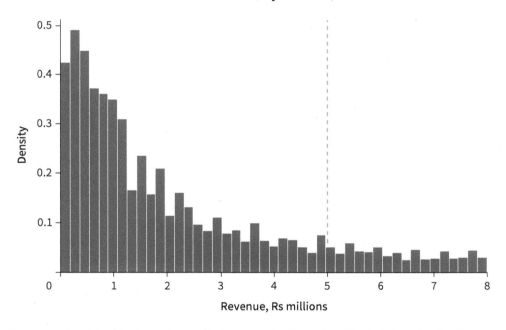

Source: Based on data of the Annual Survey of Industries and the Unorganized Manufacturing Enterprises Survey.

To quantify the difference between formal firms and informal firms, the following reduced form model was estimated using the combined ASI and UME firm-level datasets.

$$y_{isj} = formal_{isj} + \alpha_s + \gamma_j + \varepsilon_{isj}, \tag{3E.1}$$

where y_{isj} is the characteristics of firm i in sector s and state j, including log revenue, log number of employees, log value added, and log wage rate; $formal_{isj}$ is the dummy variable that equals 1 if firm i is registered with the tax authorities. (See table 3E.1.) The analysis also controlled for the ownership dummy, sector fixed effects, and the state fixed effect.

On average, formal firms are larger than informal firms in revenue, number of employees, wage rate, and value added (table 3E.2). Table 3E.3 augments an interaction term between the formal dummy and the downstream index. It shows that the differences in revenue, labor, value added, and wage rate between the formal and the informal sectors are more salient downstream. This implies stronger distortions in the downstream, which raises the entry threshold of the formal sector. The results are robust if the unweighted sample that is representative of the manufacturing sector in India is used or if the sample is restricted to the state of West Bengal.

Hsieh and Klenow (2009) show that registered Indian industrial firms grow slowly even after years of operation. The relative employment of a formal firm is less than 20 percent in India relative to a US firm. This is particularly true in the informal sector, where firm size grows even more slowly than in the formal sector. Table 3E.4 shows the correlation between firm age and firm size. An informal firm produces 9 percent less and employs a similar workforce compared with a new informal firm after 10 years of operation. The interaction term between the formal dummy and age is significantly positive, suggesting that formal firms grow more quickly, but still only slowly in an absolute sense relative to informal firms. A 10-year-old formal firm employs only 4 percent more workers and has a similar output compared with a new formal firm.

TABLE 3E.1 **Firm Value Characteristics, by Size**

Size	ln(VA per worker)	ln(K per worker)	ln(wage)
Informal firms			
1	10.62	11.52	9.27
	(0.99)	(0.99)	(1.25)
5	11.19	11.77	10.52
	(0.89)	(0.89)	(0.88)
10	11.89	13.04	11.22
	(1.31)	(1.31)	(0.54)
Formal firms			
20	12.74	13.76	11.64
	(0.89)	(0.89)	(0.66)
50	12.87	13.30	11.88
	(1.24)	(1.24)	(0.69)
100	13.02	13.32	12.07
	(1.18)	(1.18)	(0.76)
>100	13.14	13.93	12.03
	(1.11)	(1.11)	(0.83)

Source: Based on data of the Annual Survey of Industries and the Unorganized Manufacturing Enterprises Survey.
Note: ln(VA per worker) refers to the log form of value-added per worker; ln(K per worker) refers to the log form of fixed assets per worker; ln(wage) refers to the log form of salary.

TABLE 3E.2 **Differences between Formal and Informal Firms**

Variable	(1) ln(revenue)	(2) ln(labor)	(3) ln(VA)	(4) ln(wage)
Formal	1.468*** (0.018)	0.535*** (0.006)	0.947*** (0.016)	0.490*** (0.010)
Industry fixed effects	Y	Y	Y	Y
State fixed effects	Y	Y	Y	Y
Ownership fixed effects	Y	Y	Y	Y
Observations	51,529	60,696	49,705	59,661
R-squared	0.486	0.447	0.460	0.307

Source: Based on data of the Annual Survey of Industries and the Unorganized Manufacturing Enterprises Survey.
***p < .001.
Note: ln(VA per worker) refers to the log form of value-added per worker; in(wage) refers to the log form of salary;
Y = Yes.

TABLE 3E.3 **Differences between Formal and Informal Firms, by Production Stages**

Variables	(1) ln(revenue)	(2) ln(labor)	(3) ln(VA)	(4) ln(wage rate)
Formal	0.914*** (0.043)	0.347*** (0.015)	0.445*** (0.038)	0.400*** (0.023)
Formal × downstream index	0.631*** (0.044)	0.214*** (0.016)	0.572*** (0.039)	0.102*** (0.024)
Downstream index	0.043 (0.138)	0.073 (0.051)	0.099 (0.123)	−0.074 (0.089)
Industry fixed effects	Y	Y	Y	Y
State fixed effects	Y	Y	Y	Y
Ownership fixed effects	Y	Y	Y	Y
Observations	51,529	60,696	49,705	59,661
R-squared	0.531	0.561	0.473	0.542

Source: Based on data of the Annual Survey of Industries and the Unorganized Manufacturing Enterprises Survey.
***p < .001.
Note: ln(VA per worker) refers to the log form of value-added per worker; in(wage) refers to the log form of salary;
Y = Yes.

The informal sector in India is persistent. Among firms over 10 years old, more than 97 percent are informal, suggesting a persistent informality among firms that thereby evade tax obligations (figure 3E.6). The large share of informality among older firms coincides with the observation of Hsieh and Klenow (2014) that, in the United States, the average 40-year-old plant employs more than seven times as many workers as a corresponding 5-year-old or younger plant, while, among firms in the corresponding age range in India and Mexico, the surviving firms are only twice as large as the younger firms. However, this does not mean that the exit rate is low among informal firms. The literature indicates that informal firms often operate irregularly, which may mean that

TABLE 3E.4 **Differences between Formal and Informal Firms, by Age**

Variables	(1) ln(revenue)	(2) ln(labor)	(3) ln(VA)	(4) ln(wage rate)
Formal	1.386*** (0.024)	0.491*** (0.009)	0.940*** (0.021)	0.437*** (0.013)
Formal × age	0.008*** (0.001)	0.004*** (0.001)	0.002 (0.001)	0.005*** (0.001)
Age	−0.009*** (0.001)	−0.001*** (0.000)	−0.007*** (0.001)	−0.003*** (0.000)
Industry fixed effects	Y	Y	Y	Y
State fixed effects	Y	Y	Y	Y
Ownership fixed effects	Y	Y	Y	Y
Observations	51,529	60,696	49,705	59,661
R-squared	0.529	0.562	0.472	0.544

Source: Based on data of the Annual Survey of Industries and the Unorganized Manufacturing Enterprises Survey.
***p < .001.
Note: ln(VA per worker) refers to the log form of value-added per worker; in(wage) refers to the log form of salary; Y = Yes.

they exit the market if faced with negative shocks but return to the market once the shock has passed.

The practice of informal firms and their formal counterparts also differs significantly (figure 3E.7). The analysis restricts the sample in this case to firms with 3–10 employees in all sectors in the UME data. It finds that informal firms are less likely than formal firms to maintain bank accounts. The respective shares of bank account holders are 55 percent and 93 percent. Only 10 percent of informal firms undertake regular bookkeeping, while the corresponding share among formal firms is more than 70 percent. Informal firms are also less likely than formal firms to use computers and access the internet. However, both types of firms have limited access to finance; 10 percent of informal firms and 8 percent of formal firms report access to finance as the most important challenge. Only 2 percent of each type of firm receives government assistance. Among informal firms, 11 percent report that they sometimes work on a contract basis, while only 4 percent of formal firms do so.

The typical practices of small informal firms also reflect the low productivity of these firms. Figure 3E.8 compares the distribution of value added per worker in India's formal and informal sectors. Formal firms exhibit a higher average value added per worker relative to informal firms, which is captured by the rightward crest of the distribution of formal firms. Value added per worker and capital per worker grow as firms hire more workers.

FIGURE 3E.6 **Distribution of Informal Firms, by Age, 2015**

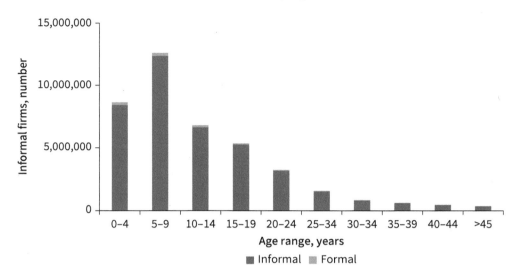

Source: Based on data of the Annual Survey of Industries and the Unorganized Manufacturing Enterprises Survey.

FIGURE 3E.7 **A Comparison of Practices between Formal and Informal Firms, 2015**

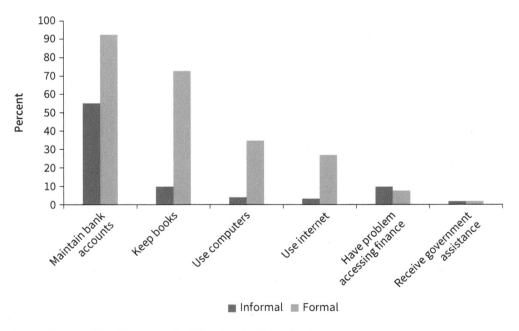

Source: Based on data of the Unorganized Manufacturing Enterprises Survey.

FIGURE 3E.8 **The Distribution of Value Added per Worker, 2015**

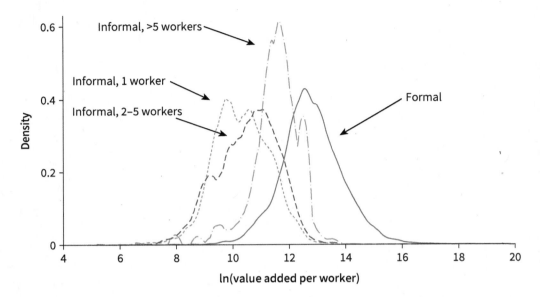

Source: Based on data of the Annual Survey of Industries and the Unorganized Manufacturing Enterprises Survey.

Annex 3F: The Simulated Method of Moments Estimator

Following Ulyssea (2018), the analysis considers S = 50 simulated data sets containing a mass of M = 30,000 potential entrants each. For each potential entrant, an observed productivity and a misperception of productivity are drawn. The stochastic components of the model are drawn only once—at the beginning of the procedure—and are kept fixed during the estimation.

To save computational time, 200 equally spaced grids are used as a representative sample of the whole population. Firms with productivity near one grid are categorized into the same grid. The economic behavior of these 200 representative firms is then calculated. The behavior of firms in the entire sample are then recovered through a spline proxy to map their productivity onto economic outcomes.

One difficulty in the estimation of discrete choice models using a simulation-based method is that simulated choices will be a step function of the parameter vector given the random raw data. Because these discontinuities are inherited by the objective function, this also precludes the use of derivative-based methods, which are more rapid and more accurate than derivative-free methods or random search algorithms (Bruins et al. 2018). To overcome these challenges, the analysis relies on the following smoothing function to correct for the choppiness of the policy function.

$$h\left(\bar{V}(\varphi), m, \lambda\right) = \frac{\overline{V_m}(\varphi) / \lambda}{1 + \sum_k \overline{V_k}(\varphi) / \lambda}, \tag{3F.1}$$

where $\bar{V}(\varphi)$ is the set of net payoffs attached to the choices of firms. As the smoothing parameter l goes to zero, $h(\cdot)$ goes to 1 if alternative m provides the highest payoff, and zero otherwise. In choosing λ, the analysis follows the method of Ulyssea (2018) to balance bias and smoothness. The analysis sets $\lambda = .05$ and $S = 50$.

The estimator is given by the following:

$$\hat{\varphi} = argmin_\varphi Q(\varphi) = \left\{ g_{NS}(\varphi)' \widehat{W} g_{NS} g_{NS}(\varphi) \right\}, \tag{3F.2}$$

where $g_{NS}(\varphi) = \widehat{m}_N - \widetilde{m}_s(\varphi)$. For notational convenience, the conditioning arguments are omitted.

The conditions for consistency are close to the conditions for the extremum estimator. For an extensive discussion of the weight matrix, see Gourinchas and Parker (2002), Newey and McFadden (1994), and Ulyssea (2018).

Annex 3G: Moments and Cutoff Productivity

Moments are illustrated in table 3G.1.

In the model, the analysis assumes that firms form their expectations about the productivity cutoff between the formal and informal sectors, beyond which a firm will choose to formalize. In equilibrium, the realized productivity cutoff confirms the expectations of the firms. Similarly, firms have expectations about the productivity cutoff in the informal sector below which a firm will exit the market. Table 3G.2 shows the expected productivity cutoff and the realized productivity in equilibrium, which confirms that the expectations of firms about the productivity cutoff are correct.

TABLE 3G.1 **Moments and Cutoff Productivity**
percent

Moments		Data	Standard deviation
Share of informality, number	Downstream	98	0.38
	Upstream	92	0.64
Share of informality, outputs	Downstream	31	3.08
	Upstream	16	2.90
Share of inputs from formal suppliers	Formal firms	80	0.14
	Informal firms	29	1.71
Share of output to formal buyers	Formal firms	48	0.16
	Informal firms	16	0.81
Distribution of informal downstream firms: relative size toward the average formal firm	5th percentile	0.02	0.01
	25th percentile	0.14	0.06
	50th percentile	0.46	0.14
	75th percentile	1.20	0.32
	95th percentile	3.35	0.86
Distribution of informal upstream firms: relative size toward the average formal firm	5th percentile	0.16	0.06
	25th percentile	0.38	0.11
	50th percentile	0.64	0.21
	75th percentile	1.50	0.46
	95th percentile	5.92	1.96
Distribution of formal downstream firms: relative size over the average formal firm	5th percentile	7.91	4.88
	10th percentile	9.70	5.85
Distribution of formal upstream firms: relative size over the average formal firm	5th percentile	1.42	0.51
	10th percentile	2.07	0.68
Standard deviation, divided by the mean	Downstream	24.5	2.0
	Upstream	24.4	2.3
Inputs/revenue	Downstream	71	2.19
Share of informal labor	Upstream	77	2.05

Source: Original compilation for this publication.

TABLE 3G.2 **Expected and Realized Productivity Cutoffs**

Parameter	Description	Expected productivity	Realized productivity
Delta low	Least productive informal upstream firm	2.0	2.04
Delta high	Least productive formal upstream firm	4.4	4.42
Theta low	Least productive informal downstream firm	1.0	1.01
Theta high	Least productive formal downstream firm	2.8	2.83

Source: Original compilation for this publication.

Notes

1. See Enterprise Surveys, National Data Archive, Data Informatics and Innovation Division, Ministry of Statistics and Program Implementation, New Delhi, http://microdata.gov.in /nada43/index.php/catalog/ENT.

2. Keen (2014) and Keen and Lockwood (2010) discuss the noncascading feature of the VAT. Chelliah (1994) and NIPFP (1994) discuss how VAT adoption would streamline the cascading taxes in India. Fajgelbaum et al. (2019), Gadenne, Nandi, and Rathelot (2019), Gérard and Naritomi (2018), Gérard, Naritomi, and Seibold (2018), Gordon and Li (2009), Papp and Takáts (2008), and Prado (2011) discuss the intersectoral trade structure and the welfare effect after the adoption of VAT.

3. Bruhn (2013), Bruhn and McKenzie (2014), Dabla-Norris, Gradstein, and Inchauste (2008), De Giorgi and Rahman (2013), de Mel, McKenzie, and Woodruff (2013), Henrique de Andrade, Bruhn, and McKenzie (2013), and Hsieh and Klenow (2009) study the causes of informality, while Banerji and Jain (2007), Fotoniata and Moutos (2013), Gelb et al. (2009), Ihrig and Moe (2004), Kaplan, Piedra, and Seira (2007), Loayza and Rigolini (2006), Medvedev and Oviedo (2013), and Steel and Snodgrass (2008) study the consequences of being informal.

4. See ASI (Annual Survey of Industries) (dashboard), Industrial Statistics Wing, National Statistical Office, Ministry of Statistics and Program Implementation, Kolkata, http://www .csoisw.gov.in/CMS/En/1023-annual-survey-of-industries.aspx.

5. Each year, all establishments with more than 100 employees and at least 12 percent of the others are surveyed, using a representative sample at the state and four-digit industry code level.

6. India currently has 36 states and union territories. The union territory of Lakshadweep and the state of Mizoram did not have registered manufacturing enterprises in 2015.

7. Seven interaction terms are augmented into the equation to compare the evolvement of informality with the trend prior to VAT adoption. The treatment group dummy is interacted with five dummy variables corresponding to the ith year after VAT adoption. If VAT adoption generates a consecutive decrease in informality in the subsequent five years, the decrease would be captured by these interaction terms.

8. The production function can also be rewritten as $y_0 = \theta^d \left\{ \int_0^N [x(i)\beta(i)^{1/\rho}]^\rho \, di \right\}^{\frac{\alpha}{\rho}}$. $\beta(i)$ may be interpreted as the share of inputs that are usable. Because informal firms produce lower-quality goods, $\beta(i)$ is smaller in the case of informal firms relative to formal firms.

9. The model assumes a fixed supply of labor.

10. That the expansion of formal firms may be driven by new entrants is a concern. To address this concern, the analysis is replicated in the informality-neutral scenario so that the extensive margin of the formal sector does not change. The results hold in the informality scenario.

References

Agrawal, David R., and Laura Zimmermann. 2019. "Production and Evasion Responses with Limited State Capacity: Evidence from Major Tax Reforms in India." IGC Working Paper S-89411-INC-1 (June), International Growth Centre, London School of Economic and Political Science, London.

Antràs, Pol, and Davin Chor. 2013. "Organizing the Global Value Chain." *Econometrica* 81 (6): 2127–2204.

Banerji, Arup, and Sanjay Jain. 2007. "Quality Dualism." *Journal of Development Economics* 84 (1): 234–50.

Besley, Timothy J., and Torsten Persson. 2013. "Taxation and Development." In *Handbook of Public Economics*, vol. 5, edited by Alan J. Auerbach, Raj Chetty, Martin Feldstein, and Emmanuel Saez, 51–110. Handbooks in Economics Series. Amsterdam: North Holland.

Bruhn, Miriam. 2013. "A Tale of Two Species: Revisiting the Effect of Registration Reform on Informal Business Owners in Mexico." *Journal of Development Economics* 103 (July): 275–83.

Bruhn, Miriam, and David McKenzie. 2014. "Entry Regulation and the Formalization of Microenterprises in Developing Countries." *World Bank Research Observer* 29 (2): 186–201.

Bruins, Marianne, James A. Duffy, Michael P. Keane, and Anthony A. Smith Jr. 2018. "Generalized Indirect Inference for Discrete Choice Models." *Journal of Econometrics* 205 (1): 177–203.

Chelliah, Raja Jesudoss. 1994. "Agenda for Comprehensive Tax Reform." *Indian Economic Journal* 41 (3): 38.

Dabla-Norris, Era, Mark Gradstein, and Gabriela Inchauste. 2008. "What Causes Firms to Hide Output? The Determinants of Informality." *Journal of Development Economics* 85 (1–2): 1–27.

De Giorgi, Giacomo, and Aminur Rahman. 2013. "SME's Registration: Evidence from an RCT in Bangladesh." *Economics Letters* 120 (3): 573–78.

de Mel, Suresh, David McKenzie, and Christopher Woodruff. 2013. "The Demand for, and Consequences of, Formalization among Informal Firms in Sri Lanka." *American Economic Journal: Applied Economics* 5 (2): 122–50.

de Paula, Áureo, and José A. Scheinkman. 2010. "Value-Added Taxes, Chain Effects, and Informality." *American Economic Journal: Macroeconomics* 2 (4): 195–221.

De Soto, Hernando. 1989. *The Other Path: The Invisible Revolution in the Third World*. New York: Harper and Row.

Emran, M. Shahe, and Joseph E. Stiglitz. 2005. "On Selective Indirect Tax Reform in Developing Countries." *Journal of Public Economics* 89 (4): 599–623.

Fajgelbaum, Pablo D., Eduardo Morales, Juan Carlos Suárez Serrato, and Owen Zidar. 2019. "State Taxes and Spatial Misallocation." *Review of Economic Studies* 86 (1): 333–76.

Farrell, Diana. 2004. "The Hidden Dangers of the Informal Economy." *McKinsey Quarterly* 3 (July 1): 27–37.

Fotoniata, Eugenia, and Thomas Moutos. 2013. "Product Quality, Informality, and Child Labor." *Review of Development Economics* 17 (2): 268–83.

Gadenne, Lucie, Tushar K. Nandi, and Roland Rathelot. 2019. "Taxation and Supplier Networks: Evidence from India." CEPR Discussion Paper DP13971 (August), Centre for Economic Policy Research, London.

Gelb, Alan, Taye Mengistae, Vijaya Ramachandran, and Manju Kedia Shah. 2009. "To Formalize or Not to Formalize? Comparisons of Microenterprise Data from Southern and East Africa." Working Paper 175 (July 20), Center for Global Development, Washington, DC.

Gérard, François, and Joana Naritomi. 2018. "Value Added Tax in Developing Countries: Lessons from Recent Research." IGC Growth Brief 15 (May), International Growth Centre, London.

Gérard, François, Joana Naritomi, and Arthur Seibold. 2018. "Tax Systems and Inter-Firm Trade: Evidence from the VAT in Brazil." Technical report, London School of Economics, London.

Gordon, Roger, and Wei Li. 2009. "Tax Structures in Developing Countries: Many Puzzles and a Possible Explanation." *Journal of Public Economics* 93 (7–8): 855–66.

Gourinchas, Pierre-Olivier, and Jonathan A. Parker. 2002. "Consumption Over the Life Cycle." *Econometrica* 70 (1): 47–89.

Henrique de Andrade, Gustavo, Miriam Bruhn, and David McKenzie. 2013. "A Helping Hand or the Long Arm of the Law? Experimental Evidence on What Governments Can Do to Formalize Firms." Policy Research Working Paper 6435, World Bank, Washington, DC.

Hoseini, Mohammad, and Océane Briand. 2020. "Production Efficiency and Self-Enforcement in Value-Added Tax: Evidence from State-Level Reform in India." *Journal of Development Economics* 144 (May): 102462.

Hsieh, Chang-Tai, and Peter J. Klenow. 2009. "Misallocation and Manufacturing TFP in China and India." *Quarterly Journal of Economics* 124 (4): 1403–48.

Hsieh, Chang-Tai, and Peter J. Klenow. 2014. "The Life Cycle of Plants in India and Mexico." *Quarterly Journal of Economics* 129 (3): 1035–84.

Ihrig, Jane, and Karine S. Moe. 2004. "Lurking in the Shadows: The Informal Sector and Government Policy." *Journal of Development Economics* 73 (2): 541–57.

Investment Yogi. 2015. "10 Taxes You Should Know About." *Business Standard*, August 22, 2015. https://www.business-standard.com/article/pf/10-taxes-you-should-know-about -114041100175_1.html.

Kanbur, Ravi. 2017. "Informality: Causes, Consequences, and Policy Responses." *Review of Development Economics* 21 (4): 939–61.

Kanbur, Ravi, and Michael Keen. 2014. "Thresholds, Informality, and Partitions of Compliance." *International Tax and Public Finance* 21 (4): 536–59.

Kaplan, David S., Eduardo Piedra, and Enrique Seira. 2007. "Entry Regulation and Business Start-Ups: Evidence from Mexico." Policy Research Working Paper 4322, World Bank, Washington, DC.

Keen, Michael. 2014. "Targeting, Cascading, and Indirect Tax Design." *Indian Growth and Development Review* 7 (2): 181–201.

Keen, Michael, and Ben Lockwood. 2010. "The Value Added Tax: Its Causes and Consequences." *Journal of Development Economics* 92 (2): 138–51.

KPMG. 2017. "Catalysing MSME Entrepreneurship in India: Capital, Technology, and Public Policy." Whitepaper (June), KPMG, Mumbai. https://assets.kpmg/content/dam/kpmg/in /pdf/2017/07/Catalysing-MSME-Entrepreneurship-India.pdf.

La Porta, Rafael, and Andrei Schleifer. 2014. "Informality and Development." *Journal of Economic Perspectives* 28 (3): 109–26.

Levy, Santiago. 2008. *Good Intentions, Bad Outcomes: Social Policy, Informality, and Economic Growth in Mexico.* Washington, DC: Brookings Institution Press.

Loayza, Norman V., and Jemele Rigolini. 2006. "Informality Trends and Cycles." Policy Research Working Paper 4078, World Bank, Washington, DC.

Luttmer, Erzo G. J. 2007. "Selection, Growth, and the Size Distribution of Firms." *Quarterly Journal of Economics* 122 (3): 1103–44.

Maloney, William F. 2004. "Informality Revisited." *World Development* 32 (7): 1159–78.

Medina, Leandro, and Friedrich Schneider. 2018. "Shadow Economies around the World: What Did We Learn over the Last 20 Years?" IMF Working Paper WP/18/17 (January), International Monetary Fund, Washington, DC.

Medvedev, Denis, and Ana María Oviedo. 2013. "Informality and Profitability: Evidence from a New Firm Survey in Ecuador." Policy Research Working Paper 6431, World Bank, Washington, DC.

Newey, Whitney K., and Daniel Little McFadden. 1994. "Large Sample Estimation and Hypothesis Testing," In *Handbook of Econometrics*, vol. 4, edited by Robert F. Engle and Daniel Little McFadden, 193–281. Handbooks in Economics Series 2. Amsterdam: North-Holland.

NIPFP (National Institute of Public Finance and Policy, India). 1994. "Reform of Domestic Trade Taxes in India: Issues and Options." NIPFP, New Delhi.

Papp, Tamás K., and Elöd Takáts. 2008. "Tax Rate Cuts and Tax Compliance: The Laffer Curve Revisited." IMF Working Paper WP08/7 (January), International Monetary Fund, Washington, DC.

Pomeranz, Dina. 2015. "No Taxation without Information: Deterrence and Self-Enforcement in the Value Added Tax." *American Economic Review* 105 (8): 2539–69.

Prado, Mauricio. 2011. "Government Policy in the Formal and Informal Sectors." *European Economic Review* 55 (8): 1120–36.

Rao, R. Kavita, and Sacchidananda Mukherjee. 2019. *Goods and Services Tax in India*. With the contribution of Amaresh Bagchi. Cambridge, UK: Cambridge University Press.

rediff.com. 2003. "VAT to Be Implemented from June 1." *Business*, April 8, 2003. https://www.rediff.com/money/2003/apr/08vat2.htm.

Ring, Raymond J., Jr. 1999. "Consumers' Share and Producers' Share of the General Sales Tax." *National Tax Journal* 52 (1): 79–90.

Rocha, Rudi, Gabriel Ulyssea, and Laísa Rachter. 2018. "Do Lower Taxes Reduce Informality? Evidence from Brazil." *Journal of Development Economics* 134 (September): 28-49.

Singh, Kanhaiya, and M. R. Saluja. 2018. "Input–Output Table for India 2013–2014: Based on the New Series of National Accounts Statistics and Supply and the Use Table." *Margin: The Journal of Applied Economic Research* 12 (2): 197–223.

Steel, William F., and Donald Snodgrass. 2008. "Raising Productivity and Reducing Risks of Household Enterprises: Diagnostic Methodology Framework." Africa Region Analysis on the Informal Economy (November 4), World Bank, Washington, DC.

Tokman, Victor E. 2007. "Modernizing the Informal Sector." DESA Working Paper 42 (June), Document ST/ESA/2007/DWP/42, Department of Economic and Social Affairs, United Nations, New York.

Ulyssea, Gabriel. 2018. "Firms, Informality, and Development: Theory and Evidence from Brazil." *American Economic Review* 108 (8): 2015–47.

Responses of Firms to Taxation and the Link to Informality: Evidence from India's GST

PIERRE BACHAS, LUCIE GADENNE, DAVI BHERING, AND RADHIKA KAUL

Introduction

The COVID-19 pandemic is reconfirming the need for governments to mobilize tax revenue in an equitable manner in the short and medium terms. Lower-income countries collect less tax revenue as a share of gross domestic product (GDP) than countries of the Organisation for Economic Co-operation and Development (OECD); they rely, to a large extent, on taxes on consumption rather than taxes on income. The issue of low revenue collection and reliance on consumption taxes is particularly acute in South Asia. The government of India collects only 12 percent of GDP in taxes; over 40 percent of this revenue is derived from taxes on consumption, similar to the share among neighboring countries.

This chapter analyzes the revenue efficiency of India's main consumption tax—the goods and services tax (GST)—and the impact of the size of the informal sector on the efficiency of the tax. The key efficiency parameter of government revenue is the elasticity of taxable income (ETI) to the tax rate. The parameter measures the percentage changes in sales that firms report for a 1 percent change in the tax rate. In the context of a tax on consumption, the ETI captures two main margins. First, it captures a drop in demand. As the tax rate on the products sold by a firm increases, consumers might reduce their purchase of those products, which would lead to a drop in the firm's sales.

Second, the ETI captures an increase in tax evasion. As the rate rises, firms might report less of their sales to the tax administration. Both margins of response generate lower reported sales following a tax rate hike and thereby lower revenue collection.

Meanwhile, registered firms selling products also sold by unregistered (informal) firms could display a different elasticity relative to firms competing only with other registered firms. First, competition from the informal sector may imply that the sales of registered firms are more sensitive to tax rates. Second, the price elasticity of lower-quality products (with larger shares of informality) may be larger than the price elasticity of higher-quality products. Third, sectors with a large share of informality may sell products that are more easily concealed to evade taxes. These mechanisms suggest that a product with a higher informal market share raises the tax elasticity of registered firms selling the same product. However, the correlation between tax elasticities and informality shares may conceivably act in the other direction if, for example, registered firms in high informality sectors are selected because they are large and compliant. The sign of the relationship between tax elasticities and informality shares is thus an open empirical question with important implications for tax policy. A large correlation between the informality share and the tax elasticity of registered firms selling a product implies that, to limit tax revenue loss, the tax rate on products often sold in the informal sector should remain low.

To study these issues, the analysis uses the variation at the product level arising in the context of the largest tax reform in India in past decades: the GST. In July 2017, the GST unified the patchwork of consumption taxes in the states of India into a single federal tax, the revenues of which were apportioned to the state and federal governments. Other taxes on interstate transactions were eliminated. The GST was designed to include several product tax brackets, ranging from 0 percent to 28 percent. Over the 18 months after the introduction of the tax, many products were reclassified across tax brackets, typically to a lower bracket.

The data used for the analysis consist of the universe of administrative tax return data from the state of Karnataka. These returns, which are filed on a monthly basis, contain information on the sales and tax liabilities reported by each firm and the products each firm sells. For the analysis, these administrative tax return data are combined with product tax-rate data that have been collected from various data sources. Each rate change on these taxes is confirmed on the basis of announcements reported in the monthly minutes of the GST Council.

The empirical strategy of the study is to estimate the ETI with respect to the tax rate by comparing—before and after a rate change (difference in differences setting)—the trends in reported sales among firms selling products affected by a rate change and the reported sales among firms selling products that are not so affected. Because effective tax rates (ETRs) are self-reported by firms and thus potentially endogenous, the changes in ETR are instrumented with the reform-induced changes in statutory tax rates. The identifying assumption of the analysis is that the changes in statutory tax rates are not decided on the basis of the economic situations of firms and that the sales of firms—the products of which face a rate change—would have trended parallel to the sales of firms whose tax rate is constant, absent the rate change. The plausibility of this assumption is validated by showing parallel trends across treated and untreated firms in the months before the tax cut.

The study finds that, on average, assigning a product to a lower tax bracket reduces its ETR by a bit under 2 percentage points, leading to an increase in reported sales of 4 percent. These impacts translate into a precisely estimated elasticity of sales to the tax rate of −2.6, meaning that, as the ETR declines by 1 percentage point, firms report a 2.6 percent rise in sales. This represents a large elasticity with direct implications for the level of the tax rate that the government should consider. The simple Laffer curve argument states that any tax rate above a top rate is suboptimal because the government could collect more revenue by lowering the tax rate, and the resulting expansion in the base would compensate for the rate reduction. The elasticity estimate of the analysis puts this top rate at 27 percent to 28 percent, close to the top rate in the GST schedule. Understanding to what extent this large elasticity is driven by changes in demand, changes in reporting, or relabeling of products across categories is beyond the scope of the current paper, but it matters for the welfare impact of tax policy.

The study then investigates how elasticities correlate with the informal market share of a sector. To measure informal market shares across sectors, the analysis combines two surveys—the Annual Survey of Industries (ASI), conducted by the Ministry of Statistics and Program Implementation, and the Unorganized Manufacturing Enterprises Survey (UME), conducted by the National Sample Survey Organization as a part of the 62nd round of the National Sample Survey during July 2005–June 2006. The analysis finds that, together, they provide a plausibly representative picture of Indian manufacturing firms.[1] Firms are classified in the ASI as formal if they report that they make value added tax (VAT) payments, while firms in the UME are, by construction, assumed to be informal.

With these data, the analysis correlates the sector-specific elasticities to the formal market shares of each sector. It finds that sectors with high elasticities are more and not less formal. This result invalidates the hypothesis that the sales of formal firms are more elastic in sectors exhibiting more intensive competition from the informal sector; this finding could be because informal and formal firms operate in segmented markets and are not in direct competition. Thus, no efficiency rationale exists for applying lower tax rates to products sold by formal firms in sectors with high informality.

Tax Policy and Informality in South Asia and India

CONTEXT

Low revenue collection is a perennial issue in the South Asia region. India collects only 12 percent of its GDP in taxes, a level analogous to its neighbors—Bangladesh 8.8 percent, Pakistan 11.8 percent, Sri Lanka 11.6 percent—and substantially below the level in countries in other parts of the world with similar incomes. The low revenue collection limits the provision of public goods and social insurance and the potential of redistribution. The narrow tax base of direct taxes (personal income and corporate income taxes) is a key driver of the low tax revenue collection in South Asia. For example, in India, only 3 percent of the population pays the personal income tax; the share is about 1 percent in Bangladesh, Nepal, and Pakistan (Gupta 2015). As a result, indirect taxes account for a large share of revenue collection. On average, in the region, 46 percent of tax revenue is collected through taxes on goods and services.[2] However, exemptions and rate differentiation are common and can erode the tax base and reduce revenue collection. The agriculture sector, self-employment, and small-scale family firms represent a large share of activity in South Asia and are inherently difficult to tax whether through direct or indirect taxes.

Most South Asian countries in recent years have expanded the tax base, simplified and strengthened tax administration, and initiated reforms of indirect taxes, such as the adoption of broader-based VATs. Adopting a single consumption tax rate for all goods and services limits the scope for tax evasion and tax avoidance and is optimal if redistribution can be achieved through income taxes and transfers. However, given the narrow base, the income tax only performs a limited redistributive role in South Asia; consumption taxes are thus often designed with multiple rates, depending on the products. Relative to the standard rate, necessity goods face lower rates, and luxury goods face higher rates. For example, Bangladesh and Sri Lanka have a reduced rate, a zero rate, and a tax-exempt category, in addition to the standard rate of 15 percent. The tax regime with the most rates across products is India's GST.

CONSUMPTION TAX REFORM IN INDIA: THE GOODS AND SERVICES TAX

The GST is the main indirect tax applicable to the consumption of goods and services. It operates like a tax on value added. It was introduced across India on July 1, 2017, and it replaced all indirect taxes (except international customs duties) at central and state levels that had applied previously (that is, the central excise duty, service tax, VAT, luxury tax, other sales taxes). It transformed indirect taxes from source-based taxes into destination-based taxes. All state GSTs collected ordinarily accrues to the state where the consumer of the goods or services sold resides. The GST introduction is seen as one of the most important tax reforms of past decades. It is aimed at eliminating the cascading effect of taxes, especially in interstate trade (taxes levied on a product at every step of the sale), simplifying tax filing and registration thanks to the online GST Network platform, and reducing the burden of regulatory compliance. When GST was introduced, GSTN was a separate website for firms to submit their tax returns; the GST council is a separate entity that is a one-stop shop for all the laws and rules associated with GST, in addition to records of recommendation of GST revisions since 2017.

Despite the objective to simplify and unify tax rates, the GST maintained the multiple-rate design that had previously existed in most states. Multiple rates tend to improve the equity of the tax system. Necessities are taxed at a lower rate, and luxuries at a higher rate. The GST was introduced with rates ranging from 5 percent to 28 percent; specific goods and services (such as fresh produce) were eligible for a 0 percent rate.

Some categories of luxury goods and services, such as vehicles, coal, tobacco, and aerated beverages, also face an excise tax known as the compensation cess.[3] The current modal tax rate is the 18 percent tax bracket, although many items are subject to reduced rates and fall under the 0 percent, 5 percent, or 12 percent tax bracket. The 28 percent tax bracket for luxuries initially covered many products, which were eventually reclassified at lower brackets.

All decisions on the design of the GST—including the assignment of products to tax brackets, tax exemptions, and tax return filing rules—are made by the GST Council. The council is chaired by the union finance minister and is completed by the finance ministers of each state. The council usually meets every month. The council meetings in November 2017, January 2018, July 2018, December 2018, and February 2019 led to multiple changes in product tax rates. The principal motivation was that the initial rates were deemed to be too high. Over the first two years of the GST's existence, many products were reclassified from the 28 percent tax rate to the 18 percent rate and from the 18 percent rate to the 12 percent rate.

INFORMALITY IN INDIA

A large share of India's economy operates in the informal sector. Salapaka (2019) estimates that the informal economy accounts for roughly 50 percent of India's GDP and 80 percent to 90 percent of employment in India. Firms in the informal sector are typically not registered with government authorities and do not remit taxes. Accordingly, the firms observed in the data are thus, by definition, not part of the informal sector. Yet, the existence of a large informal sector has implications for how formal firms respond to tax rates.

Formal firms that operate in sectors characterized by large informality may react to tax rate increases differently than firms operating in mostly formal industries. Competition with informal firms may make formal firms more willing to underreport their tax liabilities (that is, the intensive margin of tax evasion), to keep their costs low and to react to changes in tax rates. Moreover, the type of industries in which it is easier for firms to operate informally—such as industries with only small firms or with low capital requirements—may also be the type of industries in which formal firms find it easier to hide part of their production from tax authorities.[4] This is more true, the higher the tax rate. Accordingly, there are reasons to believe that firms will respond more actively to changes in tax rates in industries characterized by widespread informality. This would have stark implications for policy: the higher the ETI, the higher the efficiency cost of taxation and the lower the optimal level of taxation. From an efficiency perspective, a finding that higher elasticities exist in industries with large informal sectors would suggest that these sectors should be taxed at a lower rate.

However, the correlation between the size of the informal sector and the elasticity across industries might go in the other direction if, for example, firms that operate formally in more informal industries are precisely those that are intrinsically more tax compliant and less likely to evade more frequently (or start evading) if taxes increase. This selection effect is plausible because the decision of firms to register (the extensive margin of tax compliance) may be correlated with other factors that determine the responsiveness to taxes.[5] The sign of this correlation is therefore an empirical question of major policy importance.

Data

This chapter combines three main sources of data. First, data were assembled on product-specific tax rates in the GST over time. Second, data were accessed on administrative tax returns for all GST-registered firms in the state of Karnataka. Third, the ASI is used as a proxy for the size of the informal segments of various activity and product sectors.

TAX RATE CHANGES ON PRODUCTS

An important undertaking of the chapter is the construction of a novel database of tax rates associated with India's GST at the month-product level, beginning at the introduction of the GST in July 2017. Products are classified according to the Harmonized System Nomenclature (HSN), defined at the 2-digit (chapter), 4-digit (heading), 6-digit (subheading), and 8-digit (full HSN code) levels.[6] Furthermore, the product-level descriptions are aggregated up to 15 groups and sectors. Table 4.1 shows an example good, phosphoric acid (fertilizer grade only). Product-specific tax rates can sometimes apply to the precise HSN code, but, most often, the rates concern the heading or subheading levels. In table 4.1, products are considered as subheadings of the HSN classification.

TABLE 4.1 **Examples of Products, Harmonized System Nomenclature**

Level description	Item code	Level	Level digit
Phosphoric acid, fertilizer grade only	28092010	Full HSN code	8
Phosphoric acid; polyphosphoric acids, whether or not chemically defined	280920	Subheading	6
Diphosphorus pentaoxide; phosphoric acid; polyphosphoric acids, whether or not chemically defined	2809	Heading	4
Inorganic chemicals, organic or inorganic compounds of precious metals, rare-earth metals, radioactive elements, or isotopes	28	Chapter	2
Product of the chemical industry or allied industry	5	Group	NA

Note: The "group" variable is a variable by construction. The authors constructed the group code numbered "5" based on HSN chapter codes. HSN = Harmonized System Nomenclature.

The analysis involves the amalgamation of several datasets to obtain a panel of statutory tax rates associated with products at the month-subheading level. The key hand coded input is the information pertaining to data on product-level rate changes in the GST Council press releases on the 23rd, 25th, 28th, 31st, 33rd, 36th, 37th, 38th, and 39th meetings of the council. The press releases contain the names of all products that faced rate changes, the new tax rates, and, sometimes, the old tax rates. In addition, the analysis relies on the records kept on the ClearTax website, which allows the name of a product to be entered and the current associated tax rate to be observed.[7] This exercise serves as a check to corroborate the data across a government source and a government service provider (GST Suvidha Provider).[8] The analysis also relies on the ClearTax GST rate finder to assign an HSN code to all products that underwent a rate change but was not associated with a code in the press release document.[9]

Data that allow tax rates to be observed by product in the July 2017 cross section and in the July 2020 cross section were obtained from the Central Board of Indirect Taxes and Customs.[10] Combining this data frame with the data on changes in tax rates produces a dataset that contains tax rates on all products (at the subheading level) in July 2017 and July 2020 that underwent a rate change, including the month of the change. These data still face limitations and can be improved, although some measurement issues are inherent in the setting. In particular, some products with rate changes described in the GST Council meetings do not correspond to a precise product in the HSN; some other products do not span a given product category neatly but correspond partially to each of several subheadings.

Figure 4.1 shows the distribution of tax rates at the subheading level (5,390 unique subheadings) in July 2017 and March 2019. Over this period, a shift in rates may be observed from the 28 percent tax bracket to the 18 percent and the 12 percent tax brackets. Figure 4.2, panel a, shows the distribution of rate changes. Overall, around 800 subheadings faced a rate change over the 21 months. The average change was a 9 percent drop in tax rates. The main spike corresponded to changes in tax rates of −10 percent, and smaller spikes corresponded to changes in tax rate of −6 percent. Figure 4.2, panel b, shows the cumulative changes in tax rates at the subheading level. A few rate changes occurred in September and October 2017, followed by a large number of changes in November 2017. Fewer changes occurred in subsequent months, and then another round of rate changes occurred in August 2018.

ADMINISTRATIVE TAX RETURNS AT THE FIRM LEVEL

The analysis used administrative tax return data from the state of Karnataka that cover all GST-registered firms in the state.[11] The data cover monthly tax returns filed by firms over 21 monthly periods between July 2017 and March 2019. They include details on firm registrations, goods and services supplied by the firms, tax returns, interstate supplies and supplies received by the firms, investment tax credit eligibility, and tax payment methods. These data are mainly taken from two tax forms: the GSTR-3B,

FIGURE 4.1 **Distribution of Statutory Tax Rates, July 2017 and July 2020**

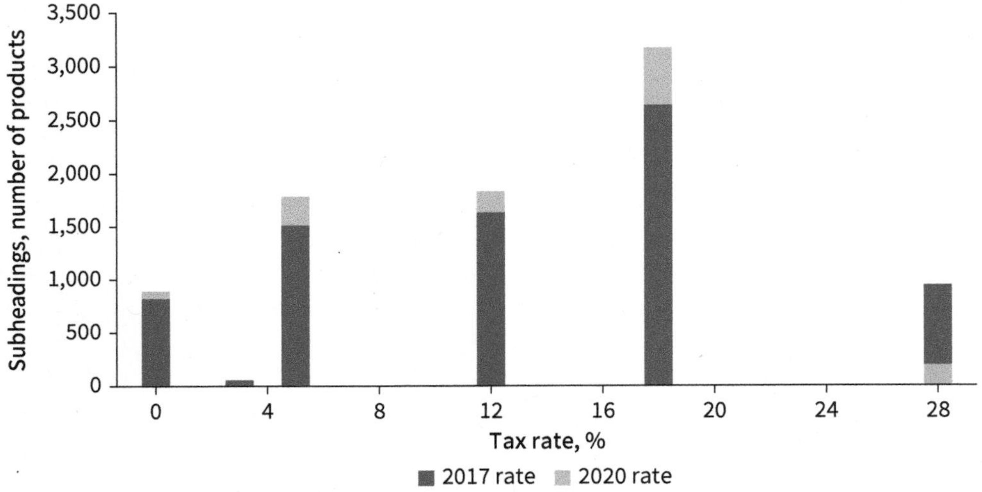

Source: GST council and Central Board of Indirect Taxes and Customs.
Note: The figure shows the distribution of tax rates for the 5,390 product subheadings of the HSN in July 2017 and July 2020. The tax rates span five major tax rate slabs: 0 percent, 5 percent, 12 percent, 18 percent, and 28 percent. GST = goods and services tax. HSN = Harmonized System Nomenclature.

a monthly self-declared summary of GST liabilities that is filed by registered GST dealers, along with other tax return forms, and the GST-REG-01, a form that the typical firm must file to register for the GST.

To make the analysis possible, important sample restrictions were adopted. Only single-product firms that reported sales in all 21 months on which the data are available were included. This gives a sample of 45,000 firms. The focus was on single-product firms for two reasons. First, the opportunities for tax avoidance are more limited among such firms than among multiproduct firms, which can relabel or misclassify their various products to receive the lower tax rate. Second, the data do not reveal the share of reported sales by product but only by total firm sales. Accordingly, the precise sales of a given product cannot be assigned, which becomes an issue among firms selling two or more products. To abstract from the extensive margin of firm entry and exit, the analysis was also working with a balanced sample of firms that reported positive sales in all 21 months of the data.

Single-product firms represent 31 percent of all GST-registered firms and 20 percent of total sales in Karnataka.[12] Table 4.2 presents summary statistics on the single-product firms in the sample for the January 2018 cross section. The outcomes of interest are the taxable value of supplies shipped by the firms (taxable sales) and the tax liability. The ratio of the tax liability over the taxable sales provides the ETR paid by each firm. The table shows that the mean (median) ETR of the GST in January 2018 was 13 percent (14 percent), with substantial variation across firms: the 25th percentile of the ETR was 5 percent, and the 75th percentile was 18 percent.

FIGURE 4.2 Rate Changes at the Subheading Level, July 2017 to March 2019

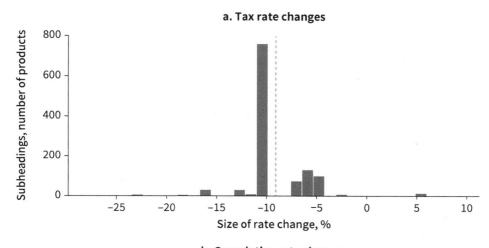

a. Tax rate changes

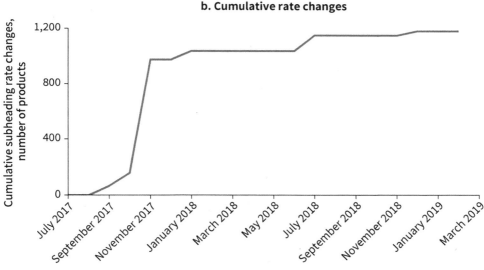

b. Cumulative rate changes

Source: GST council and Central Board of Indirect Taxes and Customs.
Note: Panel a shows that, of the 5,390 product subheadings, 1,181 faced a rate change, and a majority of the rate changes corresponded to tax cuts of 10 percent and a mean rate change across all periods of around 9 percent (the broken blue line). Panel b shows that many of these tax cuts occurred in November 2017. GST = goods and services tax.

Table 4.3 shows the number of firms and the ranked contribution to total sales by sector of activity whereby the economy has been divided into 15 large sectors. The single largest sector is base metals, which accounts for 41 percent of all sales. The second largest sector is electrical parts and electronics, which covers 11 percent of sales, followed by mineral products at 10 percent.

TABLE 4.2 Summary Statistics on All Single-Product Firms, Karnataka, January 2018

Indicator	Mean	Standard deviation	Percentile 25th	Percentile 50th	Percentile 75th
Taxable value of all sales and services provided, Rs, millions	6.11	461.23	0.21	0.60	1.82
Tax payable on all sales and services provided, Rs, millions	0.41	6.54	0.02	0.06	0.18
Effective tax rate	0.14	0.86	0.05	0.14	0.18
Log of taxable value	13.38	1.68	12.27	13.31	14.42
Log of tax payable	10.48	2.97	9.68	10.93	12.08

Source: Based on GST Tax returns data, Development Data Lab.
Note: The sample consists of all 44,529 GST-registered firms in Karnataka that sell a single product and that report positive sales in all 21 months of the data (balanced panel). GST = goods and services tax.

TABLE 4.3 Share of Total Sales, by Sector, Karnataka, January 2018

Product group	Firms, number	Share of total sales, %
Base metal products	3,578	41.06
Electrical parts	3,743	10.95
Mineral products	3,716	9.86
Animal and vegetable products	3,516	6.17
Industrial machinery	3,861	4.32
Inorganic and organic compounds	4,745	4.06
Textile or shoe articles	3,811	3.79
Glass articles	2,960	3.34
Leather and wood articles	3,259	3.18
Transportation vehicles	1,341	3.02
Beverages and tobacco	2,442	2.76
Prepared foodstuff	1,560	2.03
Plastics and rubber articles	2,165	1.95
Essential oils, cosmetics, toilet preparations	1,395	1.77
Other goods	2,437	1.74
Total goods	44,529	100.00

Source: Based on GST Tax returns data provided by Development Data Lab.
Note: The sample consists of all 44,529 GST-registered firms in Karnataka that sell a single product and that report positive sales in all 21 months of the data (balanced panel). Firms are aggregated based on the International Standard Industrial Classification of All Economic Activities. The share of total sales is based on January 2018 tax returns. GST = goods and services tax.

Data description

Data from two firm surveys—the ASI and the UME—were combined to compute the share of informality in each sector in India. The ASI covers all factories employing 10 or more workers using power and all factories employing 20 or more workers without using power.[13] It also covers all industrial establishments with more than 100 employees, as well as a random sample of establishments with fewer than 100 employees. The primary unit of enumeration is an establishment. The analysis relies on the 2014–15 round (collected between April 1, 2014, and March 31, 2015). The dataset consists of 61,339 firms.

The UME sampling frame consists of unincorporated nonagricultural enterprises with fewer than 10 employees.[14] The analysis uses the 73rd round (collected between July 2015 and June 2016). The dataset consists of 141,744 enterprises.

The study follows the existing literature and combines these two datasets using survey weights (for example, see Hsieh and Klenow 2014). This approach enables the construction of statistics that are representative of all manufacturing establishments in India. The ASI is not designed to survey establishments in the service sector. In practice, the only service firms that emerge in the ASI survey are construction firms. Services are therefore excluded from the study.

A proxy for informality

The study uses the above two datasets to construct a proxy for the share of firms paying the VAT in a sector and correlate this with the ETI at the sector level. By the construction of the survey, firms in the UME are unlikely to be paying the VAT. By definition, they are small and operate in the unorganized sector. The National Sample Surveys, of which the UME is a part, collect information on the sum of all taxes and fees paid by firms, but only 4 percent of firms report that they pay any taxes. This is likely an upper bound on the share of firms paying the VAT, because this variable also includes local taxes and fees. The study therefore assumes that all firms in the UME are informal.

In the ASI survey, firms are asked about the amount of the VAT that they pay on sales. The analysis classifies firms as formal if this amount is positive and as informal otherwise. Self-reported tax payment information in surveys should be treated with caution, because firms may be reluctant to report confidential information truthfully to the survey enumerators, and the firm employee responding to the survey may not be well informed on the firm's tax status. It is nonetheless reassuring that, among firms in the ASI, there is a positive correlation between a firm's size (measured by the number of employees) and the likelihood that the firm reports that it pays any VAT (figure 4.3, panel a).

FIGURE 4.3 **Survey Data on Firms: Share of Formality, by Sector**

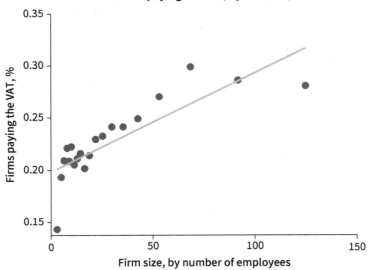

a. Firms paying the VAT, by firm size, %

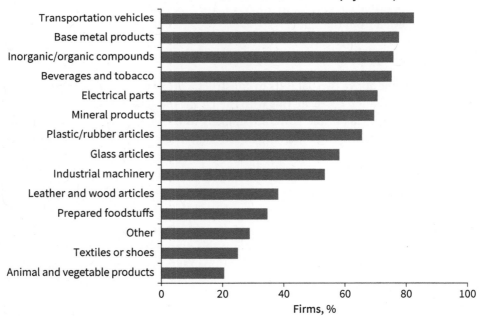

b. Formal market share, by sector, %

Source: Based on ASI and NSS-UME data.
Note: Panel a plots the average share of firms reporting that they pay the VAT in the ASI data as a function of firm size. The sample is divided into 20 bins of equal size. Each dot corresponds to 5 percent of the total observations. Survey sampling weights are used. The top 10 percent of firms are excluded from the panel. Panel b plots the formal market share in each sector among firms in the combined ASI and UME data. The definition of formality applied classifies a firm as formal if the firm reports in the ASI that it had paid the VAT; all other firms, including all firms in the UME, are classified as informal. Each observation is weighted using the firm's total sales and survey sampling weight. ASI = Annual Survey of Industries; NSS = National Sample Survey; UME = Unorganized Manufacturing Enterprises Survey; VAT = value added tax.

Average firm size in a sector is a proxy for informality and for evasion opportunities that is often used in the literature (Kumler, Verhoogen, and Frías 2020). There are good theoretical reasons for using this proxy. Thus, Kleven, Kreiner, and Saez (2016) argue that taxes become more difficult to enforce as the number of employees in a firm grows because the probability that any employee acts as a whistle-blower increases. In addition, ample evidence suggests that tax administrations devote more resources to monitoring larger firms and that larger firms are more likely to use accounting records and electronic forms of payment, generating the kind of information trails that help tax officials assess tax liabilities (Bachas, Fattal Jaef, and Jensen 2019; Basri et al. 2019).

It is assumed that all firms in the UME are informal, while firms in the ASI are formal only if they report that they paid the VAT. The two datasets are combined using the sampling weights of firms to obtain a representative sample of firms in India. Firms are also weighted using total sales to obtain the formal market share by sectors of activity. Figure 4.3, panel b plots the resulting formal market share by sector. Capital-intensive sectors (transport, metals) exhibit the highest formality share, while textiles and agricultural industries (notoriously more difficult to tax) show the lowest formality share.

Elasticity of Sales to the Tax Rate

EMPIRICAL STRATEGY

The objective of the analysis is to measure the ETI to the tax rate. The ETI is the percentage change in taxable income after a 1 percent increase in the tax rate. In the context here, the taxable income corresponds to the sales reported by GST-registered firms. Two types of tax rates may be observed in the data: the statutory tax rate that is based on the tax code and that should apply to a product sold by a firm, τ^{Stat}, and the ETR self-reported by the firm in the firm's tax return, τ^{Eff}. If these two rates were exactly the same and if effective rates only changed together with changes in statutory tax rates, a simple panel regression could be implemented to measure the ETI, as follows:

$$ln(y)_{ipt} = \alpha_i + \gamma_t + \beta.ln(1 + \tau_{pt}) + \in_{ipt}, \qquad (4.1)$$

where $ln(y)_{ipt}$ is the log of sales of firm i selling product p in month t; $ln(1 + \tau_{pt})$ is the log of 1, plus the tax rate; and α_i and γ_t are, respectively, firm and time-fixed effects.

Although statutory tax rates and ETRs are positively correlated, they differ in practice for several reasons. First, ETRs are filed directly by the firms and can thus be manipulated. Second, the law might not systematically be known or enforced, and reported ETRs might not react to statutory rate changes. Third, the statutory rates collected for the analysis may be subject to measurement error, given the difficulty in assigning product descriptions to specific product codes.

Thus, if the ETI is measured using the observed ETRs, the panel regression estimate will likely be biased because the changes in ETRs are partly driven by the choices of firms. To address this issue, an instrumental variable strategy was run in the analysis whereby the reform-induced changes in ETRs were used to measure the elasticity of the reported sales of firms. The identification assumption is now that (1) the changes in statutory tax rates are not decided on the basis of the economic situations of firms and that (2) the sales of firms the products of which face a rate change would have trended parallel to the sales of firms on which the tax rate is constant, absent the rate change. This is the standard parallel trends assumption for which support may be provided by looking at pretrends.

The first stage regresses the log of the ETR on the log of the statutory tax rate, which only changes after a reform. A similar, alternative instrument is a dummy taking the value of 1 in the months after the rate change among firms selling a treated product.

$$ln(1+\tau^{Eff})_{ipt} = \alpha_i + \gamma_t + \beta.ln(1+\tau^{Stat}_{pt}) + \in_{ipt}. \tag{4.2}$$

The second stage then regresses the predicted change in the ETR on sales, as follows:

$$ln(y)_{ipt} = \alpha_i + \gamma_t + \phi ln(1+\tau^{Eff})^{pred}_{ipt} + \in_{ipt}. \tag{4.3}$$

The reduced form regression is a regression of the log sales on the log of the statutory tax rate. It is equivalent to a generalized difference in differences or generalized event study with a pure control group that compares changes in sales before a tax rate cut versus after the cut among firms that faced a cut versus firms that did not face a change in the tax rate. Formally, this gives the following:

$$ln(y)_{ipt} = \alpha_i + \gamma_t + \sum_{k=\alpha}^{b} \psi ln(1+\tau^{Stat}_{pt}) + \in_{ipt}. \tag{4.4}$$

To show the dynamic effects, the analysis also ran a period by period event study of the changes in sales relative to the month after the reform, as follows:

$$ln(y)_{ipt} = \alpha_i + \gamma_t + \sum_{k=\alpha}^{b} \psi^k D^k_{pt} + \in_{ipt}, \tag{4.5}$$

where $ln(y)_{ipt}$ are log sales of firm i selling product p at time t; α_i and γ_t are, respectively, firm and month fixed effects; D^k_{pt} is a dummy indicating that product p faced a rate change exactly k periods ago at time t; and $a < 0 < b$ are periods relative to the tax rate cut for product p. The analysis included measurement of the effects relative to a period previous to the tax rate change and omitted $k = -3$ as the base period. Firms selling products that never face a rate change thus show a value for the dummy D_{pt} equal to zero for all k.

The identifying assumption in interpreting ψ^k as the causal impact of the tax rate cut on reported sales is the classic parallel trends assumption invoked in difference in differences. It implies that, in the absence of a tax rate cut, the sales of firms that faced a rate cut and of firms that did not face a rate cut would have trended similarly. While this is not testable, an analysis may compare the behavior of firms in the periods before a tax change by looking at the coefficients on $k < 0$. This specification also allows an observation of dynamic trends in the impact of tax cuts on sales over time by comparing the effects at impact ($k = 0$) with the effects several months after the reform.

The equivalent dynamic effects regressions may also be run from equation 4.5 by instrumenting the change in the ETR with the reform dummy. The interpretation of the coefficient of this regression then becomes the interpretation of an elasticity of taxable sales: after a 1 percent drop in the ETR because of a reform-induced cut in the statutory tax rate, by how much do firms increase their reported sales?

To interpret the coefficients as the structural elasticity of income, this empirical design also implicitly assumes limited (or diffuse) substitution among goods that face a rate change and goods that do not face a rate change. This is likely to be erroneous if one compares products within narrow groups. To account for this issue in estimating sector-level elasticities, the analysis keeps all untreated firms in the control group, not only the firms in the sector in which the elasticity is being measured.

RESULTS

Figure 4.4 displays the main results of the analysis. Figure 4.4, panel a, shows the first stage of the regression: the impact of a tax cut on the ETR reported by treated versus control firms relative to the period of the tax cut. The dashed vertical line in each panel corresponds to the month of the announcement of the reform, and the solid vertical line in each panel represents the application of the reform one month later. The month of application of the rate change is normalized to zero to count all other months relative to the reform month.

A slight anticipation effect may be observed in the lines. This is likely because firms (erroneously) applied the lower statutory tax rate at the time of the announcement of the tax cut, one month prior to its application. Upon application of the reform, the average reported ETR dropped by 1.7 percentage points and continued to drop slightly in subsequent months, thereby approaching a 2 percentage point drop. The pretrends in ETRs were small. They suggest that the drop in ETRs was slightly overestimated, which implies that elasticities were underestimated in absolute value.

Figure 4.4, panel b shows the main result, which is estimated from equation 4.5, that is, following a tax cut, sales increased by an average of 4 percent. There are no pretrends. In the periods before the rate change, the period dummies are close to zero. Firms selling products that faced a tax cut thus reported substantially more sales postreform than firms that did not face a rate change. Combining both panels allows an approximation of the ETI. The tax cuts led to a decline in the ETR by slightly less than 2 percent, which was associated with a 4 percent rise in sales. Dividing the reduced form by the first stage produces an elasticity slightly above 2.

The analysis formally ran the regression of log sales on the ETR (table 4.4). The coefficient is the elasticity of sales with respect to a firm's tax rate. Column (1) shows the results from the panel ordinary least squares (OLS) regression. It reveals a large elasticity of −6.1: as the reported ETR drops by 1 percent, reported sales increase by 6.1 percent.

FIGURE 4.4 Impact of Tax Rate Cuts on Effective Tax Rates and Sales

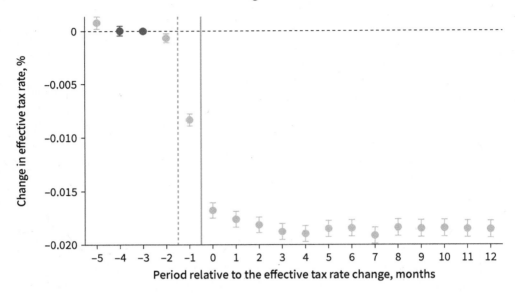

a. Change in effective tax rates

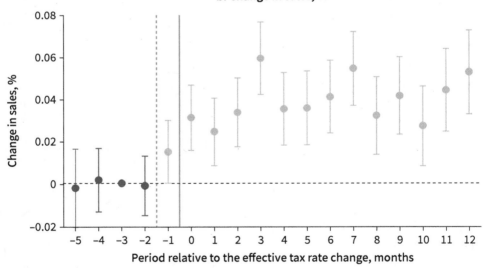

b. Change in sales, %

Source: Based on GST Tax returns data provided by Development Data Lab.
Note: The figure shows the impact of tax cuts at the product level on effective tax rates (panel a) and sales (panel b). The dashed vertical line corresponds to the month of the announcement of the tax rate cut, and the solid vertical line in each panel represents the month of the application of the rate change. The latter is normalized to zero to count all other months relative to the month of the tax cut. Each dot measures the difference between treated and control firms in a given month relative to three months before the firms faced a rate change. The difference is normalized to zero. The coefficients are obtained by running equation 4.5. The bars attached to the dots correspond to the 95 percent confidence interval. The sample consists of all GST-registered firms in Karnataka that sell a single good and that report positive sales in all 21 months of the data (balanced panel). GST = goods and services tax.

TABLE 4.4 **Elasticity of Taxable Sales**

Outcome: log sales	(1) OLS	(2) Reduced form	(3) Instrumental variable = statutory tax rate	(4) Reduced form	(5) Instrumental variable = postreform
Effective tax rate	−6.138		−2.589		−2.471
Robust standard error	(0.083)		(0.201)		(0.200)
Statutory tax rate		−0.507			
Robust standard error		(0.040)			
Postreform				0.042	
Robust standard error				(0.003)	
First stage			0.196		−0.017
Robust standard error			(0.002)		(0.000)
Observations, number	935,109	935,109	935,109	935,109	935,109
Firms, number	44,529	44,529	44,529	44,529	44,529

Source: Based on GST data provided by Development Data Lab and statutory tax rates based on the GST council minutes.
Note: The table shows the results of the regressions on firm sales (in log) on the effective tax rates of firms (in log). All regressions include firm and month fixed effects. The sample consists of all GST-registered firms in Karnataka that sell a single product and that report positive sales in all 21 months of the data (balanced panel). The instrumental variable used is either the statutory tax rate of the product sold by the firm (column 3) or a dummy that takes the value of 1 postreform among firms the products of which faced a rate change (column 5). GST = goods and services tax; OLS = ordinary least squares.

The panel OLS elasticity cannot be interpreted causally because the reported ETRs can be chosen endogenously by firms.

The ETR is thus instrumented either by the statutory tax rate of the product sold by the firm (column 3) or by a dummy indicator taking the value of 1 if the product sold by the firm faced a rate change (column 5). The first stage shows that the statutory tax rate and ETRs are positively correlated, with a coefficient of 0.196 (column 3), and that, after the tax cut, the ETRs dropped by an average of 1.7 percent (column 5). Using the statutory tax rate instrument, the analysis estimates an elasticity of −2.59, with narrow confidence bands; the 95 percent confidence interval is (−2.98, −2.20). Thus, for a 1 percent drop in the tax rate, firms respond by reporting 2.6 percent higher sales. This is a substantial elasticity, which may be driven by different types of behavior, including higher demand and production or lower tax evasion, which are not separated out here. The elasticity estimated with the dummy postreform instrument gives a similar elasticity of −2.47.

INFORMALITY AND TAX ELASTICITY AT THE SECTOR LEVEL

The analysis estimated a large elasticity of −2.6 ETI across all firms. The estimation is now repeated at the sector level to obtain sector-specific sales elasticities. The instrumental variable estimation of the ETI—equations 4.2 and 4.3—is run for the main sectors listed in figure 4.3, panel b. This empirical exercise requires that, within each

TABLE 4.5 **The Elasticity of Taxable Sales, by Sector of Activity**

Sector of activity	(1) Instrumental variable	(2) First stage
Beverages and tobacco	−1.015	0.190
	(0.591)	(0.007)
Mineral products	−2.707	0.197
	(0.483)	(0.005)
Drugs and pharmaceuticals	−2.040	0.452
	(0.249)	(0.004)
Cosmetics	−2.869	0.153
	(0.904)	(0.006)
Plastics	−0.681	0.163
	(0.923)	(0.007)
Leather and wood	−2.660	0.236
	(0.722)	(0.007)
Stone and cement	−1.371	0.300
	(0.462)	(0.007)
Metal products	−7.946	0.161
	(1.107)	(0.006)
Industrial machinery	−8.356	0.142
	(1.102)	(0.005)
Electronics	−5.374	0.157
	(0.697)	(0.004)
Vehicles	−8.572	0.032
	(3.774)	(0.004)
Other	−1.152	0.241
	(0.587)	(0.006)

Source: Based on GST data provided by Development Data Lab and statutory tax rates based on the GST council minutes.
Note: The table shows sector-specific sales elasticities to the tax rate. The control group is composed of all firms in any sector that never face a rate change. The treated firms belong to the specific sector of interest. GST = goods and services tax.

economic sector, a share of the products face a rate change. Given this constraint, the analysis is left with 12 economic sectors (out of 15) that have a sufficient number of firms facing a rate change. In the regressions, the analysis retains all firms that never face a rate change in the control group, as well as the untreated firms within the same sectors of activity as the treated firms. This is done to mitigate the issue that the control group may be adversely affected because the products it sells may be readily substituted by the products sold by the treated firms.

The results are reported in table 4.5 for the 12 large sectors in which at least a share of the products faces a tax change. Important variations in the ETI may be observed that range from around −1 in some sectors (for example, beverages and tobacco or plastics) to −8 in other sectors (such as metal products, machinery, and vehicles).

The analysis then tests the correlation between sector elasticities and the informal market share of a sector. One hypothesis is that formal firms operating in industries with substantial competition from informal firms might be more reactive to changes in tax rates, compared with firms operating in a sector in which firms are mostly registered. One might then expect a positive correlation between estimated elasticities that are negative and the formal market share at the sector level.

To test this hypothesis, the analysis correlated the sector-specific elasticities to the formality shares in each sector (figure 4.5). The exercise reveals a negative relationship. For example, the leather and wood sector, which is highly informal, exhibits moderate elasticity, comparable with the elasticity of the drugs and pharmaceutical product sector, which is much more formal. At the other end of the spectrum, metal products and vehicles, the two most formal sectors, have some of the largest elasticities.

This result invalidates the hypothesis that the sales of formal firms are more elastic in sectors with more competition from the informal sector. This may be because informal and formal firms operate in segmented markets and are not in direct competition. What might then explain the negative correlation between formal market shares and the ETI? A possibility is that the formal firms in the highly informal sectors are largely selected. Thus, these are precisely the firms in which the directors have decided to register and which are more compliant at baseline or more differentiated in terms of product quality.

FIGURE 4.5 **Correlation between Informality and Elasticities, by Sector**

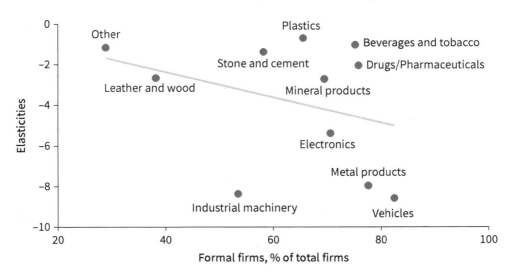

Source: Based on GST data provided by Development Data Lab and statutory tax rates based on the GST council minutes.
Note: The x-axis represents the formal market share in a sector based on the definition of formality used in the analysis. Of the 15 sectors, only 11 are ranked. For the other 4, either variation in tax reform is lacking at the sector level, or the current first stage is too noisy to be informative (F-statistic less than 10). These sectors are not currently included. GST = goods and services tax.

Another possibility, linked to the nature of the sectors, is that precisely the more formal sectors are those in which the elasticity of demand is large and which show an increase in demand following tax cuts. An important caveat is that the proxy for informality used by the analysis at the sector level is imperfect.

Implications for Tax Policy in the Region

Following a series of tax cuts to a range of products in the GST, firms in Karnataka responded by increasing their reported sales. The analysis estimated a large elasticity of taxable sales with respect to the tax rate of around −2.5. This elasticity implies that, if tax rates rise by 1 percent, reported sales will shrink by 2.5 percent. However, the analysis found no support for the widely held hypothesis that firms active in more informal sectors are also more elastic.

These results have policy implications that are relevant for India and the region. The large elasticity revealed by the analysis has direct implications for the level of the tax rate that the government of India should consider. A large elasticity implies that, as the tax rate increases, the tax base shrinks quickly. The simple Laffer curve argument states that any tax rate above the Laffer rate is suboptimal because the government could collect more revenue by lowering the tax rate, and the resulting increase in the tax base would compensate for the rate reduction. The top of the Laffer curve rate is $\tau^{Laffer} = \dfrac{1}{1+\in}$, where e is the ETI. Using the elasticity estimate, the analysis finds that the top of the Laffer curve is around 27 percent to 28 percent. This finding is close to the top rate chosen under the GST schedule in India. The fact that it applied to fewer and fewer products over time potentially reflects the concerns. We note, however, that this assumes that all the results are not due to relabeling of goods across sectors, in which case the optimal rate would need to consider the rates of neighboring products and the spillover effects that rate changes have on other tax bases.

The high efficiency cost uncovered by the analysis puts a limit on the maximum rate governments should use. Beyond the top rate, India's GST system is characterized by tax rates differentiated across products. What do the results attest about such a tax design? If registered firms operating in sectors with high shares of informality had larger elasticities, this would provide an efficiency rationale to apply lower rates to the products sold by these firms. However, firms in sectors with high informality have elasticities that are smaller in absolute value. One possible conclusion is that formal and informal firms operate in fairly segmented markets and are not in direct competition. Thus, the existence of a large informal sector does not impose additional restrictions on how governments should tax formal firms, which removes the rationale of using differentiated tax rates for efficiency purposes. Of course, the desirability of differentiation among tax rates across goods depends also on the equity gains—if necessities are taxed at a low rate, and luxuries are taxed at a high rate—and on the avoidance possibilities that differentiation creates. (The additional welfare considerations of multiple tax rates are outside the scope of the study, which is focused on efficiency.)

To what extent could the results apply to the rest of India and to other countries in the region? The elasticity is estimated using a wide range of products and thus has wider validity than if it were focused on a rate change for a single product. Diverse products face a rate change. For instance, some of the products that were important in terms of total sales and numbers of firms and that faced rate changes are cement, bottled water, prepared foods, and paints. Although there is some variation, the elasticity is substantial in most sectors.

The large elasticity may reflect (1) the high sensitivity of demand to formal prices or (2) substantial evasion and avoidance of tax rates. One may speculate about how the characteristics of the state of Karnataka—richer than the average Indian state, with a manufacturing and information technology hub and a well-functioning administration—might impact the two mechanisms leading to a large elasticity. Regarding the first channel, there is no reason to believe that demand would not be as elastic in other Indian states for the same products. However, the Karnataka industrial mix is heavy in the most elastic sectors (such as electronics; see figure 4.5), which may contribute to the large aggregate elasticity. By contrast, richer households are considered to be less price sensitive; households and firms in poorer states might then exhibit even larger demand increases following tax cuts.

Regarding the second channel, Karnataka is considered to have a well-functioning administration and so may offer fewer evasion possibilities than other states in India or other countries in the region. However, relative to equivalent taxes in other countries, the design of India's GST is more complex, and the analysis estimates the elasticity during the period immediately after the introduction of the GST, at a time when taxpayers and administrations might still have been adjusting to the new tax system.

Notes

This chapter is part of a review on informality prepared by the Office of the Chief Economist, South Asia Region, World Bank. The authors thank Maurizio Bussolo, Ravi Kanbur, Martin Kanz, and Siddharth Sharma for their feedback and Sam Asher and the Development Data Lab for their partnership.

1. See ASI (Annual Survey of Industries) (dashboard), Industrial Statistics Wing, National Statistical Office, Ministry of Statistics and Program Implementation, Kolkata, http://www.csoisw.gov.in/CMS/En/1023-annual-survey-of-industries.aspx; "India: Unorganised Manufacturing Enterprises Survey [List Frame], July 2005–June 2006, NSS 62nd Round" (data portal), National Data Archive, National Sample Survey Office, Ministry of Statistics and Programme Implementation, New Delhi, http://microdata.gov.in/nada43/index.php/catalog/112/overview.

2. 2017 data of GFS (Government Finance Statistics) (dashboard), International Monetary Fund, Washington, DC, http://data.imf.org/?sk=a0867067-d23c-4ebc-ad23-d3b015045405.

3. In India, a cess is a tax especially on a commodity or for a special purpose, such as a tea cess, a road cess, or an education cess.

4. See Gordon and Li (2009) for a discussion of industry characteristics and formality.

5. The fear of paying taxes and of interacting with tax officials is cited as a barrier to firm formalization. See Bruhn and McKenzie (2013) for a review of the determinants of formalization. The firms observed in the analysis are thus a selected sample of firms that have chosen or been obliged to register.

6. Harmonized System Database, World Customs Organization, Brussels, http://www.wcoomd .org/en/topics/nomenclature/instrument-and-tools/tools-to-assist-with-the-classification -in-the-hs/hs-online.aspx.

7. ClearTax (dashboard), Clear, Defmacro Software Private Ltd., Bangalore, India, https:// cleartax.in/.

8. "GST Suvidha Provider (GSP): An Overview," Clear, Defmacro Software Private Ltd., Bangalore, India, https://cleartax.in/s/gsp-gst-suvidha-provider.

9. ClearGST (dashboard), Clear, Defmacro Software Private Ltd., Bangalore, India, https:// cleartax.in/gst.

10. CBIC (Central Board of Indirect Taxes and Customs) (website), Department of Revenue, Ministry of Finance, New Delhi, https://www.cbic.gov.in/.

11. The data have been shared by partners at the Development Data Lab. See DDL (Development Data Lab) (dashboard), DDL, Washington, DC, https://www.devdatalab.org/.

12. Given the economic importance of multiproduct firms, future work plans to incorporate them.

13. Formally, it includes (1) manufacturing units, excluding those registered under the Factories Act, 1948, Sections 2m(i) and 2m(ii) and manufacturing enterprises registered under the Factories Act, 1948, Section 85; (2) enterprises engaged in cotton ginning, cleaning, and baling that are not covered by the ASI; and (3) units engaged in trading, noncaptive electricity generation and transmission, and other service activities.

14. This corresponds to firms registered under the Factories Act, 1948, Sections 2m(i) and 2m(ii). The Factories Act was superseded by the Occupational Safety, Health, and Working Conditions Code, 2020.

References

Bachas, Pierre, Roberto N. Fattal Jaef, and Anders Jensen. 2019. "Size-Dependent Tax Enforcement and Compliance: Global Evidence and Aggregate Implications." *Journal of Development Economics* 140 (September): 203–22.

Basri, Muhamad Chatib, Mayara Felix, Rema Hanna, and Benjamin A. Olken. 2019. "Tax Administration vs. Tax Rates: Evidence from Corporate Taxation in Indonesia." NBER Working Paper 26150 (August), National Bureau of Economic Research, Cambridge, MA.

Bruhn, Miriam, and David J. McKenzie. 2013. "Entry Regulation and Formalization of Microenterprises in Developing Countries." Policy Research Working Paper 6507, World Bank, Washington, DC.

Gordon, Roger H., and Wei Li. 2009. "Tax Structures in Developing Countries: Many Puzzles and a Possible Explanation." *Journal of Public Economics* 93 (7–8): 855–66.

Gupta, Poonam. 2015. "Generating Larger Tax Revenue in South Asia." MPRA Paper 61443, University Library of Munich, Munich.

Hsieh, Chang-Tai, and Peter J. Klenow. 2014. "The Life Cycle of Plants in India and Mexico." *Quarterly Journal of Economics* 129 (3): 1035–84.

Kleven, Henrik Jacobsen, Claus Thustrup Kreiner, and Emmanuel Saez. 2016. "Why Can Modern Governments Tax So Much? An Agency Model of Firms as Fiscal Intermediaries." *Economica* 83 (330): 219–46.

Kumler, Todd, Eric Verhoogen, and Judith Frías. 2020. "Enlisting Employees in Improving Payroll Tax Compliance: Evidence from Mexico." *Review of Economics and Statistics* 102 (5): 881–96.

Salapaka, Venkata Ramana Murthy. 2019. "Measuring Informal Economy in India." Paper presented at the International Monetary Fund's Seventh Statistical Forum, "Measuring the Informal Economy," Washington, DC, November 14–15, 2019.

CHAPTER 5

Small Businesses and Online Sales in India

MARTIN KANZ AND ROMINA QUAGLIOTTI

Introduction

Over the past decade, e-commerce has grown exponentially in India and many other emerging markets. This growth has opened up new sales channels for many small and medium enterprises that were previously confined to their local markets. This development may be especially beneficial for small and informal firms that would not otherwise have the resources to reach customers in a wider geographical market.

The overall effect of e-commerce on the growth prospects of small and informal businesses is, however, ambiguous. On the one hand, access to e-commerce could relax growth constraints for small businesses by allowing them to reach a larger market and increase sales revenues without incurring additional fixed costs. On the other hand, it is possible that the rise of e-commerce reduces the local market power of small businesses, shrinks profit margins, and generates disadvantages for businesses that are less experienced in using the technology. Another open question is whether e-commerce sales are sufficiently stable to serve as a reliable source of revenue and as a potential engine of business growth. It therefore remains unclear whether the rise of e-commerce merely exacerbates existing inequalities, or whether it represents a development that can effectively level the playing field and generate new growth opportunities for small and informal businesses.

Studying the impacts of e-commerce is difficult for a number of reasons. Information on e-commerce transactions is generally proprietary and not available to researchers. Even where such data are available, it is not usually possible to link data on e-commerce transactions to data on the characteristics of the firms or entrepreneurs using e-commerce sales channels. As a result, little is currently known about the characteristics of businesses that select into the use of e-commerce sales channels, how these businesses transact once they are signed up on an e-commerce platform, and which types of businesses manage to use e-commerce to grow their sales revenues. This also makes it difficult to assess whether businesses are able to generate sufficiently stable revenue streams for e-commerce to serve as a realistic source of longer-term revenue and business growth.

The analysis in this chapter overcomes these challenges by using new and previously unexplored data from a large e-commerce platform in India. It combines data on the universe of transactions from a leading Indian e-commerce platform that traces individual sales over a period of four years with data from a survey that captures the characteristics of the businesses and entrepreneurs transacting on the platform. This dataset is especially well suited to tracking the behavior of small and informal firms that are not covered in standard databases: the median firm in the dataset has three employees and an estimated annual revenue of about Rs 3 million (US$40,000). The analysis uses this dataset to follow the transactions of small businesses on the platform and examine, in particular, the extent to which sales and revenue outcomes differ between formal and informal firms, as well as firms with greater experience on the platform.

Although the firms represented in the data are diverse and range from large multiproduct firms to small single-product firms with no employees, the analysis places special emphasis on small and informal firms, which one might expect to experience the largest gains from adopting online sales channels. Because no universally accepted definition of business formality exists, the analysis follows the standard approach in the literature and defines a business as "informal" based on its size measured as the number of employees. In particular, a size cutoff is used that is roughly similar to that used in Indian official statistics. A business is defined as informal if it has fewer than five employees. To assess the robustness of the results, the analysis also applies alternative size cutoffs and definitions of informality (for example, definitions based on sales revenue) and finds that these do not materially change the results.

The chapter shows that both formal and informal businesses are able to grow sales and the geographical size of their markets steadily through the use of online sales channels. However, the benefits of online sales channels are larger among small informal firms, which attain higher online sales per employee and more online revenue per employee relative to formal firms. Businesses that are new to online sales experience a more rapid expansion in the size of the markets they serve; however, there is no evidence that the increase in geographical market size served differs between formal and informal businesses.

Aside from business size, the most important determinant of sales growth is experience using online sales channels, as measured by the number of months a business has been using the e-commerce platform. This is the combined effect of two channels: first, businesses that have been active on the platform for longer may be better at pricing to market and using the advertising tools available on the platform. Second, there is significant attrition; firms that are unsuccessful at growing their sales become inactive on the platform. This is a form of survival bias that gives rise to a mechanical relationship between experience and sales outcomes—a pattern that is similar to that observed in other online markets, such as online trading by retail investors in the stock market (Campbell, Ramadorai, and Ranish 2014).

The analysis additionally examines whether online sales are a sufficiently stable source of income to contribute plausibly to business growth. It finds that online sales are relatively stable and also become more stable over time. The probability that a business experiences a month with no online sales is 19 percent among businesses that have been active for less than six months and 5 percent among businesses that have been active on the e-commerce platform for more than one year. This finding suggests that adopting online sales channels is especially useful for small and informal businesses and can plausibly serve as an engine of sales and revenue growth.

This study is related to several strands of research. First, it contributes to a small but growing literature on e-commerce. Much of this work has studied price setting (Cavallo and Rigobon 2016; Gorodnichenko and Talavera 2017) and reputation (Fan, Ju, and Xiao 2016; Li, Tadelis, and Zhou 2016; Tadelis 2016) in online markets, but has found it difficult to link behavior in online markets to the characteristics of entrepreneurs because the data that online marketplaces collect about such characteristics are typically limited. One study that makes progress on this dimension is Cavallo (2018), who uses microprice data from multichannel retailers (see also Cavallo and Rigobon 2016), combined with scraped product descriptions from Amazon.com to examine how online competition has changed the pricing behavior of firms. The study finds that online competition has changed the frequency of price changes and the degree of uniform pricing across locations in the United States over the past decade.

Second, this study is related to research on the impacts of improved business practices. Studies in this literature have looked at the effects of consulting services, business training, and technology adoption on the performance of small businesses (Anderson and McKenzie 2021; Bloom et al. 2020). Although there is much survey evidence, to date no rigorous evaluations have measured the impact of e-commerce adoption on small businesses. While this study is not designed to identify the causal impact of e-commerce on business performance, one advantage of the setting is that the analysis can match self-reported data on business characteristics to data on actual transactions, which are observed free of measurement error.

Third, this study contributes to a literature on business informality and the benefits of formalization (Bruhn 2011, 2013; Kanbur 2017) and the impact of digitization on business informality (Klapper, Miller, and Hess 2019). One effect of small businesses shifting their sales transactions to online markets is that these transactions become more transparent. This improved transparency makes sales revenue easier to tax, but it also unlocks some benefits of formality to businesses. For example, it enables them to use these documented income streams as collateral for formal credit that can support business growth. Evidence from a World Bank survey among small businesses that are active on the Chaldal online platform in Bangladesh, for instance, suggests that signing up for an online platform increases the incentives for business formalization and helps entrepreneurs gain access to bank financing (Bussolo et al. 2021).

Background: Online Retail in India

India is home to one of the most rapidly growing e-commerce markets in the world. With 697 million internet users (approximately 40 percent of the population), India has the world's second largest internet user base, behind only China (*Times of India* 2014). However, the penetration of online sales—while difficult to measure in a way that is comparable across countries—is still less extensive in India than in more developed markets such as the United States, where more than 80 percent of households use online retail channels and online sales account for about 12 percent of total retail sales (Smith and Anderson 2016; US Census Bureau 2021). Today, 5 percent of all retail sales in India (US$46 billion) are e-commerce sales, and the number of e-commerce transactions is expected to grow by 20 percent annually in coming years (IBEF 2021).

Significant consolidation has occurred recently in the number of online retail platforms serving the Indian market. In a first wave of consolidation, mergers and acquisitions among local e-commerce platforms created a number of local providers with national reach. In a second wave of consolidation, international retailers—such as Alibaba, Amazon, and Walmart—entered the Indian market and acquired local online retailers. This process has made online retail channels more attractive for small businesses that can now reach a larger market by selling their products through one online retail platform. It has also given rise, however, to some concerns about the market power wielded by large online retailers. In an effort to address these concerns, the government of India introduced new regulations in February 2019 that were intended to curb the market power of international retailers. These new regulations prohibit, for example, international retailers from holding inventory in their own warehouses and limit their role to that of a marketplace that intermediates between vendors and customers. In addition, the new regulations place limits on vertical integration. International retailers are, for instance, prohibited from selling products of companies in which they hold an equity stake; they are also prohibited from entering into exclusive sales agreements with vendors, which are common in many online marketplaces.

The use of online sales channels in India has been growing rapidly among small businesses. Data from the Consumer Pyramids Household Survey (CPHS), a survey of a representative sample of small businesses, indicate that, among family businesses, 11 percent of those with five or more employees and 7 percent of those with fewer than five employees use e-commerce.[1] According to most definitions, these businesses would be considered informal, and it has been argued that the increasing use of online retail is a development that may facilitate business formalization in the longer run. For example, since the introduction of the goods and services tax in India in 2017, all large online retailers require vendors to list their tax identification number to transact on the platform. Although the vast majority of online retail payments in India is processed through cash-on-delivery channels, the use of mobile payments is increasing and will add to the formalization of business revenues in the longer term.

Data and Descriptive Statistics

DATA SOURCES AND MAIN VARIABLES

To study which types of business are using online sales channels most successfully to expand their market reach and grow their sales, the analysis combines administrative data on the universe of transactions on the partner firm's e-commerce website with survey data on the characteristics of business and entrepreneurs that use the platform. In addition, the analysis uses data from the CPHS database to study how the firms in the data compare with the wider population.[2]

The administrative data contain the universe of transactions made on the e-commerce platform between June 2016 and June 2020. The dataset contains a total of 29 million completed sales transactions made by 20,145 unique firms. The data have one observation per transaction and include the following variables: date of the transaction, company postal code (merchant location), customer postal code (customer location), transaction status (complete, canceled, return to origin), price, quantity, product category, and identifiers for the product and company. From these, the following variables were generated: experience on the platform (number of months the firm remains active on the platform, that is, has at least one completed transaction), monthly sales (number of completed transactions by month), monthly revenue (revenue from completed transactions by month in rupees), monthly number of products (number of different products offered through the platform by month), monthly number of pin codes with sales (number of different customer postal codes with completed transactions by month), and monthly number of states with sales (number of different customer states with completed transactions by month). Each of these variables is calculated at the company level for each month that a given firm is observed in the data.

The analysis additionally uses data from a survey with merchants who are active on the platform. This provides additional information on entrepreneur and firm characteristics for a sample of 2,316 active businesses that use the partner firm's platform. The survey was conducted between June 2019 and April 2020. In principle, the survey questions could be answered by any member of the business; however, the respondent was the owner or manager in 87.2 percent of cases. The survey records the age, gender, education, and business experience of respondents, as well as the number of employees of the business, the share of the firm's total sales managed through the online platform, the business age, and the type of business. Using the number of employees, two additional outcome variables were generated for the study: monthly sales per employee and monthly revenue per employee.

Because there is no universally accepted definition of business formality and measuring business formality objectively is difficult through administrative records, the analysis follows related work and proxies informality by business size (see, for instance, Nataraj 2011). Specifically, for the analysis, a business is defined as formal if it has five or more employees, and as informal if it has fewer than five employees. This definition is similar to that applied in official surveys in India, which classify a business in the manufacturing sector as formal if it has 10 employees or more if the establishment uses electricity and 20 workers or more if the establishment does not use electricity. Based on this information and considering that businesses in e-commerce can be assumed to have access to electricity, the analysis relies on thresholds of five employees and 15 employees (which are the thresholds recorded in the survey). The results do not materially change if firms are defined as informal if they have fewer than five or fewer than 15 employees, but the analysis uses the more conservative definition of five employees throughout. Using this definition, 34 percent of businesses in the sample are categorized as formal and 66 percent are categorized as informal.

To evaluate how the sample compares with the wider population of small businesses in India, the analysis uses data from the most recent round of the CPHS micro, small, and medium enterprises module and compares the characteristics of the sample with the characteristics of businesses nationwide. Individuals in the CPHS are considered a business if the main occupations of respondents were recorded as businessman, self-employed entrepreneur, qualified self-employed professional, or small trader or businessman without fixed premises.

FIRM CHARACTERISTICS AND TRANSACTIONS ON THE PLATFORM

Table 5.1 presents descriptive statistics on entrepreneur demographics and firm characteristics. The summary statistics show that entrepreneurs in the sample are young (the average entrepreneur is 32 years old), highly educated (77 percent have a college degree), and overwhelmingly male (80 percent). For firm size, the number of employees of firms in the sample ranges from zero to more than 250. The average number of employees is about 13, while the median firm in the sample has 3 employees, which is fairly representative of small informal businesses in India. Most of the businesses in the sample match the definition of micro or small enterprises. Figure 5.1, panel a, shows that 95 percent of firms in the sample have fewer than 50 employees. Table 5.1 also indicates that 66 percent of the firms in the sample are informal, according to the size-based definition. Only 12 percent of the firms are woman-owned, and the average age of these businesses is about 6 years. Of these businesses, 50 percent are merchants, 27 percent are producers, and 23 percent are distributors.

Figure 5.1, panel b, shows the percentage of total sales that firms manage through the online platform. Approximately one-half of the firms in the sample manage 10 percent

TABLE 5.1 **Summary Statistics on Demographics and Firm Characteristics**

Indicator	(1) Mean	(2) Standard deviation	(3) Median
Demographics			
Woman	0.21	0.41	—
Age	31.81	8.06	30
Elementary school or less	0.04	0.18	—
Secondary	0.05	0.23	—
Senior secondary	0.14	0.35	—
University or more	0.77	0.42	—
Firm characteristics			
Formal	0.34	0.47	—
Woman-owned	0.12	0.33	—
Employees, number	12.94	33.32	3
In business, years	5.57	5.74	4
Distributor	0.23	0.42	—
Merchant	0.50	0.50	—
Producer	0.27	0.45	—
Observations	2,316	2,316	2,316

Sources: Administrative data on transactions and business and entrepreneur characteristics associated with a partner firm website; data at CPHS (Consumer Pyramids Household Survey) (dashboard), Consumer Pyramids$_{dx}$, Centre for Monitoring Indian Economy, Mumbai, https://consumerpyramidsdx.cmie.com/.
Note: The table reports summary statistics on demographics and firm characteristics, based on survey data. The demographic variables correspond to the individual who completed the survey, 87.16 percent of whom are the firm owner or manager. — = not applicable.

or more of their sales through the platform; about 30 percent of firms manage more than 20 percent of their sales through the platform; and about 15 percent of firms make more than one-half their total sales through the platform. Because there are multiple large online retailers in India and many firms use more than one of these in parallel, these numbers are a lower bound estimate of the total share of sales that businesses make through online sales channels.

Table 5.2 reports descriptive statistics on sales transactions for firms in the survey data (column 1) and all firms on the platform (column 2). The analysis first examines the number of months during which sales transactions were recorded for a given firm. This provides information on the level of attrition after firms first register on the platform. The table shows that a nontrivial share of firms, 8.6 percent, exits the online platform within one month of registering. However, the average firm remains active for more than a year (17 months).

The study next considers the number of sales per month. The average firm makes about 65 sales per month on the platform, with a high standard deviation of 212 sales. Firms also offer, on average, about 13 products per month and make sales to customers located in 53 distinct postal codes. These numbers are somewhat different between

FIGURE 5.1 Firm Characteristics

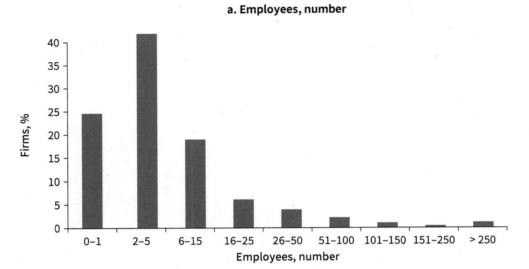

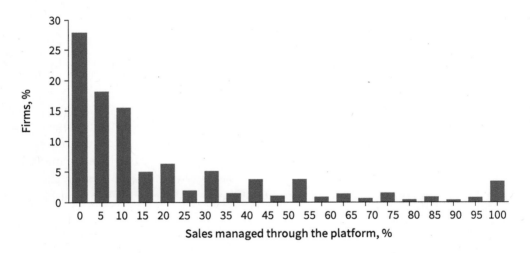

Sources: Administrative data on transactions and business and entrepreneur characteristics associated with a partner firm website; data at CPHS (Consumer Pyramids Household Survey) (dashboard), Consumer Pyramids$_{dx}$, Centre for Monitoring Indian Economy, Mumbai, https://consumerpyramidsdx.cmie.com/.
Note: Based on the survey data, the figure shows the distribution of the number of employees and the share of total sales firms manage to achieve through the e-commerce platform.

TABLE 5.2 **Summary Statistics on Transactions**

Indicator	(1) Firms in the survey data	(2) All firms
Experience on the platform	17.14	10.78
	(14.74)	(11.79)
Exits in the first month, %	8.64	12.58
	(28.09)	(33.16)
Sales per month	65.04	42.99
	(212.29)	(193.89)
Sales growth per month, %	27.71	25.62
	(44.64)	(200.57)
Products in the first month, number	6.31	5.24
	(33.52)	(21.39)
Products per month, number	12.61	8.46
	(28.21)	(23.52)
Growth in number of products per month, %	20.94	18.42
	(33.09)	(41.71)
Pin codes with sales, number	53.49	35.40
	(174.06)	(170.80)
States with sales, number	6.67	4.62
	(7.52)	(6.41)
Observations	2,316	20,145

Sources: Administrative data on transactions and business and entrepreneur characteristics associated with a partner firm website; data at CPHS (Consumer Pyramids Household Survey) (dashboard), Consumer Pyramids$_{dx}$, Centre for Monitoring Indian Economy, Mumbai, https://consumerpyramidsdx.cmie.com/.
Note: The table reports summary statistics on transactions based on administrative data. The first column reports statistics on firms in the survey data. The second column reports on all firms on the platform with at least one completed transaction during June 2016–June 2020.

the universe of businesses in the transaction data and the businesses covered by the survey. Businesses in the survey data have, on average, more experience on the platform (17 months versus 11 months), a lower share of exits in the first month (8.6 percent versus 12.6 percent), and more sales per month (65 versus 43). They also sell to customers in a larger geographical area (53 postal codes versus 35 postal codes served). These differences reflect survival bias among respondents, given that, to be included in the survey, the respondent business was required to have made at least one online sale in the previous three months.

Businesses that are active on the platform sell a wide variety of products. Most sell goods in the two largest meta categories: household items and clothing (figure 5.2). Together, these categories account for about 50 percent of total sales. Electronics also represent a significant share of the products sold on the platform, but the product categories are more concentrated. For instance, within electronics, mobile phones,

FIGURE 5.2 **Trends in the Share of Each Product Category in Total Sales**

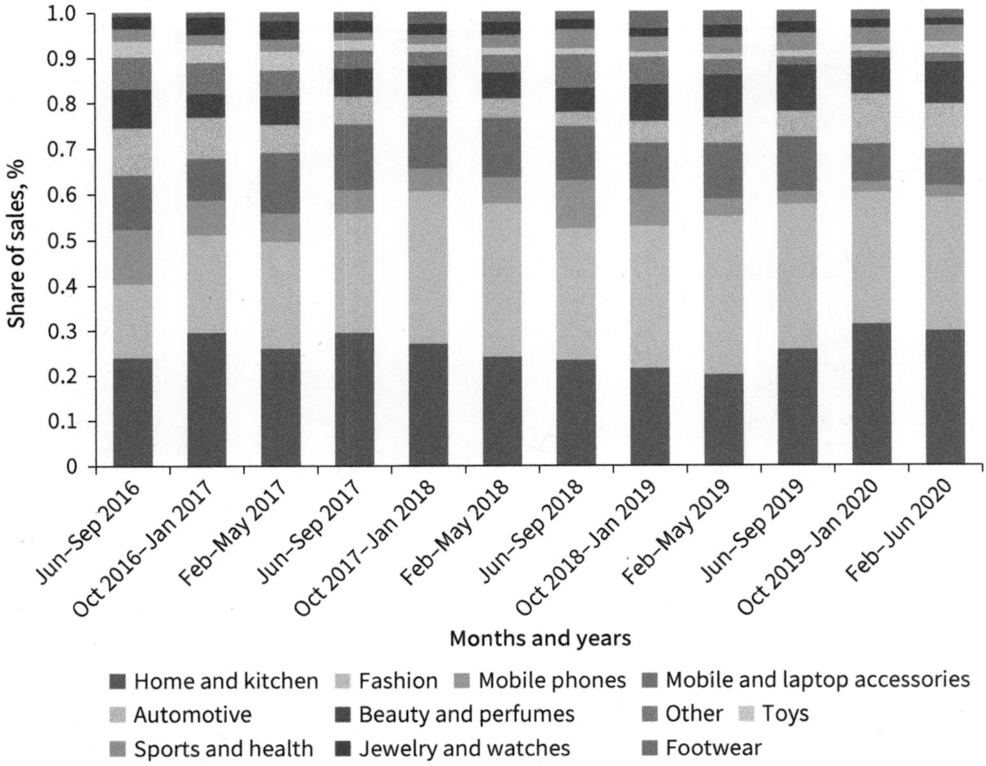

Sources: Administrative data on transactions and business and entrepreneur characteristics associated with a partner firm website; data at CPHS (Consumer Pyramids Household Survey) (dashboard), Consumer Pyramids$_{dx}$, Centre for Monitoring Indian Economy, Mumbai, https://consumerpyramidsdx.cmie.com/.
Note: The figure shows the share of each product category in total sales based on administrative data.

computer tablets, and laptop accessories alone account for about 10 percent of sales on the platform.

Finally, the study examines the geographical location of transactions. Figure 5.3 shows the distribution of sales and purchases by state. One interesting pattern that emerges is that customers are much more geographically dispersed than sellers. The vast majority of merchants is located in the metropolitan areas of Delhi and Mumbai and, to a lesser extent, in the state of Gujarat. Between 40 percent and 50 percent of total sales are made by businesses located in greater Delhi. The customers on the other end of these transactions are, however, much more geographically dispersed (figure 5.3, panel b). The states with the highest share of online purchases are Maharashtra, Tamil Nadu, Karnataka, and Uttar Pradesh (mostly postal codes outside of greater Delhi), and none of these locations has a share of more than 15 percent of total purchases. Postal codes outside the states with the 10 highest shares of purchases account for about 30 percent of total purchases.

FIGURE 5.3 Distribution of Sales and Purchases, by State and Union Territory

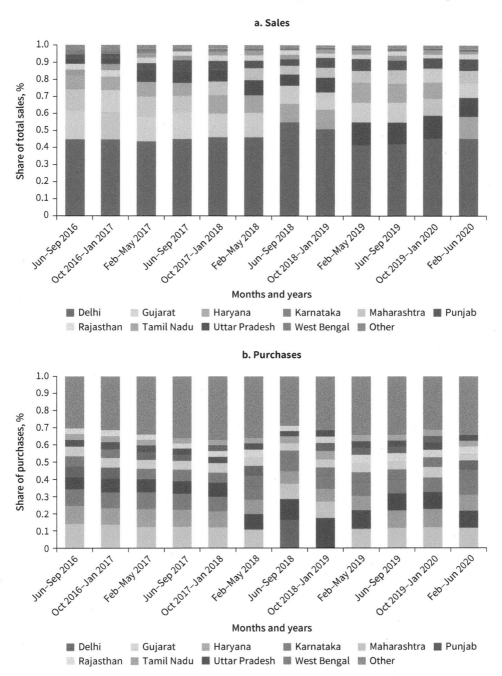

Sources: Administrative data on transactions and business and entrepreneur characteristics associated with a partner firm website; data at CPHS (Consumer Pyramids Household Survey) (dashboard), Consumer Pyramids_{dx}, Centre for Monitoring Indian Economy, Mumbai, https://consumerpyramidsdx.cmie.com/.
Note: The figure shows the geographical distribution of sales and purchases on the platform based on administrative data.

Results

SELECTION INTO E-COMMERCE AND DURATION ON THE PLATFORM

The analysis first examines the types of sellers who chose to select into online sales channels and the factors that determine how long the sellers stay active on the platform. To do so, it compares sellers in the sample with a sample of entrepreneurs from the CPHS that is representative of the population in terms of age, gender, and educational attainment. The descriptive statistics in table 5.3 indicate that entrepreneurs selecting into the e-commerce platform are substantially younger, better educated, and more likely to be women than the overall population of business owners. The average age of sellers in the sample is about 32; it is around 44 in the CPHS sample. Most of entrepreneurs in the sample have a university degree; the share of respondents with tertiary education in the CPHS data is between 15 percent and 40 percent, depending on the size of the firm. The share of women entrepreneurs in the sample—while still only 20 percent—is much higher than the 2 percent–4 percent share in the CPHS data. These differences indicate that there is substantial selection into the use of online sales channels and that younger, more educated, and women entrepreneurs are in a better position to harness the benefits of online sales channels.

The analysis next turns to attrition and survival among businesses that register on the e-commerce platform. Figure 5.4 plots survival functions for all firms that register on the platform and for formal and informal firms separately. The plotted functions estimate the probability that a firm remains on the platform beyond a given time after

TABLE 5.3 Demographics and Firm Characteristics: A Comparison of Survey Data

Indicator	Partner firm survey data			Consumer Pyramids Household Survey		
	0–1 employee	2–5 employees	6–15 employees	0–1 employee	2–5 employees	6–15 employees
Woman	0.20	0.19	0.22	0.04	0.02	0.02
Age	30.83	32.43	32.26	43.90	45.63	44.68
Elementary school or less	0.03	0.02	0.04	0.17	0.06	0.06
Secondary	0.08	0.05	0.04	0.43	0.32	0.25
Senior secondary	0.19	0.13	0.11	0.23	0.35	0.24
University or more	0.70	0.80	0.80	0.15	0.26	0.44
Observations	555	945	428	21,789	3,203	234

Sources: Administrative data on transactions and business and entrepreneur characteristics associated with a partner firm website; data at CPHS (Consumer Pyramids Household Survey) (dashboard), Consumer Pyramids$_{dx}$, Centre for Monitoring Indian Economy, Mumbai, https://consumerpyramidsdx.cmie.com/.
Note: The table compares demographic variables among businesses between the survey data and the micro, small, and medium enterprise module of the Consumer Pyramids Household Survey.

FIGURE 5.4 **Duration of Firms on the e-Commerce Platform**

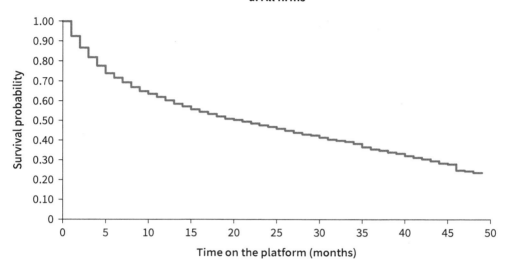

a. All firms

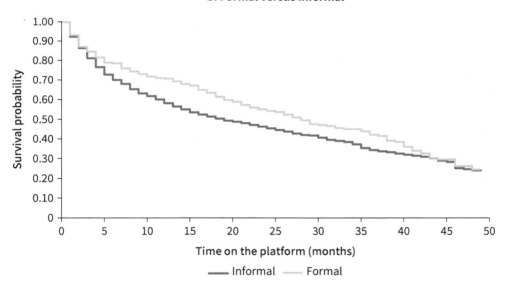

b. Formal versus informal

Informal ——— Formal

Sources: Administrative data on transactions and business and entrepreneur characteristics associated with a partner firm website; data at CPHS (Consumer Pyramids Household Survey) (dashboard), Consumer Pyramids$_{dx}$, Centre for Monitoring Indian Economy, Mumbai, https://consumerpyramidsdx.cmie.com/.
Notes: The figure shows the Kaplan-Meier estimates for the survival functions of firms on the platform.

first signing up (in this case, for more than 1 month, more than 2 months, and so on, up to more than 49 months). Data on 49 months of transactions are available, and this is the maximum amount of time during which firms may be observed on the platform. The probability that a firm remains on the platform for at least one month is about 91 percent, meaning that about 9 percent of firms exit within a month of joining the platform. After the first six months, this probability drops to 70 percent. The probability of staying on the platform for more than one year is 60 percent; only about 50 percent of firms remain active on the platform for more than two years. Accordingly, the figure highlights a relatively high rate of churn and exit among firms, especially during the first months on the platform. Figure 5.4, panel b, shows that formal firms tend to remain active on the platform longer than informal ones. However, the difference in the survival probability between formal and informal firms is not statistically significant once one controls for other characteristics of the firm and entrepreneur (gender, education, age, years in business, and business type), which implies that the differential survival probabilities are the result of factors other than business size or formality alone.

MONTHLY SALES, REVENUE, AND NUMBER OF PRODUCTS

One of the main questions examined in this study is whether there are meaningful differences in the extent to which formal and informal businesses can grow their sales and revenues by using online sales channels. To answer this question, the analysis uses a series of regressions of the form:

$$y_{i,t} = \alpha + \beta_1 \cdot formal_i + \beta_2 \cdot experience_{i,t} + \gamma \cdot X_i + \lambda_t + \epsilon_{i,t}, \qquad (5.1)$$

where $y_{i,t}$ is an outcome of interest such as sales, sales revenue, or its month-on-month growth rate; and X_i is a matrix of controls that includes entrepreneur and business characteristics, such as the age, education, and gender of the business owner and the age and type of the business. The variable *formal* takes a value of 1 if firm i is formal according to the size-based definition described above and 0 otherwise; *experience* is the number of months firm i has been active on the platform until period t; and λ_t are time fixed effects. The main parameters of interest are β_1, which, for each outcome variable, measures the difference between formal and informal businesses, and β_2, which measures the effect of an additional month of experience on the platform on the outcome variable. The error term $\epsilon_{i,t}$ is assumed to be correlated for observations within the same firm and standard errors are therefore clustered at the firm level.

Sales

The analysis first examines the relationship between business formality, online experience, and sales. Table 5.4, columns 1 to 3, present the results with monthly sales as the dependent variable. The results show that formal businesses have, on average, more monthly sales relative to informal businesses. In particular, a formal business is

SMALL BUSINESSES AND ONLINE SALES IN INDIA | 161

TABLE 5.4 Relationship between Monthly Sales and Experience on the Platform, Demographics and Firm Characteristics

	Dependent variable: Monthly sales			Dependent variable: Monthly growth in sales (%)			Dependent variable: Monthly sales per employee			Dependent variable: Monthly growth in sales per employee (%)		
	(1)	(2)	(3)	(4)	(5)	(6)	(7)	(8)	(9)	(10)	(11)	(12)
Formal	35.740 (23.330)		48.851* (28.148)	0.006 (0.006)		0.016** (0.006)	−37.042*** (5.937)		−34.696*** (6.259)	−0.006* (0.004)		0.001 (0.004)
Experience on the platform (months)		4.843*** (1.031)	5.354*** (1.457)		−0.005*** (0.000)	−0.005*** (0.000)		1.158*** (0.317)	1.291*** (0.413)		−0.003*** (0.000)	−0.004*** (0.000)
Woman-owned			−39.047 (28.145)			0.004 (0.009)			−3.596 (9.537)			−0.001 (0.007)
Years in business > median			−46.388* (26.963)			−0.000 (0.006)			−10.475 (7.114)			−0.001 (0.005)
Secondary			44.836 (79.554)			−0.051*** (0.017)			0.576 (13.630)			−0.033*** (0.013)
Senior secondary			100.375 (80.263)			−0.031** (0.015)			15.720 (19.192)			−0.019* (0.010)
University or more			−1.492 (47.813)			−0.026** (0.013)			−5.543 (8.972)			−0.018** (0.009)
Age			−1.995 (1.448)			−0.000 (0.000)			−0.929** (0.451)			−0.000* (0.000)
Merchant			23.097 (34.747)			−0.003 (0.008)			11.105 (8.941)			−0.001 (0.006)
Producer			−27.171 (31.190)			−0.003 (0.009)			−3.352 (6.662)			−0.002 (0.006)
Observations	38,576	39,687	29,779	33,150	34,115	25,713	38,576	38,576	29,779	33,150	33,150	25,713
Number of businesses	2,261	2,316	1,709	1,971	2,023	1,489	2,261	2,261	1,709	1,971	1,971	1,489

Notes: Each column corresponds to a separate OLS regression. The dependent variable in columns (1), (2), and (3) is the number of monthly sales, in columns (4), (5), and (6), the first difference in the logarithm of monthly sales, in columns (7), (8), and (9), the number of monthly sales per employee, and in columns (10), (11), and (12), the first difference in the logarithm of monthly sales per employee. All regressions include fixed effects by time. Clustered standard errors by firm in parentheses. * $p < 0.1$; ** $p < 0.05$; *** $p < 0.01$.

expected to have an average of 49 more sales transactions per month than an informal firm with similar characteristics (p-value = .083).

However, there is almost no difference between formal and informal enterprises in the growth rate of monthly sales (columns 4 and 6). Figure 5.5, panel a, complements these results by showing the average number of monthly sales among formal and informal businesses. The average number of online sales is greater among formal businesses, but the growth rate of sales does not seem to be so different among formal and informal businesses. Figure 5.5 also shows that the average number of sales grows steadily during the first 12 months on the platform among both formal and informal businesses. This finding suggests that online sales channels offer opportunities for growing sales to both informal and formal enterprises.

Because formal firms are larger, it is thus natural to expect them to generate more sales. Sales per employee might therefore be an outcome that more meaningfully captures the impact of e-commerce on business growth. The study thus uses this productivity measure as an additional outcome in table 5.4, columns 7 to 12. The results indicate that, although formal businesses report higher sales on average, they are less productive than informal businesses. In particular, a formal business is found to have 35 fewer sales per employee than an informal business with similar characteristics (p-value < .001). Table 5.4, columns 10 and 12, also show that growth in sales per capita is—if anything—slightly lower for larger formal businesses. This suggests that informal businesses use online sales channels more effectively and perform better in relative terms than formal businesses.

In addition, the results show that firms with greater experience on the e-commerce platform generate more monthly sales (see table 5.4, column 3). A firm with one additional month on the platform is expected to have about five additional monthly sales (p < .001). Similarly, firms with more experience on the platform show more monthly sales per employee on average (see column 9). Taken together, these results suggest that firms may learn how to use the platform and are able to increase sales as they gain experience. The exact mechanism through which this result occurs is, however, not clear and may reflect either a supply- or a demand-side channel. It may be, for instance, that more experienced entrepreneurs learn how to pursue more effective pricing and marketing strategies that increase sales by making their products more visible on the platform. It may also be the case, however, that businesses that have been active on the platform for longer are able to increase their sales through reputation effects. For example, it may be that customers are more likely to buy products from merchants with more customer reviews, which would disproportionally benefit firms that have been active for longer.

Finally, while in table 5.4, column 3, indicate that newer businesses have higher monthly sales, the analysis does not find any differences in the growth rate of monthly sales. One may wonder whether the ability to grow sales and sales revenues is a function of the entrepreneurs' education. If there were such an effect, this might indicate that the experience effects documented result from deliberate choices of the entrepreneur and

FIGURE 5.5 Sales Statistics, Formal and Informal Firms, First Three Years on the Platform

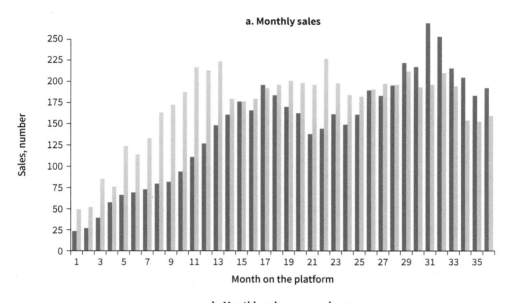

a. Monthly sales

b. Monthly sales per employee

■ Informal ■ Formal

Sources: Administrative data on transactions and business and entrepreneur characteristics associated with a partner firm website; data at CPHS (Consumer Pyramids Household Survey) (dashboard), Consumer Pyramids$_{dx}$, Centre for Monitoring Indian Economy, Mumbai, https://consumerpyramidsdx.cmie.com/.
Note: The figure shows the average number of sales (panel a) and sales per employee (panel b) by month on the platform among formal and informal businesses.

are not an artifact of greater visibility resulting from a longer presence on the online platform. Although the data suggest that there is no significant difference in sales or sales growth by level of education, it is worth noting that there is not much variation in educational attainment in the sample. Most entrepreneurs in the sample have completed tertiary education. The absence of an education effect in this sample is therefore not evidence of the absence of such an effect in the wider population.

Revenue

The analysis next examines sales revenue, which is the main outcome that can reveal the extent to which online sales support the growth of small, informal businesses. The results, reported in table 5.5, are in line with the results on sales reported in the previous section. The results show that, overall, formal businesses enjoy higher monthly revenue than informal businesses (column 3). In particular, the monthly revenue of formal business is, on average, 71 percent higher than the monthly revenue of informal businesses (p < .001).

Interestingly, however, there are no differences in the growth rate of monthly revenue between formal and informal enterprises (column 6). Figure 5.6, panel a, shows that formal businesses have higher average monthly revenue than informal firms in almost every month, but their monthly revenue does not grow more quickly than that of informal businesses. The results also show that average monthly revenue grows steadily among both formal and informal businesses during their first year on the platform.

When comparing businesses in terms of monthly revenue per employee, however, informal businesses do perform better than formal businesses (see table 5.5, column 9). In particular, monthly revenue per employee in an informal business is approximately double that of a formal business with similar characteristics (p < .001). This result indicates that informal businesses are also more productive if one considers monthly revenue. This suggests that small, informal businesses have proportionally more to gain from using online sales channels relative to larger businesses. This is reasonable, given that online sales allow small businesses to access a larger market without any of the overhead costs, such as networks of local sales agents, that larger businesses may have already incurred.

The results on the relationship between experience on the platform and sales per employee similarly mirror the results on sales transactions. Firms with more experience have, on average, greater monthly revenue and also more monthly revenue per employee (see table 5.5, columns 3 and 9). Businesses with one additional month on the platform are expected to have monthly revenue that is approximately 9.4 percent higher and revenue per employee that is approximately 8.5 percent higher (both with p < .001).

As noted in the previous section, this may be either the result of supply-side factors (learning how to market one's products more effectively) or demand-side factors (increased likelihood that customers buy from firms with a longer track record on the platform). Additionally, the results show that woman-owned businesses have lower monthly revenue, on average, while younger entrepreneurs have higher monthly revenue, both significant at the 5 percent level (p = .045 and p = .038, respectively).

TABLE 5.5 Relationship between Monthly Revenue and Experience on the Platform, Demographics and Firm Characteristics

	Dependent variable: Logarithm of monthly revenue			Dependent variable: Monthly growth in revenue (%)			Dependent variable: Logarithm of monthly revenue per employee			Dependent variable: Monthly growth in revenue per employee (%)		
	(1)	(2)	(3)	(4)	(5)	(6)	(7)	(8)	(9)	(10)	(11)	(12)
Formal	0.785*** (0.126)		0.714*** (0.138)	0.003 (0.007)		0.011 (0.008)	-1.156*** (0.124)		-1.144*** (0.136)	0.003 (0.007)		0.006 (0.008)
Experience on the platform (months)		0.103*** (0.004)	0.094*** (0.005)		-0.006*** (0.000)	-0.006*** (0.000)		0.083*** (0.004)	0.085*** (0.005)		-0.006*** (0.000)	
Woman-owned			-0.369** (0.183)			-0.011 (0.012)			-0.210 (0.186)			-0.011 (0.012)
Years in business > median			-0.087 (0.142)			0.004 (0.007)			-0.151 (0.143)			0.000 (0.008)
Secondary			0.525 (0.386)			-0.072*** (0.017)			0.648 (0.400)			-0.077*** (0.019)
Senior secondary			0.343 (0.326)			-0.049*** (0.015)			0.413 (0.328)			-0.052*** (0.016)
University or more			0.137 (0.279)			-0.042*** (0.013)			0.178 (0.285)			-0.043*** (0.014)
Age			-0.017** (0.008)			-0.001 (0.000)			-0.019** (0.008)			-0.001* (0.000)
Merchant			0.359** (0.167)			0.005 (0.009)			0.452*** (0.167)			0.003 (0.009)
Producer			-0.054 (0.180)			0.012 (0.010)			0.052 (0.180)			0.011 (0.010)
Observations	38,576	39,687	29,779	30,011	30,879	23,405	38,576	38,576	29,779	30,011	30,011	23,405
Number of businesses	2,261	2,316	1,709	1,764	1,813	1,342	2,261	2,261	1,709	1,764	1,764	1,342

Notes: Each column corresponds to a separate OLS regression. The dependent variable in columns (1), (2), and (3) is the logarithm of monthly revenue, in columns (4), (5), and (6), the first difference in the logarithm of monthly revenue, in columns (7), (8), and (9), the logarithm of monthly revenue per employee, and in columns (10), (11), and (12), the first difference in the logarithm of monthly revenue per employee. All regressions include fixed effects by time. Clustered standard errors by firm in parentheses. * $p < 0.1$; ** $p < 0.05$; *** $p < 0.01$.

FIGURE 5.6 **Revenue Statistics, Formal and Informal Firms, First Three Years on the Platform**

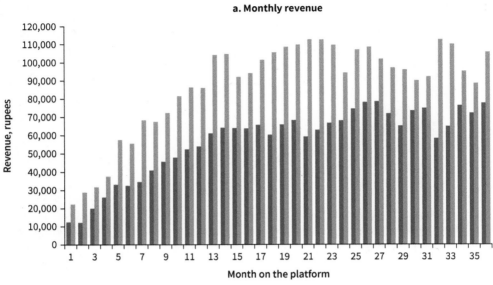

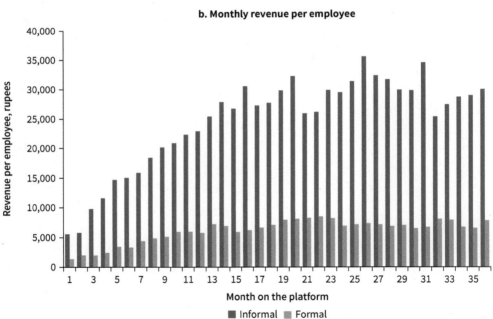

Sources: Administrative data on transactions and business and entrepreneur characteristics associated with a partner firm website; data at CPHS (Consumer Pyramids Household Survey) (dashboard), Consumer Pyramids$_{dx}$, Centre for Monitoring Indian Economy, Mumbai, https://consumerpyramidsdx.cmie.com/.
Note: The figure shows the average revenue (panel a) and revenue per employee (panel b) by month on the platform among formal and informal businesses.

Number of products

To understand whether entrepreneurs change their behavior or sales strategies as they gain experience on an e-commerce platform, the study examines the impact of business type and business experience on the number of products offered. The results, reported in table 5.6, indicate that formal businesses have a higher number of products, on average. In particular, a formal business is expected to offer about nine more products than an informal business in any given month; this difference is statistically significant at the 1 percent level (p = .009). Although experience on the platform correlates with the addition of new products, it does not reduce the difference in the size of the product portfolios offered by formal and informal firms. Figure 5.7 illustrates the growth in the average number of products offered by formal and informal businesses during their first three months on the platform. It shows that a firm with one additional month of online sales experience is expected to offer one additional product (p < .001). However, the number

TABLE 5.6 Relationship between Monthly Number of Products and Experience on the Platform, Demographics and Firm Characteristics

	Dependent variable: Monthly number of products			Dependent variable: Monthly growth in the number of products (%)		
	(1)	(2)	(3)	(4)	(5)	(6)
Formal	7.907*** (2.835)		8.830*** (3.399)	0.001 (0.004)		0.010** (0.005)
Experience on the platform (months)		0.844*** (0.076)	0.791*** (0.099)		−0.005*** (0.000)	−0.005*** (0.000)
Woman-owned			1.616 (3.654)			−0.000 (0.007)
Years in business less than 5			−0.445 (3.348)			0.004 (0.005)
Secondary			18.359** (9.009)			−0.022* (0.013)
Senior secondary			10.398** (4.789)			−0.013 (0.010)
University or more			5.989 (4.411)			−0.008 (0.009)
Age			−0.368** (0.175)			−0.001** (0.000)
Merchant			−2.707 (5.008)			0.005 (0.006)
Producer			−8.774 (5.567)			0.004 (0.007)
Observations	38,576	39,687	29,779	33,150	34,115	25,713
Number of businesses	2,261	2,316	1,709	1,971	2,023	1,489

Notes: Each column corresponds to a separate OLS regression. The dependent variable in columns (1), (2), and (3) is the monthly number of products offered by the firm, and in columns (4), (5), and (6), the first difference in the logarithm of monthly number of products. All regressions include fixed effects by time. Clustered standard errors by firm in parentheses. * p < 0.1; ** p < 0.05; *** p < 0.01.

FIGURE 5.7 **Product Statistics, Formal and Informal Firms, First Three Years on the Platform**

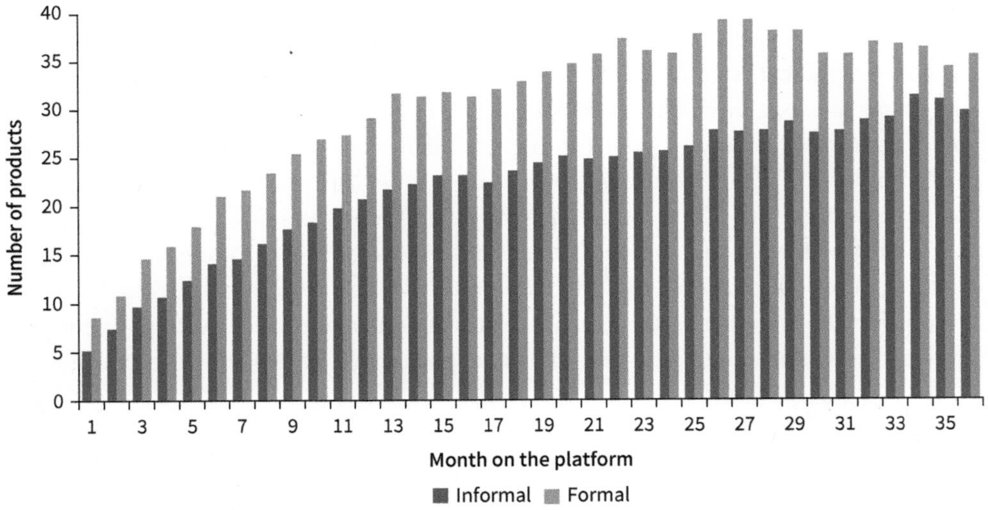

Sources: Administrative data on transactions and business and entrepreneur characteristics associated with a partner firm website; data at CPHS (Consumer Pyramids Household Survey) (dashboard), Consumer Pyramids$_{dx}$, Centre for Monitoring Indian Economy, Mumbai, https://consumerpyramidsdx.cmie.com/.
Note: The figure shows the average number of products by month on the platform among formal and informal firms.

of products offered grows steadily among both formal and informal enterprises, so that, even after one year on the platform, formal firms still offer a larger product variety than informal firms.

SALES STABILITY

So far, the analysis has revealed that both formal and informal businesses are able to grow their sales and revenues through an e-commerce platform and that informal businesses perform better in terms of sales and revenue per employee. In addition, the results document that experience on a platform is another key predictor of how effective firms are in increasing their sales through online channels.

If online sales channels are to serve as a source of business growth, another important aspect to consider is whether online sales are a sufficiently large and stable source of income to support the revenue base of small businesses. To address this question, the study first defined two additional variables based on the transaction data. The first of these outcomes is the number of months in which a business was registered on the e-commerce platform but recorded zero sales. The second outcome measure is the ratio of months with no sales to total months on the platform for each firm in the sample. Figure 5.8, panel a, plots this variable. The figure shows that the share of months with no sales was below 20 percent for about 65 percent of the firms in the sample, and 40 percent of the firms in

FIGURE 5.8 **Sales Stability**

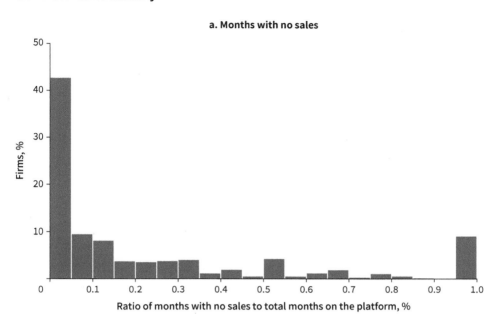

a. Months with no sales

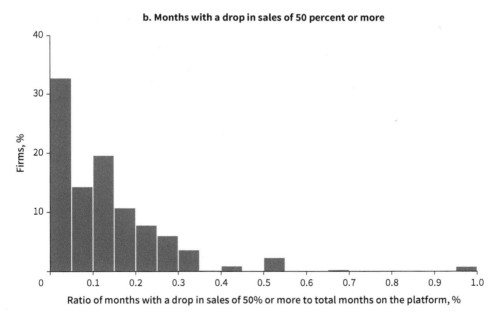

b. Months with a drop in sales of 50 percent or more

Sources: Administrative data on transactions and business and entrepreneur characteristics associated with a partner firm website; data at CPHS (Consumer Pyramids Household Survey) (dashboard), Consumer Pyramids$_{dx}$, Centre for Monitoring Indian Economy, Mumbai, https://consumerpyramidsdx.cmie.com/.
Note: The figure shows the share of months with no sales (panel a) and the share of months with a drop in sales of 50 percent or more (panel b) among firms in the sample, based on administrative data.

the sample had sales in more than 95 percent of the months of their presence on the platform. The firms that recorded no sales in any of the months on the platform are firms that left the platform in the first or second month after they registered.[3]

Second, to study whether online sales fluctuate significantly from month to month, the analysis considered for each firm the proportion of months with a drop in sales of 50 percent or more relative to the previous month and calculated the ratio of months with a drop in sales of 50 percent or more to total months on the platform. Figure 5.8, panel b, plots this ratio. It shows that about 32 percent of the firms did not experience any months with online revenue drops of this magnitude, while 75 percent of the firms did not have a drop in sales of this magnitude in 80 percent of the months in which they were active on the platform. This finding suggests that, for most businesses, online sales revenues are relatively stable.

Taken together, the results indicate that, for most businesses, online sales represent a relatively stable source of income. More than 65 percent of the firms on the platform experienced almost no months with zero sales, and large month-on-month fluctuations in sales were also relatively rare. These estimates are upper bounds on sales drops because most businesses that use online sales channels are active on more than one platform, while the study only observed sales and sales drops on one platform. In any case, the results suggest that e-commerce can be a reliable source of revenue that allows firms to expand their business, especially small, informal enterprises.

EXPANSION IN GEOGRAPHICAL MARKET SIZE

The final question addressed by this study is the extent to which online sales channels allow small businesses to expand sales by reaching consumers in a larger geographical area. Intuitively, online sales channels might increase sales in two ways. First, it may be that there is a substantial home bias among consumers, and online channels increase sales by making it easier for consumers to buy products from local merchants that they already know. Second, it may be that online channels increase sales by making a merchant's products visible to a larger geographical market. Which of these channels dominates has important implications for competition, market power, and, potentially, for how online markets should be regulated.

To examine how registering on an e-commerce platform expands the geographical reach of businesses, the study relies on the geographical identifiers contained in the transaction data. Specifically, the analysis uses as the outcome of interest the number of postal codes (pin codes) and states in which a given firm's customers are located, and estimates regressions identical to equation 5.1, with monthly number of pin codes with any sales, monthly growth in the number of pin codes with sales, monthly number of states with sales, and monthly growth in the number of states with sales as the dependent variables.

Table 5.7 presents the results and shows that formal businesses sell in more postal codes and more states on average (table 5.7, columns 3 and 9). The average formal firm

TABLE 5.7 Relationship between Monthly Number of Pin Codes with Sales and Experience in the Platform, Demographics and Firm Characteristics

	Dependent variable: Monthly number of pin codes with sales			Dependent variable: Monthly growth in the number of pin codes (%)			Dependent variable: Monthly number of states with sales			Dependent variable: Monthly growth in the number of states (%)		
	(1)	(2)	(3)	(4)	(5)	(6)	(7)	(8)	(9)	(10)	(11)	(12)
Formal	25.237* (14.717)		34.133* (17.727)	0.004 (0.006)		0.011* (0.007)	1.767*** (0.467)		1.799*** (0.525)	0.001 (0.004)		0.006 (0.005)
Experience on the platform (months)		3.472*** (0.582)	3.738*** (0.789)		-0.006*** (0.000)	-0.006*** (0.000)		0.275*** (0.015)	0.259*** (0.018)		-0.004*** (0.000)	-0.004*** (0.000)
Woman-owned			-33.952* (18.920)			-0.009 (0.011)			-1.117 (0.713)			-0.005 (0.008)
Years in business > 5			-28.454 (17.651)			0.004 (0.007)			-0.685 (0.548)			0.003 (0.005)
Secondary			29.377 (55.327)			-0.071*** (0.017)			1.421 (1.521)			-0.041*** (0.012)
Senior secondary			54.783 (47.848)			-0.047*** (0.014)			1.485 (1.230)			-0.029*** (0.010)
University or more			-0.458 (34.823)			-0.044*** (0.013)			0.430 (1.045)			-0.027*** (0.009)
Age			-1.318 (0.963)			-0.001* (0.000)			-0.083*** (0.031)			-0.000 (0.000)
Family business			21.652 (17.817)			0.013** (0.006)			0.520 (0.494)			0.008* (0.004)
Merchant			12.041 (21.809)			0.004 (0.008)			1.200* (0.632)			0.006 (0.006)
Producer			-23.073 (20.908)			0.009 (0.009)			-0.377 (0.687)			0.009 (0.006)
Observations	38,576	39,687	29,779	30,011	30,879	23,405	38,576	39,687	29,779	30,011	30,879	23,405
Number of businesses	2,261	2,316	1,709	1,764	1,813	1,342	2,261	2,316	1,709	1,764	1,813	1,342

Notes: Each column corresponds to a separate OLS regression. The dependent variable in columns (1), (2), and (3) is the monthly number of pin codes with sales, in columns (4), (5), and (6), the first difference in the logarithm of monthly number of pin codes with sales, in columns (7), (8), and (9), the monthly number of states with sales, and in columns (10), (11), and (12), the first difference in the logarithm of monthly number of states with sales. All regressions include fixed effects by time. Clustered standard errors by firm in parentheses.
* $p < 0.1$; ** $p < 0.05$; *** $p < 0.01$.

sells in 34 more postal codes and two more states than the average informal firm with similar characteristics (p = .054 and p = .001, respectively). However, there are no differences in the growth rate of geographical market reach between formal and informal enterprises (columns 6 and 12). Experience is a strong predictor of the geographical market size served by a business. Having one additional month of experience on the platform is associated with selling to customers in an additional four postal code areas (p < .001).

Figure 5.9 shows that the number of postal codes with sales grows steadily during the first year of a firm's presence on the platform among both formal and informal businesses. In the first month, formal firms sell, on average, in about 30 different postal codes, while informal firms sell in about 15 postal codes. After one year on the platform, these numbers increase to 150 and 115, respectively. These results indicate that both formal and informal firms are able to expand their markets through e-commerce and that this expansion occurs steadily, rather than discontinuously, mainly during the first year in which a business is active on the platform.

FIGURE 5.9 Postal Codes with Sales, Formal and Informal Firms, First Three Years on the Platform

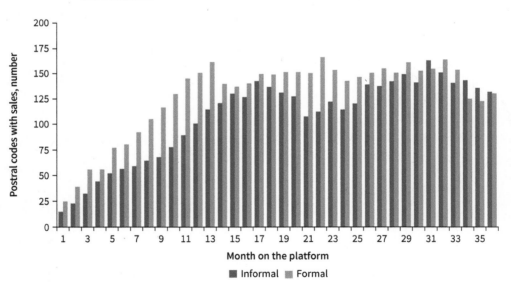

Sources: Administrative data on transactions and business and entrepreneur characteristics associated with a partner firm website; data at CPHS (Consumer Pyramids Household Survey) (dashboard), Consumer Pyramids$_{dx}$, Centre for Monitoring Indian Economy, Mumbai, https://consumerpyramidsdx.cmie.com/.
Note: The figure shows the average number of postal codes (pin codes) with sales by the number of months of presence on the platform among formal and informal businesses.

Conclusion

The increased use of online sales channels in recent years is one of the most important developments for small businesses in emerging markets. In contrast to many other innovations, the growth of online sales has the potential to be especially transformative for small businesses that would otherwise lack the resources to access a larger market and thereby grow their sales. Because data on online sales are not readily available and often lack the depth to link information on transactions with the characteristics of businesses and entrepreneurs, many important questions remain unanswered: Are the relative benefits of online sales larger for small enterprises than for large businesses? Which types of businesses and entrepreneurs are best able to harness the benefits of online sales? Do online sales provide revenue that is sufficiently stable to serve as a plausible source of business growth?

This chapter attempts to answer some of these questions using new data on online sales merged with business and entrepreneur characteristics. The study combines a large proprietary dataset on the transactions on one of India's largest e-commerce platforms with survey data on the firms and entrepreneurs that use the platform. The analysis finds that, in the first year on the platform, businesses were able to grow their sales and revenue rapidly. This is relatively more beneficial for small, informal businesses, which have persistently higher sales and revenue per employee including after they have been active on the platform for more than a year. The study also examines which business and entrepreneur characteristics are most predictive of success on the online platform. It finds that the single largest determinant of online sales and revenues is an entrepreneur's experience on the platform.

Taken together, the results suggest that online sales channels can serve as a promising source of additional revenue that is especially useful as a potential engine of growth for small, informal businesses. One limitation of the study is that these results are based on observational data. Thus, it cannot show conclusively the extent to which the results are driven by endogenous selection into the platform. Randomized studies that can demonstrate the causal effect of online sales on business growth would therefore be a promising direction for future research.

Notes

The authors are grateful for comments from Pierre Bachas, Maurizio Bussolo, Arti Grover, Siddharth Sharma, Chris Woodruff, and seminar participants at the World Bank for helpful comments and suggestions. The opinions expressed in this chapter do not necessarily represent the views of the World Bank, its executive directors, or the countries they represent.

1. See 2020 data at CPHS (Consumer Pyramids Household Survey) (dashboard), Consumer Pyramidsdx, Centre for Monitoring Indian Economy, Mumbai, https://consumerpyramidsdx.cmie.com/.

2. See CPHS (Consumer Pyramids Household Survey) (dashboard), Consumer Pyramidsdx, Centre for Monitoring Indian Economy, Mumbai, https://consumerpyramidsdx.cmie.com/. This is a nationally representative survey of Indian households that has been conducted since 2014.

3. The analysis did not observe whether a month with no sales reflects an absence of supply (the merchant decided not to post any inventory for sale) or an absence of demand (the merchant posted inventory, but no customers made a purchase that month).

References

Anderson, Stephen, and David J. McKenzie. 2021. "Improving Business Practices and the Boundary of the Entrepreneur: A Randomized Experiment Comparing Training, Consulting, Insourcing, and Outsourcing." *Journal of Political Economy.* Published ahead of print, August 26, 2021. https://doi.org/10.1086/717044.

Bloom, Nicholas, Aprajit Mahajan, David J. McKenzie, and John Roberts. 2020. "Do Management Interventions Last? Evidence from India." *American Economic Journal: Applied Economics* 12 (2): 198–219.

Bruhn, Miriam. 2011. "License to Sell: The Effect of Business Registration Reform on Entrepreneurial Activity in Mexico." *Review of Economics and Statistics* 93 (1): 382–86.

Bruhn, Miriam. 2013. "A Tale of Two Species: Revisiting the Effect of Registration Reform on Informal Business Owners in Mexico." *Journal of Development Economics* 103 (July): 275–83.

Bussolo, Maurizio, Akshay Dixit, Anne Marie Golla, Jean Nahrae Lee, and Siddharth Sharma. 2021. "How Selling Online Is Affecting Small Firms in South Asia." Policy Research Working Paper, World Bank, Washington, DC.

Campbell, John Y., Tarun Ramadorai, and Benjamin Ranish. 2014. "Getting Better or Feeling Better? How Equity Investors Respond to Investment Experience." NBER Working Paper 20000 (March), National Bureau of Economic Research, Cambridge, MA.

Cavallo, Alberto F. 2018. "More Amazon Effects: Online Competition and Pricing Behaviors." Paper presented at the Federal Reserve Bank of Kansas City's Jackson Hole Economic Policy Symposium, "Changing Market Structures and Implications for Monetary Policy," Jackson Hole, WY, August 23–25, 2018.

Cavallo, Alberto F., and Roberto Rigobon. 2016. "The Billion Prices Project: Using Online Prices for Measurement and Research." *Journal of Economic Perspectives* 30 (2): 151–78.

Fan, Ying, Jiandong Ju, and Mo Xiao. 2016. "Reputation Premium and Reputation Management: Evidence from the Largest e-Commerce Platform in China." *International Journal of Industrial Organization* 46 (May): 63–76.

Gorodnichenko, Yuriy, and Oleksandr Talavera. 2017. "Price Setting in Online Markets: Basic Facts, International Comparisons, and Cross-Border Integration." *American Economic Review* 107 (1): 249–82.

IBEF (India Brand Equity Foundation). 2021. "Indian E-Commerce Industry Analysis." *Indian E-Commerce Industry Report*, July 2021. IBEF, New Delhi. https://www.ibef.org/industry /ecommerce-presentation.

Kanbur, Ravi. 2017. "Informality: Causes, Consequences, and Policy Responses." *Review of Development Economics* 21 (4): 939–61.

Klapper, Leora F., Margaret Miller, and Jake Hess. 2019. "Leveraging Digital Financial Solutions to Promote Formal Business Participation." World Bank, Washington, DC.

Li, Lingfang (Ivy), Steven Tadelis, and Xiaolan Zhou. 2016. "Buying Reputation as a Signal of Quality: Evidence from an Online Marketplace." NBER Working Paper 22584 (September), National Bureau of Economic Research, Cambridge, MA.

Nataraj, Shanthi. 2011. "The Impact of Trade Liberalization on Productivity: Evidence from India's Formal and Informal Manufacturing Sectors." *Journal of International Economics* 85 (2): 292–301.

Smith, Aaron, and Monica Anderson. 2016. "Online Shopping and e-Commerce." Pew Research Center (blog), December 19, 2016. https://www.pewresearch.org/internet/2016/12/19/online -shopping-and-e-commerce/.

Tadelis, Steven. 2016. "Reputation and Feedback Systems in Online Platform Markets." *Annual Review of Economics* 8 (1): 321–40.

Times of India. 2014. "Online Shoppers in India to Cross 100 Million by 2016: Study." *Technology News*, November 20, 2014.

US Census Bureau. 2021. "Quarterly Retail e-Commerce Sales: 2nd Quarter 2021." *U.S. Census Bureau News*, August 19, 2021. https://www2.census.gov/retail/releases/historical /ecomm/21q2.pdf.

CHAPTER 6

What Is the Role of Socioemotional Skills in Supporting South Asia's Informal Sector Poor: Insights from Pakistan and Sri Lanka

SYUD AMER AHMED, PINYI CHEN, ZAINEB MAJOKA, AND JYOTIRMOY SAHA

Introduction

Informality is ubiquitous in the labor markets of South Asia, and it may be argued that the high rates of informality have implications for income growth and other features of economic development. In the five larger economies in the region collectively, more than 80 percent of the labor market is in the informal sector.[1] For example, in Bangladesh, India, Nepal, and Pakistan, the informal sector accounts, respectively, for 95 percent, 88 percent, 81 percent, and 82 percent of economic activity; Sri Lanka is an exception: only 68 percent of economic activity is informal. The high rates of informality may be associated with slower economic growth based on the global evidence on informality and economic development. For example, Ulyssea (2018, 2020) finds that lower rates of informality may be (but are not necessarily) associated with higher output, productivity, or welfare. More recently, Ohnsorge and Yu (2021) argue that economies with larger informal sectors tend to have less access to finance for the private sector, lower labor productivity, slower physical and human capital accumulation, and smaller fiscal resources.

At the same time, poverty reduction remains a major policy objective of many South Asian economies. Many economies are considering the role of labor market and economic inclusion programs in poverty reduction. Poverty rates are higher in South Asian economies than in many other economies, barring Sub-Saharan African economies, despite recent progress (World Bank 2020). Implementing measures that support sustained poverty reduction is thus a policy priority in the region. In many cases, these economies are now considering the development or scale-up of labor market programs targeted to poverty—such as means-tested technical and vocational training and economic inclusion programs—following the approach of BRAC's Targeting Ultra-Poor graduation programs (Andrews et al. 2021).[2] For example, Pakistan revamped its approach to social protection and poverty programming in 2019 through a cabinet-level restructuring that led to the creation of the Ehsaas (Compassion) platform and the Poverty Alleviation and Social Safety Division to promote coherent safety nets for vulnerable groups, as well as new interventions to support livelihoods and jobs among the poor.[3] Poverty reduction as an explicit goal also features prominently in national planning documents more generally, as seen in Bangladesh's five-year plans.

This chapter explores the role that socioemotional skills play in the determination of the earnings of the informal sector poor. The examination focuses on Pakistan and Sri Lanka primarily through the use of two microdatasets on labor market outcomes, education, and skills (technical, cognitive, and socioemotional): (1) the Pakistan Labor and Skills Survey (LSS) and (2) the Sri Lanka Skills toward Employment and Productivity survey (STEP). The analysis delineates the heterogeneity of socioemotional skills and earnings across various segments of the labor market in each country. The following section reviews the role of socioemotional skills in labor market outcomes, with a focus on developing economies and South Asia. The subsequent section presents an empirical analysis of data on socioemotional skills in Pakistan and Sri Lanka. The final section discusses the implications of the findings for programs designed to target the informal poor.

The (New) Role of Socioemotional Skills in the Labor Market

Although the importance of general education, work experience, and social norms in boosting the incomes of the poor is well recognized, there is a growing interest in exploring the potential of socioemotional skills to improve labor market outcomes (Acosta and Muller 2018; Heckman, Stixrud, and Urzua 2006) (box 6.1). Jencks (1979) shows that socioemotional skills are at least as important as cognitive skills, socioeconomic background, and educational attainment in predicting incomes later in life. More recent research finds that people with higher levels of socioemotional skills have better labor market outcomes (Saltiel et al. 2017). Heckman and Rubinstein (2001) find that individuals with General Education Development certificates are less likely to hold a job after they become adults and are more likely than high school graduates to engage in risky behaviors (teenage pregnancy, smoking, and drug use), even though they probably have similar levels of cognitive abilities. They adopt these behaviors presumably because of poorer socioemotional skills, such as discipline, patience, and motivation.[4]

> ### BOX 6.1 **The Big Five Socioemotional Skills**
>
> Socioemotional skills can be categorized in several ways, but the Big Five categorization is among the most common and often features in empirical analyses of socioemotional skills and labor market outcomes. The Big Five aims to capture personality traits, such as perseverance, self-control, trust, self-esteem, empathy, hostility, and the ability to engage productively in society (Heckman, Jagelka, and Kautz 2019). The Big Five includes the following: (1) agreeableness, which is the willingness to help people and act in accordance with other people's interests, as well as the degree to which an individual is cooperative, warm, and agreeable rather than cold, disagreeable, and antagonistic; (2) conscientiousness is the preference for following rules and schedules and for keeping engagements and the attitudes associated with being hardworking, organized, and dependable, as opposed to lazy, disorganized, and unreliable; (3) emotional stability encompasses dimensions such as nervous versus relaxed and dependent versus independent and addresses the degree to which the individual is insecure, anxious, depressed, and emotional rather than calm, self-confident, and cool; (4) extroversion is the preference for human contacts, empathy, gregariousness, and assertiveness and the wish to inspire people; and (5) openness measures the degree to which a person needs intellectual stimulation, change, and variety (Brunello and Schlotter 2011).
>
> The data on the Big Five are self-reported, and this process may induce a reference bias. For example, West et al. (2016), using longitudinal data, find paradoxical results in their study on eighth graders. They find that conscientiousness, self-control, and grit are positively related with test score gains but that this relationship disappears at the school level. They conclude that, with the changing circumstances, respondents redefine their notion of the meaning of conscientiousness or grit and therefore may rate themselves more critically. Because the value of these skills may vary across cultures and labor markets, any analysis using these measures should be contextualized to explain their relevance. Moreover, most of the research on socioemotional skills is based on data from high-income countries; so, it is unclear how much socioemotional skills matter in the labor markets of low-income countries.

The literature is mixed on the relative importance to earnings of cognitive versus socioemotional abilities. This is difficult to distinguish because people with high socioemotional skills also tend to have high levels of both cognitive skills and education. Socioemotional skills tend to be rewarded in the formal education system. For example, the researcher who controls for cognitive skills and coursework mastery discovers that the grades awarded by middle-school teachers are influenced by behaviors, such as paying more attention in class, spending more time on homework, completing homework, and avoiding disruptive conduct in class (Farkas 1996; Lleras 2008). In US data, Lleras (2008) finds that high-school students who have better social skills and work habits are more likely to complete higher levels of education. It is possible that socioemotional skills indirectly lead to higher cognitive abilities through behaviors, such as motivation and conscientiousness, that would make students study more assiduously and pay more attention to the tests that measure cognitive abilities (Borghans et al. 2016). Evidence suggests that high cognitive test scores are associated not only with high cognitive skills but also with socioemotional attributes, such as high motivation (Brunello and Schlotter 2011).

A few studies present evidence that greater socioemotional skills are associated with better labor market outcomes in developing countries. Gunewardena et al. (2018) use STEP surveys in Armenia, Bolivia, Colombia, Georgia, Ghana, Kenya, Serbia, Ukraine, and Vietnam to find statistically significant relationships between cognitive and socioemotional skills and earnings. Cunningham, Acosta, and Muller (2016) find that socioemotional skills influence labor force participation and tertiary education attendance in Bolivia, Colombia, El Salvador, and Peru. In Colombia, adults with higher cognitive and socioemotional skills do better in the labor market, where socioemotional skills impact outcomes through various channels (Acosta, Muller, and Sarzosa 2020).

The evidence on the role of socioemotional skills in labor market outcomes in South Asia remains underexplored more generally, but there are a few studies on Bangladesh. Nomura and Adhikari (2017) find a positive correlation between emotional stability and wages and a negative correlation between grit and wages among employees of formal sector manufacturing firms in Bangladesh. Hilger, Nordman, and Sarr (2018) find that workers in Bangladesh hired over formal channels benefit from higher returns to openness to experience, while workers hired through networks enjoy higher wages for greater levels of emotional stability. Kotikula, Hill, and Raza (2019) find that, among poor workers in slum and nonslum areas of Dhaka, Bangladesh, socioemotional skills influence the choice of employment but not necessarily earnings. They also find that women workers who are better at adapting to changes or who are more self-disciplined are more likely to engage in wage employment, whereas women who are more persistent and willing to persevere through challenges are more likely to be self-employed. These patterns may reflect the impact of Bangladesh's sociocultural dynamics and structure on firm management practices and the extent to which production workers are expected to be compliant with management directives.

The relationship between agreeableness and labor market outcomes is two-sided. Agreeableness implies cooperation and compassion and is often correlated with low levels of criminal behavior, strong social networks, and higher levels of community involvement. It has an inconsistent relationship, however, with educational achievement because its facets may influence academic success in various ways. Its positive impact is mostly observed in adverse environments where agreeableness prevents students from interacting with deviant peers or from engaging in antisocial behavior (Nieuwenhuis 2018). It also has a positive effect if strong social networks are able to help students perform better. However, the flexibility aspect of agreeableness negatively impacts educational outcomes (Noftle and Robins 2007). Similarly, Nießen et al. (2020) suggest that, because low agreeableness is often accompanied by high task orientation, which is relevant to success, higher levels of agreeableness lead to higher drop-out rates in vocational training programs.

Based on the studies on the relationship between socioemotional skills and labor market outcomes, one might expect that socioemotional skills are likely to be positively related to labor market outcomes, although distinguishing the influence of socioemotional skills from that of cognitive skills may be challenging. The next section tests these relationships in Pakistan and Sri Lanka.

Insights from Pakistan and Sri Lanka

To capture the impact of socioemotional skills on the earnings of poor workers, this analysis distinguishes between formal sector workers and informal sector workers. Informal sector workers in South Asia tend to be poorer than formal sector workers. In Pakistan, 63 percent of informal wage workers receive monthly wages that are below the minimum wage of PRs 15,000, while the share among formal wage workers is 14 percent. Formal sector and informal sector workers also differ across other characteristics. For example, 47 percent of informal wage workers have no education versus only 13 percent of formal wage workers; only 6 percent of informal wage workers have completed tertiary education compared with 38 percent of formal wage workers.

UNDERSTANDING THE SOCIOEMOTIONAL PROFILES

This chapter uses the 2014 Pakistan LSS and the 2012 Sri Lanka STEP survey to study how socioemotional skills affect earnings and the formality status of workers in the labor market. The surveys are nationally representative household surveys that gather information on all household members through interviews with one member age 15–64 in each household. They contain information on demographics, employment, incomes, and skills (cognitive, socioemotional, and technical). The information on socioemotional skills is based on the Big Five categories, along with measures of grit, perceptions of hostility, and decision-making; cognitive skills—working memory and reasoning—are measured by Raven scores, which are only available in Pakistan.[5] The Sri Lanka STEP survey includes a literacy assessment that provides measures of literacy proficiency.[6] The 2014 Pakistan LSS has 2,354 observations covering all urban and rural areas except for Baluchistan and the erstwhile Federally Administered Tribal Areas. The Sri Lanka STEP survey also covers all urban and rural areas with a sample size of 2,989 observations.

Two outcomes of interest for the analysis are derived from these surveys: formality and observed earnings. Because of data availability, workers in Pakistan are considered formal if they have a legal contract, whereas, in Sri Lanka, workers are considered formal if they have access to benefits, such as pensions. Both the LSS and the STEP record monthly earnings in local currency units.

Here, the analysis considers simple correlations between socioemotional skills and education, earnings, participation in the informal versus formal sectors, and income levels. The next section estimates the relationship between socioemotional skills and earnings, controlling for other influences on earnings.

In both Pakistan and Sri Lanka, socioemotional skills are correlated with high educational attainment (see annex 6A, figures 6A.1 and 6A.2). At a disaggregated level, socioemotional skills such as extroversion, openness, decision-making, and emotional stability are greater among respondents with postsecondary and tertiary education than among respondents with lower educational attainment. This finding is consistent with the literature (figure 6.1). Heckman, Stixrud, and Urzua (2006) find that personality

FIGURE 6.1 **Socioemotional Skills Differ Based on Educational Attainment**

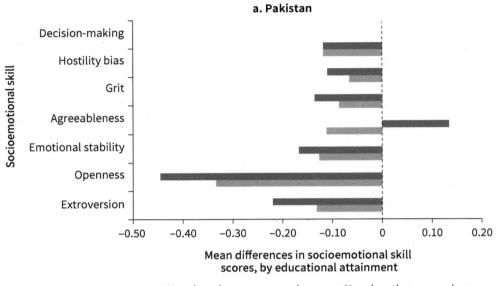

a. Pakistan

Mean differences in socioemotional skill scores, by educational attainment

■ Δ No education: postsecondary ■ Δ No education: secondary

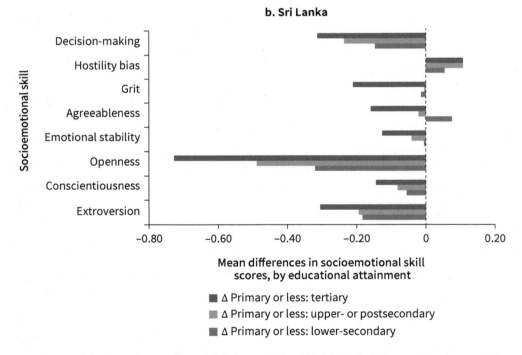

b. Sri Lanka

Mean differences in socioemotional skill scores, by educational attainment

■ Δ Primary or less: tertiary
■ Δ Primary or less: upper- or postsecondary
■ Δ Primary or less: lower-secondary

Source: Data of the 2013 Pakistan Labor and Skills Survey (LSS) and 2012 Sri Lanka Skills toward Employment and Productivity (STEP).

traits such as emotional stability and self-esteem, even after controlling for cognitive skills, significantly increase the probability of completing more advanced studies. In the United Kingdom, extroversion and conscientiousness have a positive impact on educational attainment (Lenton 2014). Conscientiousness is also the best predictor of grades and the second-best predictor of years of education, and openness to experience is the best predictor of years of education (Borghans, ter Weel, and Weinberg 2006). The differences in the level of conscientiousness by educational attainment are statistically significant only in Sri Lanka, whereas openness to experience is significant in both Pakistan and Sri Lanka.

Socioemotional skills are correlated with earnings. The relationships may be either direct or indirect and may depend on the sociocultural contexts of the economies. If the relationship is direct, the implication is that individuals with higher socioemotional skills are more productive. If the relationship is indirect, the implication is that individuals with higher socioemotional skills decide to invest in schooling and work experience, which are valued more highly in the labor market and exhibit higher returns.[7]

In Pakistan, extroversion is positively correlated with monthly earnings, which indicates that workers with higher social skills are likely to fare better in navigating a cultural context where job matching relies on interpersonal relationships. Similar associations were seen in the United Kingdom, where more sociable and assertive people are 25 percent more likely to be employed in high-earning jobs, though the returns are higher among men than women, reflecting social norms around sex (Heineck 2011). Earnings in Pakistan are also correlated with openness to experience and innovation, which is in line with the conclusions of Acosta, Muller, and Sarzosa (2020) on Colombia.

However, in the labor markets in both Sri Lanka and Pakistan, the relationship between socioemotional skills and earnings varies based on whether the sector of employment is formal or informal. Among formal sector wage workers in Pakistan, extroversion and agreeableness are negatively correlated with earnings (figure 6.2). This echoes findings in the Netherlands, where workers who are extroverted or agreeable are likely to earn less. One reason for this outcome may be that agreeable people are poor wage negotiators or that they self-select into jobs that are often low-paying (Nyhus and Pons 2005). In contrast to the case in Pakistan, agreeableness is positively correlated with earnings among formal sector workers in Sri Lanka, which implies that high levels of kindness and compliance are considered important in career success (de Vries and Rentfrow 2016). Among informal wage workers, conscientiousness is positively correlated with earnings in Pakistan, while, in Sri Lanka, emotional stability has a positive correlation. This finding is in line with experiences in other countries (Almlund et al. 2011; Heckman, Stixrud, and Urzua 2006; Nyhus and Pons 2005).

Socioemotional skills are rewarded differently in the formal and informal sectors, but this may also imply that the types of jobs available in these sectors require distinct abilities (figure 6.3). In Pakistan, formal sector workers show more hostility bias whereby they perceive others to be more hostile toward them. This suggests that competitiveness is more rewarding in the formal sector than in the informal sector. In Sri Lanka, the

FIGURE 6.2 Correlation: Socioemotional Skills, Earnings, and Formality Status

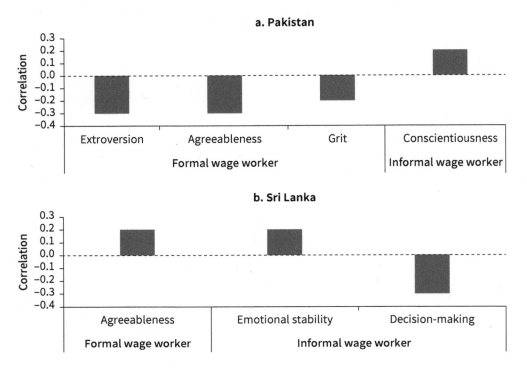

Source: Data of the 2013 Pakistan Labor and Skills Survey (LSS) and 2012 Sri Lanka Skills toward Employment and Productivity (STEP).

opposite is found: workers with higher hostility bias are more likely to be in the informal sector, which echoes the findings in Colombia, where less hostility bias is significantly associated with a 3 percent greater chance of employment in the formal sector (Acosta, Muller, and Sarzosa 2020). Informal sector workers in Pakistan are more likely to score higher on decision-making and grit. Informal sector workers in Sri Lanka exhibit lower levels of all socioemotional skills other than the hostility bias.

In both Pakistan and Sri Lanka, the top quintile has greater socioemotional skills, with the exception of the bottom quintile in Sri Lanka, which shows slightly more hostility bias than the top quintile (figure 6.4). Nyhus and Pons (2005) point out that the advantages of growing up in high-income households include more than superior education and welfare. These households also transmit soft skills, such as motivation and discipline, that are rewarded eventually by employers (Dunifon and Duncan 1998). People in higher-income households are less likely to experience stress or instability at home, while children in poorer households are more likely to live in crowded homes and in underserved neighborhoods. This experience has an impact on socioemotional skills. Individuals in higher-income households thus report greater levels of extroversion and conscientiousness (de Vries and Rentfrow 2016).

FIGURE 6.3 **Socioemotional Skills of Formal and Informal Workers Differ**

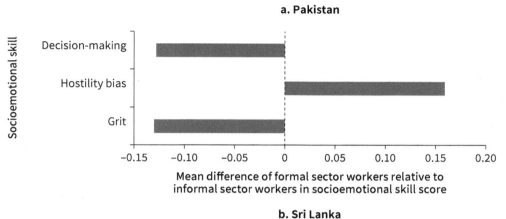

a. Pakistan

Mean difference of formal sector workers relative to
informal sector workers in socioemotional skill score

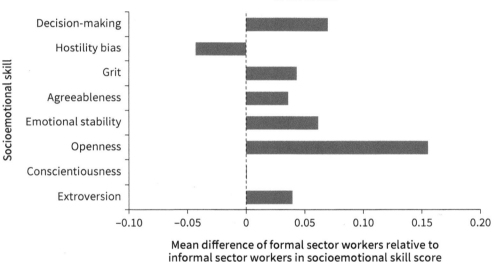

b. Sri Lanka

Mean difference of formal sector workers relative to
informal sector workers in socioemotional skill score

Source: Estimates based on data of the 2013 Pakistan Labor and Skills Survey (LSS) and 2012 Sri Lanka Skills toward Employment and Productivity (STEP).
Note: Only statistically significant results are reported.

ESTIMATING THE IMPACT OF SOCIOEMOTIONAL SKILLS ON EARNINGS

The analysis estimates the relationship of cognitive and socioemotional skills with earnings while controlling for basic demographic characteristics and a few labor market variables. The Heckman selection model is used for Pakistan because, in an ordinary least squares regression, the impact of demographics and skills on wages can only be observed among those respondents whose wages are recorded. This can potentially

FIGURE 6.4 Socioemotional Skills Differ between the Top and Bottom Wealth Quintiles

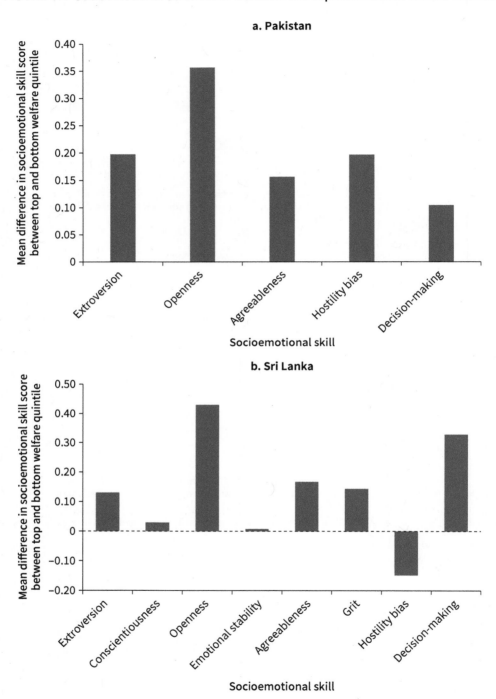

Source: Estimates based on data of the 2014 Pakistan LSS and 2012 Sri Lanka STEP.
Note: Only statistically significant results are reported.

create a selection bias given that there are many possible reasons that the value of the wages of other respondents may be missing and that it is theoretically likely that unobservable or unmeasured factors may affect both the wages and the probability of observing a wage. The Heckman selection model is used to correct for this bias by first identifying variables that affect the probability of observing wages—not the actual wages—and then estimating the prospective wages without selection bias. The selection variable in this model is the probability that workers will have an observed wage, while the outcome variable is observed wages. However, the ordinary least squares regression model based on the Mincer equation is used for Sri Lanka because the Wald test of independent errors from selection and outcome equations is not rejected, that is, error terms from selection and outcome equations are not correlated. Thus, the nonselection hazard measured by the inverse Mills ratio will have no impact on the outcome, conditional on the observation of the wage, thereby making the use of the Heckman selection equation on the data unjustified.

There may be measurement bias in most socioemotional skill indicators because these indicators are self-reported. In Peru, Cunningham, Parra Torrado, and Sarzosa (2016) find differing results in the ordinary least squares and the structural model. They conclude that there is a strong measurement bias in most socioemotional skills measures in the data used. Their paper illustrates the significant impacts of socioemotional skills on labor market outcomes, although the patterns are nonuniform by methodology and labor market outcome. For example, the perseverance of effort (grit) was strong in most outcomes regardless of methodology. However, plasticity—a composite of openness to experience and emotional stability—was only correlated with employment and only if the structural latent model was used.

In Pakistan, the returns to socioemotional skills are mostly statistically insignificant, except for agreeableness (figure 6.5). After controlling for cognitive skills (measured by Raven scores), educational attainment, parental education, wealth, work experience, nature of the employment, access to finance, and location, only the impact of agreeableness remains statistically significant. However, it is associated with negative returns to earnings. The impact of agreeableness on earnings may vary by culture. For instance, Lee and Ohtake (2016) find that Japanese men who reported a higher level of agreeableness earned more, whereas American men with a higher level of agreeableness experienced a penalty. However, in both countries, agreeableness had a positive impact on earnings among individuals working in companies with more than 1,000 employees. This finding also suggests that agreeableness improves job performance and productivity directly, rather than indirectly through occupational choice. Because the majority of the jobs in Pakistan are created by small and medium enterprises, it is possible that personality traits linked with competitiveness may be valued more than agreeableness. However, the penalty is relatively small: with every unit increase in agreeableness, the monthly wage declines by only 0.3 units.

In Sri Lanka, socioemotional skills are not significantly related to earnings in the informal sector (figure 6.6). However, in the formal sector, emotional

FIGURE 6.5 **Heckman Selection Model, Pakistan**

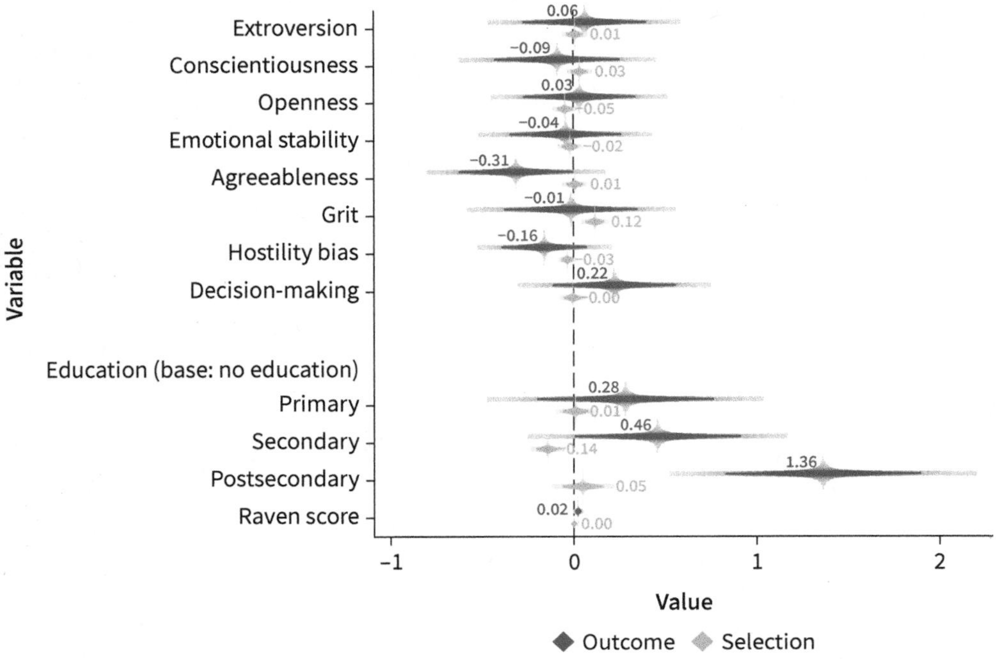

Source: Pakistan Labor Skill Survey.
Note: Only statistically significant results are reported. Full results are shown in annex 6B, table 6B.1.

stability, decision-making, and extroversion have a positive impact on earnings (annex 6B, table 6B.2). The results on the formal sector are consistent with Nyhus and Pons (2005), who find a close association between emotional stability and wages, while decision-making has a positive impact on earnings because of its association with the degree of control and leadership, which enables one to persuade others. Nyhus and Pons also argue that the impact of extroversion depends on the occupation. Extroversion may be beneficial among individuals in people-facing jobs, such as sales representatives or teachers, but not among scientists or accountants. The results on the formal sector in Sri Lanka are similar to the results on Bangladesh, where individuals in the formal sector with greater perseverance and emotional stability earn a starting salary that is 1.8 percent to 2.5 percent higher than that of individuals with fewer of these skills (Hilger, Nordman, and Sarr 2018).

The substantial gender gaps in earnings in Pakistan and Sri Lanka may be related to differences in socioemotional skills. In Pakistan, the monthly earnings of men workers are estimated at 109 percent of the monthly earnings of women workers, on average, conditional on observation of the earnings.[8] However, such a substantial gender gap in earnings may be biased because of the hugely skewed gender distribution in the sub-sample of observed wages, 93 percent of which is accounted for by men. In the overall

FIGURE 6.6 Mincerian Regression to Measure Returns, Sri Lanka

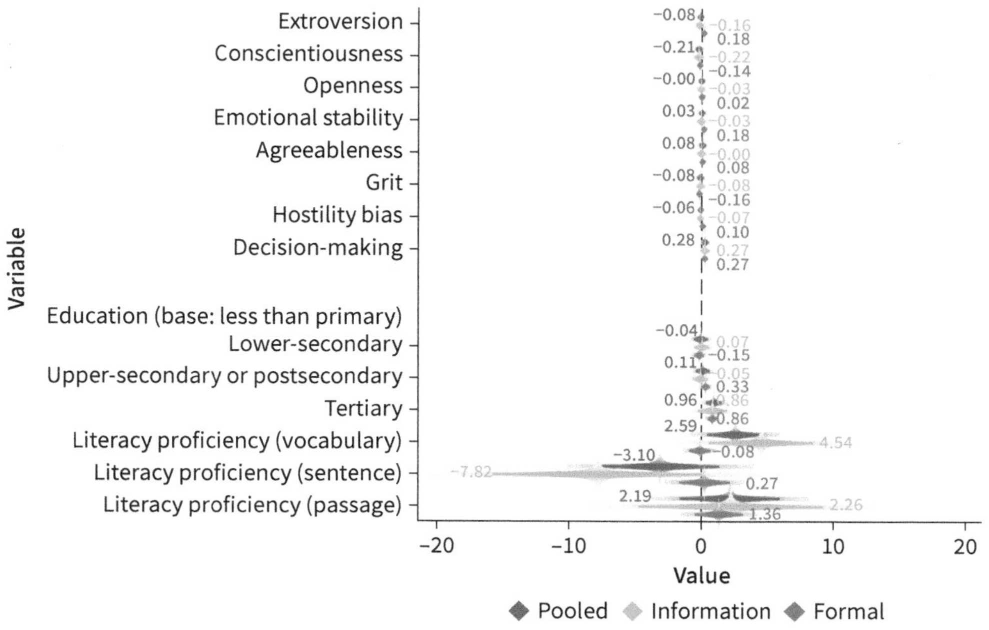

Source: STEP Sri Lanka.
Note: Only statistically significant results are reported. Full results are shown in annex 6B, table 6B.2.

sample in Sri Lanka, it is estimated that the hourly earnings of a typical man worker surpass the hourly wages of a typical woman worker by 81 percent. This gap widens (narrows) to 112 percent (25 percent) in the informal (formal) sector, indicating that the gender disparity in earnings is more pronounced in the informal sector than in the formal sector. Among the well-known causes of the gender wage gap are the social norms, the underrepresentation of women in leadership positions, the reduced working hours associated with the greater care responsibilities of women, the differences in education, and the undervaluation of the jobs held by women. However, these factors do not account for the entire gap (ILO 2019). Another reason may also be the low levels of socioemotional skills among women. In Sri Lanka, men survey respondents report higher socioemotional skills, whereas, in Pakistan, women survey respondents report greater hostility bias, agreeableness, and extroversion, while the other socioemotional skills are more prevalent among men (figure 6.7).

The results confirm that both cognitive skills and educational attainment are strong predictors of earnings.[9] As measured by Raven scores, cognitive skills in Pakistan increase earnings by 2.3 percent, conditional on the observation of monthly earnings. Cognitive skills proxied by proficiency in understanding vocabulary in Sri Lanka boost hourly earnings by 259 percent and 454 percent in the overall sample and in the informal subsample, respectively, but they do not affect participants in the formal subsample.

FIGURE 6.7 Socioemotional Skills Differ between Men and Women

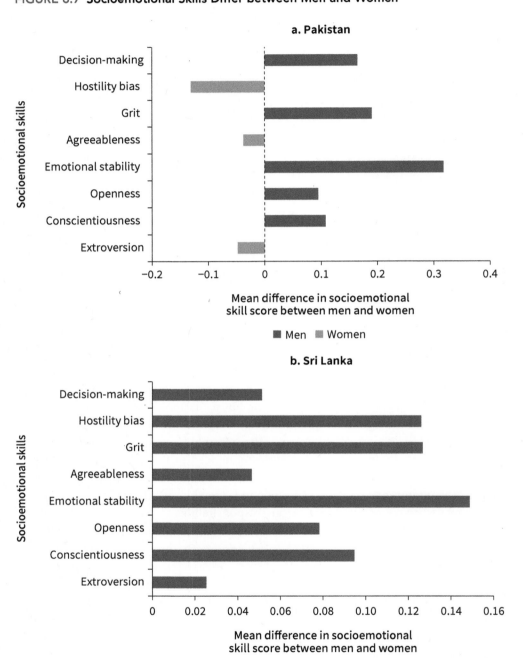

Source: Estimates based on data of the 2014 Pakistan Labor and Skills Survey (LSS) and 2012 Sri Lanka Skills toward Employment and Productivity (STEP).
Note: Only statistically significant results are reported.

These results are consistent with the results of Murnane et al. (2000), who find that US men who are high school graduates with better cognitive skills earn 30 percent more than their counterparts with lesser cognitive skills. The relationship between earnings and educational attainment holds even after controlling for cognitive abilities. This echoes the results of Lleras (2008) using US data, which suggests that schooling may strengthen socioemotional skills, which later foster greater social and economic mobility.

A sensitivity analysis shows that most of the development of socioemotional skills occurs outside of the school environment, in homes and social circles and in the workplace. The education variables in regressions are choice variables correlated with socioeconomic background, and they are endogenous to wage equations (Heckman, Stixrud, and Urzua 2006). For example, people with better cognitive and socioemotional skills may be more likely to achieve better education outcomes to promote these skills (Hansen, Heckman, and Mullen 2004). Parental education can also be endogenous because, relative to their less well-educated peers, more well-educated parents may exhibit a greater probability of passing superior abilities on to their children (Chevalier et al. 2013). Concerned with the endogeneity of education variables, the estimates presented in figure 6.5 (annex 6B, table 6B.1) and figure 6.6 (annex 6B, table 6B.2) are repeated, but with and without these indicators (see annex 6B, tables 6B.3 and 6B.4; see also tables 6B.5 and 6B.6). The reestimated coefficients of socioemotional and cognitive skills reflect both the direct and the indirect effects exerted through schooling (Heckman, Stixrud, and Urzua 2006). However, in both Pakistan and Sri Lanka, the changes in the estimates without education included relative to the corresponding estimates with education included are small, and few of the changes are statistically different from zero. This indicates that the interdependence between socioemotional and cognitive skills and education variables is limited, which is in line with the slight correlation among these variables (see annex 6A, figures 6A.1 and 6A.2). Moreover, the lack of association implies that socioemotional skills are usually developed in families, with friends, in the living environment, and in the workplace rather than in school (Heckman and Mosso 2014).

EXPLANATIONS OF THE VARYING IMPORTANCE OF DIFFERENT SOCIOEMOTIONAL SKILLS

Two explanations for the differences in various socioemotional skills and labor market outcomes may be considered. First, the relative importance of different socioemotional skills may depend on the structure of an economy. Acosta, Muller, and Sarzosa (2020) use evidence from Colombia to argue that the importance of socioemotional skills depends on the employment structure, the type of jobs available, the level of human development, and the differences in economic growth. For instance, evidence suggests that extroversion is positively correlated with earnings or with type of employment in the context of a service-rich economy such as the United States (Fletcher 2013).

Deming (2017) finds that the returns to social skills in the US labor market have been growing, suggesting that the importance of various socioemotional skills is changing as the US economy undergoes structural transformation and adopts new technologies.

There is evidence that the impact of socioemotional skills on labor market outcomes varies by sector. In Pakistan and Sri Lanka, workers in agriculture, manufacturing, and services do not have the same profile of socioemotional skills, which means either workers acquire skills that are valued in their respective sector or they learn these skills as a by-product of working in these jobs and occupations (figure 6.8). In Pakistan, workers in agriculture have more grit than workers in manufacturing or services. This finding reflects the nature of employment in agriculture, which requires perseverance more than other socioemotional skills. In contrast, jobs in services call for intellectual curiosity, innovation, and interaction with other people; service sector workers exhibit higher levels of openness and extroversion in both Pakistan and Sri Lanka. Service workers also show greater hostility bias. A good match between skills and jobs may contribute to labor productivity. However, Sahn and Villa (2016) find that, in Madagascar, socioemotional skills improve labor market outcomes not by boosting productivity but by increasing the chances that people with better socioemotional skills would obtain jobs that pay more.

Similarly, the pervasive informality in Pakistan, where more than one-half of all workers are employed in the informal sector, may drive differences in the returns to skills. Extroversion is the only socioemotional skill that is positively correlated with earnings in Pakistan. This finding is quite different from the conclusions of studies on most high-income countries, where conscientiousness, emotional stability, and grit have a significant impact on wages and other labor market outcomes. Extroverted people may have more success in taking advantage of the personal relationships that are critical in the informal sector. Alternatively, if most informal sector jobs require social interaction, extroverted people may be more successful.

The second explanation for the differences in various socioemotional skills and labor market outcomes revolves around the demands of employers. Thus, Yamauchi et al. (2018) find that Indian employers prefer organized, calm, imaginative, and quiet (less extroverted) applicants over easygoing, sensitive, or outgoing applicants. Kotikula, Hill, and Raza (2019) find that, among urban poor in Dhaka, Bangladesh, persistence, grit, self-discipline, knowledge seeking, and the ability to adapt to change are significantly correlated with a woman worker's choice between wage employment or self-employment. Women workers who are better at adapting to change or who are self-disciplined are more likely to engage in wage employment. Alternatively, women who are persistent and willing to persevere through challenges are more likely to be self-employed. These patterns in Bangladesh may reflect the impact of sociocultural dynamics, the structure of firm management practices, and, in particular, the importance employers assign to the compliance by production workers with management directives.

FIGURE 6.8 **Socioemotional Skills Vary by Sector of Employment**

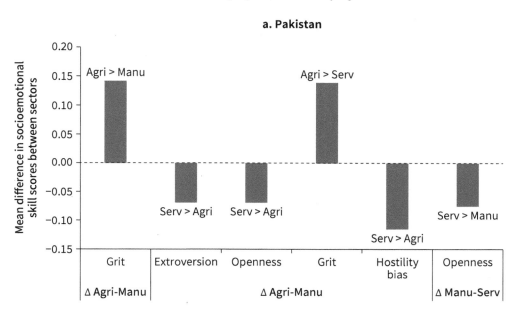

a. Pakistan

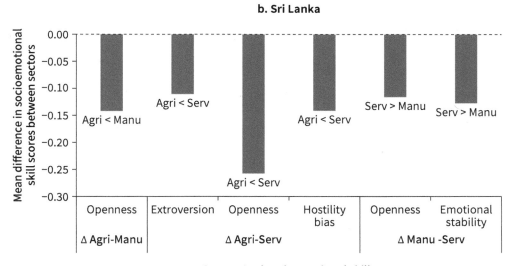

b. Sri Lanka

Source: Estimates based on data of the 2014 Pakistan Labor and Skills Survey (LSS) and 2012 Sri Lanka Skills toward Employment and Productivity (STEP).
Note: Only statistically significant results are reported. Agri = agriculture; Manu = manufacturing; Serv = services.

Enhancing Socioemotional Skills through Programs among the Informal Poor

Efforts to strengthen the socioemotional skills of poor workers to support, for example, their entry into the formal sector should reflect three considerations. First, different socioemotional skills are valued in different ways across South Asian economies, and the values placed on the skills may change as the structure of these economies changes. An increasing share of the employment in services, which tend to require more collaboration and communication relative to manufacturing or agriculture, could raise the demand for skills involving the openness skill. In addition, technological advances could change the skills demanded. Autor, Levy, and Murnane (2003) describe how the demand for cognitive skills in the US economy is changing based on changes in the task structure of jobs; Orrell (2018) argues that the demand for socioemotional skills among US employers is also changing. Deming (2017) finds that the returns to social skills in the US labor market have been growing as the US economy undergoes structural transformation. As South Asia economies adopt skill-biased technologies and automate production, the demand for different skills may be expected to evolve.

Second, interventions to improve socioemotional skills among poor workers should be undertaken across the life cycle, including early childhood development among the youngest, general education among individuals of school age, and labor market or economic inclusion programs among workers. Heckman, Stixrud, and Urzua (2006) note that the most critical period in the development of socioemotional skills is ages 6–11. Acosta et al. (2017) note in a review that optimal time periods are associated with the development of different socioemotional skills. Highlighting the importance of early childhood nutrition on the formation of socioemotional skills, Dercon and Sanchez (2011), using panel data from Ethiopia, India, Peru, and Vietnam, conclude that height-for-age at ages 7–8 is linked with self-efficacy, self-esteem, and educational aspirations measured at ages 11–12.[10] Using the same dataset, Sánchez (2017) finds that height at an early age—as a proxy for nutrition—impacts cognitive and socioemotional skills. Heckman (2005) finds that, primarily by supporting socioemotional skills, enriched childcare centers, coupled with home visitations, are successful in alleviating some of the initial disadvantages experienced by children born into adverse family environments.

Given the importance of the early years in socioemotional skill formation, a case can be made for poverty-targeted interventions among children, given that the income status of a child's household influences socioemotional skill acquisition during the school years and in later economic life (Fletcher and Wolfe 2016; Kautz et al. 2014). Many different poverty-targeted early years interventions focusing on nutrition, early childhood stimulation, and education are already being implemented in the region.[11] For instance, in Bangladesh, the government has been implementing a conditional cash transfer program that provides income support to poor rural mothers who have been identified using proxy-means testing. The transfer is conditional on the mothers with children ages under 2 years participating in growth monitoring services and taking up training in parenting and early childhood stimulation.[12] Similarly, in Pakistan, Ehsaas Nashonuma is a conditional cash transfer program aimed at pregnant and lactating mothers with children under age 2 years. The cash transfer is provided based on participation in immunization and regular attendance at health awareness sessions. Conditional cash transfer programs have generally been found to be effective in improving child nutritional and health outcomes (Leroy, Ruel, and Verhofstadt 2009; Owusu-Addo and Cross 2014).

Third, the incorporation of support for the development of socioemotional skills in economic inclusion programs can have a positive impact on the earnings potential of poor workers. Socioemotional skills are increasingly becoming a focus within the package of services provided to the poor in a broad range of economic inclusion programs, such as BRAC's Targeting the Ultra-Poor Program. A feature common to all of these programs is that they are based on a core intervention (for example, a cash transfer, microfinancing, or a training activity) that involves many complementary services. Andrews et al. (2021) recently concluded a meta-analysis of impact evaluations of economic inclusion programs. They find that a majority of programs that combined several interventions had a significant impact on measures of livelihoods and poverty, such as income, consumption, and employment diversification, as well as on measures of psychosocial well-being, child education, and child health and nutrition.

Annex 6A: Correlation Coefficients between Variables, Pakistan LSS and Sri Lanka STEP

FIGURE 6A.1 Correlation Coefficients, Pakistan

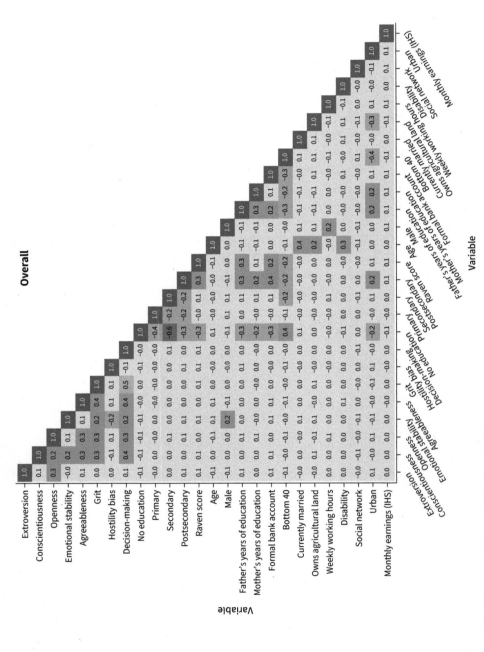

Source: Data of the 2014 Pakistan Labor and Skills Survey (LSS).
Note: IHS = inverse hyperbolic sine.

FIGURE 6A.2 **Correlation Coefficients, Sri Lanka**

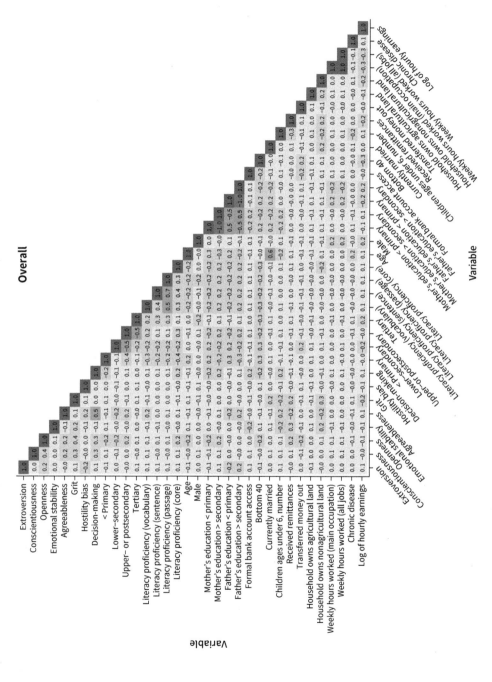

Source: Data of the 2012 Sri Lanka Skills toward Employment and Productivity (STEP).

Annex 6B: Estimation of the Impacts of Socioemotional Skills

TABLE 6B.1 **Heckman Selection Model, Pakistan**

Variable	Outcome equation	Selection equation
	Marginal effects on monthly IHS-transformed earnings conditional on being observed (selected)	Probability of observed earnings
Education (reference: no education)		
Primary	0.283 (0.293)	0.009 (0.041)
Secondary	0.459* (0.276)	−0.142*** (0.0361)
Postsecondary	1.363*** (0.325)	0.049 (0.066)
Parental education, years		
Father	0.003 (0.029)	−0.005 (0.004)
Mother	0.105*** (0.036)	−0.011 (0.008)
Raven total score	0.023** (0.011)	0.001 (0.001)
Male	1.092** (0.468)	1.079*** (0.035)
Age	0.159*** (0.057)	0.074*** (0.008)
Age-squared	−0.002** (0.001)	−0.001*** (0.0001)
Urban	0.344 (0.235)	−0.105*** (0.030)
Personality intensity		
Extroversion	0.064 (0.205)	0.009 (0.027)
Conscientiousness	−0.087 (0.209)	0.034 (0.027)
Openness	0.033 (0.187)	−0.045* (0.025)
Emotional stability	−0.042 (0.186)	−0.018 (0.027)
Agreeableness	−0.313* (0.189)	0.007 (0.027)
Grit	−0.013 (0.221)	0.117*** (0.029)
Hostility bias	−0.159 (0.142)	−0.034* (0.020)
Decision-making	0.223 (0.204)	−0.005 (0.028)
Agricultural land ownership	−0.062 (0.047)	0.080* (0.046)
Having at least one disability	0.032 (0.040)	−0.041 (0.049)
Currently married	−0.119** (0.057)	0.153*** (0.049)
Household with a bank account	0.035 (0.034)	−0.045 (0.043)
Observations	3,333	3,333
Heckman is valid; Wald test (rho = 0): (Prob > chi2) < 0.05	Yes	Yes

Source: Data of 2014 Pakistan Labor and Skills Survey (LSS).
Note: The dependent variable is the IHS-transformed monthly wage in local currency units. Marginal effects are reported. IHS = inverse hyperbolic sine.
Standard errors in parentheses; *p < .1 **p < .05 ***p < .01.

TABLE 6B.2 **Mincerian Regression to Measure Returns, Sri Lanka**

Variable	Pooled sample	Informal	Formal
Socioemotional			
Extroversion	−0.085 (0.118)	−0.157 (0.172)	0.182*** (0.0669)
Conscientiousness	−0.211 (0.149)	−0.219 (0.207)	−0.140 (0.091)
Openness	−0.004 (0.123)	−0.032 (0.159)	0.022 (0.106)
Emotional stability	0.028 (0.130)	−0.027 (0.179)	0.183*** (0.067)
Agreeableness	0.0808 (0.142)	−0.00279 (0.181)	0.0836 (0.0956)
Grit	−0.0777 (0.134)	−0.0755 (0.173)	−0.163 (0.105)
Hostility bias	−0.0588 (0.097)	−0.0720 (0.127)	0.0969 (0.071)
Decision-making	0.279* (0.148)	0.272 (0.194)	0.266*** (0.0873)
Cognitive			
Literacy proficiency (vocabulary)	2.586** (1.297)	4.544* (2.386)	−0.0805 (0.490)
Literacy proficiency (sentence)	−3.100 (2.726)	−7.816 (4.794)	0.270 (1.155)
Literacy proficiency (passage)	2.187 (2.306)	2.259 (4.231)	1.356 (1.103)
Education (reference: < primary)			
Lower-secondary	−0.040 (0.314)	0.068 (0.342)	−0.151 (0.222)
Upper-secondary or postsecondary	0.105 (0.317)	−0.051 (0.347)	0.334* (0.188)
Tertiary	0.956*** (0.361)	0.863 (0.657)	0.857*** (0.209)
Socioeconomic controls			
Age	0.130*** (0.045)	0.157*** (0.054)	0.019 (0.028)
Age-squared	−0.002*** (0.001)	−0.002*** (0.001)	−0.001 (0.001)
Male	0.806*** (0.161)	1.115*** (0.225)	0.248*** (0.088)
Father's education ≥ secondary	−0.098 (0.188)	−0.155 (0.240)	0.125 (0.093)
Mother's education ≥ secondary	0.152 (0.169)	0.206 (0.232)	0.117 (0.104)
Currently married	−0.125 (0.180)	−0.185 (0.243)	0.140 (0.112)
Children ages under 6, number	−0.0125 (0.112)	0.0299 (0.150)	−0.076 (0.0855)
Household owns agricultural land	0.400** (0.183)	0.558** (0.233)	−0.128 (0.104)
Household owns nonagricultural land	−0.201 (0.244)	−0.250 (0.309)	0.0689 (0.182)
Received remittances	0.251 (0.227)	0.197 (0.287)	0.186 (0.149)
Transferred money out	−0.120 (0.148)	−0.001 (0.220)	−0.146 (0.119)
Chronic disease	−0.088 (0.186)	0.0102 (0.241)	0.150 (0.151)
Observations	1,090	685	405

Source: 2012 Sri Lanka Skills toward Employment and Productivity (STEP) survey.
Note: The dependent variable is log of hourly wages. Marginal effects are reported.
Standard errors in parentheses; *p < .1 **p < .05 ***p < .01.

TABLE 6B.3 Heckman Selection Model, with and without Education, Pakistan

Variable	With education		Without education	
	Outcome equation	Selection equation	Outcome equation	Selection equation
	Marginal effects on monthly IHS-transformed earnings conditional on observation (selection) of earnings	Probability of observed earnings	Marginal effects on monthly IHS-transformed earnings conditional on observation (selection) of earnings	Probability of observed earnings
Education (base group: no education)				
Primary	0.283 (0.293)	0.001 (0.041)		
Secondary	0.459* (0.276)	−0.142*** (0.036)		
Postsecondary	1.363*** (0.325)	0.049 (0.065)		
Parental education, years				
Father	0.003 (0.028)	−0.005 (0.004)		
Mother	0.105*** (0.035)	−0.011 (0.008)		
Raven total score	0.0228** (0.011)	0.001 (0.001)	0.037*** (0.001)	−0.001 (0.001)
Male (1 if male; 0 if female)	1.092** (0.468)	1.079*** (0.035)	0.971** (0.451)	1.050*** (0.033)
Age	0.159*** (0.0569)	0.0740*** (0.00768)	0.164*** (0.058)	0.077*** (0.008)
Age-squared	−0.002** (0.001)	−0.001*** (0.0001)	−0.002** (0.0001)	−0.001*** (0.0001)
Urban (1 if urban; 0 if rural)	0.344 (0.235)	−0.105*** (0.0298)	0.618*** (0.225)	−0.128*** (0.029)
Personality intensity				
Extroversion	0.063 (0.205)	0.009 (0.027)	0.086 (0.205)	0.007 (0.027)
Conscientiousness	−0.087 (0.209)	0.0341 (0.027)	−0.082 (0.208)	0.041 (0.026)
Openness	0.033 (0.187)	−0.045* (0.025)	0.114 (0.186)	−0.057** (0.025)
Emotional stability	−0.042 (0.186)	−0.018 (0.027)	0.027 (0.185)	−0.014 (0.027)
Agreeableness	−0.313* (0.189)	0.007 (0.027)	−0.269 (0.188)	0.004 (0.027)
Grit	−0.013 (0.221)	0.117*** (0.029)	−0.036 (0.219)	0.119*** (0.028)
Hostility bias	−0.159 (0.142)	−0.034* (0.020)	−0.139 (0.142)	−0.034* (0.020)
Decision-making	0.223 (0.204)	−0.005 (0.0278)	0.179 (0.206)	−0.007 (0.025)
Agricultural land ownership	−0.062 (0.047)	0.080* (0.046)	−0.070 (0.049)	0.085* (0.046)
Having at least one disability	0.032 (0.0401)	−0.041 (0.049)	0.034 (0.042)	−0.041 (0.048)
Currently married	−0.119** (0.057)	0.153*** (0.049)	−0.139** (0.061)	0.168*** (0.049)
Household, w/o bank account in a formal institute	0.035 (0.034)	−0.045 (0.043)	0.052 (0.037)	−0.063* (0.038)
Heckman is valid; Wald test (rho = 0); (Prob ≥ chi 2) < 0.05	Yes	Yes	Yes	Yes
Observations	3,333	3,333	3,365	3,365

Note: The dependent variable is the IHS-transformed monthly wage in local currency units. Marginal effects are reported. IHS = inverse hyperbolic sine.
Standard errors in parentheses; *$p < .1$ **$p < .05$ ***$p < .01$.

TABLE 6B.4 Mincerian Regression to Measure Returns, with and without Education, Sri Lanka

Dependent variable = Log hourly earnings in local currency unit	With education			Without education		
	Overall	Informal	Formal	Overall	Informal	Formal
Socioemotional						
Extroversion intensity	−0.085 (0.118)	−0.157 (0.172)	0.182*** (0.067)	−0.081 (0.104)	−0.149 (0.147)	0.161** (0.071)
Conscientiousness intensity	−0.211 (0.149)	−0.219 (0.207)	−0.140 (0.090)	−0.228* (0.133)	−0.259 (0.182)	−0.064 (0.093)
Openness intensity	−0.004 (0.123)	−0.032 (0.159)	0.022 (0.106)	0.006 (0.104)	−0.063 (0.132)	0.157 (0.097)
Emotional stability intensity	0.028 (0.13)	−0.027 (0.179)	0.183*** (0.067)	0.181 (0.118)	0.130 (0.160)	0.202*** (0.080)
Agreeableness intensity	0.081 (0.142)	−0.003 (0.181)	0.0836 (0.096)	0.0301 (0.132)	−0.0587 (0.165)	0.122 (0.092)
Grit intensity	−0.078 (0.134)	−0.076 (0.173)	−0.163 (0.105)	−0.137 (0.118)	−0.153 (0.152)	−0.229** (0.095)
Hostility bias intensity	−0.056 (0.097)	−0.072 (0.127)	0.0969 (0.071)	−0.065 (0.086)	−0.0821 (0.113)	0.076 (0.067
Decision-making intensity	0.279* (0.148)	0.272 (0.194)	0.266*** (0.087)	0.217 (0.135)	0.209 (0.171)	0.273*** (0.095)
Cognitive						
Literacy proficiency (vocabulary)	2.586** (1.297)	4.544* (2.386)	−0.0805 (0.490)	2.997** (1.250)	4.226** (2.082)	0.235 (0.580)
Literacy proficiency (sentence)	−3.100 (2.726)	−7.816 (4.794)	0.270 (1.155)	−2.128 (2.591)	−7.304* (4.209)	1.777 (1.297)
Literacy proficiency (passage)	2.187 (2.306)	2.259 (4.231)	1.356 (1.103)	5.589** (2.309)	5.088 (3.955)	4.214*** (1.262)
Education (base: ≤ primary)						
Lower-secondary	−0.040 (0.314)	0.068 (0.342)	−0.151 (0.222)			
Upper/postsecondary	0.105 (0.317)	−0.051 (0.347)	0.334* (0.188)			
Tertiary	0.956*** (0.361)	0.863 (0.657)	0.857*** (0.209)			
Socioeconomic controls						
Age	0.130*** (0.045)	0.157*** (0.054)	0.0189 (0.028)	0.0996** (0.039)	0.095** (0.048)	0.043 (0.029)
Age-squared	−0.002*** (0.001)	−0.002*** (0.001)	−0.001 (0.001)	−0.001** (0.001)	−0.001* (0.001)	−0.001 (0.001)
Male	0.806*** (0.161)	1.115*** (0.225)	0.248*** (0.0881)	0.781*** (0.145)	1.061*** (0.205)	0.274*** (0.086)

(continued)

TABLE 6B.4 Mincerian Regression to Measure Returns, with and without Education, Sri Lanka (continued)

Dependent variable = Log hourly earnings in local currency unit	With education			Without education		
	Overall	Informal	Formal	Overall	Informal	Formal
Father's education ≥ secondary (base: ≤ primary)	-0.097 (0.188)	-0.155 (0.240)	0.125 (0.093)			
Mother's education ≥ secondary (base: ≤ primary)	0.152 (0.169)	0.206 (0.232)	0.117 (0.104)			
Currently married	-0.125 (0.180)	-0.185 (0.243)	0.140 (0.112)	-0.110 (0.162)	-0.097 (0.213)	0.106 (0.116)
Children ages under 6, number	-0.0125 (0.112)	0.0299 (0.150)	-0.077 (0.085)	-0.006 (0.101)	0.033 (0.135)	-0.069 (0.086)
Household owns agricultural land	0.400** (0.183)	0.558** (0.233)	-0.128 (0.104)	0.478*** (0.175)	0.655*** (0.222)	-0.152 (0.110)
Household owns nonagricultural land	-0.201 (0.244)	-0.250 (0.309)	0.069 (0.182)	-0.253 (0.231)	-0.266 (0.281)	-0.041 (0.185)
Received remittances	0.251 (0.227)	0.197 (0.287)	0.186 (0.149)	0.180 (0.207)	0.139 (0.258)	0.241 (0.148)
Transferred money out	-0.120 (0.148)	-0.00996 (0.220)	-0.146 (0.119)	-0.081 (0.143)	0.058 (0.198)	-0.141 (0.106)
Chronic disease	-0.088 (0.186)	0.010 (0.241)	0.150 (0.151)	-0.207 (0.183)	-0.187 (0.234)	0.109 (0.145)
Observations	1,090	685	405	1,362	892	470

Note: Marginal effects are reported. The individual or class is informal if any of the following three assumptions hold, and formal otherwise: (1) individuals who are currently working and reported they do not have social security or benefits; (2) individuals who reported they are unpaid workers and have household businesses; (3) individuals who reported they are self-employed and the reported size of their establishments is 1. Wage informal = employed who are currently working, but without social security or benefits. Wage formal = employed who are currently working and have social security. Self-informal = self-employed, currently working, without social security or benefits, and establishment size is 1. Self-formal = self-employed, currently working, and with social security. There is no Raven score available for Sri Lanka. However, the 2012 Sri Lanka Skills toward Employment and Productivity (STEP) survey conducts a literacy assessment of respondents, an essential part of which is to ask respondents relevant questions to evaluate their literacy proficiency in vocabulary, sentence, and passage. Literacy proficiency in vocabulary, sentence, and passage is defined as the number of questions answered correctly, divided by the time used to answer. Standard errors in parentheses; *p < .1 **p < .05 ***p < .01.

TABLE 6B.5 P-Values of Tests: Do Coefficients Differ across Regressions with and without Education Variables at the 95% Confidence Level in Pakistan?

Variable	Outcome equation	Selection equation
Male	0.51	0.02
Age	0.32	0.09
Age-squared	0.24	0.27
Urban	0.00	0.06
Raven score	0.00	0.18
Extroversion intensity	0.42	0.59
Conscientiousness intensity	0.72	0.16
Openness intensity	0.10	0.14
Emotional stability intensity	0.01	0.35
Agreeableness intensity	0.14	0.53
Grit intensity	0.49	0.68
Hostility bias intensity	0.42	0.77
Decision-making intensity	0.19	0.59
Owns agricultural land		0.58
Disability		0.97
Currently married		0.11
Formal bank account		0.34

TABLE 6B.6 P-Values of Tests: Do Coefficients Differ across Regressions with and without Education Variables at the 95% Confidence Level in Sri Lanka?

Variable name	Overall	Informal	Formal
Extroversion intensity	0.94	0.91	0.70
Conscientiousness intensity	0.83	0.72	0.18
Openness intensity	0.89	0.74	0.02
Emotional stability intensity	0.03	0.08	0.64
Agreeableness intensity	0.48	0.56	0.50
Grit intensity	0.30	0.32	0.14
Hostility bias intensity	0.88	0.86	0.66
Decision-making intensity	0.26	0.46	0.91
Literacy proficiency (vocabulary)	0.47	0.78	0.43
Literacy proficiency (sentence)	0.51	0.84	0.09
Literacy proficiency (passage)	0.01	0.16	0.00
Age	0.14	0.02	0.25
Age-squared	0.15	0.03	0.36
Male	0.70	0.52	0.62
Currently married	0.85	0.45	0.58
Children under age 6, number	0.90	0.96	0.88
Household owns agricultural land	0.28	0.31	0.69
Household owns nonagricultural land	0.65	0.92	0.30
Received remittances	0.37	0.56	0.33
Transferred money out	0.57	0.53	0.93
Chronic disease	0.37	0.22	0.69

Notes

1. Based on ILOSTAT data. The International Labour Organization defines the informal economy as all economic activities by workers and economic units, for instance, firms that are de jure or de facto not covered or insufficiently covered by formal arrangements. See ILOSTAT (dashboard), International Labour Organization, Geneva, https://ilostat.ilo.org/.

2. Andrews et al. 2021 provide a useful definition of economic inclusion as the gradual integration of individuals and households into broader economic and community development processes. This integration is achieved by addressing multiple constraints or structural barriers faced by the poor at different levels: the household (for example, human and physical capacity), the community (social norms), the local economy (access to markets and services), and formal institutions (access to political and administrative structures).

3. The division is a ministry-level body headed by a federal minister. The division houses Pakistan's flagship unconditional cash transfer program, the Benazir Income Support Program and related cash transfer programs, as well as the Pakistan Poverty Alleviation Fund.

4. It is possible that the poorer labor market earnings of General Education Development graduates reflect a belief among employers that high school graduates have better skills, rather than actual differences in socioemotional or cognitive skills between these two groups.

5. The Raven score or Raven's Progressive Matrices measures learning outcomes that capture the level of intelligence and motivation needed to complete a task (Hanushek and Woessmann 2008).

6. An essential part of the assessment involves asking respondents relevant questions to evaluate their literacy proficiency in understanding vocabulary, sentence, and passage. Literacy proficiency in this case is defined according to the number of questions answered correctly, divided by the time used to answer. The quantitative analysis covered in this chapter controlled these three variables in the Sri Lanka regressions as proxies for cognitive skills. See annexes 6A and 6B for details on the Pakistan LSS and Sri Lanka STEP survey data and the quantitative analysis.

7. This is the intuition described by Heckman, Stixrud, and Urzua (2006).

8. Inverse hyperbolic sine (IHS) transformation was applied to the earnings variable, which is used frequently for variables that have zero or negative values. It can be approximately interpreted as the natural log transformation.

9. Work experience—measured by age and age-squared—also has a significant impact on earnings. In Pakistan, one more year of work experience increases monthly earnings by 16 percent, conditional on the observation of monthly earnings. In Sri Lanka, the marginal effect of work experience on hourly earnings is 13 percent in the overall sample, which increases to 16 percent in the formal sector and becomes insignificant in the informal sector. These findings are similar to those of Jedwab (2019), although he also finds that the returns to work experience are lower in low-income countries than in high-income countries.

10. Using the same dataset, López Bóo (2016) finds that preschool attendance, early nutrition, the caregiver's education, and primary school attendance are among the factors that influence cognitive development.

11. Sánchez Puerta, Valerio, and Gutiérrez Bernal (2016) provide a cross-country review of programs that aim to boost socioemotional skills.

12. This is the Jawtno (Care) Program administered by the Local Government Division.

References

Acosta, Pablo A., Takiko Igarashi, Rosechin Olfindo, and Jan Rutkowski. 2017. *Developing Socioemotional Skills for the Philippines' Labor Market*. Directions in Development: Human Development Series. Washington, DC: World Bank.

Acosta, Pablo A., and Noël Muller. 2018. "The Role of Cognitive and Socio-emotional Skills in Labor Markets." IZA World of Labor 453 (October), Institute of Labor Economics, Bonn, Germany.

Acosta, Pablo A., Noël Muller, and Miguel Alonso Sarzosa. 2020. "Adults' Cognitive and Socioemotional Skills and Their Labor Market Outcomes in Colombia." *Revista de economía del Rosario* 23 (1): 109–48.

Almlund, Mathilde, Angela Lee Duckworth, James J. Heckman, and Timothy D. Kautz. 2011. "Personality Psychology and Economics." In *Handbook of the Economics of Education*, vol. 4, edited by Eric Alan Hanushek, Stephen J. Machin, and Ludger Woessmann, 1–181. Handbooks in Economics Series. Amsterdam: North-Holland.

Andrews, Colin, Aude de Montesquiou, Inés Arévalo Sánchez, Puja Vasudeva Dutta, Boban Varghese Paul, Sadna Samaranayake, Janet Heisey, Timothy Clay, and Sarang Chaudhary. 2021. *The State of Economic Inclusion Report 2021: The Potential to Scale*. Washington, DC: World Bank.

Autor, David H., Frank Levy, and Richard J. Murnane. 2003. "The Skill Content of Recent Technological Change: An Empirical Exploration." *Quarterly Journal of Economics* 118 (4): 1279–1333.

Borghans, Lex, Bart H. H. Golsteyn, James J. Heckman, and John Eric Humphries. 2016. "What Grades and Achievement Tests Measure." IZA Discussion Paper DP 10356 (November), Institute of Labor Economics, Bonn, Germany.

Borghans, Lex, Bas ter Weel, and Bruce A. Weinberg. 2006. "People People: Social Capital and the Labor-Market Outcomes of Underrepresented Groups." NBER Working Paper 11985 (January), National Bureau of Economic Research, Cambridge, MA.

Brunello, Giorgio, and Martin Schlotter. 2011. "Non Cognitive Skills and Personality Traits: Labour Market Relevance and Their Development in Education and Training Systems." IZA Discussion Paper DP 5743 (May), Institute of Labor Economics, Bonn.

Chevalier, Arnaud, Colm P. Harmon, Vincent O'Sullivan, and Ian Walker. 2013. "The Impact of Parental Income and Education on the Schooling of Their Children." *IZA Journal of Labor Economics* 2 (1), article 8.

Cunningham, Wendy V., Pablo A. Acosta, and Noël Muller. 2016. *Minds and Behaviors at Work: Boosting Socioemotional Skills for Latin America's Workforce*. Directions in Development: Human Development Series. Washington, DC: World Bank.

Cunningham, Wendy V., Mónica Parra Torrado, and Miguel Alonso Sarzosa. 2016. "Cognitive and Non-Cognitive Skills for the Peruvian Labor Market: Addressing Measurement Error through Latent Skills Estimations." Policy Research Working Paper 7550, World Bank, Washington, DC.

Deming, David J. 2017. "The Growing Importance of Social Skills in the Labor Market." *Quarterly Journal of Economics* 132 (4): 1593–1640.

Dercon, Stefan, and Alan Sanchez. 2011. "Long-Term Implications of Under-Nutrition on Psychosocial Competencies: Evidence from Four Developing Countries." Young Lives Working Paper 72 (October), Young Lives, Department of International Development, University of Oxford, Oxford, UK.

de Vries, Robert P., and Peter Jason Rentfrow. 2016. "A Winning Personality: The Effects of Background on Personality and Earnings." January, Sutton Trust, London.

Dunifon, Rachel, and Greg J. Duncan. 1998. "'Soft-Skills' and Long-Run Labor Market Success." *Social Psychology Quarterly* 61 (1): 33–48.

Farkas, George. 1996. *Human Capital or Cultural Capital? Ethnicity and Poverty Groups in an Urban School District*. Social Institutions and Social Change Series. New York: Aldine de Gruyter.

Fletcher, Jason M. 2013. "The Effects of Personality Traits on Adult Labor Market Outcomes: Evidence from Siblings." *Journal of Economic Behavior and Organization* 89 (May): 122–35.

Fletcher, Jason M., and Barbara L. Wolfe. 2016. "The Importance of Family Income in the Formation and Evolution of Non-Cognitive Skills in Childhood." NBER Working Paper 22168 (April), National Bureau of Economic Research, Cambridge, MA.

Greene, William H. 2008. *Econometric Analysis*, 6th ed. Upper Saddle River, NJ: Pearson Education.

Gunewardena, Dileni, Elizabeth King, and Alexandria Valerio. 2018. "More than Schooling: Understanding Gender Differences in the Labor Market when Measures of Skills are Available." Policy Research Working Paper 8588, World Bank, Washington DC.

Hansen, Karsten T., James J. Heckman, and Kathleen J. Mullen. 2004. "The Effect of Schooling and Ability on Achievement Test Scores." *Journal of Econometrics* 121 (1–2): 39–98.

Hanushek, Eric Alan, and Ludger Woessmann. 2008. "The Role of Cognitive Skills in Economic Development." *Journal of Economic Literature* 46 (3): 607–68.

Heckman, James J. 2005. "Invited Comments." In *Lifetime Effects: The High/Scope Perry Preschool Study through Age 40*, ed. Lawrence J. Schweinhart, Jeanne Montie, Zongping Xiang, W. Steven Barnett, Clive R. Belfield, and Milagros Nores, 229–33. Monographs of the High/Scope Educational Research Foundation, 14. Ypsilanti, MI: High/Scope Press.

Heckman, James J., Tomáš Jagelka, and Timothy D. Kautz. 2019. "Some Contributions of Economics to the Study of Personality." NBER Working Paper 26459 (November), National Bureau of Economic Research, Cambridge, MA.

Heckman, James J., and Stefano Mosso. 2014. "The Economics of Human Development and Social Mobility." *Annual Review of Economics* 6 (August): 689–733.

Heckman, James J., and Yona Rubinstein. 2001. "The Importance of Noncognitive Skills: Lessons from the GED Testing Program." *American Economic Review* 91 (2): 145–49.

Heckman James J., Jora Stixrud, and Sergio S. Urzua. 2006. "The Effects of Cognitive and Noncognitive Abilities on Labor Market Outcomes and Social Behavior." *Journal of Labor Economics* 24 (3): 411–82.

Heineck, Guido. 2011. "Does It Pay to Be Nice? Personality and Earnings in the United Kingdom." *ILR Review* 64 (5): 1020–38.

Hilger, Anne, Christophe Jalil Nordman, and Leopold R. Sarr. 2018. "Cognitive and Non-Cognitive Skills, Hiring Channels, and Wages in Bangladesh." IZA Discussion Paper DP 11578 (June), Institute of Labor Economics, Bonn, Germany.

ILO (International Labour Organization). 2019. "Understanding the Gender Pay Gap." Women in Business and Management Brief, ILO, Geneva.

Jedwab, Remi. 2019. "Wage Returns for Work Experience: Development and Urbanisation." *Cities* (blog), February 22, 2019. https://www.theigc.org/blog/wage-returns-for-work-experience-development-and-urbanisation/.

Jencks, Christopher, ed. 1979. *Who Gets Ahead? The Determinants of Economic Success in America.* New York: Basic Books.

Kautz, Timothy D., James J. Heckman, Ron Diris, Bas ter Weel, and Lex Borghans. 2014. "Fostering and Measuring Skills: Improving Cognitive and Non-Cognitive Skills to Promote Lifetime Success." NBER Working Paper 20749 (December), National Bureau of Economic Research, Cambridge, MA.

Kotikula, Aphichoke, Ruth Vargas Hill, and Wameq Azfar Raza. 2019. "What Works for Working Women? Understanding Female Labor Force Participation in Urban Bangladesh." World Bank, Washington, DC.

Lee, Sun Youn, and Fumio Ohtake. 2016. "Is Being Agreeable a Key to Success or Failure in the Labor Market?" ISER Discussion Paper 960 (February), Institute of Social and Economic Research, Osaka University, Osaka, Japan.

Lenton, Pamela. 2014. "Personality Characteristics, Educational Attainment, and Wages: An Economic Analysis Using the British Cohort Study." Sheffield Economic Research Paper SERPS 2014011 (August), Institute for Economic Analysis of Decision-Making, Department of Economics, University of Sheffield, Sheffield, UK.

Leroy, Jef L., Marie Ruel, and Ellen Verhofstadt. 2009. "The Impact of Conditional Cash Transfer Programmes on Child Nutrition: A Review of Evidence Using a Programme Theory Framework." *Journal of Development Effectiveness* 1 (2): 103–29.

Lleras, Christy. 2008. "Do Skills and Behaviors in High School Matter? The Contribution of Noncognitive Factors in Explaining Differences in Educational Attainment and Earnings." *Social Science Research* 37 (3): 888–902.

López Bóo, Florencia. 2016. "Socio-Economic Status and Early Childhood Cognitive Skills: A Mediation Analysis Using the Young Lives Panel." *International Journal of Behavioral Development* 40 (6): 500–08.

Mincer, Jacob A. 1974. *Schooling, Experience, and Earnings.* Vol. 2 of *Human Behavior and Social Institutions.* Cambridge, MA: National Bureau of Economic Research; New York: Columbia University Press.

Murnane, Richard J., John B. Willett, Yves Duhaldeborde, and John H. Tyler. 2000. "How Important Are the Cognitive Skills of Teenagers in Predicting Subsequent Earnings?" *Journal of Policy Analysis and Management* 19 (4): 547–68.

Nießen, Désirée, Daniel Danner, Marion Spengler, and Clemens M. Lechner. 2020. "Big Five Personality Traits Predict Successful Transitions from School to Vocational Education and Training: A Large-Scale Study." *Frontiers in Psychology* July 31. https://www.frontiersin.org/articles/10.3389/fpsyg.2020.01827/full.

Nieuwenhuis, Jaap. 2018. "The Interaction between School Poverty and Agreeableness in Predicting Educational Attainment." *Personality and Individual Differences* 127 (June 1): 85–88.

Noftle, Erik E., and Richard W. Robins. 2007. "Personality Predictors of Academic Outcomes: Big Five Correlates of GPA and SAT Scores." *Journal of Personality and Social Psychology* 93 (1): 116–30.

Nomura, Shinsaku, and Samik Adhikari. 2017. "The Influence of Non-Cognitive Skills on Wages within and between Firms: Evidence from Bangladesh's Formal Sector." Policy Research Working Paper 8053, World Bank, Washington, DC.

Nyhus, Ellen K., and Empar Pons. 2005. "The Effect of Personality on Earnings." *Journal of Economic Psychology* 26 (3): 363–84.

Ohnsorge, Franziska L., and Shu Yu, eds. 2021. *The Long Shadow of Informality: Challenges and Policies*. Advance edition. Washington, DC: World Bank.

Orrell, Brent. 2018. "STEM without Fruit: How Noncognitive Skills Improve Workforce Outcomes." November, American Enterprise Institute, Washington, DC.

Owusu-Addo, Ebenezer, and Ruth Cross. 2014. "The Impact of Conditional Cash Transfers on Child Health in Low- and Middle-Income Countries: A Systematic Review." *International Journal of Public Health* 59 (4): 609–18.

Sahn, David E., and Kira M. Villa. 2016. "Labor Outcomes during the Transition from Adolescence to Adulthood: The Role of Personality, Cognition, and Shocks in Madagascar." IZA Discussion Paper DP 10359 (November), Institute of Labor Economics, Bonn, Germany.

Saltiel, F., M. Sarzosa, and S. Urzúa. 2017. "Cognitive and Socio-Emotional Abilities." In *Handbook of Contemporary Education Economics*, edited by G. Johnes, J. Johnes, T. Agasisti, and L. López-Torres. Cheltenham, UK: Edward Elgar Publishing.

Sánchez, Alan. 2017. "The Structural Relationship between Early Nutrition, Cognitive Skills, and Non-Cognitive Skills in Four Developing Countries." *Economics and Human Biology* 27 (Part A): 33–54.

Sánchez Puerta, Maria Laura, Alexandria Valerio, and Marcela Gutiérrez Bernal. 2016. *Taking Stock of Programs to Develop Socioemotional Skills: A Systematic Review of Program Evidence*. Directions in Development: Human Development Series. Washington, DC: World Bank.

Ulyssea, Gabriel. 2018. "Firms, Informality, and Development: Theory and Evidence from Brazil." *American Economic Review* 108 (8): 2015–47.

Ulyssea, Gabriel. 2020. "Informality: Causes and Consequences for Development." *Annual Review of Economics* 12 (August): 525–46.

West, Martin R., Matthew A. Kraft, Amy S. Finn, Rebecca E. Martin, Angela L. Duckworth, Christopher F. O. Gabrieli, and John D. E. Gabrieli. 2016. "Promise and Paradox: Measuring Students' Non-Cognitive Skills and the Impact of Schooling." *Educational Evaluation and Policy Analysis* 38 (1): 148–70.

World Bank. 2020. *Poverty and Shared Prosperity 2020: Reversals of Fortune*. Washington, DC: World Bank.

Yamauchi, Futoshi, Shinsaku Nomura, Saori Imaizumi, Ana Carolina Areias, and Afra Rahman Chowdhury. 2018. "Asymmetric Information on Noncognitive Skills in the Indian Labor Market: An Experiment in Online Job Portal." Policy Research Working Paper 8378, World Bank, Washington, DC.

CHAPTER 7

Workers at Risk: Panel Data Evidence on the COVID-19 Labor Market Crisis in India

MAURIZIO BUSSOLO, ANANYA KOTIA, AND SIDDHARTH SHARMA

Introduction

There is growing concern about the vulnerability of informal workers, who number more than 1.6 billion worldwide, to the adverse labor market impacts of the COVID-19 crisis (ILO 2020a, 2020b; World Bank 2020). Informal workers are not covered by formal employment protection laws and social insurance programs; they are typically concentrated in microenterprises or small firms that have limited cash reserves for paying employees in the event of insufficient earnings. Informal workers may have limited access to relief measures introduced by governments in response to the COVID-19 crisis. It is also likely that they have less capacity than formal workers to cope with this shock, owing to their lower levels of savings and poorer access to credit.

This chapter contributes to the knowledge base on the impact of the COVID-19 crisis on informal workers in low- and middle-income economies by presenting a difference in differences event study analysis using a large, nationally representative panel dataset. The setting of this study is India, where informal employment accounts for more than 85 percent of total employment (World Bank 2020). The focus is on a specific group of informal employment: the informal wage workers, namely, workers who receive a remuneration for their services but have no formal work contract and tend to have temporary engagements (as the daily wage workers). Informal employment also includes people who are self-employed. This chapter compares and contrasts the impact of COVID-19 on three groups: informal wage workers, self-employed, and formal workers. The Indian economy was hit hard by the onset of the pandemic and by the stringent lockdown measures taken to control the spread of the disease. The unemployment rate exceeded 23 percent by early April 2020, and the gross domestic product (GDP) declined by 23.9 percent year-on-year during the second quarter (April to June) of 2020 (Vyas 2020).

The chapter first documents a sharp overall decline in employment by April 2020 following the imposition of a comprehensive national lockdown in late March that lasted until early May. Only 59 percent of those individuals who were employed in December 2019 were still employed as of April 2020. The magnitude of this drop in the employment rate is consistent with estimates reported in other recent studies on the impact of COVID-19 on India (for example, Bertrand, Krishnan, and Schofield 2020; Deshpande 2020; Dhingra and Machin 2020; Lee et al. 2020). It is also a stark departure from pre-COVID times. For instance, in contrast to the precipitous decline in the employment rate between December 2019 and April 2020, about 95 percent of those who had been employed in August 2019 were still employed in December 2019.

Informal wage workers experienced a more severe shock relative to formal workers. Only 43 percent of those who were in informal jobs in December 2019 were still employed in April 2020. The corresponding employment retention rate among those initially in the formal sector was 72 percent. Furthermore, households headed by an informal wage worker experienced a significantly higher drop in per capita household income compared with households headed by formal wage workers.

Any interpretation of this observed differential labor market shock affecting informal wage workers needs to consider the fact that the vulnerability of jobs to the COVID-19 pandemic and the associated lockdown measures has varied across industries and occupations. For example, jobs involving tasks that are inherently less amenable to remote work have been more vulnerable during the crisis (Dingel and Neiman 2020). Could it be that informal wage workers experienced more adverse outcomes than formal workers during the early COVID-19 period—not because of their informal work status but because they happen to be concentrated in more vulnerable industries or occupations?

To examine this question, the analysis estimates the differential experiences of post-COVID shocks between formal and informal wage workers through difference in differences event study regressions that control for shocks specific to industries, occupations, and locations (districts). The results indicate that some of the excess vulnerability of informal wage workers in the early phase of the COVID-19 crisis can be accounted for by the greater vulnerability of the industries and occupations in which these workers are concentrated. However, a substantial portion of the differential experiences between formal and informal wage workers persists despite the additional controls. For instance, between December 2019 and April 2020, after one controls for industry-wave and district-wave fixed effects, households headed by informal wage workers underwent a decline in per capita household income that was 10 percentage points larger than the corresponding decline among households headed by formal workers. This finding suggests that informal wage employment was inherently more vulnerable during the early COVID-19 shock.

Furthermore, even the self-employed fared better than informal wage workers in the early phase of the COVID-19 crisis. After one controls for industry-wave and district-wave fixed effects, there is no statistically discernible difference in the employment retention rates or incomes of the self-employed relative to formal workers. Self-employment may also have served as a fallback for wage workers who had lost their jobs. Thus, about 18 percent of wage workers who were in the formal sector or the informal sector in December 2019 were in self-employment by April 2020.

The differential labor market shock experienced by informal wage workers during the national lockdown in India did not persist. After April–May 2020, labor market outcomes began recovering toward pre-COVID levels more rapidly among informal workers than among formal workers. By August 2020, there was no longer a significant differential between informal and formal wage workers in the decline in the employment rate or in income relative to pre-COVID levels. Indeed, if one controls for industry-wave, occupation-wave, and location-wave fixed effects, the gap between the incomes of household heads in the formal sector and households heads in the informal sector was substantially smaller by June 2020 than it had been pre-COVID. This suggests that informal workers quickly caught up once the lockdown had been lifted.

The chapter adds to the mounting global evidence that the labor market impacts of the COVID-19 crisis have been unequal. The crisis appears to have reduced employment and income disproportionately among less well-educated or lower-wage workers, women, migrants, and more contingent workers (Abraham, Basole, and Kesar 2021; Adams-Prassl et al. 2020; Bhalotia, Dhingra and Kondirolli 2020; Deshpande 2020; Gulyas and Pytka 2020; Guven, Sotirakopoulos, and Ulker 2020; Kikuchi, Kitao, and Mikoshiba 2021; Mattana, Smeets, and Warzynski 2020). As most of this evidence is derived in the context of high-income countries, a key contribution of this chapter is the fact that it addresses the important dimension of informality in low- and middle-income countries.

In related work in the context of India, Abraham, Basole, and Kesar (2021) and Lee et al. (2020) find that the crisis affected daily-wage workers more severely than workers with more permanent job contracts, and Dhingra and Machin (2020) conclude that workers with greater guaranteed job tenure experienced relatively smaller declines in employment and earnings.[1] Nevertheless, this chapter appears to be the first analysis to rely on nationally representative panel data to explore differences in post-COVID outcomes between formal and informal workers systemically.

Because the dataset used here spans a relatively long post-COVID period (up to December 2020 in the case of employment), the analysis is also able to investigate the trajectory of labor markets several months after the onset of the crisis and associated lockdown measures. In this sense, the chapter echoes work on the United States by Lee, Park, and Shin (2021), who find that, while the early labor market impact of the pandemic differed across sex, age, and education, these differentials had disappeared by November 2020.

The analysis here also contributes to the broader literature on the effect of informality in the labor market on the response of economies to shocks. In particular, the more elastic response of informal wage employment that one may observe may be related to the more contingent or flexible nature of informal employment relationships compared with the more regulated and inflexible nature of formal employment. Data limitations impeded the ability to test this hypothesis, but there is prior evidence that the employment protection provisions of India's industrial labor laws, which apply to formal (permanent) workers, constrain employers in adjusting their formal workforce in response to local weather-related shocks and shift the burden of adjustment to the informal (temporary) workforce (Adhvaryu, Chari, and Sharma 2013; Chaurey 2015). A similar asymmetry in labor adjustment along the formal and informal margins is possible in the face of macroshocks. For example, unemployment in European countries during the global economic crisis of 2007–11 was concentrated among temporary workers and, to a greater extent, in countries with more stringent employment protection laws for permanent workers relative to temporary workers (Bentolila et al. 2012; Sharma and Winkler 2018). Alfaro, Becerra, and Eslava (2020), meanwhile, model the impact of the COVID crisis in economies with a prevalence of informality and small firms and use the model to conduct a counterfactual analysis relying on pre-COVID data on Colombia and the United States. Their analysis, too, suggests that informal employment was at greater risk in the early stages of the crisis because of the low cash reserves among small firms and the lack of employment protection. However, informal employment may recover more rapidly than formal employment because of the greater flexibility in hiring and firing and the lower dependence on organizational and physical capital in informal employment.

The idea that the informal sector can be both vulnerable and a source of resilience because of its greater flexibility is not new (Loayza and Rigolini 2011). Yet, the chapter contributes to a long-standing debate on flexibility as a salient characteristic of informality (for instance, see Maloney 2004). Moreover, our finding that self-employment served as a buffer during the COVID-19 crisis adds to the literature on how poor households cope with large aggregate shocks (for example, McKenzie 2003; Skoufias 2003).

The chapter concludes with two additional findings that are worth examining in future research. First, the analysis finds that the differential response of informal wage employment to the COVID-19 lockdown was primarily an urban occurrence. Both rural and urban areas witnessed a major labor market shock during the lockdown, evident in the unemployment rates crossing 20 percent in April and May 2020 (Vyas 2020). Unlike urban areas, however, rural areas did not experience a statistically significant difference in the post-COVID trajectories of formal and informal workers. The analysis confirms that this difference in how COVID-19 affected rural and urban labor markets did not arise because of differing industrial and occupational profiles. Unlike their urban counterparts, workers in rural areas have access to a jobs guarantee scheme, the Mahatma Gandhi National Rural Employment Guarantee Program (MGNREGA), which has cushioned rural job losses during the COVID-19 crisis (Afridi, Mahajan, and Sangwan 2021).[2] However, there was a lockdown on MGNREGA activities until April 20, 2020.[3] This suggests that the urban-rural difference in the impact of the lockdown shock in April reflects some other, unobserved urban-rural differences in labor market conditions or institutions.

Second, the analysis has highlighted an intriguing inconsistency between the relative declines in income and consumption across households headed by informal and formal wage workers. In contrast to income, the percentage drop in per capita household consumption expenditure in the early phase of COVID-19 was significantly larger in households headed by formal workers (who tend to be richer) than in households headed by informal workers. This inconsistency is puzzling in light of standard theories of how household consumption responds to temporary income shocks. These theories predict that households will use savings or borrowing to smooth consumption intertemporally if the incomes of the households fall temporarily. Relative to informal households, formal households are expected to have better access to consumption-smoothing mechanisms. Yet, the patterns the analysis has uncovered suggest that the former were able to smooth consumption more efficiently during the early COVID-19 income shock.

Although a full investigation of this issue is beyond the scope of this chapter, the analysis has reviewed potential explanations. The first explanation relates to the fact that the lockdown shock not only affected household incomes but also directly restricted household consumption opportunities. Specifically, it may be that the lockdowns imposed more restrictions on the consumption possibilities of richer formal households because these households tend to consume disproportionately more nonessentials. A second explanation relates to a potential differential mismeasurement of real consumption. Thus, it may be that the prices of items consumed more intensively by informal households rose more quickly during the lockdowns so that the real consumption of these households fell relatively more precipitously than suggested by the drop in nominal household expenditures. According to a third explanation, it may be that formal households expected the initial COVID-19 income shock to last longer, while informal households did not have this same expectation. Consequently, the former adjusted their consumption expenditure by larger amounts, leading to a larger decline in these expenditures. This is also consistent with the observation that the incomes of households headed by informal workers eventually recovered more quickly.

The rest of the chapter is organized as follows. A brief timeline of the pandemic and the lockdowns is summarized in the next section. The subsequent section describes the data, the variables used in the analysis, and the sample. The section entitled "Descriptive Analysis" presents relevant descriptive statistics. The section entitled "Empirical Specification: Event Study Analysis" introduces the empirical specification. The final section concludes and sets out the results of the difference in differences event study.

Background: Onset of COVID-19 and the Government Response

The timeline of COVID-19 in India begins on January 30, 2020, when the first COVID-19 case was confirmed in the state of Kerala (Andrews et al. 2020). The daily number of new, confirmed cases reached about 100 by March 30; 1,000 by April 15; 5,000 by May 20; and 10,000 by June 10.[4]

The federal government announced a nationwide lockdown in late March, effective March 25 to April 14.[5] Although a stepwise, limited easing of lockdown conditions commenced in late April, the nationwide lockdown was ultimately extended until May 18. Even after this lockdown lapsed, many state governments continued to impose lockdowns until late July.

The first phase of the lockdown was among the most stringent in the world (Hall, Jones, and Klenow 2020). Only essential businesses, such as banks, internet services, and shops selling food, were allowed to operate. All educational institutions and nonessential public and private establishments were closed, including nonessential transport and hospitality establishments. Large gatherings were prohibited. In late April, the government announced some easing of restrictions in areas that had not yet experienced COVID-19 cases. For example, agricultural activities, rural public works, and some industrial activities were permitted in these areas. By early May, districts were being categorized by the government as green, orange, or red zones, based on their COVID-19 risk profile. Restrictions on mobility and economic activity were the most stringent in red zones. In mid-May, state governments were given more leeway in tailoring lockdown criteria. By late July, the lockdown restrictions had generally been lifted everywhere except in containment zones.

Indicators of mobility based on smartphone tracking showed a sharp decline in mobility during the lockdown. For example, when the lockdown was implemented in late March, the estimated presence of workers at the workplace declined by a rate between 50 and 70 percent, while the presence of individuals at places of residence rose. The estimated presence at the workplace had recovered partially by the end of May, but it was still one-third lower than pre-COVID levels (Beyer, Franco-Bedoya, and Galdo 2021).

Data

The main dataset is the Consumer Pyramids Household Survey (CPHS), which is implemented by the Center for Monitoring Indian Economy (CMIE). The CPHS is administered on a panel of more than 170,000 households across India three times a year. The survey is typically conducted face-to-face; however, owing to the COVID lockdown in India after the third week of March, the face-to-face interview format was replaced with a telephone survey, allowing CMIE to continue gathering data. The response rate relative to the planned execution was a little over 60 percent during the lockdown, compared with over 95 percent before the lockdown (Vyas 2020).

The CMIE maintains that, even with the reduced sample, the data are representative of the population across several dimensions. Thus, the rural-urban divide of the CPHS sample is typically about 37:63. In the first week of the lockdown (ending March 31), this had shifted to 46:54, but it was restored to prelockdown levels by week 3.

SAMPLE SELECTION

The full CPHS sample of over 170,000 households is normally surveyed over a four-month period, called a "wave," during which the survey team is continuously in the field. Each wave of the survey is representative of the Indian population. A new CPHS wave begins immediately after the previous wave ends, and every household in the panel is potentially resurveyed at approximately a four-month interval.

Within a wave, the execution of the survey is planned such that the households surveyed during a month are well distributed over the country. In this sense, the set of households covered in one full month of the survey may be considered a representative subsample of the full panel. Every such monthly cohort reappears in the CPHS panel at four-month intervals.

India imposed a lockdown in the third week of March, which fell in the middle of wave 19 of the survey. To capture the impact of the COVID shock, the analysis therefore focused the sample on the households that were interviewed in the month of April 2020, as part of wave 19. Previously, this set of households—the April 2020 cohort—had been interviewed in December 2019 (wave 18), August 2019 (wave 17), April 2019 (wave 16), and December 2018 (wave 15). The April 2020 cohort was reinterviewed in August 2020 (wave 20) and December 2020 (wave 21). Including only those households from the April 2020 cohort that responded to the survey in all these waves, a balanced panel of 14,695 individuals of working age (ages 15 or older) in 4,862 households from December 2018 to December 2020 (waves 15–21) was created for the analysis. Given the balanced rollout of the survey, this sample spans 28 states of India.

VARIABLES

The analysis used individual-level data on employment status, employment arrangement, district, industry, and occupation. Individuals are considered unemployed if they report their employment status as "unemployed, willing, and looking for a job." They are considered out of the labor force if they report their employment status as "unemployed, not willing, and not looking for a job" or "unemployed, willing, but not looking for a job."

The CPHS asks individuals to report only their employment status during the current month. Employment outcomes are thus observed at four-month intervals. Specifically, for the main panel of individuals, employment outcomes are observed in the pre-COVID months of December 2018 (wave 15), April 2019 (wave 16), August 2019 (wave 17), and December 2019 (wave 18), and in the post-COVID months of April 2020 (wave 19), August 2020 (wave 20), and December 2020 (wave 21). The analysis of employment relies on a panel of 14,695 individuals at a frequency of four months. Of these individuals, 7,467 are unemployed or out of the labor force throughout the sample period. The analysis is based on the remaining 7,182 individuals.

In contrast to the employment data, the CPHS provides household income and consumption data at a monthly frequency. For example, households visited in April 2020 report income and consumption for not only April 2020 but also March, February, and January 2020. Hence, household income and consumption are observed each month. The analysis of income and consumption thus uses a monthly panel of 4,632 households from October 2019 to August 2020.

The CPHS describes the employment arrangement of each employed individual as follows: (1) permanent, salaried; (2) temporary, salaried; (3) self-employed; and (4) daily wage or casual. Individuals are defined as informal if they are either daily wage workers or temporary salaried workers. Permanently salaried individuals are treated as formal workers.[6]

The analysis seeks to clarify how the pandemic affected these worker types differentially. The focus is therefore on the employment status of individuals during the last prepandemic wave of the CPHS, that is, December 2019. The employment arrangement of an individual is defined as a time-invariant individual characteristic, which is fixed at the initial December 2019 level.[7] Doing this allows a study of the differential labor market patterns among workers who were initially employed in the formal sector rather than self-employed or employed as informal workers using the difference in differences event study methodology. Similarly, the income and consumption analysis categorizes households as formal, informal, or self-employed, based on the employment arrangements of the household heads.

Table 7.1 shows key summary statistics for each worker type in the balanced panel sample during the last prepandemic wave, that is, December 2019.[8] Although all worker categories exhibit similar levels of employment, informal workers earn and consume a lot less than their formal and self-employed counterparts. The average per capita household income among informal workers is less than one-half the

TABLE 7.1 **Descriptive Statistics of Outcome Variables, by Worker Type**

Worker type	Employed, %	Per capita household income, Rs	Per capita household consumption, Rs	Rural, %	Women, %	Completed high school, %	In high face-to-face industries, %
Formal	79.01	10,195	4,879	17.2	17.9	82.5	49.3
Informal	72.98	4,958	3,015	28.8	20.8	36.6	79.1
Self-employed	76.61	7,321	3,640	30.2	10.5	55.3	50.0

Source: Statistics based on a balanced sample of 7,467 individuals and 4,632 households in the 7-wave balanced panel in December 2019.
Note: Completed high school = passing the grade 10 examinations. High face-to-face industries are communication, education, entertainment and sports, hotels and restaurants, media and publishing, personal and professional services, personal nonprofessional services, post and courier, public administrative services, retail trade, travel and tourism, and wholesale trade. Rs = rupees.

corresponding average among formal workers, and the average per capita consumption among the informal is only 62 percent of the corresponding average among formal households. Compared with formal workers, a larger share of informal workers and their self-employed counterparts is rural residents. The share of women is slightly higher among informal workers than among formal workers, but it is nearly twice the share among the self-employed. Informal workers are the least well educated among the three worker groups; only 37 percent of informal workers have completed high school, compared with 82 percent of formal workers and 55 percent of the self-employed. Informal workers are also significantly more likely than the other worker types to be employed in face-to-face contact-intense industries (80 percent, versus about 50 percent among the other two types). Because such industries were inherently more vulnerable to the early COVID-19 shock, controlling for industry-specific shocks is important in assessing the relevance of informality in isolation from relevance of industry.

Descriptive Analysis

The unprecedented labor market shock from the onset of COVID-19 and the sudden imposition of a national lockdown in late March 2020 are evident in figure 7.1, which illustrates the estimated employment transition in two successive four-month intervals using the panel of individuals. (See annex 7A, table 7A.1 for the corresponding transition matrix.)

The flows describe the transitions among working-age individuals across four labor market categories: formal wage employment, self-employment, informal wage employment, and unemployment/out of the labor force (Unemp/OLF). Figure 7.1, panel a, represents the pre-COVID August 2019–December 2019 period; figure 7.1, panel b, presents the transitions from a pre-COVID starting point (December 2019) to a postlockdown end point (April 2020). Figure 7.1, panel a, is used as a benchmark of typical worker transitions for comparison with the situation during the postpandemic churning in India's labor markets.

Overall, about 41 percent of the individuals employed in December 2019 were unemployed or out of the labor force by April 2020. This is a far higher rate of job loss than the typical prelockdown flows out of employment. For example, only about 5 percent of those employed in August 2019 were out of employment as of December 2019.

Figure 7.1 also highlights that there was considerable heterogeneity in the COVID shock. Accordingly, the likelihood of employment loss was greater among individuals initially working in the informal sector than among those initially in formal jobs. Informal workers are also more vulnerable than the self-employed. Among individuals in informal jobs in December 2019, over 57 percent were not in employment in April 2020. Those initially self-employed in December 2019 showed a 33 percent chance of

FIGURE 7.1 Labor Market Churning Before and During the Lockdown

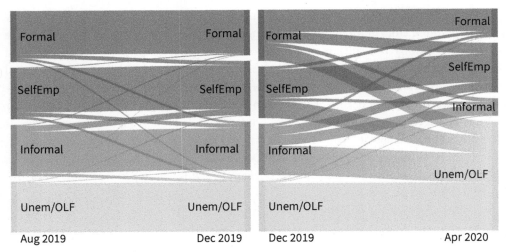

Source: Based on CPHS data.
Note: The figure shows transition flows, in percentages, between successive survey waves among the four worker categories in the data. Panel a shows typical transition patterns before the pandemic, between August and December 2019. Panel b shows transitions during the pandemic, between December 2019 and April 2020. See annex 7A, table 7A.1 for the corresponding transition matrix. SelfEmp = self-employed; Unem/OLF = unemployed or out of the labor force.

not being employed in April 2020, while those formally employed in December 2019 showed a 28 percent chance of being unemployed or out of the labor force in April 2020.

As indicated by the prepandemic flows illustrated in figure 7.1, panel a, transitions between formal and informal jobs are rare in normal times. In particular, only 1.6 percent of individuals in the informal sector move into the formal sector during a typical four-month interval. Thus, in normal times, informality is a persistent status, and upward mobility is rare. This partly justifies treating informality as a predetermined attribute in the analysis of the COVID shock.

After the lockdown, a strikingly larger share of individuals initially working in the formal sector transitioned into the informal sector or self-employment. Likewise, an unusually large share of individuals initially employed in informal wage jobs transitioned into self-employment. Overall, among individuals in formal or informal wage jobs in December 2019, about 18 percent were in self-employment in April 2020.

Transition matrices for the April 2020–December 2020 period—not presented here for the sake of brevity—show that there was a recovery in aggregate employment after May 2020. However, this aggregate recovery masks ongoing churning across job categories. Individuals continued moving out of formal or informal wage jobs into self-employment at unusually high rates compared with pre-COVID times. Moreover, an unusually large share of individuals who were either unemployed or out of the labor force in April 2020 reported that, by August 2020, they had moved, not into wage jobs, but into self-employment.

As a result, by August 2020, six months into the COVID crisis in India, employment among individuals as a share of the total working-age population had nearly recovered to pre-COVID levels, although the composition of employment had shifted radically toward self-employment (figure 7.2). Expressed as a share of total employment, formal wage employment shrank by nearly 30 percent between December 2019 and August 2020. Informal wage employment also shrank, although only marginally, while self-employment expanded from 48.2 percent of the total employed in December 2019 to 55 percent in August 2020.

Post-COVID trends in per capita income largely mirror the trajectory of employment rates. Figure 7.3 compares the trajectory of per capita incomes across formal and informal households in the panel dataset. Households are divided into formal wage earners, informal wage earners, and the self-employed, based on the baseline employment status of the household head in December 2019. The mean per capita income (in logs) is estimated for each group in each month between July 2019 and August 2020. To facilitate the visualization of the differential income trends after the onset of COVID-19, the log

FIGURE 7.2 Cross-Sectional Breakdown of the Labor Market

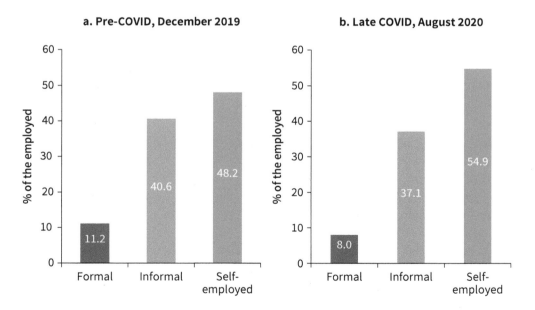

Source: Based on CPHS data.
Note: The figure shows the distribution of employed individuals in formal jobs, informal jobs, and self-employment. The data pertain to the full Consumer Pyramids Household Survey sample from wave 18 (panel a) to wave 20 (panel b).

FIGURE 7.3 **Index of Per Capita Household Income, by Worker Group, February 2020**

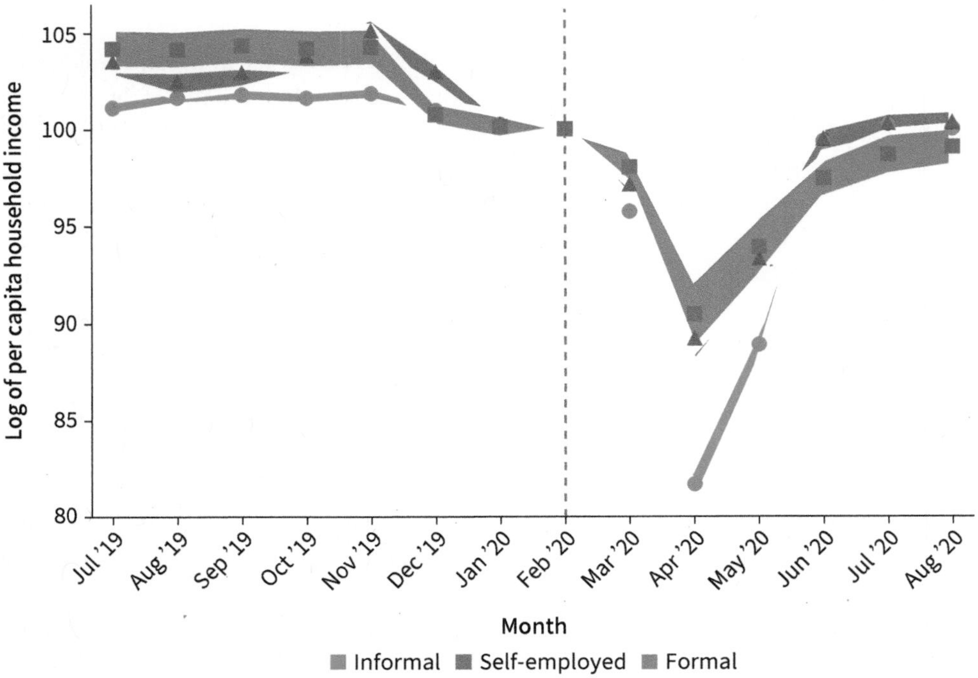

Source: Based on CPHS data.
Note: The figure shows mean levels of per capita household income (natural logarithm) by worker category. For ease of comparability, all group means are normalized to 100 in February 2020, which is used as a base because it was the last prepandemic month.
95% standard errors are reported in shaded areas around the group means.

mean per capita income of each group in February 2020—the last pre-COVID month—is normalized to 100. The figure also shows the 95 percent confidence intervals of the estimated means.

Figure 7.3 demonstrates that, while all three types of households experienced sharp drops in per capita income in April and May 2020 on average, informal wage households were affected the most severely. The log mean per capita income of informal wage households declined by nearly 20 percent between February 2020 and April 2020. In comparison, the log mean per capita income of formal wage households and self-employed households declined by 10 percent during that period.

Incomes began to recover to pre-COVID levels after May 2020. Mean per capita incomes rebounded most rapidly among informal wage households. The differential between these households and other types of households in the mean post-COVID income decline did not persist beyond May 2020.

Empirical Specification: Event Study Analysis

The formal approach adopted in the analysis to assess the differential impact of the COVID-19 crisis across groups of workers is a difference in differences event study panel regression. A multiperiod specification is used for the employment regression, as follows:

$$Employed_{it} = \alpha \, WorkerCategory_i + \Sigma_t \beta_t \, WAVE_t +$$
$$\Sigma_{t,c} \gamma_{t,c} WorkerCategory_i \times WAVE_t + \Sigma_{t,j} \lambda_{jt}(X_j \times WAVE_t) + \varepsilon_{it}, \qquad (7.1)$$

where the dependent variable is a dummy variable equal to 1 if the worker is employed and zero otherwise; $WorkerCategory_i$ is a variable representing whether a worker is informal or self-employed (formal workers are the omitted category); $WAVE_t$ is a dummy variable indicating each survey wave; $\Sigma_{t,j} X_j \times WAVE_t$ are time interacted fixed effects, specifically, $State \times Wave_t$, $Industry \times Wave_t$, $Occupation \times WAVE_t$.[9] These control for district-wave–specific shocks, such as the incidence of COVID-19 and the intensity of lockdown measures in a district over time, and time varying shocks at the industry and occupation levels.

$WorkerCategory_i$ does not have a time subscript. An individual's worker category in December 2019 defines this time-invariant attribute. The main coefficients of interest, the γ's, thus capture the differential impact of the crisis on workers who were initially informal or self-employed relative to initially formal workers.

This specification is also used for the income and consumption regressions. However, because income and consumption are observed for each month, monthly time dummies are used instead of wave dummies, as in equation 7.1.

The event study approach estimates the heterogeneous impact of COVID on different worker categories during each time period. Thus, not only can the differential impact be estimated during the lockdowns, but whether the recovery in later month differs across worker types may also be observed. For all regressions, the last observed pre-COVID time period is the omitted time dummy so that all regression coefficients are scaled with reference to this base period. For employment regressions that are at a four-month wave frequency, the base period is wave 18 of the survey (ending in December 2019); for monthly frequency regressions for income and consumption, the base period is February 2020.

Event study visuals also allow us to examine whether the assumption of parallel trends holds for the dependent variable or variables before the shock. This flexible approach exploits the time dimension of the panel data. The cost of restricting the sample to individuals who are repeatedly observed is a slightly reduced household sample size. The main results on the differential impact of COVID-19 are robust to the use of a two-period panel with a larger sample size.

Results

THE IMPACT OF COVID ON EMPLOYMENT AND INCOME

The regressions confirm the descriptive analysis, that is, the peak of the crisis in April 2020 coincides with the most stringent phase of India's lockdown. It was associated with a large loss of jobs. Most importantly, the probability of job loss was greater among informal workers than among formal workers.

The regression estimates of equation 7.1 are presented in annex 7A, table 7A.2. Column 1 of the table corresponds to a specification with only individual fixed effects. Columns 2–4 successively add district-time, industry-time, and wave-time fixed effects. Column 3, with individual, district-wave, and industry-wave fixed effects, is the preferred specification.

In the regression specification without any time-specific fixed effects (column 1), one may calculate that, in April 2020, there is a sharp rise in the probability of job loss (and a corresponding large reduction in the employment rate) for each employment group relative to December 2019. Because formal workers are the reference group, the decline among formal workers corresponds to the value of the $\beta_{Apr\ 2020}$ coefficient, which is 15 percentage points. The additional penalty for informal workers (the value of the coefficient $\gamma_{Apr\ 2020}$) is 21 percentage points, which, summed with the 15 percentage points, means that the total loss of employment among informal workers is 36 percentage points.

The magnitude of the differential impact of the pandemic falls as more fixed effects are added in columns 2–4 of table 7A.2, but it remains statistically significant and economically large: informal workers are more vulnerable even after one controls for a variety of fixed effects. The initial difference of 21 percentage points is reduced to 19 percentage points if district-wave fixed effects are added as controls (table 7A.2, column 2). These fixed effects control for factors such as the time-varying intensity of COVID-19 or the lockdown across Indian districts, and they also control for any district-time variation in the ability of local governments to contain the virus. A mere 2 percentage point reduction indicates that these factors do not play a major role in explaining the vulnerability of informal jobs during the pandemic. The magnitude of the differential impact of the pandemic falls by over two-thirds, to 6 percentage points, if both industry-time and district-wave fixed effects are controlled for (table 7A.2, column 3, also plotted in figure 7.4), and to 3.4 percentage points if occupation-time and district-wave fixed effects are controlled for (table 7A.2, column 4). This means that the COVID shock and informality are somewhat more intense in certain vulnerable industries and occupations. Controlling for these characteristics explains a significant share of the difference between informal and formal job vulnerability during the pandemic but not all of it. Even within industries or occupations, informal worker status is a significant disadvantage relative to formal worker status.

FIGURE 7.4 **Pandemic Impact on Employment Probability: Difference in Differences Estimates**

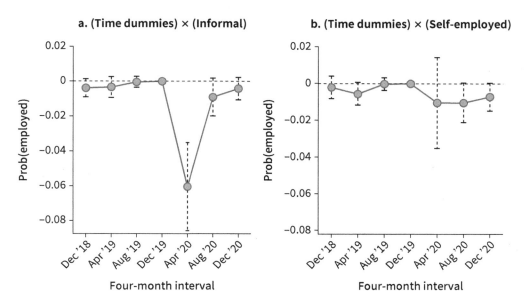

Source: Based on CPHS data.
Note: The difference in differences estimates include individual, district × wave, and industry × wave fixed effects. Informal and self-employed denotes employment status as of December 2019. Standard errors are clustered at the individual level. N = 7,182 individuals; Prob = probability.

The insights derived from the regression analysis exceed the insights derived by reproducing the patterns observed in the raw data. Figure 7.4 shows the values of the estimated $\gamma_t \times Inf$ and $\gamma_t \times SelfEmp$ coefficients (the differential impacts across employment categories) from the preferred specification (table 7A.2, column 3). Figure 7.4, panel a, shows the differential impact of the pandemic on informal wage workers and an easy inspection of pretrends in the outcome variable across informal and formal workers. The identifying assumption is that formal and informal workers were on parallel trends in employment outcomes prior to the pandemic in India and did not experience systematically different idiosyncratic shocks after the pandemic. The lack of pretrends in figure 7.4 confirms that this is a reasonable assumption.

Figure 7.4 also shows that the differential is eliminated almost completely during the recovery period. The point estimates for August and December 2020 cannot be distinguished from zero. In other words, informal workers were exposed to a greater probability than formal workers of losing employment during the peak of the crisis, but they were also able to return to employment during the recovery. By December 2020, their probability of employment was no less than the probability of employment among formal workers. The analysis cannot capture whether the workers regain the same jobs that they had lost in April 2020. Indeed, a large part of the employment gain from June to December 2020 seems to derive from new self-employed jobs. So, even though employment rates are close to pre-COVID levels, the quality of the employment recovery may not be the same.

Figure 7.4, panel b, displays the estimated differential impacts of the pandemic among self-employed individuals. The difference in the probability of job loss is much smaller and, in fact, is not statistically different from zero among the self-employed.

Estimates of the results of equation 7.1 using per capita household income as the dependent variable are presented in annex 7A, table 7A.3. Figure 7.5 displays the estimated differential impacts on informal households (panel a) and self-employed households (panel b). As with figure 7.4, the point estimates plotted in figure 7.5 correspond to the regression specification with household, district-month, and industry-month fixed effects (annex 7A, table 7A.3, column 3).

Consider first the early COVID-19 period (until May 2020). Like employment, there is a large overall negative impact on per capita household income, with an additional penalty among informal workers. The incomes of formal and informal workers fell by 59 percent and 78 percent, respectively, by April 2020 relative to February 2020 (see annex 7A, table 7A, column 1, which only controls for household fixed effects). This larger loss among informal households, as in the case of employment, partly arises

FIGURE 7.5 Pandemic Impact on Per Capita Household Income: Difference in Differences Estimates

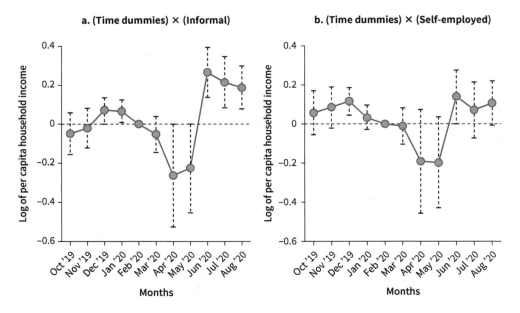

Source: Based on CPHS data.
Note: The difference in differences estimates include household, district × month, and industry × month fixed effects. Informal and self-employed denotes employment status of the household head as of December 2019. Standard errors are clustered at the household level. N = 4,623 households. The dependent variable is the log of total per capita household income.

because informal workers are concentrated in industries and occupations that are more widely affected by the COVID crisis: the magnitude of the coefficient on Informal × April 2020 in table 7A.3, column 3, which controls for industry-month and district-month fixed effects, is 40 percent lower compared with the magnitude in column 1.

Figure 7.5 highlights the same points discussed in the case of employment.[10] Thus, relative to February 2020, the informal-formal income gap was zero before the crisis, but it rose dramatically in April and May 2020. Controlling for industry and occupation reduces the magnitude of this difference. As with employment, there is an equally sharp recovery in household incomes. In fact, informal households recovered more quickly than formal workers. Controlling for district-month and industry-month fixed effects, the estimated informal-formal income difference in June, July, and August 2020 (relative to February 2020) is positive and statistically significant. In other words, the incomes of informal households relative to formal worker incomes had improved from the pre-COVID baseline.

RURAL-URBAN DIFFERENCES IN THE IMPACTS ON FORMAL AND INFORMAL WORKERS

Rural and urban areas both experienced unprecedented employment loss in the early COVID-19 period, but there is limited evidence on the differential incidence of the shock in rural areas relative to urban areas. A regression analysis conducted separately on the rural and urban subsamples indicates that the observed differential impact of the COVID-19 shock on the informal sector was driven by urban areas.

First, consider how the estimated differential employment impact in urban areas mirrors the impact on the overall sample (annex 7A, table 7A.4). The regression specification without any wave-specific fixed effects (column 1) establishes a sharp increase in the probability of job loss among each employment group in urban areas in April relative to December 2019. The estimated decline among formal workers (the reference group) is 13 percentage points, with an additional decline of 26 percentage points among informal wage workers. This differential is no longer significant by August and December 2020. This result is robust to the inclusion of wave-specific industry, occupation, and district effects.

The income impact in urban areas, too, is similar to the impact observed on the overall sample (annex 7A, table 7A.5). Relative to February 2020, the estimated difference in the per capita income of households headed by informal and formal wage workers is significantly negative in April and May 2020 and significantly positive in June and August 2020.

There was a sharp increase in the probability of job loss in April 2020 in rural areas as well. The decline among the reference group is estimated at 26 percentage points (annex 7A, table 7A.6, column 1). In this case, however, the differential between informal and formal wage workers (as well as the self-employed) is statistically not significant. Moreover, relative to February 2020, the estimated difference in the per capita income of households headed by informal and formal wage workers is significantly positive in April 2020 and insignificant in May 2020 (annex 7A, table 7A.7). These regressions suggest that, in rural areas, formal and informal workers were equally vulnerable to the early COVID-19 shock.

Evidence suggests that India's flagship rural jobs guarantee program (MGNREGA) has cushioned the impact of COVID-19 in rural areas (Afridi, Mahajan, and Sangwan 2021). Given that there was a lockdown on MGNREGA activities until at least April 20, 2020, however, it is unlikely that MGNREGA alone explains why there was no differential job loss between formal and informal workers in rural areas in April 2020. Future research is needed to look into why formal jobs were as vulnerable as informal jobs to the early COVID-19 shock in rural areas.

THE IMPACT OF COVID ON CONSUMPTION

The CMIE survey also collects panel data on consumption, which the analysis used to estimate the impact of the COVID crisis on welfare. Figure 7.6 shows trends in

FIGURE 7.6 Index of Average Per Capita Household Consumption, by Worker Group

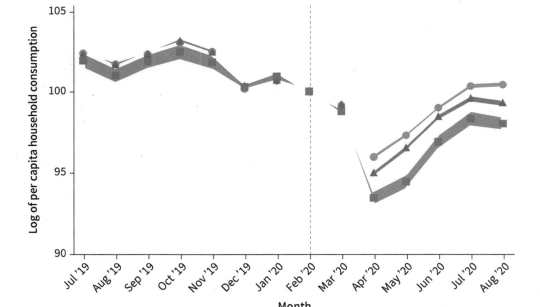

Source: Based on CPHS data.
Note: The figure shows mean per capita household consumption (natural logarithm) by worker category. For ease of comparability, all group means are normalized to 100 in February 2020, which is used as a base because it was the last prepandemic month.
95% standard errors are reported in shaded areas around the group means.

consumption per capita before, during, and after the onset of the COVID crisis by illustrating the same approach that was adopted in the case of income in figure 7.3. Specifically, total household consumption is divided by household size to calculate per capita individual consumption, and households are classified into three worker categories based on the employment status of the household head in December 2019. The log per capita consumption of each group in February 2020 is normalized to 100. The 95 percent confidence intervals of log per capita consumption are represented in the figure by the shaded bands.

As in the case of income per capita, consumption among all categories of workers was severely reduced in the months of maximum restriction linked to the pandemic. However, figure 7.6 also highlights an interesting puzzle: why do informal workers, who were exposed to larger job and income losses relative to formal workers, reduce their consumption to a lesser extent? This lower reduction is confirmed by estimations of equation 7.1 with the log of per capita consumption as the dependent variable. The results are presented in annex 7A, table 7A.8, and figure 7.7, which plots the interaction of time dummies with worker category indicators in table 7A.8, column 3.

The key message of figure 7.7 is that there is a positive, statistically significant consumption differential involving informal workers after March 2020 and a similar phenomenon (although not statistically significant) involving the self-employed. Without controlling for time-specific fixed effects, the reduction in consumption in April 2020 with respect to February 2020 was about 64 percent among formal workers (column 2 in annex table 7A.8), but it was only 45 percent among informal workers. Some of this differential is accounted for by industry-month and district-month fixed effects. The magnitude of the coefficient on Informal × April 2020 in annex 7A, table 7A.8, column 3, is 40 percent of the magnitude shown in column 1. However, even within the same industries, occupations, and districts and despite larger income losses, informal workers are affected by a smaller reduction in consumption relative to formal workers.

Three possible mechanisms may explain this puzzle: (1) forced savings, (2) differential price changes, and (3) differential adjustments to the crisis. First, the COVID economic crisis is not only an employment and income shock among households. It is also a goods and services supply shock. Some people, even if their incomes have not declined much, may be prevented from consuming certain items because some shops and services are closed or people wish to maintain voluntary social distancing. The data not only show that formal incomes are higher than informal incomes; they also show that the composition of the consumption of formal workers is quite different from that of their informal counterparts. Formal workers devote a much higher share of total consumption to nonfood items and to services, such as restaurants and other recreational services, that were unavailable during the lockdown. The unavailability of these services may have forced formal households to save a larger part of their income than they typically do.

Indeed, preliminary evidence on this forced saving effect may be seen in annex 7A, figure 7A.1. The figure plots the log of per capita income and consumption between July

FIGURE 7.7 **Pandemic Impact on Per Capita Household Consumption: Difference in Differences Estimates**

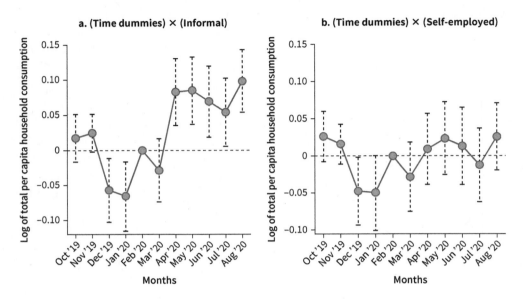

a. (Time dummies) × (Informal)

b. (Time dummies) × (Self-employed)

Source: Based on CPHS data.
Note: The difference in differences estimates include household, district × wave, and industry × wave fixed effects. Informal and self-employed denote the employment status of the household head as of December 2019. Standard errors are clustered at the household level. N = 4,623 individuals. The dependent variable is the log of total per capita household consumption.

2019 and August 2020 among households in different transition groups. The transition groups are defined according to employment status (formal, informal, self-employed, and unemployed or out of the labor force) in December 2019 and August 2020. Thus, the top left corner plots consumption income among households that were formal in December 2019 and were still in formal employment in August 2020. The panel shows that, among this specific formal-formal group, income is quite smooth, but consumption contracts during the peak of the crisis (April–May 2020), forcing these households to save a large part of their monthly incomes. Meanwhile, the informal-informal group shows the more common case of consumption smoothing (dissaving) whereby income is falling, but consumption is not.

Second, the analysis has been carried out in current prices. Suppose that the prices of food items have been affected by the crisis and increased more than the prices for other goods and services. To the extent that informal households, which tend to be poorer, spend a greater portion of their income on food items, the decline in real consumption would be greater among them. If the analysis were carried out in constant prices, then, with higher food inflation and larger food consumption shares, informal workers may indeed be less well off than formal workers. In fact, there is also evidence that this mechanism is at work because food prices did increase more rapidly than nonfood prices during the crisis (see annex 7A, figure 7A.2).

Third, formal workers may have adjusted their expected permanent income more relative to informal workers in the aftermath of the lockdown shock. Because consumption adjustment should be driven by changes in expected permanent income, this may solve the puzzle. A larger adjustment in permanent incomes among formal workers may be explained by the difficulties encountered in obtaining work in the formal sector. Losing such a job may therefore be considered a more permanent loss than losing an informal job. The finding that the incomes of informal workers have recovered more quickly than those of formal workers since May 2020 is in line with this hypothesis.

The dichotomy in the differential trajectories of consumption and income has significant policy relevance because of what it may say about the welfare impacts of the early COVID-19 crisis. For example, to the extent that this inconsistency is explained by differential price increases that were felt more among poorer, informal individuals, the welfare impact on those individuals may have been worse than that suggested by the decline in their nominal incomes. The dichotomy may also have a bearing on the expected economic recovery from the COVID-19 crisis. One might thus expect a relatively rapid recovery in consumption demand among richer households if the differential decline in their consumption during the lockdown derived from forced saving. In comparison, consumption demand might recover slowly if the differential decline in consumption among richer households arose because of a larger downward revision in the expected lifetime earnings of these households. A more in-depth analysis of these mechanisms and the associated policy implications is planned for future research.

Annex 7A: Figures and Tables

TABLE 7A.1 **Transition Matrices: Labor Market Churning, Pre- and Post-COVID Onset**

Labor categories	August 2019–December 2019				December 2019–April 2020			
	Formal	Self-employed	Informal	Unemployed	Formal	Self-employed	Informal	Unemployed
Formal	85.14	7.67	4.38	2.8	43.79	20.91	7.26	28.04
Self-employed	1.63	85.49	7.81	5.08	5.89	55.58	5.5	33.03
Informal	1.63	11.89	80.91	5.57	5.23	17.19	20.18	57.4
Unemployed	0.43	1.49	1.44	96.64	0.7	2.78	1.44	95.07

Source: Based on CPHS data.

TABLE 7A.2 **Employment Impact of COVID-19: Difference in Differences Estimates, All India**

Variable, period	(1)	(2)	(3)	(4)
December 2018	−0.0058			
	(0.011)			
April 2019	0.00066			
	(0.0096)			
August 2019	−0.017**			
	(0.0077)			
April 2020	−0.15***			
	(0.016)			
August 2020	−0.055***			
	(0.012)			
December 2020	−0.063***			
	(0.013)			
Inf December 2018	−0.027*	−0.021	−0.0038	−0.0014
	(0.014)	(0.014)	(0.0025)	(0.0031)
Inf April 2019	−0.014	−0.015	−0.0033	−0.00084
	(0.012)	(0.012)	(0.0029)	(0.0033)
Inf August 2019	0.0091	0.0052	−0.00040	0.00027
	(0.0096)	(0.010)	(0.0015)	(0.0023)
Inf April 2020	−0.21***	−0.19***	−0.060***	−0.034***
	(0.020)	(0.021)	(0.013)	(0.012)
Inf August 2020	0.011	0.012	−0.0090*	−0.0084
	(0.015)	(0.016)	(0.0054)	(0.0056)

(continued)

TABLE 7A.2 Employment Impact of COVID-19: Difference in Differences Estimates, All India (continued)

Variable, period	(1)	(2)	(3)	(4)
Inf December 2020	0.0035	0.014	−0.0041	−0.0036
	(0.015)	(0.016)	(0.0032)	(0.0037)
SelfEmp December 2018	0.0031	0.0053	−0.0021	−0.0015
	(0.013)	(0.013)	(0.0030)	(0.0046)
SelfEmp April 2019	−0.0056	−0.0091	−0.0056*	−0.0052
	(0.011)	(0.011)	(0.0031)	(0.0044)
SelfEmp August 2019	0.013	0.0071	−0.00015	−0.0027
	(0.0091)	(0.0092)	(0.0017)	(0.0029)
SelfEmp April 2020	−0.032*	−0.046**	−0.010	−0.027**
	(0.019)	(0.019)	(0.012)	(0.012)
SelfEmp August 2020	0.034**	0.026*	−0.010*	−0.015**
	(0.014)	(0.015)	(0.0054)	(0.0061)
SelfEmp December 2020	0.037**	0.042***	−0.0071*	−0.0090*
	(0.014)	(0.015)	(0.0038)	(0.0049)
Individual fixed effects	Yes	Yes	Yes	Yes
District × wave fixed effects	No	Yes	Yes	Yes
Industry × wave fixed effects	No	No	Yes	No
Occupation × wave fixed effects	No	No	No	Yes
Observations	50,165	50,151	50,148	50,151

Source: Based on CPHS data.
Note: Standard errors in parentheses are clustered at the individual level. The dependent variable is an indicator variable that takes a value of 1 if the individual is employed and zero otherwise. Inf and SelfEmp denote informal or self-employed employment status as of December 2019. This regression is run on the all-India sample. Inf = informal; SelfEmp = self-employed.
*p < .10 **p < .05 ***p < .01.

TABLE 7A.3 COVID-19 Impact on Total Household Income: Difference in Differences Estimates, All India

Variable, period	(1)	(2)	(3)	(4)	(5)
October 2019	0.29***				
	(0.033)				
November 2019	0.29***				
	(0.032)				
December 2019	0.048***				
	(0.017)				

(continued)

TABLE 7A.3 **COVID-19 Impact on Total Household Income: Difference in Differences Estimates, All India** *(continued)*

Variable, period	(1)	(2)	(3)	(4)	(5)
January 2020	−0.0021				
	(0.021)				
March 2020	−0.19***				
	(0.031)				
April 2020	−0.90***				
	(0.075)				
May 2020	−0.61***				
	(0.062)				
June 2020	−0.28***				
	(0.042)				
July 2020	−0.19***				
	(0.040)				
August 2020	−0.14***				
	(0.037)				
Inf October 2019	−0.20***	−0.17***	−0.049	−0.062	−0.090*
	(0.038)	(0.040)	(0.053)	(0.054)	(0.051)
Inf November 2019	−0.18***	−0.21***	−0.021	−0.043	−0.080
	(0.036)	(0.039)	(0.051)	(0.051)	(0.049)
Inf December 2019	0.0096	0.010	0.072**	0.052**	0.035
	(0.021)	(0.024)	(0.031)	(0.023)	(0.029)
Inf January 2020	0.0065	0.030	0.065**	0.017	0.024
	(0.024)	(0.024)	(0.029)	(0.035)	(0.026)
Inf March 2020	−0.18***	−0.21***	−0.052	−0.063	−0.055
	(0.036)	(0.035)	(0.046)	(0.050)	(0.046)
Inf April 2020	−0.63***	−0.48***	−0.26**	−0.33**	−0.42***
	(0.093)	(0.095)	(0.13)	(0.14)	(0.14)
Inf May 2020	−0.31***	−0.40***	−0.22*	−0.28**	−0.14
	(0.078)	(0.082)	(0.12)	(0.12)	(0.12)
Inf June 2020	0.18***	0.20***	0.27***	0.18***	0.23***
	(0.048)	(0.049)	(0.065)	(0.067)	(0.066)
Inf July 2020	0.17***	0.16***	0.21***	0.13**	0.20***
	(0.046)	(0.048)	(0.065)	(0.058)	(0.063)
Inf August 2020	0.100**	0.17***	0.19***	0.15**	0.083
	(0.042)	(0.046)	(0.055)	(0.062)	(0.056)

(continued)

TABLE 7A.3 **COVID-19 Impact on Total Household Income: Difference in Differences Estimates, All India** (continued)

Variable, period	(1)	(2)	(3)	(4)	(5)
SelfEmp October 2019	−0.076*	−0.077*	0.057	0.18**	0.055
	(0.041)	(0.041)	(0.056)	(0.076)	(0.053)
SelfEmp November 2019	0.013	−0.036	0.085	0.18**	0.090*
	(0.040)	(0.039)	(0.053)	(0.076)	(0.053)
SelfEmp December 2019	0.13***	0.091***	0.12***	0.15***	0.11***
	(0.025)	(0.024)	(0.034)	(0.041)	(0.034)
SelfEmp January 2020	−0.019	0.016	0.032	0.020	−0.013
	(0.026)	(0.026)	(0.030)	(0.043)	(0.028)
SelfEmp March 2020	−0.11***	−0.12***	−0.011	0.016	−0.014
	(0.037)	(0.034)	(0.046)	(0.060)	(0.047)
SelfEmp April 2020	−0.12	−0.12	−0.19	−0.092	−0.19
	(0.088)	(0.088)	(0.13)	(0.17)	(0.14)
SelfEmp May 2020	−0.029	−0.13*	−0.20*	−0.22	−0.14
	(0.075)	(0.076)	(0.12)	(0.15)	(0.13)
SelfEmp June 2020	0.16***	0.16***	0.14**	0.11	0.15**
	(0.048)	(0.048)	(0.068)	(0.092)	(0.069)
SelfEmp July 2020	0.12***	0.11**	0.071	0.070	0.085
	(0.047)	(0.048)	(0.071)	(0.086)	(0.069)
SelfEmp August 2020	0.072	0.11**	0.11*	0.15*	0.041
	(0.044)	(0.045)	(0.056)	(0.081)	(0.057)
Household fixed effects	Yes	Yes	Yes	Yes	Yes
District × month fixed effects	No	Yes	Yes	Yes	No
Industry × month fixed effects	No	No	Yes	No	Yes
Occupation × month fixed effects	No	No	No	Yes	No
Observations	43,810	43,744	43,742	43,744	43,808

Source: Based on CPHS data.
Note: Standard errors in parentheses are clustered at the household level. The dependent variable = log of total household income. Inf and SelfEmp denote informal or self-employed employment status as of December 2019. This regression is run on the all-India sample. Inf = informal; SelfEmp = self-employed.
*p < .10 **p < .05 ***p < .01

TABLE 7A.4 Employment Impact of COVID-19: Difference in Differences Estimates, Urban

Variable, period	(1)	(2)	(3)	(4)
December 2018	−0.0047			
	(0.012)			
April 2019	−0.0015			
	(0.011)			
August 2019	−0.013			
	(0.0084)			
April 2020	−0.13***			
	(0.018)			
August 2020	−0.048***			
	(0.014)			
December 2020	−0.061***			
	(0.014)			
Inf December 2018	−0.031**	−0.029*	−0.0032	0.00014
	(0.015)	(0.016)	(0.0028)	(0.0036)
Inf April 2019	−0.019	−0.022	−0.0017	0.00069
	(0.013)	(0.014)	(0.0028)	(0.0034)
Inf August 2019	−0.00089	−0.0055	0.00062	0.0012
	(0.011)	(0.012)	(0.0017)	(0.0027)
Inf April 2020	−0.26***	−0.24***	−0.070***	−0.048***
	(0.022)	(0.023)	(0.014)	(0.013)
Inf August 2020	−0.0011	−0.0088	−0.0066	−0.0057
	(0.017)	(0.018)	(0.0064)	(0.0066)
Inf December 2020	−0.0020	−0.00100	−0.0028	−0.0015
	(0.017)	(0.018)	(0.0037)	(0.0044)
SelfEmp December 2018	0.0052	0.0066	−0.0031	−0.0016
	(0.014)	(0.015)	(0.0037)	(0.0056)
SelfEmp April 2019	−0.0034	−0.0076	−0.0056*	−0.0056
	(0.012)	(0.013)	(0.0034)	(0.0053)
SelfEmp August 2019	0.010	0.0045	0.000039	−0.0032
	(0.010)	(0.010)	(0.0019)	(0.0035)
SelfEmp April 2020	−0.083***	−0.083***	−0.022	−0.028**
	(0.021)	(0.021)	(0.014)	(0.013)
SelfEmp August 2020	0.030*	0.023	−0.013**	−0.017**
	(0.016)	(0.017)	(0.0064)	(0.0074)

(continued)

TABLE 7A.4 **Employment Impact of COVID-19: Difference in Differences Estimates, Urban** *(continued)*

Variable, period	(1)	(2)	(3)	(4)
SelfEmp December 2020	0.032*	0.037**	−0.0090**	−0.011*
	(0.017)	(0.017)	(0.0043)	(0.0060)
Individual fixed effects	Yes	Yes	Yes	Yes
District × wave fixed effects	No	Yes	Yes	Yes
Industry × wave fixed effects	No	No	Yes	No
Occupation × wave fixed effects	No	No	No	Yes
Observations	36,242	36,242	36,237	36,242

Source: Based on CPHS data.
Note: Standard errors in parentheses are clustered at the individual level. The dependent variable is an indicator variable that takes the value of 1 if the individual is employed and zero otherwise. Inf and SelfEmp denote employment status as of December 2019. The regression is run on the urban sample. Inf = informal; SelfEmp = self-employed.
*p < .10 **p < .05 ***p < .01.

TABLE 7A.5 **COVID-19 Impact on Total Household Income: Difference in Differences Estimates, Urban**

Variable, period	(1)	(2)	(3)	(4)	(5)
October 2019	0.24***				
	(0.034)				
November 2019	0.25***				
	(0.032)				
December 2019	0.0097*				
	(0.0059)				
January 2020	0.014				
	(0.014)				
March 2020	−0.16***				
	(0.028)				
April 2020	−0.96***				
	(0.082)				
May 2020	−0.65***				
	(0.068)				
June 2020	−0.28***				
	(0.043)				
July 2020	−0.19***				
	(0.042)				

(continued)

TABLE 7A.5 COVID-19 Impact on Total Household Income: Difference in Differences Estimates, Urban *(continued)*

Variable, period	(1)	(2)	(3)	(4)	(5)
August 2020	−0.16***				
	(0.037)				
Inf October 2019	−0.18***	−0.17***	−0.054	−0.066	−0.087
	(0.040)	(0.042)	(0.059)	(0.060)	(0.057)
Inf November 2019	−0.16***	−0.20***	−0.056	−0.068	−0.071
	(0.037)	(0.039)	(0.056)	(0.054)	(0.055)
Inf December 2019	0.020*	0.0081	0.037	0.015	0.036
	(0.010)	(0.012)	(0.027)	(0.016)	(0.026)
Inf January 2020	0.020	0.013	0.036	0.014	0.030
	(0.016)	(0.019)	(0.024)	(0.016)	(0.020)
Inf March 2020	−0.22***	−0.26***	−0.12**	−0.12**	−0.092*
	(0.035)	(0.035)	(0.050)	(0.047)	(0.049)
Inf April 2020	−0.75***	−0.65***	−0.46***	−0.50***	−0.52***
	(0.11)	(0.11)	(0.15)	(0.15)	(0.16)
Inf May 2020	−0.45***	−0.47***	−0.30**	−0.35**	−0.18
	(0.090)	(0.091)	(0.13)	(0.14)	(0.14)
Inf June 2020	0.21***	0.21***	0.26***	0.20***	0.25***
	(0.049)	(0.051)	(0.068)	(0.068)	(0.068)
Inf July 2020	0.17***	0.15***	0.19***	0.13**	0.19***
	(0.048)	(0.049)	(0.068)	(0.058)	(0.067)
Inf August 2020	0.16***	0.16***	0.17***	0.11*	0.15***
	(0.043)	(0.044)	(0.057)	(0.058)	(0.055)
SelfEmp October 2019	−0.051	−0.065	0.085	0.19**	0.095
	(0.041)	(0.042)	(0.060)	(0.083)	(0.059)
SelfEmp November 2019	−0.010	−0.035	0.089	0.14*	0.086
	(0.039)	(0.038)	(0.058)	(0.081)	(0.058)
SelfEmp December 2019	0.053***	0.041***	0.049	0.033	0.059*
	(0.016)	(0.014)	(0.032)	(0.030)	(0.033)
SelfEmp January 2020	0.020	0.023	0.042	0.027	0.027
	(0.018)	(0.022)	(0.026)	(0.029)	(0.023)
SelfEmp March 2020	−0.17***	−0.20***	−0.065	−0.077	−0.045
	(0.034)	(0.033)	(0.049)	(0.057)	(0.050)
SelfEmp April 2020	−0.23**	−0.24**	−0.34**	−0.36*	−0.28*
	(0.099)	(0.098)	(0.15)	(0.19)	(0.16)

(continued)

TABLE 7A.5 **COVID-19 Impact on Total Household Income: Difference in Differences Estimates, Urban** (continued)

Variable, period	(1)	(2)	(3)	(4)	(5)
SelfEmp May 2020	−0.27***	−0.26***	−0.32**	−0.40**	−0.29**
	(0.084)	(0.084)	(0.13)	(0.17)	(0.15)
SelfEmp June 2020	0.19***	0.19***	0.16**	0.14	0.16**
	(0.050)	(0.049)	(0.071)	(0.093)	(0.071)
SelfEmp July 2020	0.15***	0.13***	0.077	0.070	0.083
	(0.049)	(0.049)	(0.075)	(0.087)	(0.075)
SelfEmp August 2020	0.12***	0.12***	0.10*	0.17**	0.081
	(0.044)	(0.044)	(0.058)	(0.081)	(0.057)
Household fixed effects	Yes	Yes	Yes	Yes	Yes
District × month fixed effects	No	Yes	Yes	Yes	No
Industry × month fixed effects	No	No	Yes	No	Yes
Occupation × month fixed effects	No	No	No	Yes	No
Observations	32,057	32,035	32,030	32,035	32,052

Source: Based on CPHS data.
Note: Standard errors in parentheses are clustered at the household level. The dependent variable = log of total household income. Inf and SelfEmp denote employment status as of December 2019. The regression is run on the urban sample. Inf = informal; SelfEmp = self-employed.
*p < .10 **p < .05 ***p < .01.

TABLE 7A.6 **Employment Impact of COVID-19: Difference in Differences Estimates, Rural**

Variable, period	(1)	(2)	(3)	(4)
December 2018	−0.011			
	(0.028)			
April 2019	0.011			
	(0.024)			
August 2019	−0.034*			
	(0.019)			
April 2020	−0.26***			
	(0.040)			
August 2020	−0.085***			
	(0.028)			

(continued)

TABLE 7A.6 Employment Impact of COVID-19: Difference in Differences Estimates, Rural (continued)

Variable, period	(1)	(2)	(3)	(4)
December 2020	−0.073***			
	(0.025)			
Inf December 2018	−0.013	−0.0052	−0.0073	−0.010*
	(0.031)	(0.033)	(0.0060)	(0.0062)
Inf April 2019	−0.0084	−0.0023	−0.011	−0.0063
	(0.027)	(0.028)	(0.010)	(0.0084)
Inf August 2019	0.042**	0.038	−0.0046	−0.0040
	(0.021)	(0.024)	(0.0039)	(0.0032)
Inf April 2020	−0.035	0.0013	−0.012	0.020
	(0.045)	(0.045)	(0.026)	(0.025)
Inf August 2020	0.056*	0.064*	−0.018**	−0.019**
	(0.032)	(0.036)	(0.0087)	(0.0083)
Inf December 2020	0.022	0.051	−0.011	−0.010*
	(0.030)	(0.034)	(0.0081)	(0.0059)
SelfEmp December 2018	0.0011	0.014	0.00022	−0.0056
	(0.030)	(0.032)	(0.0053)	(0.0065)
SelfEmp April 2019	−0.016	−0.0068	−0.0083	−0.0055
	(0.026)	(0.027)	(0.0086)	(0.0076)
SelfEmp August 2019	0.030	0.024	−0.0030	−0.0037
	(0.021)	(0.023)	(0.0044)	(0.0047)
SelfEmp April 2020	0.14***	0.10**	0.034	−0.011
	(0.043)	(0.044)	(0.025)	(0.024)
SelfEmp August 2020	0.060*	0.062*	−0.0049	−0.0085
	(0.031)	(0.034)	(0.0076)	(0.0076)
SelfEmp December 2020	0.055*	0.072**	−0.0051	−0.0032
	(0.028)	(0.032)	(0.0095)	(0.0071)
Individual fixed effects	Yes	Yes	Yes	Yes
District × wave fixed effects	No	Yes	Yes	Yes
Industry × wave fixed effects	No	No	Yes	No
Occupation × wave fixed effects	No	No	No	Yes
Observations	13,923	13,902	13,889	13,897

Source: Based on CPHS data.
Note: Standard errors in parentheses are clustered at the individual level. The dependent variable is an indicator variable that takes the value of 1 if the individual is employed and zero otherwise. Inf and SelfEmp denote employment status as of December 2019. The regression is run on the rural sample. Inf = informal; SelfEmp = self-employed.
*$p < .10$ **$p < .05$ ***$p < .01$.

TABLE 7A.7 COVID-19 Impact on Total Household Income: Difference in Differences Estimates, Rural

Variable, period	(1)	(2)	(3)	(4)	(5)
October 2019	0.54***				
	(0.10)				
November 2019	0.53***				
	(0.10)				
December 2019	0.25**				
	(0.10)				
January 2020	−0.093				
	(0.11)				
March 2020	−0.35***				
	(0.12)				
April 2020	−0.61***				
	(0.19)				
May 2020	−0.42***				
	(0.15)				
June 2020	−0.27**				
	(0.13)				
July 2020	−0.20				
	(0.12)				
August 2020	−0.045				
	(0.12)				
Inf October 2019	−0.36***	−0.20	0.048	0.035	−0.14
	(0.11)	(0.13)	(0.14)	(0.16)	(0.11)
Inf November 2019	−0.34***	−0.24*	0.16	0.24	−0.096
	(0.11)	(0.14)	(0.14)	(0.19)	(0.11)
Inf December 2019	−0.11	0.025	0.24*	0.30**	0.025
	(0.11)	(0.11)	(0.13)	(0.13)	(0.11)
Inf January 2020	0.018	0.11	0.10	−0.17	−0.040
	(0.11)	(0.10)	(0.14)	(0.23)	(0.12)
Inf March 2020	−0.0090	0.084	0.28**	0.26	0.14
	(0.13)	(0.13)	(0.14)	(0.23)	(0.13)
Inf April 2020	−0.48**	0.20	0.70***	0.65**	−0.034
	(0.21)	(0.20)	(0.27)	(0.32)	(0.26)
Inf May 2020	−0.054	−0.091	0.048	0.095	0.17
	(0.17)	(0.18)	(0.26)	(0.33)	(0.24)

(continued)

TABLE 7A.7 COVID-19 Impact on Total Household Income: Difference in Differences Estimates, Rural (continued)

Variable, period	(1)	(2)	(3)	(4)	(5)
Inf June 2020	0.12	0.19	0.34	0.13	0.21
	(0.14)	(0.15)	(0.21)	(0.27)	(0.21)
Inf July 2020	0.19	0.26*	0.37**	0.23	0.28
	(0.13)	(0.16)	(0.19)	(0.24)	(0.18)
Inf August 2020	−0.10	0.26	0.33*	0.45	−0.16
	(0.13)	(0.16)	(0.18)	(0.28)	(0.19)
SelfEmp October 2019	−0.26**	−0.12	0.073	0.17	−0.093
	(0.12)	(0.13)	(0.15)	(0.20)	(0.12)
SelfEmp November 2019	−0.054	−0.057	0.11	0.38*	0.11
	(0.12)	(0.14)	(0.15)	(0.22)	(0.12)
SelfEmp December 2019	0.20*	0.25**	0.39***	0.44***	0.27**
	(0.11)	(0.11)	(0.13)	(0.16)	(0.12)
SelfEmp January 2020	−0.066	0.019	−0.086	−0.31	−0.19
	(0.12)	(0.10)	(0.16)	(0.25)	(0.13)
SelfEmp March 2020	0.13	0.17	0.23	0.44*	0.19
	(0.13)	(0.13)	(0.15)	(0.24)	(0.14)
SelfEmp April 2020	−0.040	0.44**	0.74***	1.03***	0.17
	(0.20)	(0.20)	(0.27)	(0.37)	(0.26)
SelfEmp May 2020	0.41**	0.25	0.21	0.13	0.51**
	(0.17)	(0.17)	(0.27)	(0.39)	(0.25)
SelfEmp June 2020	0.085	0.059	0.085	−0.13	0.14
	(0.14)	(0.15)	(0.22)	(0.33)	(0.23)
SelfEmp July 2020	0.077	0.091	0.11	−0.015	0.14
	(0.13)	(0.16)	(0.20)	(0.31)	(0.20)
SelfEmp August 2020	−0.088	0.17	0.19	0.15	−0.12
	(0.13)	(0.16)	(0.19)	(0.30)	(0.19)
Household fixed effects	Yes	Yes	Yes	Yes	Yes
District × month fixed effects	No	Yes	Yes	Yes	No
Industry × month fixed effects	No	No	Yes	No	Yes
Occupation × month fixed effects	No	No	No	Yes	No
Observations	11,753	11,686	11,643	11,676	11,714

Source: Based on CPHS data.
Note: Standard errors in parentheses are clustered at the household level. Dependent variable = log of total household income. Inf and SelfEmp denote employment status as of December 2019. The regression is run on the rural sample. Inf = informal; SelfEmp = self-employed.
*p < .10 **p < .05 ***p < .01.

TABLE 7A.8 COVID-19 Impact on Total Consumption: Difference in Differences Estimates, All India

Variable, period	(1)	(2)	(3)	(4)	(5)
October 2019	0.097***				
	(0.012)				
November 2019	0.045***				
	(0.0084)				
December 2019	−0.063***				
	(0.016)				
January 2020	−0.0046				
	(0.019)				
March 2020	−0.19***				
	(0.016)				
April 2020	−0.64***				
	(0.016)				
May 2020	−0.56***				
	(0.016)				
June 2020	−0.36***				
	(0.017)				
July 2020	−0.24***				
	(0.017)				
August 2020	−0.27***				
	(0.014)				
Inf October 2019	0.011	−0.0086	0.017	0.025	0.051***
	(0.013)	(0.012)	(0.017)	(0.017)	(0.017)
Inf November 2019	0.020**	0.030***	0.025*	0.021	−0.0076
	(0.010)	(0.0094)	(0.013)	(0.013)	(0.015)
Inf December 2019	−0.042**	−0.059***	−0.057**	−0.031	−0.011
	(0.018)	(0.018)	(0.023)	(0.024)	(0.023)
Inf January 2020	−0.061***	−0.099***	−0.066***	−0.048**	0.0013
	(0.021)	(0.019)	(0.025)	(0.025)	(0.026)
Inf March 2020	0.0026	−0.023	−0.029	−0.0052	0.030
	(0.018)	(0.016)	(0.022)	(0.023)	(0.025)
Inf April 2020	0.20***	0.13***	0.083***	0.038	0.16***
	(0.019)	(0.017)	(0.024)	(0.025)	(0.026)
Inf May 2020	0.22***	0.13***	0.085***	0.054**	0.21***
	(0.019)	(0.017)	(0.024)	(0.025)	(0.029)

(continued)

TABLE 7A.8 COVID-19 Impact on Total Consumption: Difference in Differences Estimates, All India *(continued)*

Variable, period	(1)	(2)	(3)	(4)	(5)
Inf June 2020	0.15***	0.10***	0.069***	0.037	0.14***
	(0.019)	(0.017)	(0.025)	(0.027)	(0.028)
Inf July 2020	0.14***	0.093***	0.054**	0.019	0.13***
	(0.019)	(0.017)	(0.024)	(0.025)	(0.028)
Inf August 2020	0.17***	0.13***	0.098***	0.081***	0.14***
	(0.016)	(0.016)	(0.022)	(0.024)	(0.023)
SelfEmp October 2019	0.020	0.0049	0.026	0.042*	0.044**
	(0.013)	(0.012)	(0.017)	(0.022)	(0.017)
SelfEmp November 2019	0.019**	0.022**	0.016	0.035**	−0.0057
	(0.0095)	(0.0089)	(0.013)	(0.017)	(0.015)
SelfEmp December 2019	−0.025	−0.041**	−0.048**	−0.045	−0.0083
	(0.018)	(0.017)	(0.023)	(0.031)	(0.023)
SelfEmp January 2020	−0.055***	−0.065***	−0.050*	−0.043	−0.0053
	(0.021)	(0.019)	(0.025)	(0.034)	(0.027)
SelfEmp March 2020	0.0065	−0.0099	−0.028	−0.045	0.018
	(0.018)	(0.016)	(0.023)	(0.030)	(0.026)
SelfEmp April 2020	0.12***	0.064***	0.0093	−0.011	0.062**
	(0.018)	(0.016)	(0.024)	(0.033)	(0.026)
SelfEmp May 2020	0.15***	0.076***	0.023	0.012	0.13***
	(0.019)	(0.016)	(0.024)	(0.033)	(0.029)
SelfEmp June 2020	0.11***	0.058***	0.013	0.020	0.072**
	(0.019)	(0.016)	(0.026)	(0.035)	(0.028)
SelfEmp July 2020	0.078***	0.037**	−0.012	−0.018	0.062**
	(0.019)	(0.016)	(0.025)	(0.033)	(0.028)
SelfEmp August 2020	0.077***	0.051***	0.026	0.050*	0.057**
	(0.016)	(0.015)	(0.022)	(0.030)	(0.023)
Household fixed effects	Yes	Yes	Yes	Yes	Yes
District × month fixed effects	No	Yes	Yes	Yes	No
Industry × month fixed effects	No	No	Yes	No	Yes
Occupation × month fixed effects	No	No	No	Yes	No
Observations	57,652	57,568	57,568	57,568	57,652

Source: Based on CPHS data.
Note: Standard errors in parentheses are clustered at the household level. Dependent variable = log of total household consumption. Inf and SelfEmp denote informal or self-employed employment status as of December 2019. This regression is run on the all-India sample. Inf = informal; SelfEmp = self-employed.
*p < .10 **p < .05 ***p < .01.

FIGURE 7A.1 Household Per Capita Income and Consumption, by Transition Category

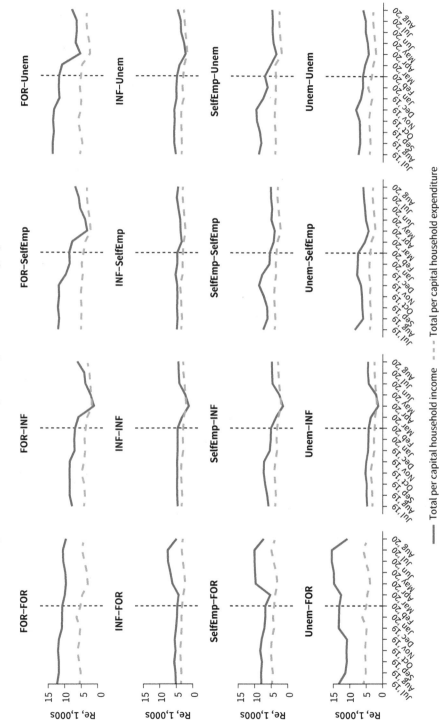

Note: The figure plots the log of per capita income and consumption between July 2019 and August 2020 among households in four transition groups. FOR = formal; INF = informal; SelfEmp = self-employed; Unem = unemployed or out of the labor force.

FIGURE 7A.2 Consumer Price Index: Inflation in Food and Nonfood Prices

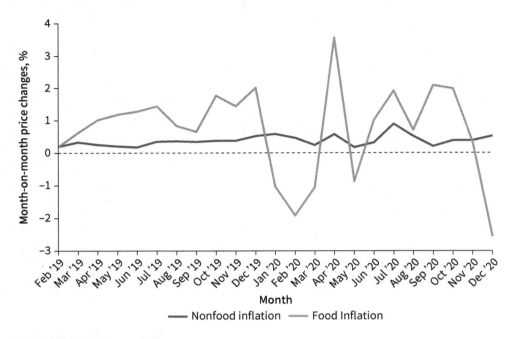

Source: World Development Indicators.

Notes

The authors thank Anirudha Dutta, Kaushik Krishnan, Sutirtha Sinha Roy, Anurati Tandon, and participants at the Center for Monitoring Indian Economy (CMIE) seminar and the 6th Turin Center on Emerging Economies Workshop for their comments and suggestions. The findings, interpretations, and conclusions expressed in this chapter are entirely those of the authors. They do not necessarily represent the views of the World Bank.

1. Also in the context of India, Deshpande (2020) examines gender differentials in the impacts of COVID-19.

2. Azam (2012), Berg et al. (2012), Deininger and Liu (2019), Dutta et al. (2012), Imbert and Papp (2015), and Zimmermann (2020) have examined the impact of the MGNREGA scheme on labor market outcomes among rural workers, especially those who are unskilled and likely to be in casual wage jobs.

3. Order 40-3/2020-DM-I(A) of the Ministry of Home Affairs allowed state governments to lift lockdowns on certain types of activities, including MGNREGA-eligible employment.

4. COVID-19 data of CRC (Coronavirus Resource Center) (dashboard), Center for Systems Science and Engineering, Johns Hopkins University, Baltimore, https://coronavirus.jhu.edu/.

5. Ministry of Home Affairs order 40–3/2020-DM-I(A).

6. As mentioned in the introduction, this study compares and contrasts the impacts of the shock on three groups: (1) informal wage workers, (2) self-employed, and (3) formal workers. For brevity, informal wage workers are labeled simply as informal workers, even if, strictly speaking, informality includes both groups (1) and (2).

7. If individuals were unemployed in December 2019, their employment arrangements were not observed in wave 18. This variable is then imputed according to the last time in the previous 10 waves that each individual was employed. If individuals were never previously employed, their December 2019 employment arrangements are imputed based on the next time each individual becomes employed (that is, in wave 19, 20, or 21). If individuals are not employed before or after wave 18, they are treated as unemployed and dropped from the estimation sample.

8. Although the CPHS dataset contains survey weights to adjust for differences in sampling probabilities across the sample, the analysis does not use them because they are designed to be applied to the full CPHS sample and are not appropriate for the balanced panel, which is a subset of the full sample. Hence, the summary statistics presented in table 7.1 may not be representative of the Indian population. For example, the unweighted balanced panel shows an urban bias; the share of rural workers is below 30 percent. This is because the CPHS oversamples urban areas.

9. Because employment is observed at four-month intervals, there is one $WAVE_t$ dummy for every fourth month starting in December 2018 and ending in December 2020.

10. There is an important caveat. Because individual-level data are not available on incomes, household per capita income must be used. Household per capita income is classified as informal or formal according to the informal or formal status of the household head. Household composition is thus ignored. This may underestimate the differential between formal and informal workers. If each household has exactly two working-age members (the head and a nonhead) whose baseline formal (F) or informal (NF) status is observed,

there are four types of households according to the baseline status of the two members. If each type is denoted by a pair dummy whereby the first term is the head's status and the second term is the nonhead's status, this gives (NF, NF), (NF, F), (F, NF), and (F, F). A household-level regression of income could then be run whereby the regressors include interactions of time with all four of the dummies. Because the individual regression on employment shows that households with the greatest number of informal members were affected most severely by the crisis, the coefficient on Time X (NF, NF) can be expected to be the most negative, while the coefficient on Time X (F, F) would be the least negative. The other two coefficients are between these two because they are mixed households. In the current specification, the nonhead member of the pair is ignored, and the coefficient on Post X NF is actually a mixture of Time X (NF, NF) and Time X (NF, F). In this sense, the impact of informality might be underestimated if it is claimed that Post X NF is equivalent to Post X (NF, NF). To the extent that there are some mixed households, ignoring the nonhead likely biases downward the estimated differential between formal and informal workers only in the sense that the difference between the two polar cases of NF, NF and F, F are not measured. Estimations with this more elaborate regression are available upon request.

References

Abraham, Rosa, Amit Basole, and Surbhi Kesar. 2021. "Tracking Employment Trajectories In the Covid-19 Pandemic: Evidence from Indian Panel Data." CSE Working Paper 35 (January), Center for Sustainable Employment, Azim Premji University, Bangalore, India.

Adams-Prassl, Abi, Teodora Boneva, Marta Golin, and Christopher Rauh. 2020. "Inequality in the Impact of the Coronavirus Shock: Evidence from Real Time Surveys." IZA Discussion Paper 13183 (April), Institute of Labor Economics, Bonn, Germany.

Adhvaryu, Achyuta, A. V. Chari, and Siddharth Sharma. 2013. "Firing Costs and Flexibility: Evidence from Firms' Employment Responses to Shocks in India." *Review of Economics and Statistics* 95 (3): 725–40.

Afridi, Farzana, Kanika Mahajan, and Nikita Sangwan. 2021. "Employment Guaranteed? Social Protection during a Pandemic." IZA Discussion Paper 14099 (February), Institute of Labor Economics, Bonn, Germany.

Alfaro, Laura, Oscar Becerra, and Marcela Eslava. 2020. "EMEs and COVID-19: Shutting Down in a World of Informal and Tiny Firms." NBER Working Paper 27360 (June), National Bureau of Economic Research, Cambridge, MA.

Andrews, M. A., Binu Areekal, K. R. Rajesh, Jijith Krishnan, R. Suryakala, Biju Krishnan, C. P. Muraly, and P. V. Santhosh. 2020. "First Confirmed Case of COVID-19 Infection in India: A Case Report." *Indian Journal of Medical Research* 151 (5): 490–92. https://doi.org/10.4103/ijmr.IJMR_2131_20.

Azam, Mehtabul. 2012. "The Impact of Indian Job Guarantee Scheme on Labor Market Outcomes: Evidence from a Natural Experiment." IZA Discussion Paper 6548 (May), Institute of Labor Economics, Bonn, Germany.

Bentolila, Samuel, Pierre Cahuc, Juan J. Dolado, and Thomas Le Barbanchon. 2012. "Two-Tier Labor Markets in the Great Recession: France Versus Spain." *Economic Journal* 122 (562): F155–F187.

Berg, Erlend, Sambit Bhattacharyya, Rajasekhar Durgam, and Manjula Ramachandra. 2012. "Can Rural Public Works Affect Agricultural Wages? Evidence from India." CSAE Working Paper WPS/2012-05, Centre for the Study of African Economies, Oxford University, Oxford.

Bertrand, Marianne, Kaushik Krishnan, and Heather Schofield. 2020. "How Are Indian Households Coping under the COVID-19 Lockdown? Eight Key Findings." Rustandy Stories, May 11, 2020, Rustandy Center for Social Sector Innovation, Chicago Booth, Booth School of Business, University of Chicago, Chicago. https://www.chicagobooth.edu/research/rustandy/stories /indian-households-coping-with-covid19-lockdown-8-findings.

Beyer, Robert C. M., Sebastian Franco-Bedoya, and Virgilio Galdo. 2021. "Examining the Economic Impact of COVID-19 in India through Daily Electricity Consumption and Nighttime Light Intensity." *World Development* 140 (April), 105287.

Bhalotia, Shania, Swati Dhingra, and Fjolla Kondirolli. 2020. "City of Dreams No More? The Impact of Covid-19 on Urban Workers in India." CEP Covid-19 Analysis Paper 008 (September), Centre for Economic Performance, London School of Economics and Political Science, London.

Chaurey, Ritam. 2015. "Labor Regulations and Contract Labor Use: Evidence from Indian Firms." *Journal of Development Economics* 114 (May): 224–32.

Deininger, Klaus W., and Yanyan Liu. 2019. "Heterogeneous Welfare Impacts of National Rural Employment Guarantee Scheme: Evidence from Andhra Pradesh, India." *World Development* 117 (May): 98–111.

Deshpande, Ashwini. 2020. "The COVID-19 Pandemic and Gendered Division of Paid and Unpaid Work: Evidence from India." IZA Discussion Paper 13815 (October), Institute of Labor Economics, Bonn, Germany.

Dhingra, Swati, and Stephen Machin. 2020. "The Crisis and Job Guarantees in Urban India." IZA Discussion Paper 13760 (October), Institute of Labor Economics, Bonn, Germany.

Dingel, Jonathan I., and Brent Neiman. 2020. "How Many Jobs Can Be Done at Home?" NBER Working Paper 26948 (April), National Bureau of Economic Research, Cambridge, MA.

Dutta, Puja Vasudeva, Rinku Murgai, Martin Ravallion, and Dominique van de Walle. 2012. "Does India's Employment Guarantee Scheme Guarantee Employment?" *Economic and Political Weekly* 47 (16): 55–64.

Gulyas, Andreas, and Krzysztof Pytka. 2020. "The Consequences of the Covid-19 Job Losses: Who Will Suffer Most and by How Much?" Discussion Paper CRC TR 224 (September), Collaborative Research Center Transregio 224, Rheinische Friedrich-Wilhelms-Universität Bonn, Bonn, Germany; Universität Mannheim, Mannheim, Germany.

Guven, Cahit, Panagiotis Sotirakopoulos, and Aydogan Ulker. 2020. "Short-Term Labor Market Effects of COVID-19 and the Associated National Lockdown in Australia: Evidence from Longitudinal Labor Force Survey." GLO Discussion Paper 635, Global Labor Organization, Essen, Germany.

Hall, Robert E., Charles I. Jones, and Peter J. Klenow. 2020. "Trading Off Consumption and COVID-19 Deaths." NBER Working Paper 27340 (June), National Bureau of Economic Research, Cambridge, MA.

ILO (International Labour Organization) 2020a. "ILO Monitor: COVID-19 and the World of Work; Updated Estimates and Analysis, Third Edition." April 29, ILO, Geneva.

ILO (International Labour Organization). 2020b. "Answering Key Questions around Informality in Micro and Small Enterprises during the COVID-19 Crisis." Policy Brief, September 14, ILO, Geneva.

Imbert, Clément, and John Papp, 2015. "Labor Market Effects of Social Programs: Evidence from India's Employment Guarantee." *American Economic Journal: Applied Economics* 7 (2): 233–63.

Kikuchi, Shinnosuke, Sagiri Kitao, and Minamo Mikoshiba. 2021. "Who Suffers from the COVID-19 Shocks? Labor Market Heterogeneity and Welfare Consequences in Japan." *Journal of the Japanese and International Economies* 59 (March), 101117.

Lee, Kenneth, Harshil Sahai, Patrick Baylis, and Michael Greenstone. 2020. "Job Loss and Behavioral Change: The Unprecedented Effects of the India Lockdown in Delhi." BFI Working Paper 2020-65 (May 15), Becker Friedman Institute for Research in Economics, University of Chicago, Chicago.

Lee, Sang Yoon (Tim), Minsung Park, and Yongseok Shin. 2021. "Hit Harder, Recover Slower? Unequal Employment Effects of the Covid-19 Shock." NBER Working Paper 28354 (January), National Bureau of Economic Research, Cambridge, MA.

Loayza, Norman V., and Jamele Rigolini. 2011. "Informal Employment: Safety Net or Growth Engine?" *World Development* 39 (9): 1503–15.

Maloney, William F. 2004. "Informality Revisited." *World Development* 32 (7): 1159–78.

Mattana, Elena, Valerie Smeets, and Frederic Warzynski. 2020. "Changing Skill Structure and COVID-19." *COVID Economics* 45 (August 28): 1–30.

McKenzie, David J. 2003. "How Do Households Cope with Aggregate Shocks? Evidence from the Mexican Peso Crisis." *World Development* 31 (7): 1179–99.

Sharma, Siddharth, and Hernán Jorge Winkler. 2018. "The Labor Market Effects of Financial Crises: The Role of Temporary Contracts in Central and Western Europe." *Economics of Transition* 26 (1): 35–60.

Skoufias, Emmanuel. 2003. "Economic Crises and Natural Disasters: Coping Strategies and Policy Implications." *World Development* 31 (7): 1087–1102.

Vyas, Mahesh. 2020. "Impact of Lockdown on Labour in India." *Indian Journal of Labour Economics* 63 (1): 73–77.

World Bank. 2020. *Beaten or Broken: Informality and COVID-19*. South Asia Economic Focus (October). Washington, DC: World Bank.

Zimmermann, Laura. 2020. "Why Guarantee Employment? Evidence from a Large Indian Public-Works Program." GLO Discussion Paper 504, Global Labor Organization, Essen, Germany.

CHAPTER 8

Social Insurance among Informal Workers in South Asia

GUSTAVO DEMARCO, ERNESTO BRODERSOHN, MIGLENA ABELS, CLÉMENT JOUBERT, AND EMILIO BASAVILBASO

Introduction

Most workers in advanced countries and workers in the formal sector in South Asia have access to pension benefits and other forms of social insurance to protect against sudden reductions in income and to provide support after retirement or in the event of loss of income because of other social risks (annex 8A). However, most South Asian workers are in the informal sector, and most informal sector workers lack good access to social insurance and face various uninsured or poorly insured risks, including illness, temporary unemployment, and income loss if they can no longer work.[1] In the region, 95 percent of the labor force does not have any form of pension, the highest rate among low- and middle-income regions, together with Sub-Saharan Africa (figure 8.1). This chapter focuses on the potential for expanding access to pensions among informal sector workers in South Asia. Because international experience shows that the possibility of reducing informality is limited, the analysis explores the potential for extending social insurance to workers who remain informal.

The most common approach to improving access is to expand existing contributory social insurance schemes to reach more workers. However, the results in most countries worldwide have been disappointing (Palacios and Robalino 2020). Reducing the size of the informal sector so more workers can be subject to payroll taxes to finance social insurance through improvements in records, administration, and compliance enforcement has had a limited impact (Palacios and Robalino 2020). Countries in Latin America have had some success in extending the coverage of contributory social insurance programs through the simplification of rules, procedures, and packages, notably, for small contributors. Typically, countries worldwide tend to focus on the introduction of pension schemes for special groups of workers, such as the self-employed or rural workers. However, the prospects for significantly increasing social insurance coverage through greater formalization or modifying current contributory programs are limited. In Sri Lanka, for instance, schemes adopted in the past 20 years have shown mixed results (box 8.1).

FIGURE 8.1 **The Labor Force without Pensions, by World Region, 2006–16**

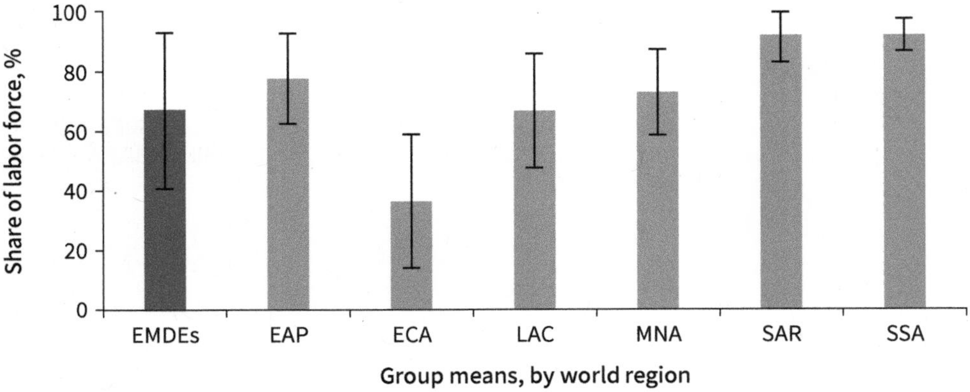

Source: Ohnsorge and Yu 2022.
Note: The whiskers indicate ± 1 standard deviation. EAP = East Asia and Pacific. ECA = Europe and Central Asia. EMDEs = emerging markets and developing economies. LAC = Latin America and the Caribbean. MNA = Middle East and North Africa. SAR = South Asia. SSA = Sub-Saharan Africa.

BOX 8.1 **Experiences in Addressing Informal Sector Pension Coverage in Sri Lanka**

In Sri Lanka, 218,000 of the 5 million informal workers are enrolled in some pension scheme. About 70,000 accounts are enrolled under the Social Security Board, which was created in 1996. Various specific pension schemes were introduced for the self-employed 10 years later, which include medical doctors, artists, journalists, and small-scale tea producers. Most of these are defined benefit schemes that may have more rigid eligibility requirements, such as minimum contributions within a year or burdensome conditions for enrollment. Some of these conditions discourage individuals from enrolling and contributing to the scheme. For instance, participants in the Fishermen's Pension defined benefit scheme cannot own more than a certain threshold of assets, such as three professional fishing craft or more than two hectares of land. The number of active members fell from 70,000 in 1995, when the scheme was launched, to 1,300 in 2016. At the same time, the scheme faced sustainability challenges. Coverage rates for this and various other, similar schemes hardly changed in the 20 years up to 2016 (figure B8.1.1).

(Box continues next page)

BOX 8.1 **Experiences in Addressing Informal Sector Pension Coverage in Sri Lanka** *(continued)*

FIGURE B8.1.1 **Pension Scheme Coverage, Working-Age Population Ages 18–60, 1996–2016**

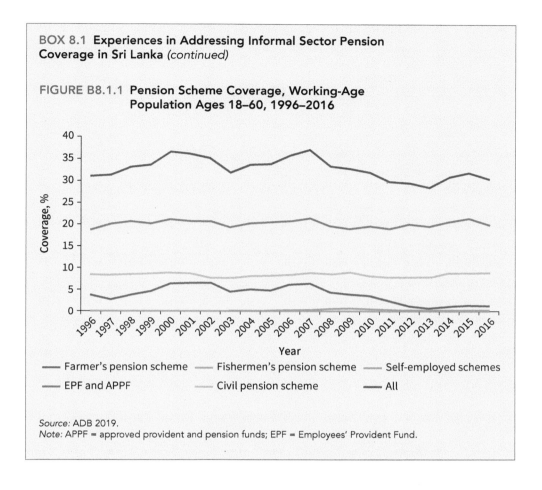

— Farmer's pension scheme   — Fishermen's pension scheme   — Self-employed schemes

— EPF and APPF   — Civil pension scheme   — All

Source: ADB 2019.
Note: APPF = approved provident and pension funds; EPF = Employees' Provident Fund.

The occupations and incomes of informal sector workers in the region are quite varied. In Sri Lanka, for example, 57.4 percent of total employment is informal, covering a wide range of occupations, such as managers, technicians, professionals, sales workers, and more (table 8.1). Although income data do not differentiate between the formal and informal sectors, a wide income dispersion may also be inferred, although average incomes are lower and the poverty rate is higher in the informal sector. In Bangladesh, which has one of the largest informal sectors in the region, official statistics reveal the diversity of activities, with shares ranging between 71.8 percent in services to more than 95.4 percent in agriculture (figure 8.2). Most of these workers are not covered by any formal contributory pension system, and coverage is limited to the means-tested system that was introduced in 1998 among workers with the lowest incomes (Hu and Stewart 2009) (annex 8B).

The main message of this chapter is that the diversity in occupations and incomes in the informal sector means that no single solution can be applied to expand the coverage of social insurance schemes. A segment of workers in the informal sector has relatively high incomes and some potential to save. For example, household surveys in Pakistan indicate that the two highest quintiles in the income distribution consist of a significant

TABLE 8.1 **Formal and Informal Employment, by Main Occupation, Sri Lanka, 2019**

Occupation	Formal		Informal	
	Number	%	Number	%
Managers, senior officials, legislators, and chief executives				
Chief executives, senior officials, legislators	26,098	93.2	1,891	6.8
Administrative and commercial managers	104,109	84.3	19,349	15.7
Production and specialized service managers	82,403	55.6	65,881	44.4
Hospitality, shop, and related service managers	99,117	30.7	223,619	69.3
Professionals	524,764	86.2	84,321	13.8
Technical and associate professionals	571,397	77	170,408	23
Clerks and clerical support workers	283,638	91.8	25,256	8.2
Services and sales workers	416,177	58.8	291,790	41.2
Skilled agricultural, forestry, and fishery workers	38,131	2.8	1,337,410	97.2
Craft and related trade workers	357,744	27.4	950,022	72.6
Plant and machine operators and assemblers	293,279	41	421,267	59
Elementary occupations	565,615	37.4	1,101,192	62.6
Armed forces occupations and unidentified occupations	29,033	83.4	5,783	16.6
Total	3,482,505	42.6	4,698,187	57.4

Source: DCS 2019.

FIGURE 8.2 **Informal Employment, by Broad Economic Sector, Bangladesh, 2016–17**

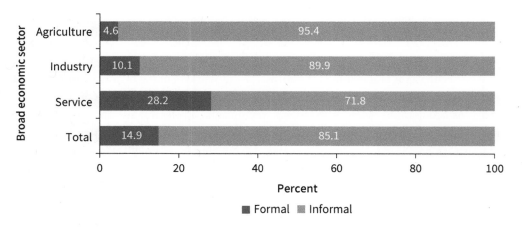

Source: BBS 2018.

share of households with self-employed individuals and skilled employees.[2] These households own a diversified portfolio of assets, including productive assets needed for self-employment that show potential for accumulation over the life cycle. In this, they are similar to formal sector households. Evidence shows that the households of informal workers in the highest deciles or quintiles hold savings. Nevertheless, these savings are not normally used to provide income security in old age, perhaps partly because of a lack of appropriate savings instruments. There is clearly room to introduce innovative contributory schemes for the less poor segment of the informal sector.

Among poor informal workers, by contrast, contributory schemes are either not feasible or not attractive. The informal workers in the lowest three quintiles of households consist mostly of paid employees in elementary occupations and some cultivators. These people own few assets besides residential housing and a little land. Their households are therefore unlikely to be able to accumulate substantial savings for old age. This groups need to be targeted by noncontributory pensions or social pensions. All countries in the region have social pension systems. The expansion of these systems is possibly the only option for reducing old-age poverty among a large group of informal workers. However, in the absence of alternative solutions, the size of these programs may end up being too large; the associated fiscal costs would be too high; and the programs may not address informality at large scale because of the low incentive to assume the costs of formal sector jobs.

Given the heterogeneity in income levels among informal workers, the chapter proposes that undertaking various approaches would help ensure adequate resources to provide long-term income support for lower and higher income quintiles. The following section discusses the potential to expand noncontributory social insurance in the region because this is the only way to reach workers with low or no capacity to contribute. The main conclusion of the section is that such an expansion may be too costly if it is not targeted, and, even if it is targeted, the benefits need to be restrained to be fiscally sustainable and not discourage formalization. The section entitled "Expanding Social Insurance to Higher-Income Informal Workers" examines the potential to integrate higher-income informal workers into existing contributory social insurance. The international experience teaches that this is possible and that simplification and lower costs may produce some modest impact. The section analyzes the potential of long-term savings for higher income workers in Pakistan.[3] Data from household surveys for that country confirm that there is space for such expansion, provided that incentives and institutional enabling conditions are also met. The section entitled "Policy Implications" explores the possibility of generalizing the conclusions of the preceding section to the rest of the South Asian countries. In the absence of comprehensive household survey data, the chapter uses indicators from Findex to infer enabling conditions in the region and concludes that three of the countries will likely meet those conditions, under similar enabling environment (annex 8C).[4]

Extending Coverage through Noncontributory Social Insurance

The expansion of noncontributory social insurance to provide all informal workers with retirement and the coverage of other long-term social insurance risks would require enormous fiscal efforts and is not recommended. Although noncontributory pensions play a necessary role in providing income security in old age for the poorer informal, fiscal constraints will limit both the size of these kinds of pensions and the age to be eligible to receive the old age benefit.[5] However, government fiscal space, the share of the elderly in the total population, and the projected rate of population aging vary considerably across the region. Accordingly, the potential for extending the coverage of noncontributory pension schemes to informal workers also varies. It is important to underscore that, even if noncontributory pensions are devised to be affordable now, a major challenge is ensuring that the program remains affordable over time, given the population aging and the potential for discretionary increases in the benefit amounts.

THE CURRENT STATE OF NONCONTRIBUTORY PENSIONS IN SOUTH ASIA

Five of the eight countries in the region have noncontributory schemes targeted at the elderly and persons with disabilities. Box 8.2 provides an overview of existing noncontributory pension programs, eligibility criteria, and benefit levels across the region. In principle, this provides a platform to potentially expand pension coverage on a noncontributory basis.

BOX 8.2 Noncontributory Pensions in South Asia

- **Bangladesh.** The Old Age Allowance is income tested and targeted at men ages 65 or more and women ages 62 or more who do not receive any other government or nongovernment allowance. Only one member of a household can receive the pension. The beneficiary's annual income cannot exceed Tk 10,000 (equivalent to US$120). A designated committee prioritizes the benefit payments to the most vulnerable and women. Of those selected, at least half must be women.

- **India.** The Indira Gandhi National Old Age Pension Scheme (IGNOAPS) is targeted at people ages 60 an older whose annual income does not exceed a certain limit, which may vary across states. A basic pension of Rs 200 a month is paid to the 60–79 age group, and a pension of Rs 500 a month is paid to the 80 and older age-group. The federal scheme is complemented by programs run by the states and territories, which provide far more extensive and generous protection among the elderly and persons with disabilities. The fragmentation and multiplicity of designs among the state programs make aggregation at the national level a complex task that would require a specialized study.

- **Maldives.** The Old-Age Basic Pension covers every citizen age 65 and older who resides in the country and who is not receiving more than twice the amount of the old age basic pension from any other pension source.

- **Nepal.** The Old Age Allowance or Senior Citizens Allowance is paid to all citizens ages 70 and older, except Dalits (lower castes) and residents of Karnali Province, who may receive the allowance at ages 60 and older.

- **Sri Lanka.** People ages 70 and older are covered by the Elderly Assistance Program if they are living in low-income households and have been receiving the samurdhi[a] subsidy or monthly public assistance allowance. Another social welfare program—the Public Welfare Assistance Allowance or pin padi program—may also benefit the elderly, although the program is not targeted specifically at this group.

Source: Various World Bank data, including Pensions: Data (dashboard), World Bank, Washington, DC, https://www.worldbank.org/en/topic/socialprotection/brief/pensions-data.
a. The samurdhi (prosperity) subsidy is a targeted food stamp program introduced in 1995.

The coverage of the elderly by noncontributory pensions varies across the region, mainly because of differences in age and income requirements (figure 8.3). The non-contributory pension in Nepal is universal, which explains why the coverage of the 70+ population is over 100 percent; it is above 100 percent likely because, in some areas, the pension can be drawn at age 60. In Maldives, even though the pension is not universal,

FIGURE 8.3 Noncontributory Pension Programs: Age of Eligibility and Coverage

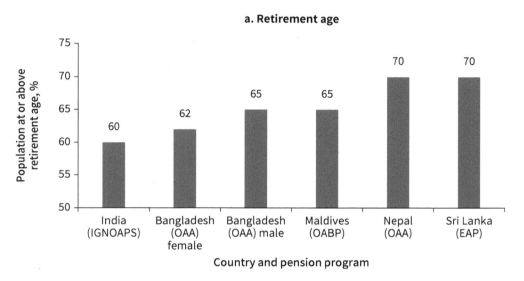

a. Retirement age

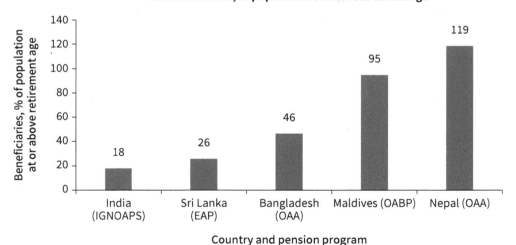

b. Beneficiaries, % population above retirement age

Sources: World Bank calculations; World Population Prospects 2019 (database), Population Division, Department of Economic and Social Affairs, United Nations, New York, https://population.un.org/wpp/.
Note: EAP = Elderly Assistance Program; IGNOAPS = Indira Gandhi National Old Age Pension Scheme; OAA = Old Age Allowance; OABP = Old Age Basic Pension.

the income threshold is quite high, which explains the near universal coverage of 95 percent of the population above the age of eligibility. In India, the threshold is low, which likely contributes to the low coverage of the program.

There is also significant variation in the monthly benefits across the five countries (figure 8.4, panel a). Pensions are highest in Maldives and Nepal, equal to 37 percent

FIGURE 8.4 Monthly Benefits

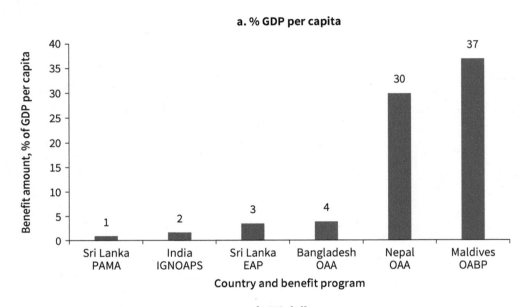

a. % GDP per capita

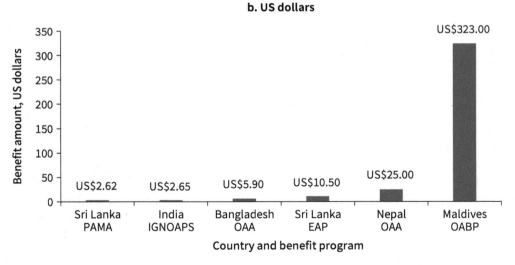

b. US dollars

Sources: World Bank calculations; ASPIRE (Atlas of Social Protection Indicators of Resilience and Equity) (dashboard), World Bank, Washington, DC, http://datatopics.worldbank.org/aspire/.
Note: EAP = Elderly Assistance Program; GDP = gross domestic product; IGNOAPS = Indira Gandhi National Old Age Pension Scheme; OAA = Old Age Allowance; OABP = Old Age Basic Pension; PAMA = Public Welfare Assistance Allowance.

FIGURE 8.5 **Expenditures on Noncontributory Pensions**

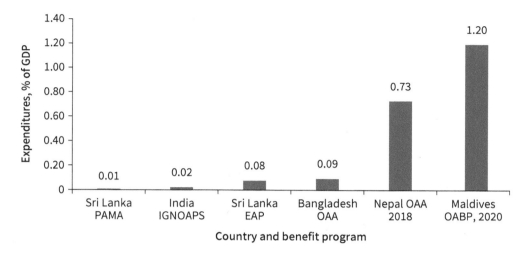

Sources: World Bank calculations; ASPIRE (Atlas of Social Protection Indicators of Resilience and Equity) (dashboard), World Bank, Washington, DC, http://datatopics.worldbank.org/aspire/; government data.
Note: EAP = Elderly Assistance Program; GDP = gross domestic product; IGNOAPS = Indira Gandhi National Old Age Pension Scheme; OAA = Old Age Allowance; OABP = Old Age Basic Pension; PAMA = Public Welfare Assistance Allowance.

and 30 percent of per capita gross domestic product (GDP), respectively. In Maldives, benefits are equal to more than 2.4 times the national poverty line.[6] In Nepal, benefit levels are equal to almost double the national poverty line.[7] This suggests that the programs are not only a poverty reducing mechanism but are also intended to support a degree of consumption smoothing throughout the life cycle. By contrast, in Bangladesh, India, and Sri Lanka, the benefits are low, accounting for a small share of the poverty line. They are estimated at around 40 percent of the national poverty line in Sri Lanka and at only 11 percent of the national poverty line in Bangladesh.[8]

Expenditure trends mirror program coverage and benefit levels (figure 8.5). Expenditure is highest in Maldives and Nepal, which also cover the largest share of individuals ages 60+ and pay the highest noncontributory pensions in the region.

FUTURE OF NONCONTRIBUTORY PENSIONS IN SOUTH ASIA

The expansion of noncontributory pensions beyond current benefit and coverage levels will be difficult in countries in which the average age of the population is rising rapidly. To examine the future fiscal impact of population aging on noncontributory pension programs in the region, the analysis relied on a projection of a first scenario based on the assumption that expenditure increases will be caused only by population aging, that is, an increase in the number of individuals above the eligibility age (figure 8.6, panel a). Coverage rates will remain constant, and benefit levels will remain at a steady share of GDP per capita.

FIGURE 8.6 **Pension Coverage and Projected Share of Population Ages 60+, 2020–50**

a. Current and projected population ages 60+

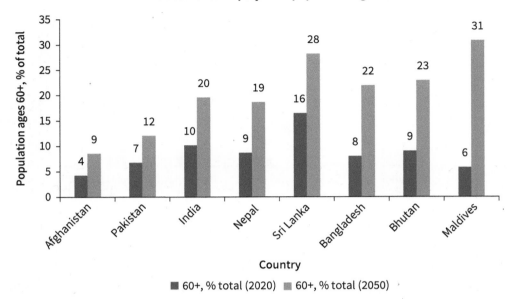

Legend: ■ 60+, % total (2020) ■ 60+, % total (2050)

b. Current pension coverage

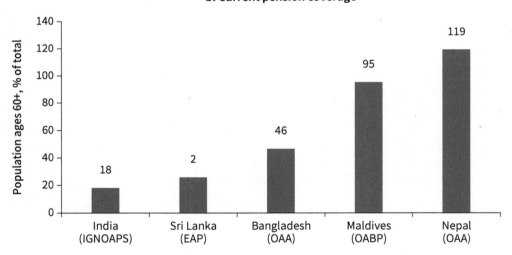

Source: Calculations based on data of ASPIRE (Atlas of Social Protection Indicators of Resilience and Equity) (dashboard), World Bank, Washington, DC, http://datatopics.worldbank.org/aspire/.
Note: EAP = Elderly Assistance Program; IGNOAPS = Indira Gandhi National Old Age Pension Scheme; OAA = Old Age Allowance; OABP = Old Age Basic Pension.

Officials in Maldives and Nepal may need to consider lowering benefit levels, introducing or improving targeting mechanisms, or raising the age of retirement to ensure that benefit program expenditures do not become unaffordable because of aging. Although expenditures are projected to rise several-fold in all countries under this purely demographic scenario, Maldives and Nepal stand out in terms of the rise in expenditures as a share of GDP because they provide almost universal coverage for the population above retirement age, as well as high benefit levels (figure 8.7). Moreover, Maldives provides the benefits from age 65, and Nepal as early as age 60 for some groups (although others must wait until age 70). Retirement at age 60 or 65 is relatively young for a noncontributory social pension and will certainly need to be revised going forward in the context of increasing life expectancy.

Meanwhile, Bangladesh, India, and Sri Lanka could consider an expansion of noncontributory pensions in terms of both greater coverage of the elderly and higher benefit levels. The numbers on India underestimate the real level of current benefits and expenditures because only the Indira Gandhi National Old Age Pension Scheme (IGNOAPS) is considered, not the additional programs in the states and territories. The costs are projected to rise because of aging, but the low to modest benefit levels and lower coverage of the elderly population mean that expenditures in federal level programs are projected to remain below 0.3 percent of GDP in all three countries through 2050 if benefits and coverage rates remain constant.[9]

FIGURE 8.7 **Projected Cost of Noncontributory Pension Programs, Demographic Scenario**

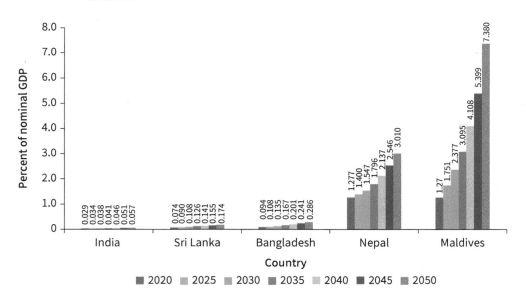

Source: Calculations based on data of ASPIRE (Atlas of Social Protection Indicators of Resilience and Equity) (dashboard), World Bank, Washington, DC, http://datatopics.worldbank.org/aspire/.
Note: The numbers represent the projected cost of noncontributory pension programs for the shown years under the demographic scenario, that is, the projected increase in cost simply due to an increase in the eligible population due to demographic changes (aging of the population).

Bangladesh and Sri Lanka may be able to improve the adequacy of the noncontributory benefits without imposing an unmanageable fiscal burden on government finances. All three countries currently provide benefits equal to less than 4 percent of GDP per capita, which suggests that benefits could be raised. The same would apply to India if only the federal IGNOAPS is considered.

The second scenario explores the projected impact on expenditures if benefits increase to reach national poverty lines. Bangladesh is projected to undergo the highest rise in expenditures relative to scenario 1 because of the ninefold increase in benefit levels from Tk 500 to Tk 4,483 per month assumed in scenario 2 (figure 8.8). This scenario still takes demographic change into account, but it does not assume an increase in coverage rates. A more modest increase in benefit levels will result in correspondingly lower expenditures.

In addition to enhancing benefit adequacy, Sri Lanka (and India, if one considers only the IGNOAPS) may also have room to boost coverage while keeping costs below 1 percent of GDP by 2050. Scenario 3 assesses the fiscal impact of increasing benefits (as in scenario 2) but also raising coverage to 50 percent of the population above retirement age (figure 8.9). Because coverage is already at 46 percent of the population above retirement age in Bangladesh, this scenario has negligible impact. It does, however, matter in the case of India and Sri Lanka, where noncontributory pension programs only cover 18 percent and 26 percent of the elderly, respectively.

FIGURE 8.8 **Projected Expenditures, Increased Benefit and Unchanged Coverage Scenario**

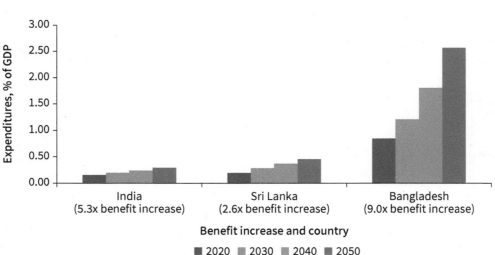

Source: Calculations based on data of ASPIRE (Atlas of Social Protection Indicators of Resilience and Equity) (dashboard), World Bank, Washington, DC, http://datatopics.worldbank.org/aspire/.

FIGURE 8.9 **Projected Expenditures, Higher Benefit and Wider Coverage**

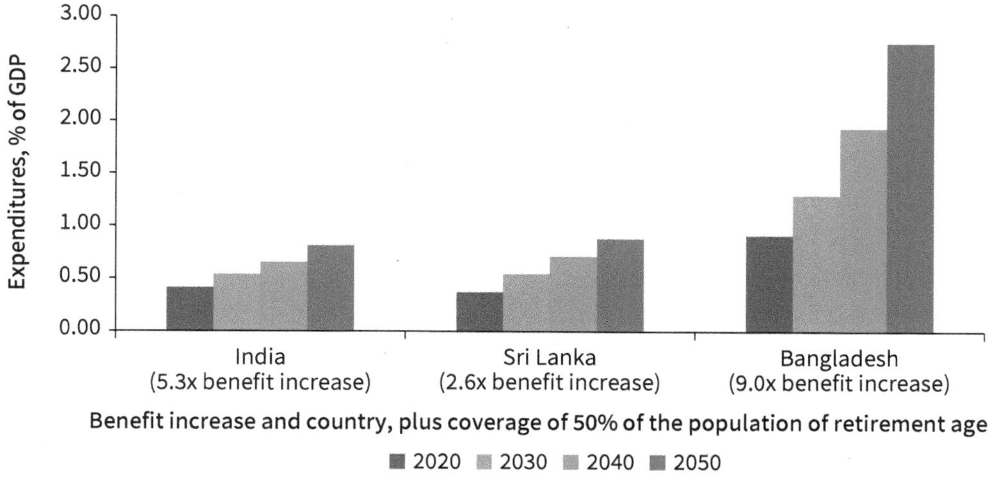

Benefit increase and country, plus coverage of 50% of the population of retirement age

■ 2020 ■ 2030 ■ 2040 ■ 2050

Source: Calculations based on data of ASPIRE (Atlas of Social Protection Indicators of Resilience and Equity) (dashboard), World Bank, Washington, DC, http://datatopics.worldbank.org/aspire/.

BOX 8.3 **Summary of the Three Scenarios**

Scenario 1, a purely demographic scenario, demonstrates the future fiscal impact of population aging on noncontributory pension programs with the current benefit and coverage levels.

Scenario 2 explores the projected impact on expenditures if benefits are increased to the national poverty line. The scenario reflects higher costs because of demographic change (as in scenario 1), but does not assume any expansion in coverage. In Bangladesh, the benefit would increase from 4 percent to 35 percent of GDP per capita (equivalent to about Tk 59,210 a year, around US$686 in 2020). In India, the benefit would be raised from the current 1.6 percent of GDP per capita to 8.0 percent (equal to the rural poverty line). In Sri Lanka, the benefit would rise from around 4 percent to 11 percent of GDP per capita (equal to the national poverty line).

Scenario 3 assesses the projected fiscal impact of population aging (scenario 1) if benefits are increased to the national poverty line (scenario 2), and coverage is raised to reach 50 percent of the population above retirement age. The current coverage is 46 percent of the population above retirement age in Bangladesh, 18 percent in India, and 26 percent in Sri Lanka.

Note: GDP = gross domestic product.

These stylized scenarios are intended to serve as an example of gauging the cost of a program under a specific set of parameters, which may not be appropriate or afford-able given country-specific factors (box 8.3). Authorities in individual countries must determine what is affordable and set benefit levels and age and other eligibility require-ments accordingly to ensure that higher benefits and greater coverage do not render these programs unaffordable over the longer term.[10] It is also important to emphasize that, even if these programs are considered affordable, the government should have the capacity to maintain the benefit levels sufficiently low to avoid disincentives to formalization.

Expanding Social Insurance to Higher-Income Informal Workers

Although a growing number of government officials are realizing that formal sector pension systems are not responding to the needs of the large informal sector, there is no clear consensus on the appropriate methods to increase social insurance coverage among those workers in the informal sector who have some capacity to contribute to insurance schemes to prevent poverty or income loss because of old age, disability, or other social risks.

Although a significant share of the informal sector does have the capacity to contribute to insurance or save for retirement, the coverage of contributory pension schemes has largely been limited to a small segment of the population in the formal sector. South Asian countries have young populations today, but the share of the population ages 60+ is projected to multiply by a factor of 2 or 3 by 2080. Without access to appropriate savings vehicles, even some higher-income informal sector workers may find their resources inadequate to finance retirement and may need to rely on income support from publicly funded social assistance. This section discusses potential avenues for involving a greater share of informal sector workers in contributory pension schemes.

INTERNATIONAL EXPERIENCE

There have been many efforts by social security agencies in low- and middle-income countries to extend coverage to the informal sector, with limited success.[11] This contrasts with the experience in upper-middle-income and high-income countries, in which most self-employed workers file income taxes and social insurance contributions jointly.

Programs to reach informal sector workers do not always fit well with the administrative structures of social security agencies, which have typically been established to support wage employment. Self-employment and wage employment are different, and any forced equivalence may overload workers with extra tax burdens as employees and employers of their own labor. The high costs are the main drivers of the failure of such attempts.

Efforts have been moderately more successful if they involve simplified enrollment, low payments, and the bundling of social insurance and other benefits to encourage informal workers (and employers) to formalize. This approach has been adopted in some countries of Latin America (see annex 8F).

Figure 8.10 offers a concise illustration of the additional structures or initiatives that social security agencies have adopted to include the coverage of the self-employed and informal sector workers with the core structures to cover the formal sector.

A voluntary structure was created in Mexico, for instance, to simplify significantly the payment of pension contributions by individuals through a network of over 15,000 convenience stores (see figure 8.10, strategy a). To facilitate enrollment among individuals, digital registration is available. Monotributo, a simplified tax regime in Argentina, includes a multirisk, multiproduct scheme that is designed to be more attractive to smaller companies and microentrepreneurs and in which compliance is much simpler than traditional social insurance (figure 8.10, strategy b). Such simplifications require specific structures that are built on core pension scheme structures as either add-ons or specifically targeted services and engagement mechanisms. Governments in other regions, such as the Middle East and North Africa, are also looking to expand current mandatory structures to create specific benefit and administrative arrangements to cover the informal sector.

In Sub-Saharan Africa, some social security agencies have built structures specifically tailored to the informal sector. In Rwanda in 2017, the Social Security Board launched EjoHeza, a long-term savings scheme with its own administrative structure within the board, to address the specific requirements of informal sector workers (figure 8.10, strategy c). Similarly, the National Trust Holding Company in Ghana will manage a fully funded voluntary provident fund and personal pension scheme that covers informal

FIGURE 8.10 **Social Security Agency Strategies to Realize Informal Sector Pension Schemes**

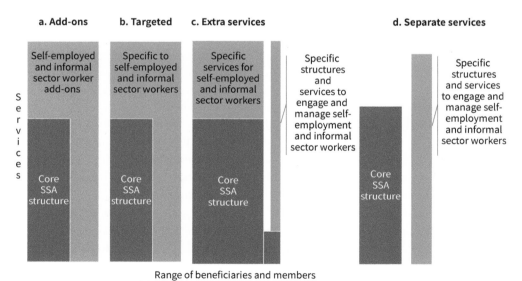

Source: Original figure produced for this publication.
Note: SSA = social security agency.

sector workers. Private initiatives have also been proliferating in the region through the introduction of voluntary schemes with the support of pension regulators. For example, Kenya's MBAO retirement benefits savings scheme provides a specific solution to meet informal sector needs (figure 8.10, strategy d).

Making the transition from a purely mandatory core social security administrative structure to the addition of specific programs and services for the informal sector may not be realistic or desirable for many organizations. It may be more practical to continue to strengthen the core service while building a parallel structure to address the informal sector. Eventually, this parallel structure could be fully integrated within the social insurance system.

Because of the limitations of the traditional approach to the formalization of self-employed and informal workers, long-term savings schemes to finance pensions and other benefits are being increasingly considered as an option in several countries. Innovative approaches even propose long-term savings schemes to finance not only pensions but also shorter-term needs, such as health care, loss of crops, and small investments.

However, most of these innovative interventions are in their infancy, and their development has been slow. In Sub-Saharan Africa, Ghana and Kenya were the first to introduce specific schemes to cover the informal sector. Additional countries considering such programs include Benin, Côte d'Ivoire, Mali, Nigeria, Rwanda, Senegal, Sierra Leone, Uganda, Zambia, and Zimbabwe. In South Asia, India has taken significant steps to extend pension coverage through several initiatives, including opening access to the National Pension Scheme to all citizens on a voluntary basis in 2009. The contributors to the scheme include people working in companies (largely middle- and high-income individuals) and people in the informal sector (largely low-income individuals) (Guven 2019).

FINANCIAL DEVELOPMENT AND THE CAPACITY OF INFORMAL WORKERS TO SAVE

The following subsections explore the potential to develop savings schemes in South Asia. Household information on Pakistan provides detailed data for analyzing the savings capacity of the informal sector. If adequate instruments are available and institutional capacity is developed, savings can be channeled effectively. In the absence of information on other countries in South Asia, financial indicators based on Global Findex data are used to infer the potential of such approaches.

Countries with substantial informality, such as most countries in South Asia, tend to exhibit limited financial development. This can be seen in the relationship between an index of financial development and informality, as well as in the relationship between indicators of financial access and informality (figure 8.11). A low level of financial development can be an important constraint on the potential to extend contributory pension systems to the informal sector. On the demand side, informal sector individuals require

FIGURE 8.11 **Financial Development, Informality, and Household Access to Finance**

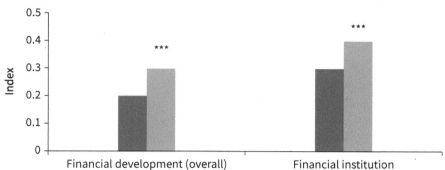

a. Informality and financial development

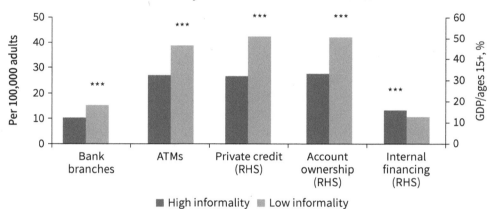

b. Informality and household access to finance

■ High informality ■ Low informality

Source: Ohnsorge and Yu 2022.
Note: Panel a: bars show simple averages for emerging markets and developing economies in 2010–18. Financial development (overall) = the aggregate financial development index from the Financial Development Index Database (dashboard), International Monetary Fund, Washington, DC, https://data.imf.org/?sk=f8032e80-b36c-43b1-ac26-493c5b1cd33b. It purports to measure the overall level of financial development in both financial institutions and financial markets. Panel b: RHS = right-hand side, that is, the y-axis on the right side of panel b.
*** Group differences are not zero at the 10 percent significance level.

much more accessible and lower-cost financial service solutions. On the supply side, specifically tailored solutions would need to be developed to provide the workers with a long-term savings vehicle, possibly supported by public interventions.

This subsection explores the potential for the introduction or expansion of instruments that provide long-term savings opportunities for income support in old age and other life-work contingencies using data from eight rounds of a representative survey of Pakistan households that span 18 years (2001–18), as reported in Joubert and Kanth (2021).[12]

The potential for long-term savings instruments among informal workers in Pakistan

A major issue is the extent to which households supported by informal sector workers tend to accumulate wealth over the life cycle and the nature of this wealth or assets. In 2017, 88.5 percent of employment in Pakistan was informal (Bossavie, Khadka, and Strokova 2018), and the formal pension coverage rate relative to the working-age population was less than 0.25 percent in 2008 (OECD 2008).[13] Savings patterns associated with age are isolated from differences between cohorts and time effects by applying the decomposition of Deaton (1997).

Three socioeconomic trends that are common to many developing countries may have strengthened the life-cycle motive for saving in Pakistan in the past three decades. First, life expectancy and thus the number of unproductive years to be covered have increased significantly throughout the developing world. In Pakistan, the rate rose from 60.1 years in 1990 to 67.1 years in 2018.[14] Second, high fertility rates in the past have meant that the elderly could expect to rely on large cohorts of active individuals within their household and community networks for support in old age. While still relatively high compared with peer countries, the fertility rate in Pakistan has declined by almost one-half over the past 30 years, from 6.2 births per woman in 1990 to 3.5 in 2018, a trend that is common to many developing countries. Finally, the large increase in GDP per capita in Pakistan—from US$371.70 in 1990 to US$1,284.70 in 2019—should have broadened the segments of the population able to set aside some income for future consumption.

To what extent these demographic and economic changes have impacted household asset accumulation over the life cycle is an empirical question. Households may have more incentive to save, but they lack the savings technology (financial inclusion) or ability (commitment or need for liquidity) to put money aside safely for decades. The Global Findex surveys reveal that only 15 percent of individuals was saving specifically for old age in 2017. However, a larger share (35 percent) reported that it generally did save, and those savings may ultimately help finance old-age consumption even if that is not the most urgent intended use. In addition, some components of household net worth, such as housing, may not be identified as savings by respondents, although they are indirectly consumed in old age in the form of, for instance, saved rent payments. Moreover, while relatively illiquid, such assets could be sold as a last resort.

Context: informality and pension coverage in Pakistan

Informality is commonplace in Pakistan, and this has largely remained unchanged over the past decade. It is also pervasive across the income distribution; 70 percent of the jobs among the top quintile is informal (PBS 2017). More than 40 percent of informal jobs in the top quintile correspond to nonagricultural self-employment. This finding suggests that a certain type of informality is associated with high earnings rather than lower productivity or poor working conditions.

Among workers, 24 percent has incomes below the poverty line, and job quality among the bottom quintiles is inadequate to meet basic consumption needs, let alone finance saving. Because most poor workers are also informally employed, they generally lack the social protection that is synonymous with formality in terms of insurance against risks and assistance during shocks. The aggregate labor market outcomes of the poor mask substantial heterogeneity across location, composition, sex, and age. Structural transformation is low. The share of rural employment (65 percent) is high and largely informal. Thus, 72 percent of rural employment is nonwage employment, compared with 44 percent in urban areas. Migration from rural to urban areas results in huge gains in employment status, particularly among people entering into formal wage employment.

Unpaid work is prevalent among youth and women, implying that they suffer greater vulnerability and lack of protection. Close to 20 percent of the employed are engaged in unpaid family work, and the share is three times higher among women than men. Unpaid work is also more prevalent among youth and likely acts as a transition into the labor force. The share of youth in unpaid work is almost 40 percent, which is high compared with other countries, according to the 2014–15 Labor Force Survey (PBS 2015). Although the rate of unpaid work among men is high at younger ages, it diminishes with age and is replaced primarily by self-employment in agriculture in rural areas and in the nonagricultural sector in urban areas. Among women, however, the share of unpaid work remains similar across age groups because transition into paid work is uncommon.

Women, especially poor women, face substantially worse labor market outcomes than men both in job quality and earnings. This is driven by social norms and care responsibilities within the household. The highest labor force participation rate among women is observed among the lowest two quintiles (24 percent in the first quintile and 16 percent in the second), suggesting that women tend to work out of necessity. Most women who work are in unpaid work throughout their lives. Among women in unpaid work, 59 percent are in rural areas, compared with 15 percent among men. When women do work in paid jobs, they tend to work under worse conditions. For instance, in manufacturing, 77 percent of women work as day laborers or casual laborers, compared with 22 percent of men, and the gender wage gap is among the highest in the world, at 34 percent in 2018 (ILO 2018a). Social norms affect women's mobility outside the household because a significant share of women in the nonagricultural sector tend to work inside their dwellings (44 percent in rural areas and 37 percent in urban areas). Women also systematically tend to work fewer hours than men because of the care responsibilities they assume within the household (Cho and Majoka 2020).

Among the poor, informal employment is associated with two major challenges: the engagement in low productivity jobs throughout their lives and the inadequate protection and safety nets they receive because of the volatility of their jobs and their low precautionary savings. In Pakistan, both of these challenges are prevalent among the poor. As shown by the analysis of survey data, lifetime skills acquisition is low because people remain in employment that is not dynamic, but that is characterized by low-skills equilibriums (Bossavie, Khadka, and Strokova 2018; PBS 2015). Informal jobs, by definition, lack access to legal protection and social security (World Bank 2012). Those employed in the informal sector are also more vulnerable to the detrimental consequences of shocks because they also tend to have more variable incomes and less access to safety nets (Stuart, Samman, and Hunt 2018). This is especially true of the poor and near poor because even a small idiosyncratic shock can push them further into poverty.

According to the Access to Finance Survey (2015), only 23 percent of the adult population in Pakistan is formally banked, that is, having transaction accounts, either conventional or mobile money accounts.[15] Financial inclusion remains low, despite the achievement of key milestones, such as the creation of a regulatory framework for microfinance banks in 2001, the expansion and modernization of the online credit information bureau in 2005, legislation on branchless banking in 2008, the establishment of a specialized microfinance credit information bureau in 2012, the launch of a nationwide financial literacy program in 2012, and subsidized lending schemes aimed at encouraging lending to the underserved. Only 18 percent of adults have an account with a formal financial institution (the South Asian average is 33 percent); 86 percent of the financially included are men; and 68 percent reside in urban areas.[16] Access to credit increases with age and education, but borrowing is mostly informal. One-third of the adult population borrows, and less than 2 percent use a formal financial institution to do so. The microfinance industry in Pakistan is a major source of credit to lower-income individuals, household enterprises (77 percent of which are informal in Pakistan), and rural communities. The industry is largely comprised of microfinance banks, microfinance institutions, and rural support programs. The industry has 6.9 million borrowers and a total portfolio of PRe 274 billion (PMN 2019).

Pensions and social insurance programs in Pakistan are limited to the few formal sector workers. At the federal level, the Employees' Old-Age Benefits Institution provides age, disability, and survivors pensions through a voluntary pension scheme on a self-registration basis that covers only a fraction of formal sector workers. At the provincial level, employees social security institutions provide health services (through social security hospitals, medical centers, and dispensaries, thereby acting more like health insurance) and some cash benefits to employees of registered establishments. The Punjab employees social security institution serves above 2.5 million patients every year and requires employers to contribute 6 percent of the wages of their employees with wages up to PRe 18,000. Both the Employees' Old-Age Benefits Institution and the employees social security institutions cater to the formal sector through registered public and private enterprises. There is no such scheme for employees in the informal sector, such as day laborers and agricultural workers, and only the Zakat charitable councils and the Bait-ul Mal charity and social welfare organization supply some relief to vulnerable groups. Currently, self-registration is not possible under the existing legislation on employees social security institutions. The institution in Sindh has already started self-registration among informal workers under the Home-Based Workers Act 2019; under the Domestic Workers Act 2019 in Punjab, employers can register domestic workers with the Punjab institution.

Some programs, such as the employees social security institutions, are intended to cover both rural and urban areas; however, implementation and enforcement show large gaps, particularly in rural areas. In addition, anecdotal evidence suggests that beneficiaries covered under some of these programs, such as the employees social security institutions, do not have great knowledge of the benefits to which they are entitled. The challenges faced by such institutions include promoting compliance to cover all workers in all economic sectors, delivering quality and timely health benefits, and providing adequate cash benefits to replace loss of income. These problems in part reflect the limited resources available to the institutions to invest in human and information technology capacity and good governance management systems. The International Labour Organization (ILO) has supported comprehensive activities in the short term to boost knowledge sharing, impart more awareness of best practices in enforcing compliance, modernize contribution collection, enhance delivery of higher-quality and timely health benefits, and strengthen tripartite governance and advocacy communication (ILO 2018b).

Methodology: estimating life-cycle household wealth accumulation

It would be useful to be able to measure how average household net worth evolves along the life cycle, but using a single cross-section of data (that is, from one specific year) severely understates household net worth accumulation. Figure 8.12 plots household

FIGURE 8.12 **Household Net Worth, by Age of Household Head, 2001, 2010, and 2018**

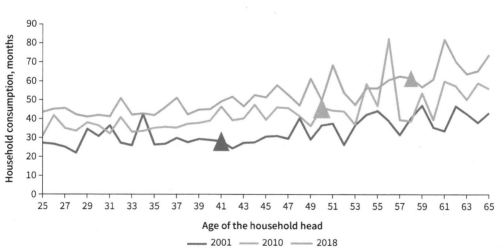

Source: Derived from data of the 2001, 2010, and 2018 survey rounds, PSLM Publications (Pakistan Social and Living Standards Measurement Publications), Pakistan Bureau of Statistics, Islamabad, Pakistan, https://www.pbs .gov.pk/pslm-publications.
Note: Triangles denote the average net worth for the cohort born in 1960.

net worth, measured in multiples of monthly household consumption, against the age of the household head in the 2001, 2010, and 2018 rounds of the Pakistan Social and Living Standards Measurement Survey. Age profiles thus constructed appear quite flat. Household net worth increases by around a year (12 months) of consumption every 20 years. However, this fails to consider that each cohort is wealthier than the next. The 2018 cross-sectional profile is shifted upward by around 20 months of consumption relative to the 2001 profile.

Pooling multiple years of data allows each cohort to be followed as they age and the true rate of net worth accumulation to be measured changes. For example, the three triangles in figure 8.12 identify household heads born in 1960, whose net worth is observed at ages 41, 50, and 58. When the 1960 cohort reaches age 58 (green triangle), its average net worth is much higher than that of a 58-year-old in 2001. The line that intersects the three data points corresponding to the 1960 cohort is therefore much steeper than the cross-sectional profiles. Across 20 years, the average net worth for the cohort rises by nearly 3 years (36 months) of consumption. Considering household net worth by age in a specific year thus significantly understates the rate at which households accumulate net worth over time. In that case, the rate in the example would appear three times (36/12) slower in figure 8.12.

The goal of this analysis is to estimate the true rate at which households accumulate wealth over the life cycle by exploiting the repeated survey cross-sections available between 2001 and 2018. To accomplish this, the age profiles of assets, log income, and log consumption are extracted using the methodology of Deaton (1997) described in Joubert and Kanth (2021). The age profile of the saving rate is obtained by subtracting log consumption coefficients from the corresponding log income coefficients.

Decomposition of average household life-cycle wealth and savings profiles

Household income begins to outpace household consumption when the age of the household head reaches the early 40s, thereby allowing the household saving rate to grow by 20 percentage points by age 55 (figure 8.13). At ages in the 20s and 30s, income and consumption grow at the same rate, which implies that the saving rate is constant throughout that age range.

The analysis finds that households, on average, accumulate net worth equivalent to around 5 years (60 months) of consumption between ages 25 and 65. Figure 8.14 shows the additional average household net worth relative to age 25. The accumulation is gradual but, consistent with the age profile of the saving rate, it accelerates significantly in the later part of the life cycle. The slope of the curve of household net worth in the figure is twice as steep at ages 45–65 compared with ages 25–45. Net worth increases by 20 months on average between ages 25 and 45 and by 40 months between ages 45 and 65.

Real estate accounts for most of the net worth households accumulate (figure 8.15, panel a). Its share in total household net worth rises by 45 months of household consumption, which represents about 75 percent of the total increase in net worth.

SOCIAL INSURANCE AMONG INFORMAL WORKERS IN SOUTH ASIA | 271

FIGURE 8.13 Age Profile, by Income, Consumption, and Savings, 2001–18

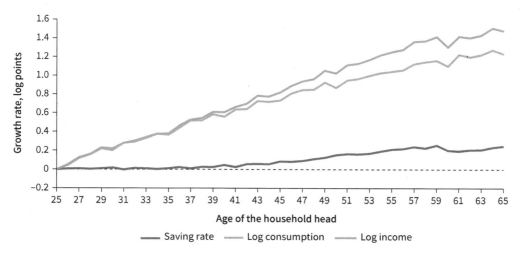

Source: Derived from data of the 2001–18 survey rounds, PSLM Publications (Pakistan Social and Living Standards Measurement Publications), Pakistan Bureau of Statistics, Islamabad, Pakistan, https://www.pbs.gov.pk /pslm-publications.

FIGURE 8.14 Household Net Worth over the Life Cycle, by Age of Household Head, 2001–18

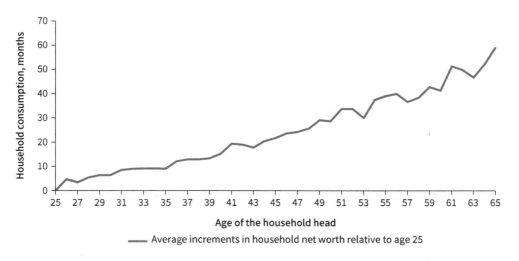

Source: Derived from data of the 2001–18 survey rounds, PSLM Publications (Pakistan Social and Living Standards Measurement Publications), Pakistan Bureau of Statistics, Islamabad, Pakistan, https://www.pbs.gov.pk/pslm -publications.

FIGURE 8.15 **Household Net Worth, by Component and Age of Household Head, 2001–18**

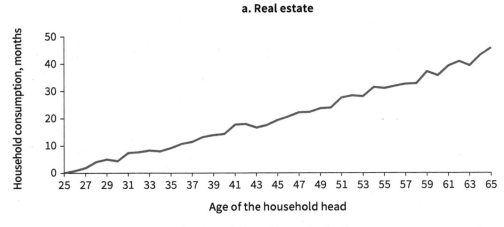

a. Real estate

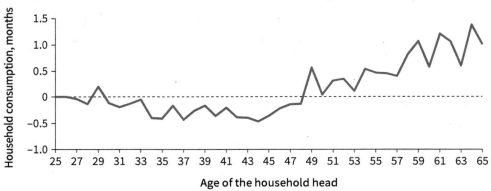

b. Financial wealth, excluding loans

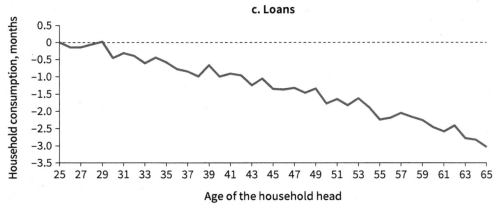

c. Loans

—— Average wealth increments relative to age 25

Source: Derived from data of the 2001–18 survey rounds, PSLM Publications (Pakistan Social and Living Standards Measurement Publications), Pakistan Bureau of Statistics, Islamabad, Pakistan, https://www.pbs.gov.pk/pslm -publications.

Although the data do not reveal the value of household dwellings separately from other real estate assets, the main residence likely accounts for most of the real estate wealth among all households except the richest. The steady rise in the value of the real estate owned by households may also reflect several distinct phenomena that are difficult to disentangle in the data, including (1) a gradual increase in the share of households that own their main residences, (2) upgrades in the main residence through renovations or moving, and (3) a rise in real estate prices above the consumer price index, which is used here to compare prices.

The value of financial wealth (panel b)—net savings and deposits, gold, silver, jewelry, and securities—tends to stagnate or decline slightly until the household head reaches age 45 and then grows at a net average increase of one month of consumption over the life cycle. This pattern may suggest that the need for liquidity does not change significantly over the life cycle, perhaps because, while wealth and therefore consumption rise, the levels of economic risk faced by households diminish. However, one may also observe that households steadily decumulate debt over the life cycle (panel c), generating an improvement in the net household position of around three months. A reduction in debt should facilitate access to new loans, which would reduce the need to hold liquid wealth and would explain why financial assets initially stagnate. Overall, financial wealth represents a negligible share of the life-cycle accumulation of net worth. It may serve to finance large expenses that arise punctually, such as funerals, or form a buffer stock of liquid funds in case of shock, but it is not sufficiently sizable to finance retirement consumption.

To obtain a more specific view beyond averages, the analysis also examines the net worth of households at several thresholds in the 2001, 2010, and 2018 survey cross-sections. It considers households with net worth above 6 months, 1 year, and 5 years of household consumption. These thresholds are somewhat arbitrary, but 6 months is a common rule of thumb among financial advisors for the amount of liquid wealth a household should have available. Households with at least 6 months in liquid wealth are assumed to be able to smooth out the impact of most short-term life shocks. Households with wealth covering at least 5 years of consumption would be able to fund a significant share of their needs in retirement to the extent that they are able to extract income from that wealth.

The net worth of most households is above 6 months of consumption. The share has grown over time (figure 8.16, panel a). However, most of this wealth is in residential real estate and therefore difficult to access quickly in the event of a shock. Gauged only by financial wealth, around 20 percent of households have a net worth above 6 months of consumption (figure 8.16, panel b). This may signal vulnerability to economic shocks, especially if there are also borrowing constraints or if family or community networks are likewise under stress, for example, in the case of aggregate shocks.

In 2001 and 2018, 20 percent and 35 percent of the households, respectively, had accumulated net worth equivalent to at least 60 months (5 years) of consumption needs by the time the household head had reached age 65 (figure 8.16, panel c). Most of the current elderly in the sample have thus not accumulated sufficient net worth to cover

FIGURE 8.16 Household Net Worth, by Consumption Reserves, 2001, 2010, and 2018

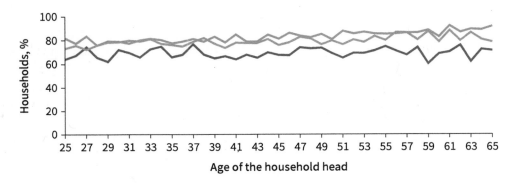

a. Net worth >6 months

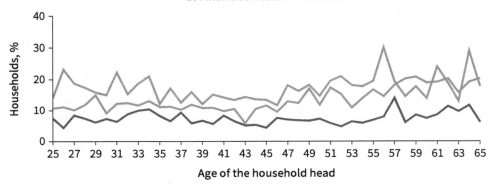

b. Financial wealth >6 months

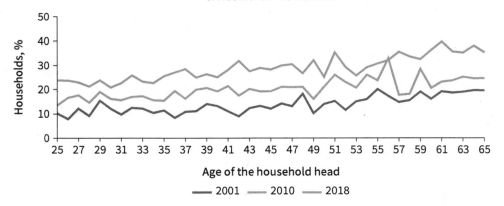

c. Net worth >60 months

Source: Derived from data of the 2001, 2010, and 2018 survey rounds, PSLM Publications (Pakistan Social and Living Standards Measurement Publications), Pakistan Bureau of Statistics, Islamabad, Pakistan, https://www.pbs .gov.pk/pslm-publications.

a sizable share of old-age consumption. However, the decomposition results and the upward shift over time apparent in figure 8.16, panel c, suggest that the share of households that have accumulated adequate net worth will grow substantially as new generations reach retirement age.

Heterogeneity in household wealth accumulation, by rural location and income quintile

The decomposition of age profiles can be disaggregated along household characteristics—such as income, educational attainment of the household head, and rural or urban location—to examine whether the patterns outlined above hold for various types of households. The analysis approximates quintiles of permanent income by computing per capita equivalent consumption quintiles over five-year age bins, as described in the data section. Because schooling strongly correlates with permanent income, only results are reported that are disaggregated by urban or rural location and permanent income quintiles.

Saving rates follow similar life-cycle progressions across all consumption quintiles. Saving rates are constant in households with heads who are in their 20s and 30s, before increasing by 15 to 30 percentage points in the second half of the life cycle (figure 8.17, panel a). Households in the bottom four quintiles exhibit stronger growth in life-cycle saving rates relative to households in the top quintile. However, they start from much lower levels.

The saving rates of rural and urban households exhibit distinct life-cycle patterns (figure 8.17, panel b). In urban areas, saving rates decline early in the life cycle before stabilizing and then rising again when household heads reach ages 45–60. In rural areas, the pattern found in the overall population holds. The data suggest that the baseline—the saving rate at age 25—is much lower among rural households than among urban households.

In line with the patterns in saving rates, the patterns in household wealth accumulation are similar across consumption quintiles 2 through 5 (figure 8.18, panels a–c). Residential real estate wealth increases at similar rates. Financial wealth stagnates early on; it picks up after household heads reach age 45 and debt burdens decline steadily. Patterns differ somewhat among the first consumption quintile. The growth in residential real estate wealth is markedly slower, even if expressed in terms of lower consumption. This finding appears to correlate closely with the urban-rural divide.

Urban and rural households exhibit the same rate of growth in residential real estate wealth, but their financial wealth trends differently (figure 8.18, panels d–f). Urban households improve their situation steadily by increasing their financial wealth and reducing their debt throughout the life cycle. Rural households see a deterioration in their financial wealth and reduce their debt at a slower rate. Several explanations are consistent with these patterns. Rural households may be exposed to more frequent or damaging shocks early in the life cycle relative to urban households, depleting their buffer stock. It is also possible that they benefit from better community networks to cope

FIGURE 8.17 **Household Saving Rates, by Age of Household Head, Quintile, and Location**

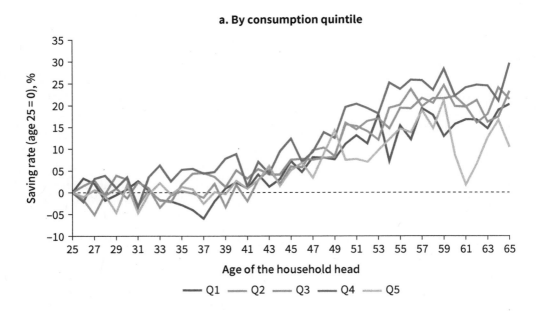

a. By consumption quintile

Saving rate (age 25 = 0), %

Age of the household head

— Q1 — Q2 — Q3 — Q4 — Q5

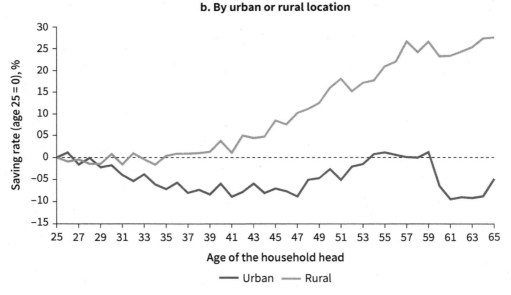

b. By urban or rural location

Saving rate (age 25 = 0), %

Age of the household head

— Urban — Rural

Source: Derived from data of the 2001–18 survey rounds, PSLM Publications (Pakistan Social and Living Standards Measurement Publications), Pakistan Bureau of Statistics, Islamabad, Pakistan, https://www.pbs.gov.pk/pslm -publications.

FIGURE 8.18 Household Wealth, by Age of Household Head, Quintile, and Location

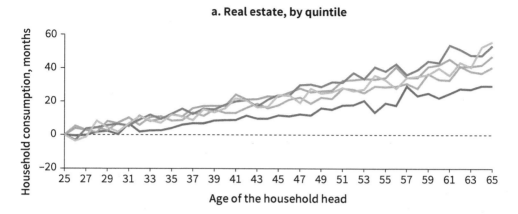

a. Real estate, by quintile

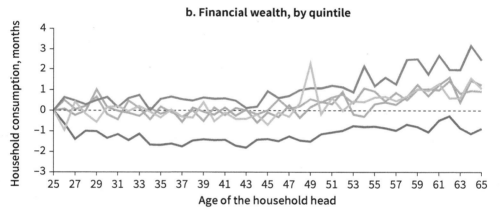

b. Financial wealth, by quintile

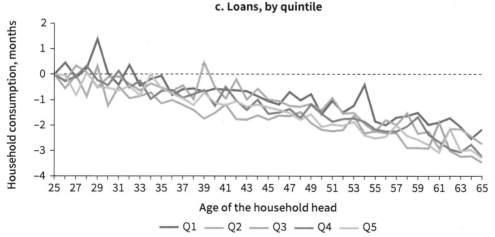

c. Loans, by quintile

━━ Q1 ━━ Q2 ━━ Q3 ━━ Q4 ━━ Q5

(Figure continues next page)

FIGURE 8.18 **Household Wealth, by Age of Household Head, Quintile, and Location**
(Continued)

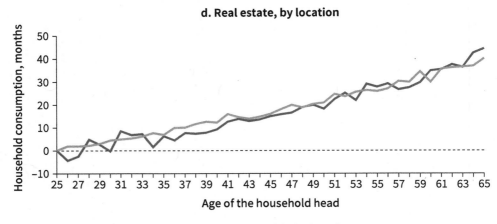

d. Real estate, by location

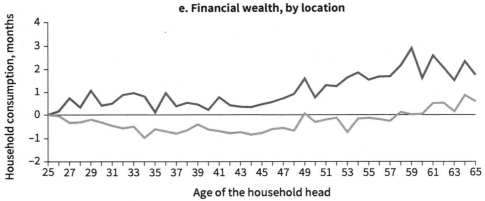

e. Financial wealth, by location

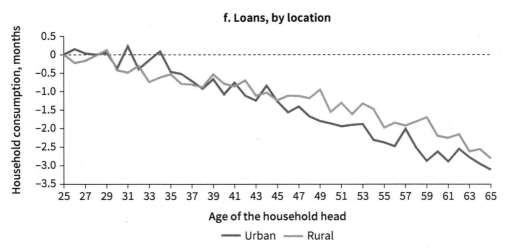

f. Loans, by location

Source: Derived from data of the 2001–18 survey rounds, PSLM Publications (Pakistan Social and Living Standards Measurement Publications), Pakistan Bureau of Statistics, Islamabad, Pakistan, https://www.pbs.gov.pk/pslm-publications.
Note: Financial wealth (panels b and e) excludes loans.

with economic uncertainty, reducing their need to accumulate liquid wealth in their 30s and 40s. Because liquid wealth is also accumulated to pay for predictable expenditures, such as schooling expenditures and ceremonial costs, the patterns exhibited by these expenditures or the availability of safe savings instruments may differ between rural and urban households.

Life-cycle savings and old age subsistence in the context of population aging and informality

Elderly men and women in Pakistan resort to a variety of strategies to finance consumption in old age (table 8.2). Labor force participation and coresidence are among the main means of support. Among men, 39.1 percent continue to participate in the labor force after age 65. The share exhibits a slight downward trend, from 40.2 percent in 2001 to 38.7 percent in 2018. In contrast, only 6.4 percent of elderly women were working in 2018, a slight decline from the 7.7 percent in 2001. Among households that include an elderly member, the main source of income is labor, equivalent to 31.2 percent of household consumption, followed by remittances (20.2 percent) and income from nonagricultural assets, such as rent or the sale of household land (18.7 percent). Income from all types of assets represents 34.6 percent of household consumption.[17]

The elderly are less likely than nonelderly adults to be living in poor households (table 8.3). The ratio appears stable or to decline slightly over time, indicating that the elderly have benefited from the reductions in poverty of the 2000s as much or perhaps more than the general population. In 2018, 94.4 percent of elderly men and women were coresiding with family members other than their spouse (table 8.3). This share did not change substantially between 2001 and 2018.

Still, the combined pressures of population aging, weakening family and community risk-sharing networks, and low formal pension coverage mean that financing consumption among the elderly will be a major challenge in the future. The increases in life expectancy and the declines in fertility in Pakistan over the past 30 years will reduce the number of family or network members who may provide support. Absent efforts by the government to extend access to pensions, formal pension coverage is likely to remain low as a share of the labor force, as large cohorts of young workers enter the labor market, exceeding the availability of formal jobs offering fringe benefits, even if GDP growth is strong (La Porta and Shleifer 2014).

Perhaps in response to these trends, a growing share of households accumulates significant net worth over the life cycle. The levels of wealth among households headed by 60- to 65-year-olds have grown significantly over time. In 2018, the median net worth among this group was equivalent to 36.8 months (3.1 years) of household consumption (table 8.3). The 25th percentile of the consumption distribution was 15.1 months (1.3 years) and the 75th percentile was 74.6 months (6.2 years). The median wealth doubled relative to 2001, when it was 18.2 months (1.5 years). A significant and growing share of the population, while not covered by formal pension schemes, therefore

TABLE 8.2 Sources of Income among Households with Elderly Members, 2001–18

Year	Labor force participation, %		Labor income	Remittances	Safety nets	% of household consumption				
	Elderly women	Elderly men				Agricultural assets	Nonagricultural assets	Financial assets	Other transfers
2001	7.7	40.2	27.4	17.0	1.3	11.0	15.4	1.4	2.6
2005	8.0	41.9	37.5	23.1	0.8	12.4	19.9	0.6	1.8
2007	5.6	40.0	34.1	16.5	0.5	10.8	24.1	0.3	4.7
2010	4.9	37.6	28.6	18.7	0.6	8.1	16.0	0.5	4.9
2011	6.3	38.3	27.5	17.2	0.3	19.5	18.1	2.5	4.6
2013	5.9	37.1	31.0	21.4	0.7	5.3	16.3	1.2	6.0
2015	6.9	39.3	34.8	22.5	0.3	9.2	19.9	1.0	3.6
2018	6.4	38.7	29.0	25.3	0.8	9.2	20.0	3.4	5.2
Average	6.5	39.1	31.2	20.2	0.7	10.7	18.7	5.2	4.2

Source: Derived from data of the 2001–18 survey rounds, PSLM Publications (Pakistan Social and Living Standards Measurement Publications), Pakistan Bureau of Statistics, Islamabad, Pakistan, https://www.pbs.gov.pk/pslm-publications.

reaches retirement with significant potential resources to maintain part of their consumption in old age.

A striking finding is that, on average, nearly 80 percent of the wealth accumulated by households by the time the household heads reach ages 60–65 consists of residential real estate. The share increased slightly over the period of the sample, from 73.0 percent in 2001 to 81.9 percent in 2018. The ability of elderly individuals to extract income from housing wealth may be a key parameter. The process may involve several methods, including renting property, selling or renting property while downsizing, and the application of sophisticated financial instruments such as reverse mortgages; it may also include implicit intergenerational arrangements in which children support their elderly parents in exchange for lodging and real estate bequests.

That households save almost exclusively in real estate, including land, signals that this is probably considered a safe investment relative to other available options. For example, housing may be a way to store resources for the long term in a way that cannot easily be stolen or appropriated. It may also reflect a lack of access to other safe, high-return, and trustworthy long-term savings instruments. Low financial literacy, low numeracy, and lack of familiarity with formal banking institutions can represent barriers to participation in other forms of saving. Pakistan has been much slower than neighboring countries in expanding financial inclusion, and the obstacles need to be addressed.

Improving the opportunities for long-term saving through government-sponsored or subsidized old-age savings instruments could yield greater independence among the elderly and reduce the burden on younger family members. The analysis finds that average net worth accumulation accelerates midway through working life, roughly around age 40. Some of this accumulation may reflect patterns in inheritance, but active saving likely plays a significant part. Household income growth starts to outpace household consumption growth around the time a household head reaches age 40, and the saving rate increases by 20 percentage points between ages 40 and 65. This suggests that programs to encourage formal saving may be most successful among individuals in that age range.

Although it is a relatively safe savings instrument, housing is also relatively illiquid, which takes resources away from short-term consumption smoothing. According to Global Findex, only 3 percent of individuals ages 15 and older in Pakistan report that they are able to rely on savings for emergency funds, while 49 percent say they are unable to produce funds in an emergency. According to 41 percent of the population ages 15 and older, the main source of emergency funds is family or friends. In the case of medical expenditures, 25 percent say borrowing is the main source. Policies that allow greater use of real estate as collateral for loans through formal financial institutions might reduce the need for liquid precautionary savings, while freeing up resources for retirement savings, but such initiatives may also encourage overindebtness and lead to evictions.

The lack of other safe, liquid forms of saving may also be a constraint on better labor market outcomes, particularly self-employment. The self-employed tend to be older

TABLE 8.3 Economic Characteristics of the Elderly, Pakistan, 2001–18

Year	Wealth, consumption, adjusted			Elderly poverty ratio	Coresidence rate	Net worth, %			Nonresidential wealth, %	
	1st quartile	Median	3rd quartile			Residential wealth	> 6 months	> 60 months	> 6 months	> 60 months
2001	5.7	18.2	43.5	0.92	94.6	73.0	71.5	16.6	21.7	8.6
2005	10.9	25.8	54.0	0.91	92.7	84.3	86.0	22.8	24.2	6.4
2007	14.0	29.8	61.1	0.84	93.8	80.3	88.4	25.5	29.6	6.9
2010	9.8	24.0	54.5	0.83	94.0	77.6	82.0	22.5	25.9	6.0
2011	12.8	27.1	55.5	0.90	94.6	80.0	87.3	22.8	26.8	5.9
2013	11.4	28.4	58.6	0.78	96.0	80.3	85.1	24.2	24.0	5.5
2015	15.7	34.6	67.7	0.79	94.3	81.4	87.0	29.6	24.4	6.1
2018	15.1	36.8	74.6	0.85	95.5	81.9	86.5	32.1	26.8	7.0
Average	11.9	28.1	58.7	0.85	94.4	79.8	84.2	24.5	25.4	6.6

Source: Derived from data of the 2001–18 survey rounds, PSLM Publications (Pakistan Social and Living Standards Measurement Publications), Pakistan Bureau of Statistics, Islamabad, Pakistan, https://www.pbs.gov.pk/pslm-publications.

Note: Coresidence rate = the share of the elderly living in households; elderly poverty ratio = the share of the elderly living in households below the national poverty line, divided by the share of households with nonelderly household heads below the national poverty line; net worth and nonresidential wealth > 6 (or 60) months = the share of households that have net worth (or nonresidential wealth) that can cover more than 6 (or 60) months of household consumption needs; residential wealth (net worth) = residential wealth as an average share of the total wealth of households.

than informal wage workers but have similar educational attainment. Almost one-half of the self-employed has no education. The older age of the self-employed might suggest that initial working years are spent acquiring start-up capital, because most self-employed enterprises are launched using personal capital (Bossavie, Khadka, and Strokova 2018; PBS 2015). According to Global Findex, only 11 percent of people ages 15 and older borrow to start or expand a business.

The one woman, one bank account policy (the Ehsaas Kafalat Program), which aims to provide full-scale branchless bank savings accounts for beneficiaries of government cash transfers, may be a vehicle for the rapid expansion of financial inclusion and may be used to provide social pensions or access to savings products. The need is greater among women, particularly older women and widows, who tend to have less agency within the household and in society. In addition, social norms around inheritance leave women vulnerable and without assets in old age. The Benazir Income Support Program has shown that providing access to financial accounts in banks significantly increases voice, agency, and self-reliance.

The potential for long-term savings among informal workers elsewhere in South Asia

In the absence of detailed household data on other South Asian countries, the financial information available through the Global Findex dataset can be used to identify variables that may provide insights into the potential to support an expansion of long-term savings among informal sector workers. The analysis presented in this subsection should be complemented by more detailed analysis of each country.

The analysis focuses on five concepts, as follows:

- *Economic inclusion:* the share of individuals with a financial account and the share of individuals who report they save for old age

- *Formalization indicator:* the share of workers who have received wages within the past year

- *Identification of the willingness and capacity to save:* the share of individuals who receive digital payments

- *Resilience and sensitivity to shocks:* borrowing for health or medical expenditures and the ability to produce funds in an emergency

- *Institutional savings gaps:* the extent to which individuals lack a financial account because of the high cost or insufficient funds.

Economic inclusion. The correlation of individuals possessing a basic bank account with the accumulation of general savings has been analyzed in various studies across regions. In Malawi and Uganda, individuals who opened and used basic bank accounts increased savings, and balances grew by 22 percent and 28 percent, respectively (Dupas et al. 2018). In Mexico, recipients of a conditional cash transfer who receive the funds through bank accounts increased savings after a six-month acquaintance and trust process with the bank account (Bachas et al. 2017). A randomized control trial in Kenya found that access to a traditional nonmobile savings account led to a 45 percent increase in productive investments (Radcliffe and Voorhies 2012). These relationships give a sense of how these governments are seeking to create enabling environments for individuals to save.

The share of the population ages 15 and older with accounts at financial institutions varies considerably across the region. India and Sri Lanka have high ratios (80 percent and 74 percent, respectively) compared with other countries in the region. In Pakistan, only 18 percent of the adult population has an account. The share of the population with an account in Afghanistan, Bangladesh, and Nepal is 15 percent, 41 percent, and 45 percent, respectively, well below the regional average of 68 percent. Given the low share of the population with a financial account across the region, it is likely that many people are saving for retirement outside of the formal financial sector, perhaps because of a lack of appropriate financial products to facilitate savings among informal workers for old age.

A look at more disaggregated inclusion indicators developed from the same Global Findex data on people with lower incomes and the three quintiles with higher incomes shows that, although there is some variation, the prevailing shares are similar to the averages in lower-middle-income countries and the averages in the region.

Additionally, the indicator on the propensity to save for old age among adults (the shares among individuals ages 25 or more) is part of the economic inclusion module. It is meaningful also as measure of financial inclusion because long-term savings schemes are among the basic mandatory or voluntary savings products in which workers participate. The data suggest that most workers, regardless of whether they are in the formal sector or informal sector, do not have a long-term savings account.

These indicators highlight the level of unsatisfied potential demand for products, mechanisms, and systems to meet the needs of the populations of countries with lower saving rates relative to the averages in the region. They also help gauge the need for efforts to sensitize individuals about the importance of long-term savings, especially in those countries in which formal vehicles for long-term savings are underused or are lacking because of high administrative costs or high barriers to the use of formal instruments. The Global Findex information shows that there is a need for financial products and services and that it is not satisfied in some of these countries. There is thus an opportunity to introduce short- and long-term savings vehicles.

Formalization indicator. This is a rough indicator derived from Global Findex data on the level of formalization. It shows the share of the population ages 15 and older that has received wages in the past year. It builds on concepts presented by Majoka and Palacios (2017), who find a substantial correlation between the share of the working-age population in a country that reports that it receives formal wages and the share of the working-age population that contributes to a mandated pension scheme. This allows a rough estimate of the size of the informal sector. Consistent with the data on formal employment, the countries with the highest share of informality are Bangladesh and Pakistan; the majority of the other countries are close to the average in the region, which is at the low end of indicators of formalization, around 20 percent. Over 80 percent of the population ages 15 and older is likely to lack access to retirement savings instruments, pensions, insurance, and other financial products designed to protect incomes from shocks. Like the analysis of economic inclusion, this indicator also implies that there is both an unsatisfied demand and an opportunity to facilitate long-term savings.

Identifying the willingness and capacity to save. Long-term saving requires creative mechanisms to reach individuals in new ways. It is unlikely there is a single route to achieve retirement savings among those who are able to save. Nevertheless, several authors agree that, similar to the effects of regular banking on savings, the use of digital payments has expanded nonbank financial services precisely among those individuals who may be close to being able to save but who have not yet been reached by the formal banking system. Digital payments and digital finance have not only facilitated economic activity; they are an integral part of a two-stage process whereby saving follows after the establishment of a digital account and a digital payment process as part of the provision of access to customized savings services. Evidence suggests that digital finance not only promotes financial inclusion among the vulnerable but also generates sizable welfare benefits among this group and in the system more widely (Radcliffe and Voorhies 2012). With the increase in the adoption of smartphones, many more channels have been opened to offer services anywhere where there is phone service. Evidence indicates that mobile money and mobile payments have improved the economic activity of developing countries and vulnerable populations and have successfully promoted financial inclusion and the introduction of savings vehicles (Donovan 2012).

Evidence also shows there is some savings capacity among the less poor in the informal sector. Global Findex data indicate that 32 percent of the population ages 15 and older in Pakistan report that it is saving some money, and 15 percent reports that it is saving for old age. However, these people have limited ability to mobilize liquid savings or self-insure and are therefore vulnerable to shocks and old-age poverty. Among this group, programs are necessary to enhance the security of savings for long-term income support and emergency contingencies.

From the Global Findex database, the analysis uses the share of the population ages 15 and older that received digital payments in the previous year as an indicator of the ability or willingness to save. The region can be divided into two groups. Bangladesh, India, and Sri Lanka have relatively high shares of individuals who received digital payments in the previous year; Afghanistan, Nepal, and Pakistan have significantly lower shares. Thus, on average, the population may be more willing to use digital channels to save in the first group than in the second group. This represents two valuable elements for the identification of savings capacity. The first is the use of digital channels to carry out financial transactions, receive payments, and make contributions. The second is that the digital payments received by respondents can constitute a part of income. This may be recurring income related to economic activity, but it also may be irregular or extraordinary income, which is a potential avenue for saving if there is a surplus in cash flow. The relevant data would also serve as an indirect indicator of a certain degree of financial literacy among individuals.

Resilience and sensitivity to shocks. Resilience and sensitivity to shocks are revealed in the Global Findex database by the share of the population ages 15 and older that borrowed to pay for health care or other medical needs and the share of this population that was able (or unable) to produce emergency funds, regardless of the nature of the emergency. The first of these helps measure resilience. The second supplies information about the ease with which people can produce emergency funds. The more that people are able to produce such funds, the greater is the likelihood that appropriate financial mechanisms are available to support such operations, including formal and informal mechanisms.

In most of the countries under study, the share of people that borrows to pay for medical services is close to the average in the region, 13 percent, although Nepal had a much higher share. The regional average is higher than the average in low- and middle-income countries, which may indicate that public health services in the countries under study are more vulnerable and that there is less capacity to cope with health crises. This finding also points to an opportunity to offer other financial services as part of informal sector pension schemes.

The capacity to produce emergency funds is much higher than the regional average in Afghanistan, Bangladesh, and Nepal and much lower than the average in India, Pakistan, and Sri Lanka. This may indicate that financial instruments designed to help people respond to emergencies in the second group are relatively underdeveloped or that their coverage is low. This is consistent with the wide coverage of microfinance in the three countries that were well above the regional average. Indeed, the share of the poorest 40 percent (the bottom 40), who are the target clients of microfinance and who considered that they could produce emergency funds, was also higher than the regional average in both Afghanistan and Bangladesh.

Institutional savings gaps. The analysis relies on two indicators derived from the Global Findex database to measure whether available financial products are adequate to support efforts to save by individuals ages 15 and older: (1) the share of this population that lacks financial accounts because opening such accounts is too expensive and (2) the share of this population that lacks financial accounts because they do not have sufficient funds. In the region, the share of the first is 24 percent, with relatively higher shares in Afghanistan, India, Nepal, and Sri Lanka and relatively lower shares in Bangladesh and Pakistan. This may indicate that the cost of financial services in the latter two countries tends to be lower than in the rest of the region. The share of the second ranges from

20 percent in Afghanistan to 72 percent in Nepal, with a regional average of 56 percent. Many of these individuals may subsist on daily wages and are unable to save. Among such individuals, there may be potential to provide a basic pension product through social security institutions or by incentivizing competition, reducing supply-side costs, or offering a more flexible range of financial products among various types of users.

Leveraging Global Findex data to evaluate the potential for long-term savings

Using aggregate data from the Global Findex database and the five concepts outlined, the analysis established a methodology for a high-level evaluation of the importance, potential impact, and opportunity of the introduction of a long-term savings scheme tailored to the informal sector in each of the countries on which information is available (see annex 8D). The methodology establishes a scale of 1 through 5 with respect to the average in the region to identify some differences among the countries, with 5 representing the greatest potential in each of the dimensions and 1 representing countries facing the greatest challenge with respect to the five concepts.

In the cobweb diagram in figure 8.19, Bangladesh, India (potentially), Pakistan, and Sri Lanka stand out as the countries with greatest potential to develop long-term

FIGURE 8.19 **Nonvulnerable Informal Sector: Opportunity for Contributory Pensions**

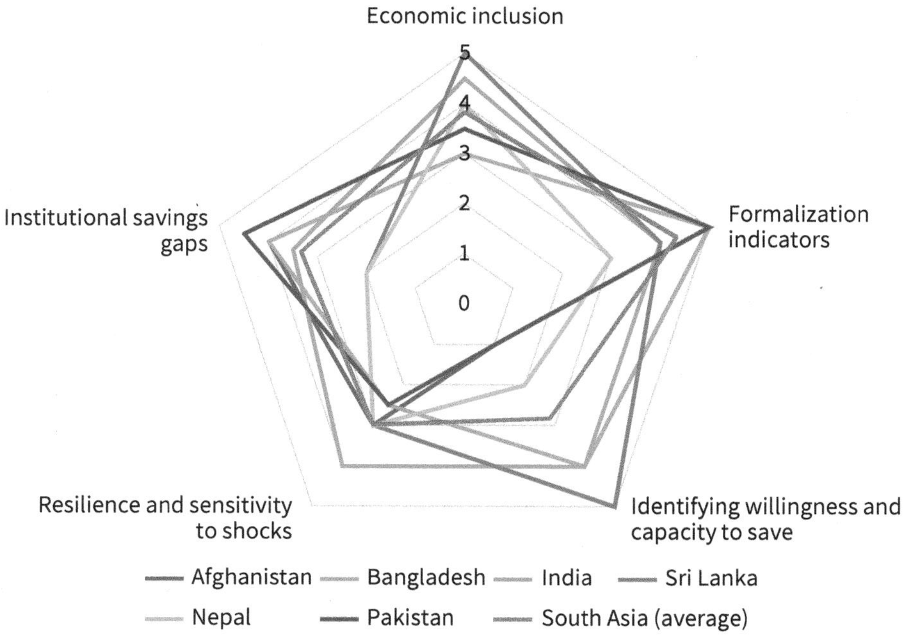

Source: Calculated based on data of Global Findex (Global Financial Inclusion Database), World Bank, Washington, DC, https://globalfindex.worldbank.org/#data_sec_focus.
Note: In the scale of 1–5 with respect to the average in the region, 5 represents the greatest potential in each of the dimensions, and 1 represents countries facing the greatest challenge with respect to the five concepts shown.

savings schemes targeted at the informal sector to cope with risks normally covered by social insurance. A detailed review of the figure has been conducted to compare each of the countries with respect to the region (see annex 8E).

The cobweb in figure 8.19 is not an absolute measurement of the potential for introducing contributory pension schemes in the nonvulnerable portion of the informal sector. It does provide a visual representation of countries in which more needs to be done to identify and initiate a policy dialogue about programs that cover the five specific dimensions presented. It is a first approximation of a comparison across countries on the main challenges in each jurisdiction that may become a focus among policy makers, other government authorities, and social protection specialists. No country has yet tackled fully the challenges of establishing a contributory pension scheme targeting the informal sector, and the comparison may help identify lessons learned.

The study applied equal weights to each of the five concepts, but more analysis of the weighting is required to fine-tune the model. For example, the measurement of financial inclusion might involve weighting based on two sorts of variables: demand-side variables and supply-side variables (Cámara and Tuesta 2014). Demand-related variables are those that reflect the potential of the population to use a financial product or a financial service to participate in the formal financial sector. Supply-related variables are those whereby financial industries, governments, and other organizations make regulations, policies, and infrastructure available for digital finance to meet the demand (Buckley and Malady 2015). New and more accurate weights should be examined as part of a calibration exercise involving work on the case of Pakistan and other countries in other regions.

South Asian countries may be addressing different needs if they seek to strengthen the environment for the development of long-term savings in the informal sector, but there is a potential to establish low-cost mechanisms now to reduce future pressures on government-financed programs to provide income support to the elderly. Offering a pension instrument to some informal workers may encourage formalization, provided that the benefits are sufficiently attractive. Although there is no definitive proof that people who open normal bank accounts also use digital services, experience does suggest that opening an account is often a first step and part of an enabling environment that can facilitate an introduction to long-term savings and even participation in an informal sector pension scheme.

This conclusion illustrates the need for much more detailed research to address factors that may support short- and long-term savings schemes among the informal sector; it opens a discussion on the importance of these factors in achieving much wider financial inclusion that might also accommodate pension coverage.

Policy Implications

Given the heterogeneity of the informal sector, the approach adopted in this chapter—consistent with similar studies on other, less well-developed regions—proposes a combination of interventions to help the informal sector cope with income losses aris-ing from a multiplicity of risks, such as old age, disability, and health shocks (Guven, Jain, and Joubert 2021). Responsiveness to different types of shocks is even more impor-tant among informal workers because of their greater vulnerability relative to formal workers.

Attempts to extend the coverage of social insurance instruments should reflect a rec-ognition that insuring informal work is intrinsically different from formal wage employ-ment. A small segment of the informal sector may choose to participate provided that the costs of the scheme is low; schemes do not require specialized knowledge or under-taking long, complex processes; and there are incentives to enroll and contribute to a bundled group of programs, including pensions, unemployment, health, and in some cases even income taxes. The Monotributo Program in Latin America is an example of the possible direction of such schemes.

The poorest informal workers, however, will not be able to enroll in any contribu-tory scheme. The size of informality in the South Asia region imposes the adoption of a pragmatic expansion of noncontributory or social pensions, but the low current level of benefits and the expected growth of the elderly population will require careful manage-ment if programs are to be sustainable. Low pensions targeted to the poorest among the elderly would reduce poverty, minimize disincentives to formalize, and keep program expenditures reasonable.

More well-off workers in the informal sector have savings capacity in most of the countries in the region. Long-term savings schemes should build on this potential to entice informal workers to join long-term savings schemes that would provide resources to finance contingencies associated with multiple social insurance risks.

To achieve these purposes, long-term savings schemes should rely on the following enabling conditions:

- Technical feasibility studies should assess the potential demand for long-term sav-ings products.

- Defined benefit plans should induce behavioral change by promoting long-term retirement savings. The plans might cover unemployment insurance, the early with-drawal of funds for emergencies, microfinance credit links, matching contributions, and other incentive features. These would be aimed at establishing appealing pack-ages focused on informal sector workers and could be used as vehicles to gain trust in long-term savings products. The benefits would respond to the needs revealed by respondents in the Global Findex surveys.

- Nontraditional instruments should be designed for low-scale savings schemes that provide easy, cost-effective mechanisms allowing informal sector workers to make small, irregular contributions.

- Sound institutional capacity should be developed, and regulatory and supervisory bodies should be instituted where necessary by leveraging the Social Insurance Administrative Diagnosis tool to assist social security agencies in enhancing their administrative capacity and ensuring compliance with regulations and proper enabling conditions of long-term savings products (Sluchynskyy 2019).

- Savings instruments should be diversified, especially those that involve entry barriers to the participation of informal workers. Doing this might involve the promotion of minimum contribution amounts, transparent but low administrative costs, and schemes tailored to specific needs, such as partial short-term withdrawals to finance shorter-term risk coping (health shocks, unemployment, loss of crops, and investment needs).

- Incentives need to be introduced based on an assessment of behavioral responses. Incentives should respond to the needs and realities of informal sector workers. In South Asia and globally, the informal sector is heterogeneous. Research on behavioral responses among different groups of informal workers should lead to the design of incentives that will eventually increase the popularity of the schemes, thereby boosting enrollment. Some of the incentives may be simple instruments, such as matched contributions, or more sophisticated instruments, such as lotteries and access to microcredit.

- Administration has to be simple and transparent. Important steps include simplifying the payment of contributions, creating links with the tax system, and designing new or adapted schemes for informal workers. Simplification is needed as a stepping-stone to formalization and to reduce costs, make the schemes sustainable, and offer solutions that are accessible to informal workers.

- Communication should be effective over channels that informal workers already use to make schemes, products, and programs visible among the target population. If the authorities and union leaders publicly provide information about the schemes, this renders the support tangible; in other countries, this approach has been a key part of a communication strategy to build the buy-in of informal sector workers.

Annex 8A: Social Insurance Schemes in South Asia

Afghanistan: Afghanistan only covers public servants. The Pension Department of the Ministry of Labor, Social Affairs, and Martyrs and Disabled operates the civil servants and military pension scheme. The Da Afghanistan Bank Pension Scheme, operated by the Pension Unit of the bank, covers employees in the public banking sector.

Bangladesh: Bangladesh has a special system for public sector employees, Grameen Pension Savings. The system serves as a short- to medium-term savings plan for known future expenditures, including marriage and education expenses. The old-age social pension (income tested) is provided to men at age 65 and to women at age 62 who do not receive any other government or nongovernment allowance. Only one member of a household receives the pension. The beneficiary's annual income must not exceed Tk 10,000. A designated committee schedules the benefit payments, giving priority to the most vulnerable and women. Among those selected, at least one-half must be women.

Bhutan: The Provident Fund covers persons employed in firms with at least five employees and with labor contracts lasting at least one year. Voluntary coverage is provided for employees of firms with up to five employees. The Provident Fund Old Age Benefit pays all employee and employer contributions, plus accrued interest, minus previous withdrawals. The benefit may be taken as a lump sum or an annuity.

The old-age settlement (provident fund) pays a lump sum of total employee contributions, plus accrued interest, minus previous withdrawals.

An old-age benefit (gratuity, employer liability) pays a lump sum of the employee's last monthly basic earnings, multiplied by the number of years of continuous employment, or the employee's total gratuity account balance, whichever is greater.

Self-employed persons and family workers are excluded from the provident fund and employer liability system.

There is a special system for military personnel, civil servants, and employees of public corporations.

India: India has mandatory social insurance pensions for private sector workers (old age, survivors, and disability) and a voluntary defined contribution scheme that is privately managed, the National Pension Scheme. In May 2021, the scheme was extended through notification to all Indian citizens, including informal sector workers on a voluntary basis. The self-employed, agricultural workers, and members of cooperatives with less than 50 workers are excluded.

Social assistance is provided for needy older persons and poor households. There are special systems for informal sector workers, certain artisans, and the rural landless.

The Indira Gandhi National Old Age Pension Scheme (IGNOAPS) is income tested (annual income must not exceed a certain limit, which may vary across states) and is limited to people ages 60 and older. The 60–79 age group receives a basic pension of Rs 200 a month, and the 80+ age group receives a pension of Rs 500 a month.

Unemployment benefits are provided through Mahatma Gandhi National Rural Employment Guarantee, a social assistance program, if a member of the household volunteers to do unskilled manual work in qualified rural areas.

Civil servants benefited from a special regime until 2004. Now, they contribute to the National Pension Scheme. A special scheme for military personnel was not subject to the 2004 reform.

Maldives: The Old Age Basic Pension covers every citizen age 65 and older who resides in the country. The Maldives Retirement Pension Scheme is a funded mandatory defined contribution scheme. The contribution rate of 14 percent is shared equally. Foreign employees and the formal sector self-employed can participate voluntarily. The Public Sector Defined Benefit Scheme is closed to new contributors, but it is still ongoing for contributors who transitioned from the old 20/40 defined benefit scheme and who will receive a double pension (defined contribution plus defined benefit), plus a top-up social pension.

A government subsidy of Rf 2,000 is paid to each of the first 5,000 self-employed workers who join the scheme each year.

The self-employed who earn less than Rf 5,000 receive a matching contribution of up to 25 percent of the yearly contribution, which is limited to 25 percent of the average pension contribution (7 percent of the pensionable wage) of government employees as a government subsidy.

Nepal: The old-age allowance (Senior Citizen's Allowance, social assistance) provident fund covers public sector employees, including civil servants and military and police personnel, and private sector employees with permanent contracts, including apprentices and students in vocational training. Voluntary coverage is provided for foreign workers.

Self-employed persons are excluded from provident fund membership.

The 2017 law established a mandatory social insurance program for private sector employees, including day workers. The program was gradually implemented starting in May 2019. Insured persons contribute 11 percent of monthly earnings, and employers contribute 20 percent of the monthly payroll. Considering the combined insured person and employer contributions, 28.33 percent of the payroll will finance old-age benefits; 1.40 percent will finance disability and work injury benefits; 0.27 percent will finance survivor benefits; and 1.00 percent will finance sickness and maternity benefits.

Pakistan: The Employees' Old-Age Benefits Institution covers employees of private sector firms with five or more workers. Self-employed persons and family workers are excluded. Special systems are provided for public sector employees, military and police personnel, and railway employees. Old-age pensions are provided to men at age

60 and to women at age 55 with at least 15 years of contributions. Miners can claim the pension earlier under certain conditions. Covered employment may continue. Early pensions (except in Sindh Province) are given to those eligible at age 55 (men) and age 50 (women) with at least 15 years of contributions.

To enable employed and self-employed individuals to provide for retirement in a regulated environment, the Securities and Exchange Commission of Pakistan introduced the Voluntary Pension System in 2005. The system is regulated by the Securities and Exchange Commission. The following should be noted with respect to schemes within the system:

- A Pakistani national age 18 and older (salaried or self-employed) with a valid computerized national identity card or a national identity card for overseas Pakistanis is eligible to participate in the system. Under the system, the employee or the employer (or both) contribute to the employee's individual pension account, which is invested for the long term. Contributions can be in a lump sum or at a regular frequency. There is no penalty for missing a payment.

- The pension fund manager opens an individual pension account in the name of the individual, who is referred to as a "participant." Each individual pension account is assigned a unique identification number. The funds accumulated are used to pay into a regular pension or lump sum on retirement.

- To protect pension fund account holders, the Voluntary Pension System separates fund management and the custody of funds through the establishment of a trust. To protect pension fund account holders through diversification, the Securities and Exchange Commission has specified an investment and allocation policy for pension funds that sets out the broad parameters for the investment of the contributions received.

- Individuals can allocate their contributions between equities, debt, money market instruments, and commodities in accordance with their investment horizon and risk appetite as reflected in their chosen allocation scheme.

Sri Lanka: Employers in the public and private sector make monthly contributions to a trust fund owned and managed by employees. The Provident Fund invests in a range of asset types and provides supplemental old-age, disability, and survivor benefits. Public and private sector employees—including apprentices and casual, temporary, contract, and piece-rate workers—participate, except for self-employed persons, family workers, civil servants, farmers, and fishermen. The trust fund system provides voluntary coverage for self-employed persons and migrant workers, except for household workers, persons working in small charitable institutions or religious organizations, and family workers. Special systems are established for public sector and local government employees, farmers, and fishermen.

Annex 8B: The Informal Sector in South Asia: Bangladesh

Over 85 percent of total employment in Bangladesh is informal (figure 8B.1).

Informal workers in the country can be easily found in agriculture, as well as among the self-employed or in small enterprises that are usually production units or household businesses. Workers are also employed by formally established companies through informal arrangements.

The pension system provides a monthly old-age pension of Tk 500 (US$5.90). The eligible population is men age 65 and older and women age 62 and older who have a monthly income of up to Tk 10,000 (table 8B.1). The beneficiary cannot be the recipient of any other type of aid or allowance, and the benefit is limited to one member per household. A designated committee determines eligibility, giving priority to the most vulnerable (SSA and ISSA 2017). Aside from this pension system, no pension coverage is available for informal workers with higher incomes, who presumably have the capacity to save, although they may also need to prepare for retirement.

According to Global Findex data, only about 10 percent of the population saves for old age. This is lower than the average in other lower-middle-income countries (13 percent) and in countries in the South Asia region (11 percent). Combined with the share of the population ages 15 and older who have bank accounts (around 40 percent, compared with the regional average of 68 percent), this provides some rationale for believing that people in Bangladesh are not generally saving for retirement because of the lack of formal pension systems able to provide them with coverage.

FIGURE 8B.1 **Informal Employment, by Economic Sector, Bangladesh, 2016–17**

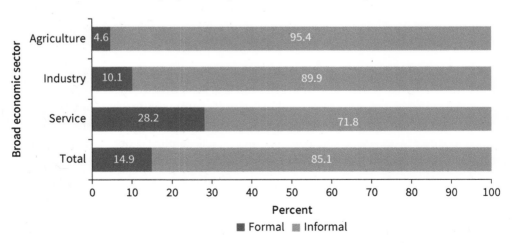

Source: BBS 2018.

TABLE 8B.1 Pensioners in Total Population above Retirement Age, Selected Countries
Percent

Country	Pensionable age	Contributory pensions	Noncontributory pensions	Total coverage
Armenia	63 men, 62.5 women	64.6	15.4	80.0
Bangladesh	65 men, 62 women	4.9	34.6	39.5
Cambodia	55	—	—	5.0
China	60 men, 55 women	32.2	42.1	74.4
Fiji	55	—	—	10.6
India	58	9.9	14.2	24.1
Indonesia	55	—	—	8.1
Korea, Rep.	60	—	—	77.6
Kyrgyz Republic	63 men, 58 women	—	—	100.0
Lao PDR	60	—	—	5.6
Malaysia	55	16.2	3.6	19.8
Mongolia	60	62.6	37.4	100.0
Nepal	58	9.2	53.3	62.5
Pakistan	60 men, 55 women	—	—	2.3
Papua New Guinea	55	—	—	0.9
Philippines	60	24.3	4.2	28.5
Sri Lanka	55 men, 50 women	—	—	17.1
Thailand	60	13.1	68.6	81.7
Uzbekistan	60 men, 55 women	97.8	0.3	98.1
Vietnam	60 men, 55 women	25.8	8.7	34.5

Sources: ILO 2014.
Note: — = not available.

In Bangladesh, 10 percent of people borrowed money to start or expand a farm or a business. This is double the average in the region and in other lower-middle-income countries. The higher share in Bangladesh may derive from the fact that microfinance is popular in Bangladesh, and the large variety of financial products that offer credit for productive purposes. This also points to a relatively higher capacity among informal workers to repay loans. It may likewise indicate a greater capacity to save for retirement and a willingness among households to use financial products to improve economic position.

The share of remittance recipients is also higher in Bangladesh (17 percent) than in the South Asia region (12 percent) and the average in other lower-middle-income countries (15 percent). This may indicate a higher savings capacity among households that receive remittances. It may also show that there is a need for formal pension arrangements for those sending the remittances because some of these people may wish to return to the country for retirement.

Annex 8C: Producing Projections on Social Pensions

The projections presented here rely on World Population Prospects to estimate the age of pension eligibility, plus population through 2050 (table 8C.1). The long-term economic assumptions include a 5 percent nominal GDP growth rate, a 2 percent annual inflation rate, and 3 percent real GDP growth. It is also assumed that pension indexation reflects 100 percent of the inflation rate, that is, projections are made in real terms.

Scenario 1: The same percentage share of the population at the eligible ages will be covered now and in the future. The purely demographic scenario will essentially show the status quo under the projected demographic trends.

Scenario 2: The same percentage share of the population at the eligible ages will be covered now and in the future, but the benefits will be increased, where pertinent, from the current level to reach the poverty line. In the case of India, for example, this means the following (see table 8C.1):

• Rural poverty line per month: Rs 1,059

• Urban poverty line per month: Rs 1,286

• Current pension amount: Rs 200 (Rs 500 for beneficiaries ages 80+)

• Monthly pension, percent rural poverty line: 19 percent

• Fivefold increase in the benefit: Rs 1,695 (using the Rs 200 base benefit)

TABLE 8C.1 **Pension Benefits and Coverage, Current and Projections**

Country	Coverage: beneficiaries, population of retirement age, %	Current benefit amount per month		Increased adequacy of benefit amount per month	Rate of increase from year 1, %
Bangladesh	46	Tk 500	US$5.90	Tk 4,483	9.0
India	18	Rs 200	US$2.65	Rs 1,059.42	5.3
Maldives	95	Rf 5,000	US$323.00	Current benefit is above the national poverty line	
Nepal	10	Nr 3,000	US$25.00		
Sri Lanka	26	SL Rs 2,000	US$10.50	SL Rs 5,177	2.6

Source: Calculated based on data of World Population Prospects (dashboard), Population Division, Department of Economic and Social Affairs, United Nations, New York, https://population.un.org/wpp/.

Annex 8D: Methodology of the Global Findex Analysis

To obtain an indicator of the potential to introduce medium- to long-term savings schemes among informal sector workers in the South Asia region, the analysis used data from the Global Findex Inclusion Database. First, the variables found in the database were surveyed to determine which might be helpful in building the relevant indicator. These variables were classified into five modules that are considered key to realizing the potential of introducing long-term savings schemes among informal workers. The five modules and the corresponding variables in the Global Findex data are illustrated in table 8D.1.

The value of the variable for each country is then compared with the average value for the region to obtain a ratio, called the "country factor" of each variable. For example, for the economic inclusion evaluation, two variables were used—the financial institution account and saved for old age. To obtain each variable's country factor, the percentage share of people with accounts in the country was rated against the regional average as follows:

$$\frac{\text{Financial institution account (\% age 15+) country}}{\text{Financial institution account (\% age 15+) region}} * (100) = \text{Financial institution account (\% age 15+) Country factor} \qquad (8D.1)$$

To standardize and simplify the calculation of the indicator, a unitary value from 1 to 5 was assigned, depending on the relationship between the variable and the potential to introduce pension systems in the sector of activity of the informal workers. The more direct the relationship, the higher the value of the variable and the greater

TABLE 8D.1 An Indicator of Informal Sector Savings Potential: Five Modules and Variables

Module	Variables (population share)
Economic inclusion	Financial institution account, ages 15+, %
	Saved for old age, older adults, ages 25+, %
Formalization indicators	Received wages in the previous year, ages 15+, %
Identifying willingness and capacity to save	Received digital payments in the past year, ages 15+, %
Resilience and sensitivity to shocks	Borrowed for health or medical purposes, ages 15+, %
	Coming up with emergency funds: possible, ages 15+, %
Institutional savings gaps, share without an account in a financial institution	No account because financial services are too expensive, ages 15+, %
	No account because of insufficient funds, ages 15+, %

Source: Calculated using data of Global Findex (Global Financial Inclusion Database), World Bank, Washington, DC, https://globalfindex.worldbank.org/#data_sec_focus.

the opportunity to introduce pension schemes in the informal sector of the country (figure 8D.1, panel a). A correspondingly higher score is therefore assigned to the higher country factors obtained. The more inverted the relationship, the lower the value of the variable and the weaker the opportunity to introduce pension schemes in the informal sector of the country (figure 8D.1, panel b). A correspondingly lower score is assigned to the lower country factors obtained.

For instance, in the case of the financial institution account variable (age 15+, percent), the more accounts, the greater the opportunity for financial inclusion. Using this relationship, a country factor score may be assigned within the range for this variable (table 8D.2).

Obtaining the module score

Once the scores for the variables that are included in each module have been obtained, the next step is to calculate a weighted average of the variable scores. The result is the score of the module evaluation, as follows:

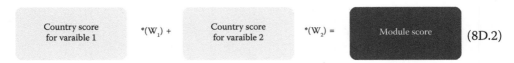

$$\text{(8D.2)}$$

Obtaining the final opportunity score for a pension scheme

To obtain the final opportunity score for each country, the weighted average of all module evaluation scores is calculated, as follows:

$$\text{(8D.3)}$$

FIGURE 8D.1 Country Factors and the Opportunity Score for Pension Schemes

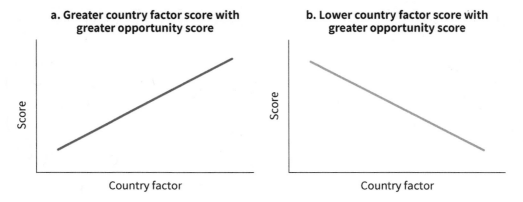

a. Greater country factor score with greater opportunity score

b. Lower country factor score with greater opportunity score

Source: Original compilation for this publication.

TABLE 8D.2 **Range of the Country Factor Score, Financial Institution Account Variable**
Percent

Score	1	2	3	4	5
Country factor value	0–25%	26–50%	51–75%	76–100%	> 100%

Source: Original compilation for this publication.

TABLE 8D.3 **Country Factors, Financial Institution Account Variable, Selected Countries**

Country	Afghanistan	Bangladesh	India	Nepal	Pakistan	Sri Lanka
Country factor, %	22	60	117	66	26	108

Source: Original compilation for this publication.

Following the methodology in a specific case

Among the variables that the researchers deemed relevant to the potential or opportunity to introduce a pension scheme for informal sector workers, two constituted the economic inclusion module, as follows:

- Financial institution account (ages 15+, percent)

- Saved for old age (ages 15+, percent)

To calculate the financial institution account variable, the percentage share of people with an account in each country was divided by the regional average. This calculation produces the country factor for each variable (see equation 8D.1). To standardize these country factors so that the country factors for all the variables can be compared across the countries, the country scores for all variables need to be obtained. For the financial institution account variable, the country factors are shown in table 8D.3.

In the case of the financial institution account variable, the higher the share of the relevant population with accounts, the greater the opportunity for financial inclusion. Using this logic, the country factor scores are calculated depending on the percentage range of the country factors for this variable (see table 8D.2). The values of the country factor range from 22 percent to 117 percent (see table 8D.3). A set of proportional ranges are set within these limits to assign a unitary country score of 1 to 5 to these values (table 8D.4).

The process is repeated to obtain the country score for the saved for old age variable (ages 25+, percent). Once the country scores for both variables have been determined, the weighted average of the two scores are calculated for each country to obtain the relevant economic inclusion module scores, as follows:

$$\boxed{\begin{array}{l}\text{Financial institution account} \\ \text{(\% age 15+) country's score}\end{array}}*(\alpha) + \boxed{\begin{array}{l}\text{Saved for old age (\% age 25+)} \\ \text{country's score}\end{array}}*(1-\alpha) = \boxed{\begin{array}{l}\text{Economic inclusion} \\ \text{country's score}\end{array}}$$

$$(8D.4)$$

Table 8D.5 summarizes the results of the process described for the case of the economic inclusion scores for each country in the analysis.

TABLE 8D.4 **Country Factors and Scores, Financial Institution Account Variable, Selected Economies**

Country	Variable value, %	Country factor, %	Country score
Afghanistan	15	22	1
Bangladesh	41	60	3
India	80	117	5
Nepal	45	66	3
Pakistan	18	26	2
Sri Lanka	74	108	5

Source: Original compilation for this publication.
Note: The variable value represents the share of the population ages 15 or older with accounts at financial institutions.

TABLE 8D.5 **Country Scores, Economic Inclusion Variable, Selected Economies**

Economy	Financial institution account, ages 15+			Saved for old age, ages 25+			Economic inclusion country score
	Variable value, %	Country factor, %	Country score	Variable value, %	Country factor, %	Country score	
Afghanistan	15	22	1	10	77	3	3
Bangladesh	41	60	3	10	77	3	3
India	80	117	5	13	98	4	5
Nepal	45	66	3	15	116	5	4
Pakistan	18	26	2	18	134	5	4
Sri Lanka	74	108	5	21	157	5	5
South Asia	68	n.a.	n.a.	13	n.a.	n.a.	n.a.

Source: Original compilation for this publication.
Note: The variable value represents the share of the population ages 15 or older with accounts at financial institutions or the share of the population ages 25 or older who save for old age. n.a. = not applicable.

The process is repeated to determine all the relevant indicators and module scores. The weighted average of each is then calculated to obtain the final score for the potential or opportunity to introduce pension schemes for informal sector workers using equal weights (0.2) (see equation 8D.3). For each variable, a country score matrix is used to provide a points evaluation (table 8D.6).

Table 8D.7 provides weighted module evaluations and final scores for each country.

TABLE 8D.6 Summary Country Score Matrix, Points Evaluation, Selected Economies

Module	Global Findex variable	Factor value and score, relationship	Points				
			1	2	3	4	5
Economic inclusion	Financial institution account, ages 15+, %	Direct	0–25%	25–50%	50–75%	75–100%	>100%
	Saved for old age, ages 25+, %	Direct	<40%	40–60%	60–80%	80–100%	>100%
Formalization indicators	Received wages in previous year, ages 15+, %	Inverted	>160%	140–160%	120–140%	100–120%	<100%
Identifying willingness and capacity to save	Received digital payments in previous year, ages 15+, %	Direct	>60%	60–80%	80–100%	100–120%	>120%
Resilience and sensitivity to shocks	Borrowed for health or medical purposes, ages 15+, %	Direct	>60%	60–80%	80–100%	100–120%	>120%
	Coming up with emergency funds: possible, ages 15+, %	Inverted	>135%	115–135%	100–115%	85–100%	<85%
Institutional savings gaps, share without an account in a financial institution	No account because financial services are too expensive, ages 15+, %	Inverted	>140%	115–140%	95–115%	70–95%	<70%
	No account because of insufficient funds, ages 15+, %	Inverted	>120%	110–120%	110–130%	90–110%	<90%

Source: Calculated using data of Global Findex (Global Financial Inclusion Database), World Bank, Washington, DC, https://globalfindex.worldbank.org/#data_sec_focus.

TABLE 8D.7 **Weighted Module and Final Scores, Selected Economies**

Economy	Economic inclusion		Formalization indicators		Identifying willingness and capacity to save		Resilience and sensitivity to shocks		Institutional savings gaps		Final score
	Score	Weight	Score	Weight	Score	Weight	Score	Weight	Score	Weight	
Afghanistan	3	20%	5	20%	1	20%	3	20%	4	20%	3
Bangladesh	3	20%	5	20%	4	20%	3	20%	4	20%	4
India	5	20%	4	20%	4	20%	4	20%	4	20%	4
Nepal	4	20%	3	20%	2	20%	3	20%	2	20%	3
Pakistan	4	20%	5	20%	1	20%	3	20%	5	20%	3
Sri Lanka	5	20%	4	20%	5	20%	3	20%	2	20%	4
South Asia	4	n.a.	4	n.a.	4	n.a.	3	n.a.	3	n.a.	n.a.

Source: Original compilation for this publication.
Note: n.a. = not applicable.

Annex 8E: Cobweb Analysis: Introducing a Contributory Pension Scheme

FIGURE 8E.1 **Contributory Pension Scheme for the Nonvulnerable, Afghanistan versus South Asia**

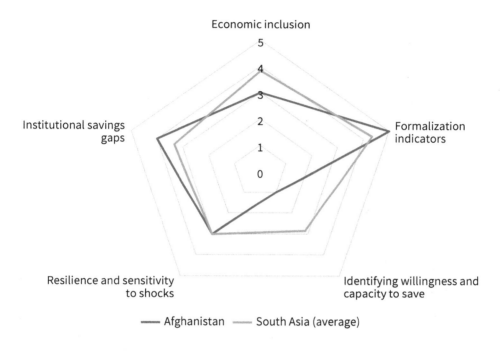

Economic inclusion: Most Afghans do not have an account in a financial institution and few have saved for retirement.

Formalization indicators: There is a great opportunity to introduce financial solutions for the highly informal population.

Willingness and capacity to save: A smaller share of the population uses digital payments in Afghanistan relative to the region, a potential indication of a lower capacity to save.

Resilience and sensitivity to shocks: Most people are capable of coming up with emergency funds, in line with the situation in other countries in the region.

Institutional savings gaps: A large share of the population does not have an account because of insufficient funds.

FIGURE 8E.2 **Contributory Pension Scheme for the Nonvulnerable, Bangladesh versus South Asia**

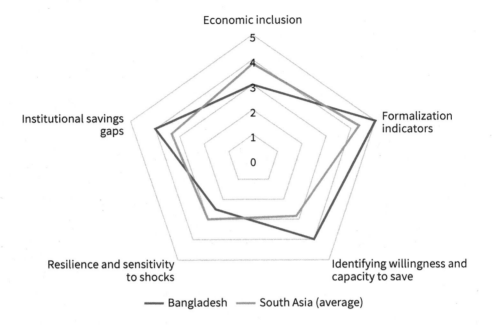

— Bangladesh —— South Asia (average)

Economic inclusion: Most Bangladeshis do not have an account in a financial institution and few have saved for retirement.

Formalization indicators: There is a great opportunity to introduce financial solutions for the highly informal population.

Willingness and capacity to save: The share of the population that is willing to save and has the capacity is close to the regional average.

Resilience and sensitivity to shocks: Most people are able to come up with emergency funds.

Institutional savings gaps: The large share of the population does not have an account because of insufficient funds.

FIGURE 8E.3 **Contributory Pension Scheme for the Nonvulnerable, India versus South Asia**

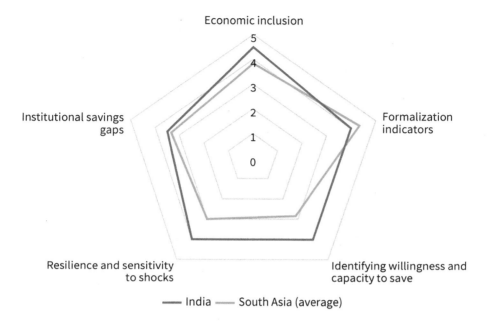

Economic inclusion: Although many people in India have accounts in financial institutions, most are not saving for old age.

Formalization indicators: Formal workers are more common in India than in the region in general; nevertheless, there is an opportunity to introduce financial instruments for informal workers.

Willingness and capacity to save: Signs are that extra income and familiarity with digital finance are not widespread.

Resilience and sensitivity to shocks: Most people are able to come up with emergency funds, and few take out loans.

Institutional savings gaps: There seems to be relatively more competition among financial institutions in India than in the region.

FIGURE 8E.4 **Contributory Pension Scheme for the Nonvulnerable, Nepal versus South Asia**

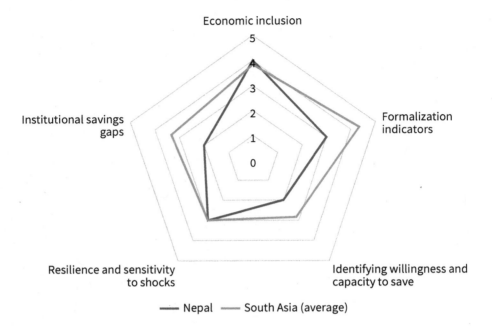

Economic inclusion: Although the share of accounts in financial institutions is relatively low, some of the accounts represent savings for old age.

Formalization indicators: The share of informal workers is low in Nepal, which means there is less potential for contributory pensions.

Willingness and capacity to save: Signs are that extra income and familiarity with digital finance are not widespread.

Resilience and sensitivity to shocks: There is a great need for products to help respond to shocks.

Institutional savings gaps: The cost of financial services is high, which represents a significant opportunity to introduce an accessible long-term savings scheme.

FIGURE 8E.5 **Contributory Pension Scheme for the Nonvulnerable, Pakistan versus South Asia**

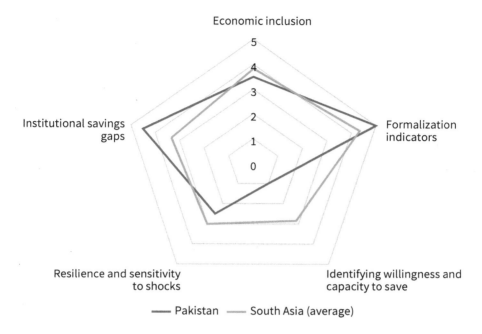

Economic inclusion: The share of accounts in financial institutions is relatively low, but some of the accounts represent saving for old age.

Formalization indicators: Pakistan has the largest share of informal workers among countries in the region for which data are available, which indicates that the market for contributory pensions may be substantial.

Willingness and capacity to save: The lack of signs of extra income and familiarity with digital finance may indicate that savings capacity is limited.

Resilience and sensitivity to shocks: The use of loans for medical purposes is low, and the share of people able to produce emergency funds is close to average. This indicates the existence of strong informal financial mechanisms and greater benefits accruing from the introduction of formal vehicles to save.

Institutional savings gaps: Indications that the cost of financial services is affordable imply that there may be viable instruments for individuals to save, though these may not be targeted to the informal sector.

FIGURE 8E.6 Contributory Pension Scheme for the Nonvulnerable, Sri Lanka versus South Asia

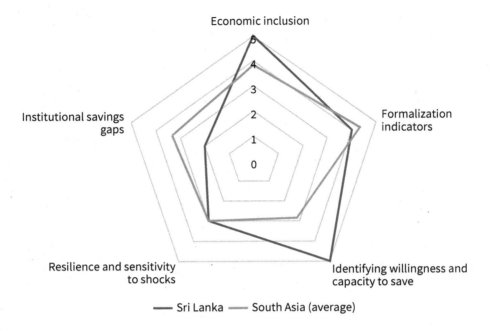

Economic inclusion: The share of accounts in financial institutions is high, and the incidence of saving for old age is above the regional average.

Formalization indicators: Sri Lanka has the lowest percentage share of informal workers among the countries under analysis.

Willingness and capacity to save: There are strong signs of extra income and familiarity with digital finance.

Resilience and sensitivity to shocks: There is some need for products to help respond to shocks.

Institutional savings gaps: The cost of financial services is high, which represents a significant opportunity to introduce an accessible, long-term savings scheme.

FIGURE 8E.7 Opportunity for Contributory Pension Schemes for the Nonvulnerable, South Asia

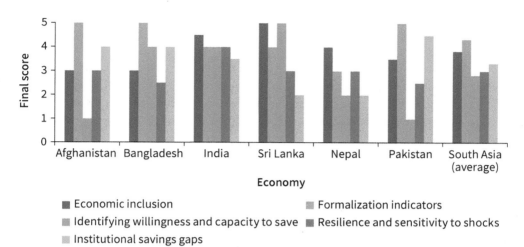

Source: Calculated based on data of Global Findex (Global Financial Inclusion Database), World Bank, Washington, DC, https://globalfindex.worldbank.org/#data_sec_focus.
Note: In the scale of 1–5, 5 represents the greatest potential in each of the dimensions, and 1 represents countries facing the greatest challenge with respect to the five concepts shown.

Annex 8F: Simplified Regimes in Latin America

Simplified regimes are single tax payment schemes available to the informal sector and individuals who pay low taxes. They involve a unique fixed fee instead of separate tax categories. To achieve greater simplification in the associated taxation systems, some countries in the South Asia region have added two key services for workers under the systems: social security benefits and optional or mandatory basic health insurance protection. These additions act as a strong incentive to encourage tax compliance.

The regimes are supported by simplified administrative and financing procedures and requirements to facilitate participation and coverage among self-employed workers. They are often managed over user-friendly web pages. A participant self-declares a projected annual income, which is verified by the revenue collection agency at the end of the tax year. The tax categories are progressive: the more you earn, the more you pay.

Simplified regimes may have different characteristics across countries, as follows:

- Tax subjects: only human persons, joint owners, and small companies.
- The small taxpayer is defined by the level of gross income or other factors, such as energy consumption or the size of the home or office.
- Some regimes are voluntary; others are compulsory.
- Some regimes replace only taxes (the value added tax or the income tax); others replace social security contributions and health insurance fees.
- The tax is a fixed fee up to a certain threshold, or the fee is variable according to the level of the categorization parameters.

Some countries have developed these simplified regimes to address the informality of self-employed workers who do not exceed an income threshold. Such programs guarantee various services against a single monthly payment. The aim of this public policy is to include small contributors who are not suitable for the typical social security regime designed for wage workers and who would otherwise probably remain informal.

The advantages of a simplified regime include the following:

- The tax responsibilities of the entire economically active population are recognized, thereby enlarging the tax base.
- The reduction in the need for audits creates a class of small taxpayers under a simplified regime that facilitates voluntary compliance and eliminates some of the burden on the tax collecting authority.
- An inclusive tax and pension system is generated that attracts economically active people who are outside the formal system. In some countries, the regime also includes basic primary health care insurance.

- The challenge of limited administrative capacity is addressed because the regimes are easy to use, for example, the Monotributo Program in Argentina and Uruguay, the Simples Program in Brazil, and the Rise Program in Ecuador.

The regimes are often coordinated and integrated along the delivery chain. Some processes are common or can be made common across multiple initiatives, such as outreach, intake and registration, assessment of needs and conditions, payments, and some aspects of beneficiary operations management (Lindert et al. 2020).

Although participation in monotax mechanisms is usually voluntary, simpler administrative procedures and, in some cases, lower contribution rates as well make this mechanism attractive (Bertranou 2007).

THE SIMPLIFIED REGIME IN URUGUAY (MONOTRIBUTO)[1]

Fixed single-tax contributions associated with the simplified regime are collected by the Social Security Institute of Uruguay, which transfers the tax share to the fiscal authority and uses the contribution share to finance social security benefits for members affiliated through the scheme and their families. Participating members have access to all social protection benefits except unemployment benefits. The introduction of the simplified regime mechanism has led to a significant expansion in social protection coverage. For instance, ride-hailing service drivers can pay their social security contribution on the go by using a phone application, supplied, in some cases, by the service provider, that allows them to deduct payments from the trip price through the single-tax mechanism and enjoy the same social security coverage as drivers in traditional economies.[2]

THE SIMPLIFIED REGIME IN ARGENTINA (MONOTRIBUTO)[3]

The monotax regime created in 1998 covers tax payments, social security, and basic health insurance. The system is seen as a good mechanism to formalize self-employed workers. There is a tendency among participants to remain in the system indefinitely because of the small contribution. A share of the monthly fee goes to the tax administration, another to the social security agency, and the rest to the health insurance provider. If the contributions are maintained up to date, the social security provision includes old age and disability pensions and family allowances. The fee depends on the annual income, although other factors, such as the energy consumption or the size of the building where the business is located, are also considered.

THE SIMPLES NACIONAL OF BRAZIL[4]

The simplified regime in Brazil is optional. The contribution is fixed by calendar year. The program covers most taxes of microenterprises and social security contributions.

The collection of taxes is covered by a single collection document, the documento de arrecadação (tax document). Users are provided with access to a digital system for the calculation of the monthly amount due and the generation of the tax document. They must present a single and simplified declaration of socioeconomic and fiscal information. The deadline for submitting the tax document is the 20th of the following month in which the gross revenue was earned. The Management Committee of the Simples Nacional consists of four representatives of unions, two representatives of the states and the Federal District, and two representatives of municipalities. The committee establishes the regulations for the scheme.

NOTES

1. See Monotributo (dashboard), Banco de Previsión Social (Social Insurance Institute), Montevideo, Uruguay, https://www.bps.gub.uy/4659/monotributo.html.

2. Data of Banco de Previsión Social (Social Insurance Institute), Montevideo, Uruguay. See Behrendt, Nguyen, and Rani (2019).

3. See Monotributo (dashboard), Administración Federal de Ingresos Públicos (Federal Administration of Public Revenues), Buenos Aires, https://monotributo.afip.gob.ar/Public/landing-monotributo.aspx.

4. See Simples Nacional (website), Secretaria da Receita Federal do Brasil (Special Department of Federal Revenue of Brazil), Brasília, http://www8.receita.fazenda.gov.br/simplesnacional/.

Notes

1. Informal employment consists of the following: (1) the informal self-employed: own-account workers, owners of informal enterprises, and contributing family workers; (2) the employees of informal enterprises, that is, unregistered or unorganized firms, which, in South Asia, generally means all firms with fewer than 20 employees, including household enterprises and microenterprises; and (3) workers holding informal jobs in formal firms, that is, jobs that are not subject to national labor legislation, income taxation, social protection, or entitlement to certain employment benefits. The main operational definition of this category is wage employment without a formal contract.

2. See PSLM Publications (Pakistan Social and Living Standards Measurement Publications), Pakistan Bureau of Statistics, Islamabad, Pakistan, https://www.pbs.gov.pk/pslm -publications.

3. "Long-term savings" is used here to refer to those savings meant to address contingencies normally covered by social insurance: old age, loss of employment, health care, and death. It can also be applied to provisions for crop loss and other risks affecting the normal flow of income.

4. See Global Findex (Global Financial Inclusion Database), World Bank, Washington, DC, https://globalfindex.worldbank.org/#data_sec_focus.

5. Although this chapter uses a broader concept of social insurance coverage, beyond old-age pensions, noncontributory or social pensions are normally designed to provide income support in old age and, in some cases, also in the event of disability. This section will therefore apply a narrower scope to social insurance, assimilating it to old-age and disability (social) pensions.

6. In Maldives, the upper-middle-income-country poverty line at US$5.50 (Rf 70) per person per day is equivalent to around Rf 2,100 a month, but the monthly benefit is Rf 5,000.

7. In Nepal, the Central Bureau of Statistics produces the poverty estimates based on the Nepal Living Standards Survey (CBS 2011). The national poverty line in Nepal was estimated at Rs 19,262 per person per year in 2010. It is an absolute poverty line based on the cost of satisfying basic food and nonfood needs.

8. The data presented on India only correspond to the Indira Gandhi National Old Age Pension Scheme, which is limited in coverage and benefit amounts, compared with the extensive network of state programs (see box 8.2).

9. No simple international benchmarks exist to compare the costs of noncontributory pensions across countries. Estimates on countries in the Latin America and Caribbean region in 2014 showed a median above 0.3 percent of GDP, which was considered low for the region, even though all the elderly were not covered (Bosch, Melguizo, and Pagés 2013).

10. Social pensions in many countries include a couple's rate, which is typically about 160 percent–170 percent of the single pensioner rate. Thus, two elderly people in the same household do not receive twice the value of a single pension but slightly less.

11. "Social security agency" refers here to the diversity of administrative bodies having a general mandate to provide pensions and other social insurance products, although social security and social insurance are not equivalent.

12. A draft of Joubert and Kanth's paper (2021), with technical details regarding the data and methodology, is available upon request from the authors (cjoubert@worldbank.org).

13. These findings are based on the Labor Force Surveys of 2007–08 and 2017–18. See Labour Force Publications, Pakistan Bureau of Statistics, Islamabad, Pakistan, https://www.pbs.gov.pk/labour-force-publications.

14. "Life Expectancy at Birth, Total (Years): Pakistan," Data, World Bank, Washington, DC, https://data.worldbank.org/indicator/SP.DYN.LE00.IN?locations=PK.

15. See "Financial Inclusion" (website), State Bank of Pakistan, Karachi, Pakistan, https://www.sbp.org.pk/finc/SR.asp.

16. See Demirgüç-Kunt et al. (2018); "National Financial Inclusion Strategy (NFIS)" (website), State Bank of Pakistan, Karachi, Pakistan, https://www.sbp.org.pk/Finc/NF.asp.

17. Other transfers, including government transfers, are minor contributors to household consumption. Because of savings, borrowing, or measurement error, total income may not equate with total consumption expenditure in the case of either variable.

References

ADB (Asian Development Bank). 2019. *Growing Old before Becoming Rich: Challenges of an Aging Population in Sri Lanka.* December. Manila: ADB.

Bachas, Pierre, Paul Gertler, Sean Higgins, and Enrique Seira. 2017. "How Debit Cards Help the Poor to Save More." NBER Working Paper 23252 (March), National Bureau of Economic Research, Cambridge, MA.

BBS (Bangladesh Bureau of Statistics). 2018. *Report on Labour Force Survey (LFS) 2016–17.* January. Dhaka, Bangladesh: BBS, Statistics and Informatics Division, Ministry of Planning.

Behrendt, Christina, Quynh Anh Nguyen, and Uma Rani. 2019. "Social Protection Systems and the Future of Work: Ensuring Social Security for Digital Platform Workers." *International Social Security Review* 72 (3): 17–41.

Bertranou, Fabio M. 2007. "Informal Economy, Independent Workers, and Social Security Coverage in Argentina, Chile, and Uruguay." Paper prepared for the "Tripartite Interregional Symposium on the Informal Economy: Enabling Transition to Formalization," International Labour Office, Geneva, November 27–29, 2007.

Bosch, Mariano, Ángel Melguizo, and Carmen Pagés. 2013. *Better Pensions, Better Jobs: Towards Universal Coverage in Latin America and the Caribbean.* Washington, DC: Inter-American Development Bank.

Bossavie, Laurent, Upasana Khadka, and Victoria Strokova. 2018. "Pakistan: A Labor Market Overview." Background paper, Jobs Diagnostic Pakistan, World Bank, Washington, DC.

Buckley, Ross P., and Louise Malady. 2015. "Building Consumer Demand for Digital Financial Services: The New Regulatory Frontier." *Journal of Financial Perspectives* 3 (3): 122–37.

Cámara, Noelia, and David Tuesta. 2014. "Measuring Financial Inclusion: A Multidimensional Index." BBVA Working Paper 14/26 (September), BBVA Research, Madrid.

CBS (Central Bureau of Statistics, Nepal). 2011. *Nepal Living Standards Survey 2010/11: Statistical Report.* 2 vols. November. Kathmandu, Nepal: National Planning Commission, CBS.

Cho, Yoonyoung, and Zaineb Majoka. 2020. "Jobs Diagnostic Pakistan: Promoting Access to Quality Jobs for All." Jobs Series 20, World Bank, Washington, DC.

DCS (Department of Census and Statistics, Sri Lanka). 2019. *Sri Lanka Labour Force Survey: Annual Report 2019*. Battaramulla, Sri Lanka: DCS, Ministry of Finance. http://www.statistics .gov.lk/Resource/en/LabourForce/Annual_Reports/LFS2019.pdf.

Deaton, Angus S. 1997. *The Analysis of Household Surveys: A Microeconometric Approach to Development Policy*. Washington, DC: World Bank; Baltimore: Johns Hopkins University Press.

Demirgüç-Kunt, Asli, Leora F. Klapper, Dorothe Singer, Saniya Ansar, and Jake Hess. 2018. *The Global Findex Database 2017: Measuring Financial Inclusion and the Fintech Revolution*. Washington, DC: World Bank. https://doi.org/10.1596/978-1-4648-1259-0.

Donovan, Kevin. 2012. "Mobile Money for Financial Inclusion." In *Information and Communications for Development 2012: Maximizing Mobile*, 61–73. Washington, DC: World Bank.

Dupas, Pascaline, Dean Karlan, Jonathan Robinson, and Diego Ubfal. 2018. "Banking the Unbanked? Evidence from Three Countries." *American Economic Journal: Applied Economics* 10 (2): 257–97.

Guven, Melis Ufuk. 2019. "Extending Pension Coverage to the Informal Sector in Africa." Social Protection and Jobs Discussion Paper 1933 (July), World Bank, Washington, DC.

Guven, Melis Ufuk, Himanshi Jain, and Clément Jean Edouard Joubert. 2021. *Social Protection for the Informal Economy: Operational Lessons for Developing Countries in Africa and Beyond*. Washington, DC: World Bank.

Hu, Yu-Wei, and Fiona Stewart. 2009. "Pension Coverage and Informal Sector Workers: International Experiences." OECD Working Paper on Insurance and Private Pensions 31 (January), Organisation for Economic Co-operation and Development, Paris.

ILO (International Labour Organization). 2014. *World Social Protection Report 2014/15: Building Economic Recovery, Inclusive Development, and Social Justice*. Geneva: International Labour Office.

ILO (International Labour Organization). 2018a. *Global Wage Report 2018/19: What Lies behind Gender Pay Gaps*. Geneva: International Labour Office.

ILO (International Labour Organization). 2018b. "South-South and Triangular Cooperation for Strengthening Workplace Injury Compensation System in Pakistan." Press Release, July 16, 2018. https://www.ilo.org/islamabad/info/public/pr/WCMS_644666/lang--en/index.htm.

Joubert, Clément Jean Edouard, and Priyanka Kanth. 2021. "Life-Cycle Saving in a High-Informality Setting: Evidence from Pakistan." World Bank, Washington, DC.

La Porta, Rafael, and Andrei Shleifer. 2014. "Informality and Development." *Journal of Economic Perspectives* 28 (3): 109–26.

Lindert, Kathy, Tina George Karippacheril, Inés Rodríguez Caillava, and Kenichi Nishikawa Chávez, eds. 2020. *Sourcebook on the Foundations of Social Protection Delivery Systems*. Washington, DC: World Bank.

Majoka, Zaineb, and Robert Palacios. 2017. "What Can We Learn about Pensions from the FINDEX Data." Social Protection and Labor Policy Note: Pensions 21 (March), World Bank, Washington, DC.

OECD (Organisation for Economic Co-operation and Development). 2008. *OECD Private Pensions Outlook 2008*. Paris: OECD.

Ohnsorge, Franziska L., and Shu Yu, eds. 2022. *The Long Shadow of Informality: Challenges and Policies*. Washington, DC: World Bank.

Palacios, Robert Joseph, and David A. Robalino. 2020. "Integrating Social Insurance and Social Assistance Programs for the Future World of Labor." IZA Discussion Paper IZA DP 13258 (May), Institute of Labor Economics, Bonn, Germany.

PBS (Pakistan Bureau of Statistics). 2015. "Labour Force Survey 2014–15." Issue 33 (November), Statistics Division, PBS, Islamabad, Pakistan.

PBS (Pakistan Bureau of Statistics). 2017. "Household Integrated Economic Survey (HIES) (2015–16)." February, Statistics Division, PBS, Islamabad, Pakistan.

PMN (Pakistan Microfinance Network). 2019. *Pakistan Microfinance Review 2018*. Islamabad, Pakistan: PMN.

Radcliffe, Daniel, and Rodger Voorhies. 2012. "A Digital Pathway to Financial Inclusion." December, Bill & Melinda Gates Foundation, Seattle, WA.

Sluchynskyy, Oleksiy A. 2019. "Social Insurance Administrative Diagnostic (SIAD): Guidance Note." World Bank, Washington, DC; International Social Security Association, Geneva.

SSA (Social Security Administration, United States) and ISSA (International Social Security Association). 2017. *Social Security Programs throughout the World: Asia and the Pacific, 2016*. SSA Publication 13-11802 (March). Geneva: ISSA; Washington, DC: SSA.

Stuart, Elizabeth, Emma Samman, and Abigail Hunt. 2018. "Informal Is the New Normal: Improving the Lives of Workers at Risk of Being Left Behind." ODI Working Paper 530 (January), Overseas Development Institute, London.

World Bank. 2012. *World Development Report 2013: Jobs*. Washington, DC: World Bank.